QUE®

D1232160

Windows® 98
Installation and
Configuration

Handbook

Rob Tidrow

Windows® 98
Installation and Configuration
Handbook

Windows 98 Installation and Configuration Handbook

International Standard Book Number: 0-7897-1510-4

Library of Congress Catalog No.: 97-075461

First Printing: April 1998

00 99 98   4 3 2 1

Trademarks

Credits

EXECUTIVE EDITOR
Jeff Koch

ACQUISITIONS EDITORS
Jane Brownlow
Stephanie McComb

DEVELOPMENT EDITOR
Mark Cierzniak

MANAGING EDITOR
Sarah Kearns

SENIOR EDITOR
Mike La Bonne

PROJECT EDITOR
Andrew Cupp

COPY EDITORS
Fran Blauw
Geneil Breeze
Charles Hutchinson
Pat Kinyon

INDEXER
Cheryl Jackson

TECHNICAL EDITORS
Walter Glenn
Ron Ellenbacher

SOFTWARE DEVELOPMENT SPECIALIST
Jack Belbot

PRODUCTION
Marcia Deboy
Michael Dietsch
Jennifer Earhart
Cynthia Fields
Maureen West

Contents at a Glance

Table of Contents

IV Configuring Multimedia for Windows 98

About the Authors

Lead Author

Rob Tidrow is a writer, Web site designer, trainer, and president of Tidrow Communications, Inc., a firm specializing in content creation and delivery. Rob has authored or co-authored over 25 books on a wide variety of computer topics, including Windows 95, Netscape Communicator 4.0, Windows NT, and Microsoft Internet Information Server 4.0. He authored *Windows 95 Registry Troubleshooting*, *Windows NT Registry Troubleshooting*, *Implementing and Supporting Windows 95*, all published by New Riders and *Windows 95 Installation and Configuration Handbook*, published by Que. He is also contributing author to *Special Edition Using Microsoft Office 97, Inside Windows 95, Deluxe Edition, Platinum Edition Using Windows 95, Inside the World Wide Web*, and *Windows 95 for Network Administrators*, all published by Macmillan Computer Publishing. He lives in Indianapolis, IN with his wife Tammy and their two sons, Adam and Wesley. You can reach him on the Internet at `rtidrow@iquest.net`.

Contributing Authors

Dean Andrews is a freelance writer living in Boston. After receiving a bachelor degree in computer science from the University of California at Berkeley, he worked as software devel- oper at IBM and was a systems consultant to small businesses in the San Francisco bay area. In 1991, he joined the computer press and has worked on staff at *InfoWorld*, as a Senior Test De- veloper, and *PC World, a*s the Manager of Usability Testing. Now, as a freelancer writer, he frequently contributes to a variety of publications including *PC World*, *Macworld*, and *Boston.com*, the online hub of the *Boston Globe*. Mr. Andrews is also a contributing author in *Peter Norton's Guide to Upgrading and Repairing PCs* and *Special Edition Using Windows 98*.

Christopher Gagnon is a network analyst and consultant with an Atlanta-based software development firm. He has worked with Digital Equipment Corporation, IBM, and several prac- tice management firms in the healthcare industry. He has served as network administrator on several occasions and knows only too well the politics and technical nuances of this unique environment. While he's not reading trade magazines and technical manuals, he enjoys playing his didgeridoo, chasing his cat, and reading about theoretical physics. He currently resides in the Atlanta suburb of Roswell, Georgia with his wife Keshly and their daughter, Paige. Christo- pher is also a contributing author in *Platinum Edition Using Windows NT 4.0*.

James M. Spann is a Microsoft Certified Professional who has spent the last six years working as a trainer and lecturer in the computer industry. James received his Bachelor of Science degree in 1984 and immediately started working as a computer and networking troubleshooter. From there James advanced to the Director of Information Systems for a large investment corporation headquartered in Orlando, Florida. In 1992, James went out on his own and began working with Spann & Associates, Inc. to provide training and consulting services to Fortune 500 companies and government clients. Since then, Mr. Spann has logged more than 5,000 hours teaching classes in both the United States and Europe. Most recently, James has started another new company in Lake Mary, Florida. This new company, Surf Solutions, Inc., is dedicated to providing networking and Internet solutions to small businesses in the Orlando metropolitan area. James can be reached at jay@surfsol.com. James is also a contributing author in *Networking Essentials Unleashed*.

Keith Underdahl is an electronic publishing specialist for Ages Software in Albany, Oregon, where he produces electronic versions of classic texts on CD-ROM. Keith is also a prolific author and personal computing consultant and has served as technical editor on numerous titles from Que. When he is not goofing off with computers, Keith is a road tester and regular contributor to *Street Bike*, a motorcycle magazine serving the western United States.

Serdar Yegulalp has been writing both as a freelancer and staffer for a number of computer publications, including *Computer Buyer's Guide and Handbook* and *Computer Retail Week*, and has contributed to other MCP books in the past, including *Platinum Edition Using Windows NT 4.0* and *Inside Windows 98*. He is currently Associate Technology Editor for *Windows* Magazine, where he writes on and researches Windows 98, Windows NT 4.0, and Windows NT 5.0. Email him at syegul@winmag.com.

Dedications

This book is dedicated to my wonderful wife, Tammy and two great boys, Adam and Wesley.

—Rob Tidrow

Acknowledgments

I would like to thank all those who have worked on this book over the past nine months to help make it happen. A big thanks to Mark Cierzniak, Jeff Koch, Jane Brownlow, and Stephanie McComb. Also, thanks to Walter Glenn and Ron Ellenbacher. Finally, thanks to my wife and kids and to all my family and friends who helped us move to our new house during this project. I couldn't have done it without you.

—Rob Tidrow

We'd Like to Hear from You!

As part of our continuing effort to produce books of the highest possible quality, Macmillan Computer Publishing would like to hear your comments. To stay competitive, we *really* want you, as a computer book reader and user, to let us know what you like or dislike most about this book or other Macmillan Computer Publishing products.

You can mail comments, ideas, or suggestions for improving future editions to the address below, or send us a fax at (317) 581-4663. Our staff and authors are available for questions and comments through our Internet site at `http://www.mcp.com` or via email at `opsys@mcp.com`.

Thanks in advance—your comments will help us to continue publishing the best books available on new computer technologies in today's market.

Introduction

What, you didn't have problems installing Windows 98? You only experienced problems when you restarted your computer to *run* Windows 98? Don't worry. You're not alone. Most Windows 98 installation problems occur after you've installed the software and when you reboot your computer. This is when the Windows Setup program configures your computer to work with Windows 98.

Windows 98 is designed to ease installation and configuration burdens. Setting up your Windows environment has never been easier. If you're new to the world of Windows, you'll find installation very easy and simple.

So why do you need this book? In short, because nothing is perfect—including Windows. It's not that Microsoft doesn't want Windows 98 to be perfect and fit every situation perfectly. The problem is that no two computer systems are alike. In fact, chances are that if you have two computers in your office or home, they have two different setups and configurations. Even if the two computers are the same make and model, they are unique and have their own idiosyncrasies. What all this means is that Windows 98 must be flexible enough to work on different configurations, yet offer a simple way to customize each individual PC.

That's where this book comes in. *Windows 98 Installation and Configuration Handbook* guides you through the entire Windows 98 installation process. You are shown how to prepare your computer before you install Windows 98, as well as how to upgrade hardware, tweak memory settings, install and uninstall software, and add other devices after Windows 98 is up and running.

For the most part, you can use Windows 98 straight out of the box and get most of your work done. If you need to change a setting (called a *property* in Windows 98), you need to dig a little deeper into the operating system and become familiar with some of Windows 98's configuration features. Some of these include the Add/Remove Software and Add New Hardware utilities, the Windows Update feature, the Device Manager, and Property sheets. You find out about all these in this book.

Who Should Use This Book

This book is designed for users who need to install Windows 98 and who want to customize and reconfigure the way Windows behaves and looks. For beginning Windows users, this book includes step-by-step procedures that guide them through setting up the Windows environment. The new Help utility available in Windows 98 is a much-welcomed addition to Windows. However, not all procedures are covered in Help, and many assumptions are left up to the user to figure out. This book attempts to fill in many of those gaps.

For experienced Windows 3.x users, this book includes customization procedures and techniques to help them configure the Windows 98 environment the way they want it. In many places in this book, comparisons to how a procedure or step was performed in Windows 3.x are included. This helps the experienced user become comfortable with Windows 98 more quickly.

Finally, those who are upgrading from Windows 95, this book shows how to install and configure many of the new features of Windows 98. These include configuring the Web View desktop, setting up multiple monitors, installing PC TV and DVD devices, and more.

Who Should Not Use This Book

Any user of Windows 98 who wants to install new hardware, add software, or reconfigure the Windows 98 environment should appreciate this book. If you need a tutorial of the way in which Windows 98 works, however, you may find that this book does not meet your needs. Although some chapters give basic overviews of how a feature works or some of the benefits of using a configuration setting versus another setting, you need another book to learn how to use Windows 98.

Fortunately, an outstanding book is available that does just this. Que's *Special Edition Using Windows 98* is full of instructions, tutorials, and reference materials to help you understand and master Windows 98. If you need to learn how to use Windows 98, you may want to pick up a copy of that book.

How To Use This Book

Use this book as you would a reference book. Unless you find your local library or bookstore lacking entertaining novels, you probably don't want to read this book from cover to cover. The best way to use this book is to look over the table of contents at the front of the book and the index in the back to find the topic you want. Turn to that chapter or section and use the instructions and discussions provided. Then close the book and start working with Windows 98.

If you have specific questions, scan the book for the troubleshooting sidebars in the book. Troubleshooting sidebars are provided in almost all chapters to help you solve many of the common problems associated with installing and configuring Windows 98.

The following is a quick look at each of the chapters in this book.

Part I: Installing Windows 98

Chapter 1, "Preparing to Install Windows 98," is the place to start if you have not installed Windows 98. Windows 98 requires you to perform several system level procedures before you start installing it. One of these is to defragment and optimize your hard disk. Chapter 1 shows you how to prepare your system for Windows 98 and introduces the new Windows 98 installation features.

Chapter 2, "Installing Windows 98 on a Desktop and Laptop," is intended for readers who have prepped their machines and want to install Windows 98 on their desktop or laptop computers. For laptop users, there are several sections geared for users who have mobile computers and want to install only those files and programs that are necessary for laptop computers. Many of these users have both a mobile PC they take with them on the road and a desktop PC that remains in the office or at home. Windows 98 includes some new components that enable mobile users to transfer files back and forth between the mobile computer and the stationary computer. This chapter shows how to configure these options.

Chapter 3, "Selecting Windows 98 Components," provides an overview of the different components you can select during or after Windows 98 Setup runs. This chapter is intended for users who are comfortable with their computer and know which components they want to install.

Chapter 4, "Installing Windows 98 from a Network Server," shows how to use the Microsoft Batch 98 utility to create an installation batch file to help you install Windows to multiple machines that will use the same setup parameters.

Chapter 5, "Installing and Configuring New Hardware and Software," shows you how to setup new hardware on your computer using the Add/New Hardware applet. You also are shown how to update device drivers using the Update Driver Wizard. Finally, you are shown how to install and uninstall applications under Windows 98.

Part II: Configuring and Customizing the Windows 98 Desktop

Chapter 6, "Configuring Windows 98 Classic and Web View Desktops," shows how to set up both the classic and new Web View desktops. The Web View desktop turns your desktop into a Web page so you can navigate it like you do Web pages, as well as display active content on it.

Chapter 7, "Configuring Monitors and Video Cards," shows you how to set resolution settings, configure color palettes, and set font sizes for your monitor. You also are shown how to set up dual monitors on your system.

Chapter 8, "Configuring the Desktop and Fonts," picks up after you have Windows 98 installed and running. You are now ready to customize your Windows 98 environment. This chapter shows how to change wallpaper, select screen savers, and create shortcuts.

Chapter 9, "Configuring the Taskbar and Start Button," helps you modify the way the Windows 98 taskbar behaves and looks. You are shown how to add programs and files to the Start menu, which gives you one-button access to them. You also are shown how to set up Windows 98's new taskbar toolbars.

Part III: Configuring Storage Devices

Chapter 10, "Installing and Configuring Hard Disk Drives," shows how to install and configure hard disk drives to work under Windows 98. You also learn how to partition and prepare a new hard drive to use with Windows 98.

Chapter 11, "Installing and Configuring Floppy Disk Drives," leads you through adding a floppy drive to your system and includes troubleshooting topics that help you configure your floppy drive for Windows 98.

Chapter 12, "Installing and Configuring CD-ROM and DVD Drives," may become dog-eared from use if you upgrade or add a CD-ROM to your system. This chapter shows you how to install and set up a CD-ROM to work with Windows 98. You also learn how to set up DVD drivers under Windows 98.

Chapter 13, "Setting Up Backup Systems," shows you how to install a backup system to work with Windows 98. Although you may not use a tape backup system, DAT system, or other backup media, you should seriously consider adding one to your system. This chapter leads you through this process.

Chapter 14, "Configuring Memory, Disks, and Devices," provides information on using system memory, modifying virtual memory, improving hard disk performance, and how to use the Device Manager.

Part IV: Configuring Multimedia for Windows 98
Chapter 15, "Installing Sound and MIDI Cards," is your guide to setting event sounds in Windows 98, setting sound volumes, and configuring MIDI sounds.

Chapter 16, "Configuring Full-Motion Video Capabilities," introduces you to setting up Windows 98's digital video support. You also learn how to use the Windows Media Player to play these digital video files.

Chapter 17, "Configuring PC TV Devices," provides coverage on how to configure television devices to work with Windows 98. You also learn how to retrieve program listings and scan for channels using the WebTV for Windows component.

Part V: Configuring Windows 98 Communication Capabilities
Chapter 18, "Configuring Modems," should be used in conjunction with the chapters on setting up online and Internet connections and configuring Microsoft Fax. You need to configure your modem before you start any of those other configurations. This chapter includes updated information about 56Kbps modems, as well as ISDN and cable modem technology.

Chapter 19, "Configuring an Internet Connection," leads you step by step to setting up Windows 98 built-in support for the Internet, including how to set up a new Internet account if you don't currently have one.

Chapter 20, "Configuring Microsoft InternetÍÁplorer 4.0," shows you how to configure the Internet Explorer 4.0 Web browser.

Chapter 21, " Configuring Outlook Express," shows how to set up and configure Outlook Express, Microsoft's Internet mail, newsreader, and address book application.

Part VI: Configuring Windows 98 In a Networked Environment
Chapter 22, "Configuring Windows 98 as a Network Client," shows how to configure Windows 98 as a Windows NT or Novell NetWare client. You also are shown how to set up user profiles to enable roving computing, enabling users to use their own system settings regardless of the computer they use to connect to the network.

Chapter 23, "Configuring Network Hardware," shows how to configure network adapters, install network cables, configure Microsoft Fax for a workgroup environment, and how to share CD-ROMs on a network using Windows 98.

Chapter 24, "Setting Up Windows 98 on a Peer-to-Peer Network," provides coverage of how to set up a peer-to-peer network that uses only Windows 98 as the network operating system. You're also shown how to set up shares to printers and files.

Chapter 25, "Configuring the Personal Web Server," shows how to configure the Personal Web Server application to serve Web pages from your desktop to other clients on a Web or intranet.

Part VII: Running Your Software on Windows 98

Chapter 26, "Using Windows 98 Software," shows some of the Windows 98 applications available on the market and how to use Windows 98 software on the Windows 98 operating system. This chapter also includes information on the Windows 98 Registry.

Chapter 27, "Using DOS Software," is intended for those users still using their favorite (or forced to use their least favorite) DOS software under Windows 98. See this chapter to set Property sheets for DOS programs.

Part VIII: Configuring Common Peripherals

Chapter 28, "Configuring Input Devices," shows how to set mouse properties, troubleshoot common problems with installing pointing devices, and how to configure your pointing device to work with Windows 98. You also learn how to configure keyboards under Windows 98.

Chapter 29, "Configuring Printers," helps you install a printer for a single computer. The Add Printer Wizard makes installation a breeze, but you may have some problems that this chapter can help you correct. You also can find information about how to obtain updated printer drivers for Windows 98.

Chapter 30, "Configuring Scanners," shows how to set up scanners to work with Windows 98. You also learn to pick out a scanner and are given some tips on getting the most out of your scanners.

Chapter 31, "Configuring Game Cards and Joysticks for Windows 98," provides information on maximizing your Windows 98 environment for games by showing how to set up joysticks and game adapters. This chapter provides updated troubleshooting information about Microsoft GamePad and SideWinder devices.

Chapter 32, "Configuring Digital Cameras," teaches you how to set up and configure digital cameras, which let you take pictures and save them on your hard drive as an image file.

Part IX: Appendixes

Appendix A, "What's New with Windows 98," leads you through all the new features of Microsoft's newest operating system.

Appendix B, "Configuring Windows Messaging and Microsoft Fax," shows you step by step how to set up Microsoft Fax prior to installing Windows 98. If you have Windows 95 and want Fax support under Windows 98, you must install Fax in Windows 95 first. Then, when you upgrade to Windows 98, Fax is supported. In this chapter, you find all the Microsoft Fax options discussed, including those intended for more advanced audiences. You also are shown how to use the Fax Cover Update to fix bugs found in the release version of Microsoft Fax.

Obtaining Additional Windows 98 Information

Other valuable sources of information for Windows 98 include Microsoft's Internet World Wide Web site (http://www.microsoft.com). You can find white papers, some technical support documents, and updated drivers for some hardware devices at those sites.

Conventions Found in This Book

You find four visual aids that help you on your Windows 98 installation journey: Notes, Tips, Cautions, and Troubleshooting.

N O T E This paragraph format indicates additional information that may help you avoid problems or that should be considered in using the described features. ■

 This paragraph format suggests easier or alternative methods of executing a procedure.

CAUTION

This paragraph format warns the reader of hazardous procedures (for example, activities that delete files).

 TROUBLESHOOTING

This paragraph format provides guidance on how to find solutions to common problems. Specific problems you may encounter are shown in bold. Possible solutions appear following the problem.

Installing Windows 98

Preparing to Install Windows 98

by Rob Tidrow

In this chapter

Before Installing Windows 98

Installing Windows 98 is not tricky, but it can be frustrating at times. You'll notice two things about Windows 98 when you start installing it. First, if you're upgrading from Windows 95, you'll have the option of preserving your Windows 95 Setup so that you can uninstall Windows 98 and return to your previous Windows 95 installation. Second, if you're upgrading from Windows 3.1, you can opt to keep this operating system intact so that you can boot to Windows 98 or Windows 3.1. To begin, you should set aside 30 to 60 minutes to install Windows 98. If you need to prepare your hard disk or you decide to customize the setup, don't be surprised if you invest two or more hours to ensure that everything is set up properly.

Windows 98 is an upgrade to Windows 95, which was released in the fall of 1995. Like Windows 95, Windows 98 provides a new installation process. Many of the options and customization procedures users had to perform with older versions of Windows after installation now are included during setup. Some of these procedures include configuring hardware devices, networking components, and online connections. The following is a list of areas that have been improved since previous versions of Windows Setup:

- Windows 98 Setup is a new, streamlined process. It provides a more user-friendly setup environment to make it less intimidating to new users, and it also gives helpful information to all users. Windows 98 Setup uses current Windows settings to speed up installation time.

- For users upgrading from other operating systems, Windows 98 includes the automatic detection of hardware—such as modems, printers, and network adapters—during setup. This capability frees users from having to configure all their hardware devices after the setup stage. Legacy hardware detection is performed during Windows 98's first boot, after all Plug and Play devices are set up.

- Windows 98 provides the Smart Recovery System to deal with an interrupted setup process. Windows 98 knows when a previous installation has failed and returns to the point of interruption to continue setup.

- A Setup log is created to verify that the system is set up properly.

- Network setup has been improved, which includes the use of batch installs across *local area networks* (LANs).

- The *emergency boot disk* (EBD) now includes a real-mode *Advanced Technology Attachment Packet Interface* (ATAPI) CD-ROM driver. This enables you to have a CD-ROM drive working if you encounter system problems and must run the EBD.

Using Installation Wizards

Wizards are onscreen guides that walk users through a particular process, such as installing Windows 98 or installing new hardware on your system (see Figure 1.1). Windows 98 continues to rely on wizards for installation and configuration concerns. If you use Microsoft Word or Access, you probably encounter wizards on a daily or weekly basis.

FIG. 1.1

Wizards offer a great deal of help as you install hardware devices or Windows itself.

Wizards are intended to help all users, not just beginners. More advanced users who feel comfortable setting configuration parameters are given opportunities in some wizards to manually set up devices. The Install New Modem Wizard, for example, enables users to select the modem name and manufacturer from lists (see Figure 1.2). Many users, however, opt for Windows 98 to automatically determine and set up their modem or other hardware device. If Windows 98 cannot detect the modem, users can manually configure the device by following onscreen instructions that guide them through the process.

FIG. 1.2

The Install New Modem Wizard enables you to select the name and manufacturer of the modem.

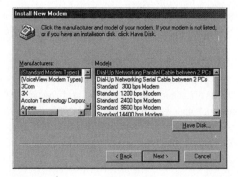

Wizards generally have three buttons along the bottom of the screen that provide navigation:

■ *Next.* Presents you with the next step in the wizard. Next is the default button on many wizard screens and can be activated by clicking it or by pressing Enter.

■ *Back.* Sends you back one screen or step. Click this button if you want to change a setting or re-read the previous step. Most wizards let you back up as far as you want in the wizard.

■ *Cancel.* Exits the wizard without performing any actions or making system changes.

N O T E Depending on the wizard and the application you are in, the screen may have a Help button. Click Help to obtain online help for that screen or function. ■

Upgrading to Windows

The type of operating system (if any) you currently have installed on your computer will dictate how you install Windows 98. Windows 98 is designed primarily as an upgrade to Windows 95 or Windows 3.1 on existing computers, but you can install Windows 98 in other operating-system scenarios.

If you purchase a new computer, Windows 98 may be preinstalled by the PC manufacturer on that computer. In that case, you won't have to worry about installing Windows 98. However, you should make sure that you obtain the Windows 98 Setup CD-ROM or floppy disks for future reference. You might need to reinstall Windows 98 in the future, for example, or you might need to access a driver or applet from the Setup disks.

The best scenario for installing Windows 98 is to do so over an existing version of Windows 95. This is because Windows 98 automatically keeps the same hardware and software settings from the Windows 95 setup. Any Windows applets you have installed—such as WordPad, Paint, and other components—will be updated under the Windows 98 installation. Components not installed under Windows 95, however, will not be installed during the Windows 98 setup process. This ensures that the Windows 98 setup time is kept to a minimum and that your Windows 98 environment will closely match your old Windows 95 setup as much as possible.

If you do not have Windows 95 installed, you can install Windows 98 on a computer running Windows 3.1. Windows 98 Setup uses the information about the applications and utilities you have set up under Windows 3.1 and updates only those.

N O T E   If your Windows 3.1 system runs on a version of DOS that is not MS-DOS 3.2 or higher, make sure that your DOS version can exceed the 32MB partition limit, which Windows 98 supports. Some *original equipment manufacturer* (OEM) versions of DOS do not meet this standard; check your system manuals to make sure that your version of DOS does. If you do not know what version of DOS you have, type **VER** at the command prompt for this information.

Also, if you plan to dual-boot between Windows 3.1 and Windows 98, you must have MS-DOS 5.0 or higher installed under Windows 3.1. ▓

If your primary operating system is Windows NT, you cannot upgrade to Windows 98 directly. You must set up Windows NT to multiboot between Windows NT and MS-DOS. During Windows 98 Setup, you must specify that Windows 98 should be installed in a directory separate from Windows NT. Also, a FAT16 or FAT32 partition is required for Windows 98; you cannot install Windows 98 on a Windows *NT file system* (NTFS) partition. Similarly, Windows NT cannot exist on a FAT32 partition, which Windows 98 supports. You can read more about these requirements in Chapter 2, "Installing Windows 98 on a Desktop and Laptop." Another operating system you might have installed is IBM OS/2. The Windows 98 Setup program will not run under OS/2, so you need to start your computer in MS-DOS mode and run Windows 98 Setup from there. If OS/2 is on a *Hewlett-Packard file system* (HPFS) partition, make sure that you have OS/2 Disk 1 handy. You'll need it during the Windows 98 Setup process.

Windows 98 also can be installed on a clean hard disk—a hard disk that has been reformatted and does not contain an operating system or other data files.

Computer Requirements for Installing Windows 98

A PC that currently runs Windows 3.1, 3.11, or Windows 95 without many performance problems should have few problems running Windows 98. A good way to judge whether your PC will perform well with Windows 98 is to open three to four applications and check the system resources. You can do this by choosing Help, About Microsoft Windows in the Windows 3.x Program Manager. To check system resources in Windows 95, run the Resource Meter by choosing Start, Programs, Accessories, System Tools, Resource Meter (see Figure 1.3).

FIG. 1.3

Run a few Windows 95 applications to test your PC's performance prior to installing Windows 98.

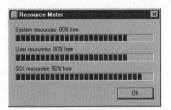

If you can run three to four applications simultaneously and keep the system resources above 50 percent, you should find your system adequate for Windows 98.

Table 1.1 lists the Microsoft minimum system requirements and recommended requirements for running Windows 98. In most cases, you'll have better performance if your system matches or exceeds the recommended requirements.

Table 1.1   Windows 98 Minimum and Recommended System Requirements

Component	Requirement	Recommended Requirement
Processor	80386 or higher	Pentium or Pentium II processor
Hard drive	120MB free space; 45MB of this space is temporary space used only during Windows 98 Setup	300MB free disk space, particularly if you want to include the optional Windows 95 uninstall file (WINUNDO.DAT)
Memory	4MB	16MB–32MB for running four or more applications
Input device	Mouse	Mouse for productivity software; digital joystick for games and entertainment software
Floppy disk drive	Required for installation from floppy disks	Required for installation from floppy disks

continued

Table 1.1 Continued

Component	Requirement	Recommended Requirement
CD-ROM drive	Required for installation from CD-ROM	Quad-speed or faster (such as 24X) for multimedia applications
Monitor	VGA	*SuperVGA* (SVGA)
Fax/modem	Required to use Microsoft Network, Remote Access, HyperTerminal (included in Windows 98), Microsoft Fax, Phone Dialer, and the Microsoft Internet Explorer 4.0 Web browser	33.3Kbps or higher speed for Internet and World Wide Web connectivity
Sound card and speakers	Not required for installation	16-bit sound card for multimedia applications, games, and World Wide Web content; speakers should be rated between 10–40 watts per channel and should have separate volume, bass, and treble controls

CAUTION

Although Windows 98 is a powerful operating system, it is designed only for Intel x86-based processors. Windows 98 also does not support multiple processors, as does Windows NT. You can install Windows 98 on a machine that has multiple processors, but only one processor can be accessed by Windows 98.

Another processor limitation you need to be aware of is that Windows 98 cannot install on a 386-based B-step processor. A B-step processor has an ID of 0303, which can be determined from your system documentation or by using a utility such as Microsoft Diagnostics from MD-DOS. Type **MSD** from the DOS command line to start the Microsoft Diagnostics program and check the CPU settings for the ID of your processor.

The recommended hard drive space in Table 1.1 does not take into consideration the disk space requirement for installing or reinstalling applications to run under Windows 98. For those requirements, refer to the documentation that comes with the specific application you plan to install.

You must decide whether you want to install Windows 98 on top of your existing Windows 3.1 installation. If you choose to install a new directory to preserve your old setup, you must reinstall all your applications to work with Windows 98. (Some applications may run under Windows 98 without reinstalling them, so you might want to try them before reinstalling them.) This means that each application must occupy space again on your hard disk if you plan to use the same application under Windows 3.x and Windows 98. For this reason, calculate the amount of hard drive space you will need for installing the same application twice on your system.

Part
I
Ch
1

Running Windows 98 System Check Software

A quick way to determine whether your system meets the minimum requirements for installing Windows 98 is to use the System Check software designed for Windows 95 and provided by Microsoft. System Check is a small utility (about 76KB) that runs on your computer and reports back to you if your hardware and software are compatible with Windows 95. In most cases, if your system is compatible with Windows 95, you should not have a problem upgrading to Windows 98.

System Check scans your computer and reports on the following items:

- *Memory.* Determines whether your system memory (*random-access memory* or RAM) meets or exceeds the minimum Windows 98 requirements.
- *Processor.* Determines whether the *central processing unit* (CPU) is compatible with Windows 98. System Check also searches for 80386 processors that might not be compatible with Windows 98.
- *Applications.* Searches the first three directory levels for applications that are known not to run well under Windows 98.
- *Hard disk space.* Determines whether your hard disk has enough space to install Windows 98. If your hard disk is compressed, System Check determines whether enough space is available to create a boot drive for the compressed volume.
- *Swap file space.* Determines whether your hard disk has enough space for a swap file (virtual memory) to be created.

NOTE System Check does a fine job of reporting the preceding items. It does not determine whether your hard disk has errors on it; whether viruses are located on your computer; whether peripherals (such as modems or CD-ROMs) are compatible with Windows; or whether network adapters, protocols, and network resources are compatible with Windows 98, though. For compatibility information on these items, see the table of contents in this book for related chapters. ∎

To install System Check and run it on your computer, you first need to download it from the Microsoft Web site at

`http://www.microsoft.com/windows95/info/w95pcready.htm`

Click the Download hyperlink to get a copy of System Check. The file is only 76KB and takes only a few seconds to download using a 28.8Kbps modem. The default filename for System Check is SYSCHECK.EXE, which is a self-extracting file that runs under Windows 3.0, Windows 3.1, Windows for Workgroups, Windows NT 3.51 or earlier, and IBM OS/2. (If System Check runs on a computer already running Windows 95, it does not scan the system; instead, it reports that your system is compatible with Windows 95, which means that Windows 98 will run on your system as well.)

The following steps show how to run System Check on a computer running Windows 3.1:

1. In File Manager, double-click the file SYSCHECK.EXE to uncompress it. This places three files on your system: W95CHECK.EXE, VER.DLL, and README.TXT. (If you are running System Check under Windows 3.0, make sure that the VER.DLL file is in the same directory as the W95CHECK.EXE file. Sometimes, these files can be in different places if you are running W95CHECK.EXE from a floppy disk.)

2. Double-click the W95CHECK.EXE file to execute it.

3. Follow the onscreen directions to run System Check on your particular operating system. After System Check runs, the Windows System Check dialog box appears and reports any compatibility problems with your system.

4. Click OK.

If System Check reports any compatibility problems with your system, you need to upgrade or replace your system before attempting to install Windows 98.

Reviewing the Windows 95 and Windows NT Logo Program Web Site

Along with the System Check utility, you also can review the Microsoft Windows Logo Program Web site to determine whether the hardware and software you have or plan to purchase are tested to run with Windows 98. Software and hardware tested to work under Windows 95 should have little or no problems running under Windows 98.

 Many applications and hardware devices include files that provide updated information about specific problems (known as *bugs*). Be sure to read these files, which are usually in TXT format and are known as README.TXT files, to find out whether any known compatibility problems exist with Windows 95 or Windows 98.

The Microsoft Windows Logo Program Web site is located on the World Wide Web at

http://www.microsoft.com/windows/thirdparty/winlogo/default.htm

Currently, more than 1,000 products have passed testing to be approved for the Microsoft Designed for Windows NT and Windows 95 Logo program. This program includes a set of recommendations and requirements for all software manufacturers to create software that is compatible with Windows 98 and Windows NT. Some of the guidelines follow:

- Provide automated installation and update features.
- Use the Windows Registry for configuration and system settings.
- Include enhanced accessibility features for people with disabilities.
- Include Java support for software distributed over networks.

After you connect to the Microsoft Windows Logo Program Web site, click the Search for Tested Software hyperlink to see a list of software that meets the Designed for Windows Logo requirements. Likewise, click the Hardware that Meets the Test hyperlink to connect to the *Windows Hardware Quality Labs* (WHQL) Web page, on which you can locate a link to the *Hardware Compatibility List* (HCL). Click this link to see a list of hardware that meets the Designed for Windows Logo program for hardware devices.

If you plan to purchase new hardware for your system, use the Hardware Compatibility List to see whether older, legacy hardware works with Windows 98. For new hardware that does not appear on the HCL, look for the Designed for Windows 95 logo on the hardware packaging. This tells you whether the device has passed the Windows 98 compatibility testing.

You also may see products that claim they "work under Windows 95." These products do not pass the Designed for Windows NT and Windows 95 logo requirements. However, these products have been shown to work with Windows 95 and, in most cases, you should not have problems running them on your system.

When you purchase software for Windows 98, you should review the Software that Meets the Test Web site to determine whether your software runs under Windows 98. Most software that runs under Windows 3.1 or Windows 95 should run fine under Windows 98. However, some applications, many of which are games, have difficulty migrating to the Windows 98 platform. When you purchase new software for Windows 98, look for the Designed for Windows 98 logo on the software packaging to ensure that it is written for Windows 98.

 At the time of this writing, Microsoft had published initial guidelines for designing products for Windows NT 5.0 and Windows 98. To read a preliminary white paper on the Designed for Windows NT 5.0 and Windows 98 logo requirements, visit

    http://www.microsoft.com/windows/thirdparty/winlogo/enterprise/
    roadmap2.htm

Hard Drive Requirements

In addition to being able to handle sheer volume, your hard drive needs to be prepared to handle Windows 98. "Preparing for Installation," later in this chapter, shows you how to optimize your hard disk before you install Windows 98. This section discusses partitioned drives and compressed drives.

Partitioned Drives

Many people use partitioned drives to organize files or to install another operating system on the same hard disk. To install Windows 98, you must have a *file allocation table* (FAT) partition on your hard disk. With the release of Windows 95, a new 32-bit, protected-mode FAT system was introduced. This same FAT system is supported by Windows 98 as well. It enables long filenames (filenames with up to 256 characters instead of the old limit of eight plus three characters) and exclusive access to disk devices, such as ScanDisk.

Windows 98 also features an enhanced file system, called FAT32, that enables you to format hard drives of more than 2GB as a single hard drive. FAT32 also is designed to use smaller clusters than older FAT file systems, enabling Windows 98 to use your hard drive in a more efficient manner. You learn more about FAT32 in Chapter 14, "Configuring Memory, Disks, and Devices."

Windows 98 installs over existing MS-DOS FAT partitions as long as you have enough space in the partition for Windows 98. You also need at least 5MB for the Windows 98 swap file. Partitions set up by third-party schemes, including Disk Manager DMDRVR.BIN and Storage Dimension's SpeedStor SSTOR.SYS, also are recognized by Windows 98. If you decide to convert your hard drive from FAT to FAT32, Windows 98 includes the FAT32 conversion utility to guide you through the conversion process.

TIP

If you use FDISK to partition removable drives, such as Bernoulli drives, you shouldn't have a problem with Windows 98 accessing those drives.

If you have IBM OS/2 installed on your system, you must have MS-DOS installed as well to install Windows 98. Windows 98 must run from MS-DOS if OS/2 is in your primary partition, which usually is the case when running OS/2 to take advantage of the OS/2 dual-boot feature.

As indicated earlier, Windows 98 does not recognize the NTFS that can be set up for Windows NT. If you are running NTFS, you can install Windows 98 on a FAT partition if enough disk space is present and then use NT's multiple-boot feature to boot into Windows 98. If you do not have a FAT partition established, set up one and then perform the Windows 98 installation. Chapter 10, "Installing and Configuring Hard Disk Drives," discusses how to set up a FAT partition.

CAUTION

If you want to delete disk partitions on your hard disk prior to installing Windows 98, do so with caution. You might want to delete a partition to free up disk space or if you no longer need a particular partition. Make sure that you have all critical data backed up and secure before deleting the partition. Keep in mind that during the partitioning stage, you will lose all the data on your hard disk and will need to reload MS-DOS on your hard drive before you can run Windows 98 Setup from an upgrade or full version.

You can use the DOS-based FDISK command to delete partitions before creating a new primary partition. You must delete partitions in the following order:

- Any non-DOS partitions
- Any logical drives in the extended DOS partition
- Any extended DOS partitions
- The existing primary DOS partition

To delete a partition or logical drive, follow these steps:

1. At the DOS prompt, enter **FDISK** to display the FDISK Options dialog box.
2. Press 3 and then press Enter. The Delete DOS Partition or Logical DOS Drive dialog box appears.

▶ **See** "Partitioning a Hard Drive," **p. 178**

3. Press the number that corresponds to the number onscreen for the kind of partition you want to delete, and then press Enter.
4. Follow the directions onscreen, and repeat the steps for deleting any additional logical drives or partitions.

T I P If FDISK cannot delete a non-DOS partition, quit FDISK, delete the non-DOS partition by using the software used to create it, and then restart FDISK.

Compressed Drives

Another hard disk situation you might encounter is the use of compression applications to increase the virtual size of your hard disk. Most compression software, such as Microsoft DriveSpace or DoubleSpace and Stac Electronics Stacker software (versions 2.x and higher), are supported by Windows 98. One point to keep in mind before you start Windows 98 Setup is to make sure that you have enough free space on an uncompressed drive for a swap file. Swap files, which Windows 98 uses as virtual memory, can be set up on compressed drives only if you use the DriveSpace 3 utility provided with Microsoft Plus! for Windows. If you do not have this utility, you must set up your swap file on an uncompressed drive.

N O T E   A Windows *swap file* is a special file on your hard disk that is used by Windows to store files temporarily as you work. Swap files also are known as *virtual memory* because they "virtually" increase the amount of storage area where information can be stored during a Windows operation. The information stored in swap files is lost when you leave Windows. ■

As a rule of thumb, you need 14MB of total memory (RAM plus virtual memory) on your system. To figure this amount, add the amount of physical memory you have to the amount of virtual memory you have (this is your swap file size). This gives you your total system memory. If you have 4MB of memory in your system, for example, you need a swap file that is at least 10MB. Free up that amount of uncompressed disk space before running Windows 98 Setup. Even if you have more than 14MB of RAM on your system, you should set aside at least 5MB of uncompressed disk space for a swap file in case you ever need it.

N O T E   For information on freeing up uncompressed disk space, consult your DOS documentation or the documentation that comes with your compression software. You also can pick up a copy of Que's *Using MS-DOS 6.2*, Special Edition for coverage of compressed disks.

If Windows 95 is on your computer and you use DriveSpace 3 to compress your hard disk, choose Drive, Adjust Free Space to change the amount of uncompressed disk space. Drag the slider to the amount of free disk space you want and click OK. If Windows prompts you to, restart your computer. ▓

Windows 98 includes built-in support for Microsoft DriveSpace 3 and is compatible with DoubleSpace, which is provided with MS-DOS 6.x. Windows 98 compression uses a 32-bit virtual device driver to give it better performance over the 16-bit product available in MS-DOS 6.x. The 32-bit driver also frees up conventional memory so that MS-DOS–based applications can use it. If you currently use DoubleSpace or DriveSpace with DOS 6.x or Windows 3.x, you do not need to make changes to the *compressed volume file* (CVF) that these applications currently are using. Likewise, if you use DriveSpace 3 with Windows 95, you do not have to make any changes for Windows 98. Except for freeing up enough space for a swap file, as pointed out earlier, you do not have to change any settings or instruct Windows 98 to install over the compressed drive. It does this automatically.

Installing on SuperStor and XtraDrive Compressed Drives

If your hard disk has been compressed by using SuperStor, you might have some problems installing Windows 98 on your drive. First try running Windows 98 Setup. If you receive a message that Setup cannot locate your startup drive, you must exit Setup, uncompress your hard disk, and remove SuperStor from your computer. See the documentation that comes with SuperStor for directions on uncompressing hard drives and uninstalling SuperStor. After you complete these tasks, restart Windows 98 Setup.

If you are upgrading from a previous version of Windows that uses XtraDrive to compress your hard drive, you first must turn off XtraDrive's write cache before attempting to start Windows 98 Setup. To do this, exit Windows and type **VMU.EXE** at the DOS prompt. This activates the XtraDrive Volume Maintenance utility. Next, perform the following steps:

1. Select Advanced Options and press Enter.
2. Change the EMS cache size to 0. Also, set the conventional cache size to 1.
3. Change the Allow Write Caching option to No.
4. Click Yes when prompted to confirm your changes and to restart your computer.
5. Exit the Volume Maintenance utility.
6. Restart your computer.

After your computer restarts, start Windows and activate Windows 98 Setup.

Online Connection Requirements

Windows 98 includes several new World Wide Web–based features to enable you to take advantage of the Internet. Some of these features include the Microsoft Internet Explorer 4.0 Web browser, NetMeeting conferencing software, Outlook Express email and newsgroup reader, and other components. When you want to use Windows 98's Internet features, you need to make sure that your system is connected to the Internet and World Wide Web. You can do this in two ways. First, you can be connected to the Internet through a connection via a LAN. The other connection possibility is to use a modem to connect to the Internet through an *Internet service provider* (ISP).

The general requirements for connecting to the Internet follow:

- *Internet account.* Regardless of how you connect to the Internet, you need to be assigned a unique address on the Internet, called an *Internet protocol* (IP) address. If you plan to send or receive email, you also need an email address. If you connect to the Internet through a LAN, ask your system administrator for your Internet account information. If you connect through a modem, you need to obtain an account with an ISP, who in turns provides you with your Internet account information. Chapter 19, "Configuring an Internet Connection," explains how to get an Internet account.

- *Physical connection.* If you use a LAN to access the Internet, your physical connection most likely will be networking cable, such as 10BASE-T or coaxial, connected to an installed network adapter card in your computer. If you use a modem, you need a standard phone line to which you can connect. If you plan to connect to the Internet for long periods of time, you might want to invest in a separate phone line for your online connections. This way, you can connect to the Internet with one line and make regular phone calls with the other line. Another type of connection is an *Integrated Services Digital Network* (ISDN) phone line that provides high-speed connections to the Internet. Windows 98 includes the ISDN Configuration Wizard, which helps you set up Windows 98 for ISDN support. You learn more about this tool in Chapter 7.

- *Connection software.* You need two types of software to connect to the Internet. First, you need software that adds the networking protocol *Transfer Control Protocol/Internet Protocol* (TCP/IP) to your system. Windows 98 includes a built-in version of TCP/IP that you can use. You also can use third-party TCP/IP software (usually called a *protocol stack*), such as FTP Software's OnNet32 2.0 for Windows 98.

  The second type of connection software you need is dial-up software. This software is used by the modem to dial your ISP and to make the connection to the Internet. You can use Windows 98's built-in Dial-Up Networking software as your dial-up software.

- *Browsing software.* This is the software you use to access resources on the World Wide Web and Internet. Microsoft's Internet Explorer 4.0 Web browser is provided with Windows 98.

Preparing for Installation

You'll find that the Windows 98 installation process goes much smoother if you do a few pre-setup tasks before you launch Windows 98 Setup. You should keep in mind that installing Windows 98 is a major upgrade to your computer. If you decide to do so, you can use Windows 98 to totally replace your existing operating system, such as Windows 95, DOS, or Windows 3.x. This section describes many of the preliminary tasks you should do before installing Windows 98 to your system.

Back Up System Files

One of the most overlooked areas of computing is performing backup procedures. You might be one of those lucky users who are connected to a LAN, and the system administrator takes care of all your backup needs. Or you might have been victim to a system crash in the past, so you now regularly run a system-wide backup every day.

If you are like many other users, though, you don't take the time to back up your data; you only think about it when you lose some critical data. Before you run Windows 98 installation, however, back up all the files you don't want to lose. It is better to assume that you will lose something instead of hoping that you won't.

As a place to start, you should back up the files shown in the following list. Back up these files to a tape backup system, a recordable CD-ROM, a network backup system, floppy disks, or other backup media. Do not back up the files to your local hard disk if that's where you are installing Windows 98. You might encounter data loss at some point and be unable to access your local drive.

- *AUTOEXEC.BAT.* As Windows 98 installs, it modifies your current AUTOEXEC.BAT file to include Windows 98–specific instructions. If a problem occurs during the Windows 98 install process, you might need to reboot into your old configuration. Having a backup of AUTOEXEC.BAT will speed up this process. You can find this file in your root directory.

- *CONFIG.SYS.* As with the AUTOEXEC.BAT file, Windows 98 modifies CONFIG.SYS during installation. A backup copy of CONFIG.SYS will save you time and headaches if you need to restore your original system. This file is located in your root directory.

- *INI files.* If you currently run Windows 3.x, you need to make sure that all your INI files are backed up. Not all INI files are stored in the same directory, so you'll need to look for them. A quick way to locate all your INI files is to run a search for *.INI in Windows File Manager.

- *Registry files.* In Windows 95, back up the SYSTEM.DAT and USER.DAT files, which make up the Windows 95 Registry. You can use these files to restore a corrupted Registry database if you experience problems during Windows 98 installation and need to return to your old Windows 95 installation. Because these files can become large, you might need to back them up to a tape backup or other large-capacity backup system. If you have access to a network server, you might place a copy of these files there as well.

- *Personal documents and files.* Often, you overlook your personal documents—such as memos, spreadsheets, drawings, and so on—during backup procedures; be sure to back up these elements. You also should back up any templates you have customized. Also remember to back up program files associated with your email client, newsgroup reader, and other utilities. In short, you should back up anything that you don't want to spend time re-creating.

- *Group files.* Group files tell Windows 3.x what to display in groups in Program Manager. Group files, denoted as GRP, are in the \Windows directory. You can use GRP files to populate the Start menu in Windows 98.

- *Network files.* Although Windows 98 has built-in networking support, many installations will rely on their existing network setups. Check with your system administrator to find out which files associated with the network you should back up.

Create a Boot Disk

Along with backing up your system, you should create a boot disk of your current system. A *boot disk* enables you to boot your system from a floppy disk in case you have a major problem during the Windows 98 installation process.

To create a boot disk in Windows 3.x, insert a floppy disk into the floppy drive from which your system boots, which usually is the A: drive. Next, in Windows File Manager, choose Disk, Make System Disk, and select the Make System Disk check box. Click OK. Store this disk in a safe place and don't copy over it.

In DOS, you can make a system disk by using the FORMAT command, such as FORMAT A:/S.

TIP When you make a DOS boot disk, you might have room to add useful DOS utilities to it. If so, add FORMAT, COPY, CHKDSK, and MSCDEX.

In Windows 95, you can make a startup disk by choosing Start, Settings, Control Panel and double-clicking the Add/Remove Programs icon. Select the Startup Disk tab and click Create Disk. Label a floppy disk **Windows 95 Startup Disk** and insert the disk into your A: drive, which is the drive from which your computer boots. Click OK to finish creating the startup disk.

Turn Off TSRs and Time-Out Features

During the Windows 98 installation process, your system may at times appear to pause or stop working. During these times, Windows 98 is preparing system files and checking your existing system configuration. For this reason, if you have power-down features, such as those in laptops, turn off those features so that the installation process is not terminated prematurely.

You also should disable *terminate-and-stay-resident* (TSR) programs and screen savers that may turn on during the install process. You need to clear out all but the necessary device drivers and batch files from memory. You can do this by remarking out (using the REM label) appropriate lines in your AUTOEXEC.BAT and CONFIG.SYS files (after you back up these files, of course). Do not delete settings for the following drivers, however: network drivers, CD-ROMs, video cards, and the mouse. You can remark out lines by starting the DOS EDIT utility, opening the appropriate file, such as AUTOEXEC.BAT, and inserting the word **REM** in front of the line you want to disable. Save the file and restart your machine for these settings to take place.

> **CAUTION**
>
> Do not turn off TSRs that are used for partitions or hard disk control, or you might encounter problems when booting your computer into the primary disk partition.

Delete the Windows Swap File

In the "Compressed Drives" section earlier in this chapter, you read that Windows 98 uses a swap file. Windows 3.x uses a temporary or permanent swap file, but Windows 95 and Windows 98 use a dynamic swap file. A *dynamic swap file* changes as needed by the system. Your old permanent swap file no longer is needed by Windows 98, so you can remove it for added hard disk space. If you are upgrading from Windows 95, do *not* delete its swap file.

> **CAUTION**
>
> Windows 98 enables you to boot into Windows 3.x and Windows 98 if you do not set up FAT32 support on the partition that contains DOS and Windows 98. If you choose to have both operating systems on your computer, *do not* delete the swap file from your system. You'll still need it for Windows 3.x to run.

Defragment and Check Your Hard Disk

After you back up and delete files from your hard disk, you should run a disk-defragment utility to clean up your hard drive. When you run a disk-defragment utility, the hard disk reorganizes files so that you get optimal performance from the drive. As you use your computer (copying, deleting, and creating files), your hard disk becomes fragmented, increasing the disk-access time. A disk-defragment utility cleans up your disk and eliminates fragmented files.

Microsoft DOS 6.0 and higher include a disk-defragment utility called DEFRAG. To run it, exit Windows 3.x and type **DEFRAG** at the DOS prompt. Follow the instructions onscreen to optimize your hard drive. Other programs, such as Norton Utilities and PC Tools, include defragment programs as well.

During the Windows 98 installation process, Windows 98 runs ScanDisk to check your drive. ScanDisk, which fixes and repairs hard drive errors, is another disk utility included with Windows 98 Setup. The problem with Windows 98 running ScanDisk during installation is that if you have a problem that ScanDisk cannot fix (which occurs many times), you might have trouble cleaning up the problem in DOS. This is because, during the initial part of the Windows 98 install (even before ScanDisk is executed), long filenames are created on your hard drive. If ScanDisk reports a hard drive error it cannot fix, the Windows 98 install stops, and you are returned to your old Windows 3.x or DOS setup. Then, when you try to run a disk-defragment utility such as DEFRAG to correct the problem ScanDisk found, you get an error when the software encounters the long filenames Windows 98 placed on your hard drive. You have to delete those files manually if this occurs. The best solution is to defragment your hard drive before starting the Windows 98 installation process.

Another utility you should run is CHKDSK. Run CHKDSK /F from the DOS prompt to analyze and fix any surface-level problems with your hard disk. If CHKDSK encounters errors or bad files, it asks whether you want CHKDSK to fix them or leave them for you to fix. You should let CHKDSK fix them in most cases.

If you have Windows 95 installed, you can run Disk Defragmenter—a tool designed to defragment your hard drive. To use Disk Defragmenter, choose Start, Programs, Accessories, System Tools, Disk Defragmenter. After the Select Drives dialog box appears, select the drive you want to defragment (such as the C: drive) and click OK.

Run Antivirus Software

Before starting the Windows 98 Setup program, run an antivirus software program on your MS-DOS and Windows 95 computer before upgrading to Windows 98. That way, if there are any virus programs on your system, you can find them before installing Windows 98 on your system. For Windows 95, a few of the programs available include McAfee VirusScan 3.0 and Norton AntiVirus 2.0. For MS-DOS, Microsoft Anti-Virus comes with MS-DOS 6.22. You also might want to purchase a copy of Norton AntiVirus for Windows 3.x, which usually locates and deletes more known viruses than Microsoft Anti-Virus.

After you run the antivirus software, turn it off and make sure that any *Complementary Metal-Oxide Semiconductor* (CMOS) or *basic input/output system* (BIOS)-based antivirus settings are disabled. If you attempt to run Windows 98 Setup with these programs enabled, you'll receive an error message, and Setup will stop. You need to consult the documentation that comes with your computer and antivirus software for instructions on disabling CMOS and BIOS-based antivirus settings.

Program Tasks

Before starting Windows 98 Setup, shut down all applications (except Windows itself), including Explorer (or File Manager in Windows 3.1) and My Computer. You need to do this to ensure that any shared files that need to be updated can be updated.

Also, remove any program icons from the StartUp folder so that those programs do not start when Windows 98 reboots during the installation process.

Finally, open WIN.INI in Notepad and remark the LOAD= and RUN= lines, such as **REM load=C:\NORTON\NORTON.EXE**.

CHAPTER 2

Installing Windows 98 on a Desktop and Laptop

by Rod Tidrow

In this chapter

Using Windows 98 Setup

You learned in Chapter 1, "Preparing to Install Windows 98," that there are steps you take to prepare your machine for Windows 98. After you make these preparations on your machine, you are ready to start installing Windows 98. The following sections show you how to install Windows 98 from Windows 98 and Windows 3.x. You also learn how to upgrade from MS-DOS, Microsoft Windows NT, and IBM OS/2—three other popular operating systems.

N O T E   If you purchase a new computer, Windows 98 already might be installed on it. To determine whether it is installed, right-click the My Computer icon and choose Properties. On the General tab, look at the information just below the System: heading. It will say Microsoft Windows 98 if Windows 98 is installed. If it is, you can bypass this chapter. ■

After you prepare your computer for Windows 98, you can start the Windows 98 Setup program. Setup is located on the Windows 98 installation disks or CD-ROM. The Windows 98 Setup program uses a Setup Wizard that displays many dialog boxes and useful prompts to help you install Windows 98 on your system.

N O T E   You'll find valuable information contained in various text files (such as README.TXT and SETUP.TXT) on the Windows 98 CD-ROM or installation disks. Read these files for information that might pertain to your specific system hardware or software. ■

Taking Your System's Inventory

Before you start Setup, make a note of the following items' configuration settings (such as IRQ, I/O, and DMA information) on your system:

- Video card and monitor type
- Mouse type
- Network configuration, including network operating system (such as IntranetWare or NetWare 4.0), network adapter name (such as NE2000 or 3Com), protocol supported (such as TCP/IP), and mapped drive specifications (such as H:).
- Printer type and port
- Modem type and port
- CD-ROM
- SCSI adapter, if installed
- Identification number of your Windows 98 disks or CD-ROM
- Other devices, including sound cards, scanners, and joystick

N O T E   The easiest way to determine your network configuration settings is to ask your system administrator for them. ■

Installation Options

Windows 98 provides you with several installation options from which to choose. Depending on the configuration of your system, you have the following setup options:

- Install Windows 98 from DOS
- Upgrade Windows 3.x to Windows 98
- Dual boot Windows 98 with Windows 3.x
- Upgrade Windows 95 to Windows 98
- Migrate from Windows NT to Windows 98
- Dual boot Windows 98 and Windows NT
- Install Windows 98 over IBM OS/2
- Install Windows 98 on a freshly formatted hard drive
- Choose different install options to determine which Windows 98 components are installed
- Install Windows 98 from across a local area network
- Create a customized and automated installation
- Maintain or update an installation

Upgrading Windows 95 to Windows 98

Probably your safest bet for getting a clean and trouble-free installation is to install Windows 98 over a copy of Windows 95. Windows 98 is designed to replace Windows 95 and does so by reusing configuration information about installed applications and Windows applets (such as Paint, WordPad, and other components). When you upgrade from Windows 95, the amount of data you must enter during the Windows 98 Setup is kept to a minimum. You do not have to fill out user information or which components to install, for example. After the file-copy stage of Windows 98 Setup completes, you do not have to input any other data until you are ready to start working in the Windows 98 environment. The only exception to this is if you have to enter a login password when Windows 98 reboots to finish the final setup stage.

When you upgrade from Windows 95, you have the option of creating a backup file of Windows 95 files in case you decide to uninstall Windows 98. When you do this, your previous Windows 95 installation is recovered, and all traces of Windows 98 are deleted from your computer. You need approximately 50MB of free space for this uninstall file (called WINUNDO.DAT), in addition to the free space devoted to Windows 98 installation files. You can place WINUNDO.DAT on your primary drive (such as drive C:), or on another drive or partition, if another is available.

If you have Windows 98 on CD-ROM, Setup runs automatically under Windows 95 if the AutoRun feature for your CD-ROM drive is activated (which it should be, unless you have explicitly disabled it). After you insert the Windows 98 CD-ROM, Setup tells you that an older version of Windows is installed and asks whether you want to upgrade to Windows 98. Click Yes to start.

If you have Windows 98 on a floppy disk, open Explorer and locate the Setup.Exe file on the first disk. Double-click this file to start Windows 98 Setup.

The Windows 98 Setup welcome screen appears, as shown in Figure 2.1.

FIG. 2.1

Installing Windows 98 begins at the Windows 98 Setup screen.

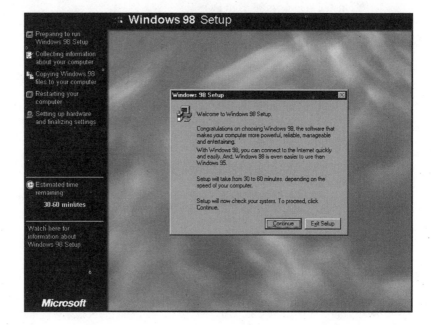

 N O T E   If you are familiar with Windows 95 Setup, you will see that the Windows 98 Setup screen differs quite a bit from the Windows 95 Setup screen. On the left side of the screen are descriptions of the stages Windows 98 Setup will go through on your machine, including the estimated time remaining for the current stage. ▉

Follow these steps to continue:

1. Click Continue. Windows 98 prepares to run Windows 98 Setup and looks at your system to determine whether other applications are running. If it finds other running applications, you're prompted to close them before continuing (see Figure 2.2). By keeping other applications running, you run the risk of certain shared files (such as dynamic link libraries and device drivers) not being updated properly.

T I P   Press Ctrl+Tab to switch to an open application. Be sure to save your work in that application, and then close it.

2. Click OK. The License Agreement screen appears (see Figure 2.3). Read the agreement and click I Accept the Agreement. If you click I Don't Accept the Agreement, you won't be allowed to continue installing Windows 98.

FIG. 2.2
Be sure to close all
other applications
before continuing to run
Windows 98 Setup.

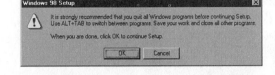

FIG 2.3
You must choose to
accept the license
agreement before
you're allowed to
continue.

3. Click Next. The Checking Your System screen appears. During this stage, the following tasks are performed:

- Windows 98 Setup collects information from your Windows 95 Registry database that Setup needs to upgrade your PC.

- Windows 98 Setup checks for the installed components from your previous Windows 95 configuration. Windows 98 Setup uses this information to install only those components during the Copying Windows 98 Files To Your Computer stage.

N O T E When upgrading to Windows 98 from Windows 95, you do not have the option of selecting or deselecting optional components. Windows 98 Setup assumes that you want the same components installed under Windows 98. Later, you can install or uninstall components as necessary by using the Add/Remove Programs Wizard. You can read about optional components in Chapter 3, "Selecting Windows 98 Components." ▪

- Windows 98 Setup prepares the Windows directory in which Windows 98 will be installed. This will be the same directory in which Windows 95 resides, usually named

- Windows 98 determines whether your PC has enough free disk space available on which to install Windows 98.

4. After the preceding tasks are performed, the Internet Channels screen appears (see Figure 2.4). Select the country in which you reside to specify the proper set of Internet channels for you.

FIG. 2.4
Internet channels provide automatically downloaded information from the World Wide Web to your desktop.

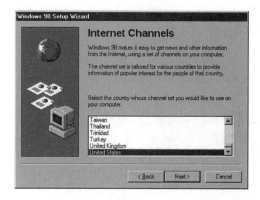

5. Click Next. The Emergency Startup Disk screen appears (see Figure 2.5). The emergency startup disk is your life preserver in case you experience problems with Windows 98 after it's installed. You use this disk to start your PC and diagnose problems using files stored on the emergency startup disk. By taking a few minutes now and using one floppy disk, you insure yourself against potential problems.

FIG. 2.5
The emergency startup disk includes diagnostic programs and important system files.

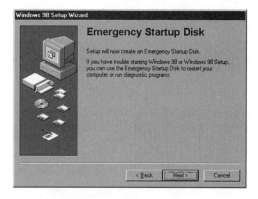

You'll need a blank floppy disk or a floppy disk that can be reformatted. All files will be lost if you choose to reformat a disk. Also, be sure the disk is one used by the floppy disk drive that boots your computer (the A: drive).

6. Click Next. Insert a floppy disk into your A: drive when prompted. Click OK to continue.

CAUTION

You also can click Cancel when prompted to insert a floppy disk if you do not want to create an emergency startup disk. This is not recommended, though, because you do not know when you'll experience problems while starting Windows 98. Go ahead and create the startup disk now and store it in a safe place. If you're installing on a laptop PC, you might want to throw a copy of this disk in your laptop carrying case.

7. Click OK after the Windows 98 Startup Disk dialog box appears, informing you that the startup disk is created. Also, remove the startup disk from your A: drive.

8. After the Start Copying Files screen appears, click Next (see Figure 2.6). Windows 98 Setup begins installing files to your computer. This process can take between 30 and 60 minutes. If you're installing from a CD-ROM, you can sit back and relax. If, however, you're installing from floppy disks, you'll need feed disks into your floppy drive as requested.

FIG. 2.6
When Windows 98 Setup has enough information to start copying files, the Start Copying Files screen appears.

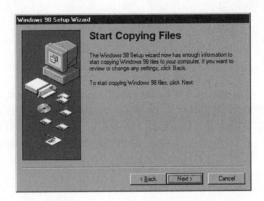

 TIP Watch the Estimated Time Remaining and file-copy progress items on the left side of the Windows 98 Setup screen to monitor the installation progress.

After Windows 98 Setup finishes copying files, Setup needs to restart your PC. It does this in one of two ways:

■ You can click the Restart Now button after Windows displays a screen telling you that Setup must restart your PC to continue the installation process.

■ Or, after 15 seconds, Setup automatically restarts your computer.

Your PC shuts down and restarts. Windows 98 then runs for the first time and updates your configuration files. Be patient, because this process might take a few minutes to complete.

The Windows 98 Setup screen appears after your files are updated. At this point, the Setting Up Hardware and Finalizing Settings stage begins. In this stage, your installed hardware is config-ured to work under Windows 98. If your devices were running properly under Windows 95, there should be no problems with them under Windows 98. However, if you do experience problems with a device, consult the chapter in this book relating to that device to fix it. Also, you might need to consult the manufacturer of that device to inquire about any new device drivers or system settings required to get the device working under Windows 98.

Part
I

Ch
2

Your machine may restart a few times during the Setting Up Hardware and Finalizing Settings stage. After your hardware is configured, the following items are set up:

- Control Panel
- Programs on the Start menu
- Windows Help
- MS-DOS program settings
- Application start tune up
- System configuration

TROUBLESHOOTING

I was running Setup, and my machine crashed. Do I have to run Setup from the beginning again?
Technically, no. Windows 98 Setup includes a smart-recovery mechanism that maintains a log file during Setup. If Setup crashes, the last entry in the Setup log identifies where Windows needs to start from to resume installation. However, the best answer for this question is yes; you should restart Setup from the beginning and install all the Windows 98 files again. This is because some files might have become corrupted during the system crash.

Again, Windows 98 Setup restarts your PC after the preceding items are set up. Windows 98 then starts for the first time (see Figure 2.7). If you need to test your Windows 98 installation or you have questions about running Windows 98 Safe mode, see the "Starting Windows 98" section, later in this chapter.

FIG. 2.7
The Welcome to Windows 98 screen is the first screen you see after Windows 98 starts.

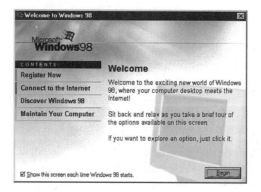

N O T E It's beyond the scope of this book to show you how to use Windows 98 and its various components. Click the Discover Windows 98 button on the Welcome to Windows 98 screen to tour Windows 98's features. Or, read *Special Edition Using Windows 98*, published by Que. ■

TROUBLESHOOTING

I can't boot into Windows. What can I do? Reboot your computer and press F8 to activate the Startup menu in MS-DOS. Select the Safe Mode option to start Windows 98 in Safe mode. Now you can boot into Windows and diagnose the problem. In many cases, you might have a device-driver conflict. To see if you do, select Start, Settings, Control Panel, and double-click the System icon. Select the Device Manager tab and review the device settings listed. If you see a big red X next to a device, select it and click the Remove button. Click OK. You'll need to reboot your machine to see whether this fixes your problem.

Starting Windows 98 Setup from Windows 3.x

One popular installation method is to install Windows 98 from Windows 3.x. When you do this, Windows 98 migrates your SYSTEM.INI, WIN.INI, and PROTOCOL.INI configuration settings and your Windows 3.x file associations into the Windows 98 Registry. The Registry entries in your Windows 3.x configuration are file and program associations. You need to preserve these to make your applications work under Windows 98.

Another conversion that takes place during the Windows 98 setup is that of Windows 3.x Program Manager to Windows 98 *folders*. Folders in Windows 98 have replaced program groups. You access program folders from the Start button in Windows 98.

By default, Windows 98 installs over your existing Windows 3.x. When this occurs, the applications installed are updated automatically. If, however, you decide to keep your existing Windows 3.x setup, you need to reinstall all your applications under Windows 98.

> **CAUTION**
>
> Before running Windows 98 Setup on Windows 3.x systems, disable all third-party memory managers, such as QEMM. Also, remove all third-party compression managers, including Stacker, from your system. You can leave Microsoft compression managers on your system, however, such as DriveSpace.

Use these steps to install Windows 98 from Windows 3.x:

1. Start your computer and run Windows 3.x. Make sure all applications are closed before running Setup.

2. For installation from floppy disk, insert the disk labeled Disk #1 into the floppy drive. If you are installing from CD-ROM, place the CD-ROM into the CD-ROM drive.

3. From Program Manager, choose File, Run. In the Run dialog box, type the letter of the drive containing the disk or CD-ROM, a colon (:), a backslash (\), and the command **SETUP**. The following command, for example, starts Setup from a floppy drive labeled A:

   A:\SETUP

4. Click OK. Setup starts, and the Windows 98 Installation Wizard initializes and begins installing Windows 98.

You're given the option of selecting the type of installation Windows 98 should take. You can choose from Typical, Custom, Portable, and Compact. Select one of these options to continue with the install process. Continue working through the Setup Wizard as explained in "Upgrading Windows 95 to Windows 98," earlier in this chapter.

TROUBLESHOOTING

Do I need to reinstall my programs when I install Windows 98? Windows 98 picks up program settings when you upgrade an existing version of Windows or Windows for Workgroups. If Windows 98 is installed in a separate directory, all Windows-based programs need to be reinstalled.

Starting Windows 98 Setup from DOS

If you do not have Windows 3.x installed on your system, you can install Windows 98 from DOS. Windows 98 first installs a mini-version of Windows on your system. The Windows 98 Setup program that runs is a 16-bit, Windows-based application, so it needs to use these files to execute. You cannot run install from an MS-DOS prompt from within Windows 3.x.

In cases in which you do not have MS-DOS installed, such as upgrading from IBM OS/2 or Windows NT, you need to install DOS on a partition and run the Windows 98 Setup program from the DOS partition.

To start Windows 98 Setup from DOS, use the following steps:

1. Start your computer.
2. For installation from floppy disk, insert the disk labeled Disk #1 in the floppy drive. If you are installing from CD-ROM, place the CD-ROM into the CD-ROM drive.
3. At the DOS command prompt, type the letter of the drive that contains the setup disks, a colon (:), a backslash (\), and the command **SETUP**. You can use the following command, for example, to start Windows 98 Setup from a floppy disk labeled A:

    A:\SETUP

4. Press Enter. Setup starts, and the Windows 98 Installation Wizard initializes and begins installing Windows 98.

You're given the option of selecting the type of installation Windows 98 should use. You can choose Typical, Custom, Portable, or Compact. Select an option to continue with the install process. Continue working through the Setup Wizard as explained in "Upgrading Windows 95 to Windows 98," earlier in this chapter.

TROUBLESHOOTING

My icons in Windows 98 are black. Is this normal? No, this is not normal and might mean that the SHELLICO file has been corrupted. This file is a hidden file and is in your Windows folder. (Open Explorer, select View, and select Folder Options. Then select the View tab, choose Show All Files in the Hidden Files Folder, and click OK.) Delete the SHELLICO file and reboot your computer. As Windows 95 restarts, the SHELLICO file rebuilds automatically, and your icons should display correctly. If this doesn't work, reboot the computer and press F8 when your computer boots. From the Startup menu, select Safe Mode and start Windows. Shut down Windows and then reboot your computer again.

Migrating from Windows NT 4.0 to Windows 98

Most installations that have Windows NT 4.0 installed will want to run both Windows NT and Windows 98 in a multiboot environment. To set up Windows 98 in this situation, boot to MS-DOS, run Setup from the DOS command prompt, and install Windows 98 in a directory separate from that of Windows NT. This method keeps Windows NT intact on your system and enables you to choose to boot into Windows NT or Windows 98 when you start up your system. The downside is that you won't be able to run Windows 98 in FAT32 mode, because Windows NT doesn't support FAT32 file systems.

N O T E If you decide to install Windows 98 in a multiboot environment with Windows NT, you must set the Windows NT file system to the *file allocation table* (FAT) system. You cannot run the *NT file system* (NTFS). In situations in which you need to have the NTFS installed (for file-level security, for example), you can set up Windows 98 and Windows NT on separate partitions or on separate hard drives.

For more information about setting up Windows NT, see *Special Edition Using Windows NT Workstation 4.0* and *Windows NT 4.0 Installation and Configuration Handbook*, both published by Que. ■

Another way you can install Windows 98 with Windows NT is to set up different partitions for each operating system. This enables you to run Windows 98 with FAT32 file support on the Windows 98 partition and to run NTFS on the other partition, for example. You just won't be able to see the NTFS partition while in the FAT32 partition, and vice versa. You can use the MS-DOS command FDISK to set up the partitions and then run the setup program for Windows 98 from one partition and the setup program for Windows NT from the other partition.

If you want to install Windows 98 over an existing version of Windows NT, boot MS-DOS from a floppy disk and run the Windows 98 Setup program. This action disables the boot option for Windows NT. If you use this method and later want to restore the Windows NT boot option, you must use the Windows NT boot repair disk that was created when you initially installed Windows NT. When you run this disk, select the Repair option to repair the boot option.

Regardless of the option you choose to install Windows 98 with an existing Windows NT installation, you must reinstall all of your applications. This is because Windows 98 and Windows NT use different Registries. When Windows 98 is installed over a Windows NT installation, settings from the Windows NT Registry are not converted automatically to the Windows 98 Registry. For more information on the Windows 98 Registry, see Chapter 26, "Using Windows 98 Software."

Installing Windows 98 on an OS/2 Computer

To install Windows 98 on a computer running IBM OS/2, you must boot to an MS-DOS prompt and then run Windows 98 Setup from the MS-DOS prompt. To boot to an MS-DOS prompt, select the DOS prompt option from the Boot Manager or, if you are upgrading from an HPFS partition, use the OS/2 Disk 1 to boot to the DOS prompt.

When you are using the Boot Manager in OS/2 and you start Windows 98 Setup, Setup disables the Boot Manager. This way, Windows 98 can restart your computer and automatically boot into Windows 98 to complete the installation process. After Windows 98 is installed, use the following steps to re-enable Boot Manager:

1. In Windows 98, choose Start, Run, and enter **FDISK** in the Run field.
2. From the FDISK list of options, select Option 2, Set Active Partition.
3. Enter the Boot Manager partition number, which is the 1MB no–MS-DOS partition. It usually is the first or last option.
4. Exit FDISK.
5. Restart your computer. Boot Manager is restored.

TIP   If you no longer want Boot Manager to start after you install Windows 98, you can remove it. Do this by booting to MS-DOS from Boot Manager and running FDISK. Next, select the MS-DOS partition as your active partition. Exit FDISK and restart your computer.

TROUBLESHOOTING

I plan to use a floppy disk to boot MS-DOS on my OS/2 computer to run Windows 98 Setup. Is there anything I should do first? Yes; before you run Windows 98 Setup, rename the AUTOEXEC.BAT and CONFIG.SYS files OS/2 uses before you run Windows 98 Setup. If you do not rename these files, you will not be able to boot OS/2 after Windows 98 is installed.

Installing Windows 98 on a Freshly Formatted Hard Drive

Windows 98 can be installed on a freshly formatted hard drive. This way, you can delete everything from your hard drive using the FDISK command from MS-DOS and rebuild your system from the ground up by using Windows 98.

To do this, use the following guidelines:

- Create a boot disk that includes the FORMAT.COM file.
- SYS your hard disk, format it, and then install real-mode CD-ROM drivers. Or, create a boot floppy disk that includes the MSCDEX and your CD-ROM's real-mode drivers. You

might be able to use the Microsoft Create System Diskette (MSCSD.EXE) utility to create a CD-aware boot disk. This utility came on systems that had Windows 95 preinstalled on it.

■ Use the FDISK command on your hard disk. Make sure that if you want to create a new partition, you do so and mark the new one as active.

■ Install your real-mode CD-ROM IDE or SCSI drivers onto a floppy disk using the CD-ROM's installation disks. You should make sure this floppy disk works before formatting your hard disk.

■ Reboot your system with the boot disk you created and format the hard disk using the FORMAT command and the /s switch.

■ Run Windows 98 Setup from the \WIN98 folder on the CD-ROM.

See "Partitioning Your New Hard Disk Drive" in Chapter 10, "Installing and Configuring Hard Disk Drives," for more details on partitioning a hard disk.

Starting Windows 98

After Setup installs Windows 98 and configures all its options, Windows 98 starts. Figure 2.8 shows the Windows 98 Welcome screen, which includes helpful suggestions for navigating Windows 98.

FIG. 2.8
The Welcome to Windows 98 screen is the first screen you see after Windows 98 starts.

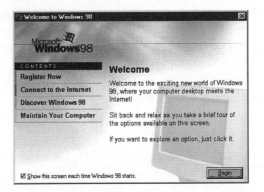

 If you do not want to see this screen the next time you boot Windows 98, disable the S̲how This Screen Each Time Windows 98 Starts check box in the Welcome dialog box. To show this screen again, double-click the Welcome application in the Windows 98 folder in Windows Explorer.

Testing Windows 98 Setup

Before you use Windows 98 for the first item, test to see whether it is installed properly. Shut down Windows and restart it by clicking the Start button at the bottom of the screen (this is called the *taskbar*) and choosing Sh̲ut Down. The Shut Down Windows dialog box appears (see Figure 2.9). Make sure the S̲hut Down option is selected and click OK. This begins the

Windows 98 shut-down procedure, which you must perform whenever you want to exit Windows 98.

When a message appears on your screen telling you it's OK to turn off your machine, press the reset button on your computer. As your PC reboots, watch the screen to see whether you notice any errors. If Windows 98 starts, your system probably works fine, and you can start using Windows 98.

If your system doesn't start, or if you get a DOS screen, your setup has encountered some problems. You can start Windows 98 in Safe mode and fix the problem.

Configuring Laptop Utilities

Windows 98 provides some utilities designed to make working on laptop PCs easier. The following sections show you how to configure Briefcase, Direct Cable Connection, PCMCIA and infrared support, and power-saving devices. Although all of these except the PCMCIA and infrared utilities can be used on desktop PCs, they are mainly used on laptop or other portable systems.

Briefcase and Direct Cable Connection

After Setup finishes installing Windows 98 and you have tested it, you can configure Briefcase and the Direct Cable Connection applications.

An option installed during the Portable Setup installation is the Windows 98 Briefcase. Mobile computing users who have both a portable and desktop PC spend several hours a week transferring files from one machine to the other. Part of this time is devoted to ensuring that the most current file is copied and being used each time the file is modified. Briefcase enables users to synchronize files and copy them between their PCs if they have a network or use the Direct Cable Connection. Briefcase helps eliminate the possibility of errors and overlooked files that users work on.

To use Briefcase, double-click its icon on the desktop to start it. There are no configuration settings for Briefcase, except for those related to setting up a network connection or the Direct Cable Connection. After you start Briefcase, drag and drop files and directories from Explorer or your desktop to the Briefcase (see Figure 2.10). This is much like carrying a briefcase or attaché to the office: You stuff your papers and folders into your briefcase to carry them home or on a trip, or back to the office. Windows 98's Briefcase extends this concept to the electronic platform.

FIG. 2.10
You can use the Windows 95 Briefcase to help you synchronize your files from your portable PC to your desktop PC.

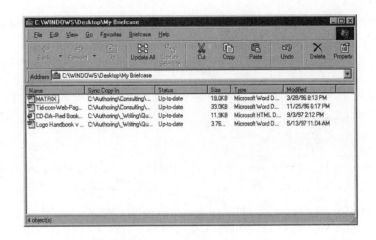

N O T E For more information on using Briefcase, see Que's *Special Edition Using Windows 98, Platinum Edition*. ▨

Another feature that mobile users can use is Windows 98 Direct Cable Connection. This feature enables users to hook together two PCs using serial or parallel-port cables. With Direct Cable Connection, you can share folders, files, or printers with another computer without being on a *local area network* (LAN). This is handy if you transfer files from a laptop PC to a desktop PC, but your laptop does not have a network adapter. If your other PC is on a network, however, the connected PC (in this case, the laptop PC) can access the network and share files or network printers.

By default, Direct Cable Connection is installed during the Portable setup (it's also installed by default during Custom and Typical setups). After Setup installs Windows 98, you need to configure the Direct Cable Connection for each computer you hook together. To do so, use these steps:

1. Choose Start, Programs, Accessories, Communications, and click Direct Cable Connection. The Direct Cable Connection Wizard starts (see Figure 2.11).

FIG. 2.11
Use the Direct Cable Connection Wizard to hook two computers together using a serial or parallel port.

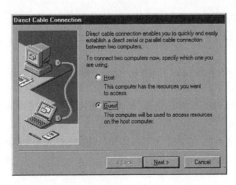

2. On the first Direct Cable Connection screen, you need to specify which computer you are configuring. You have two choices:

- *Host*. The PC that contains the files or printer connection you want to copy or share.

- *Guest*. The PC that accesses files from the host PC.

Select Host or Guest.

3. Click Next.

 TIP   Host and guest PCs must use the same port connections, such as LPT1, COM1, and so on.

4. Specify the port to which you want to connect. You can use serial (usually, COM1 or COM2) or parallel (usually, LPT1 or LPT2) ports (see Figure 2.12).

FIG. 2.12

Select the type of port each computer will use.

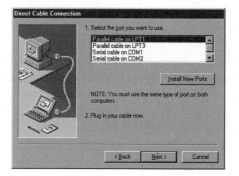

N O T E   If you need to add a port to your computer, click Install New Port. Windows 98 searches your system for the new port and configures it. If Windows cannot find a new port on your system and you recently installed one, shut down Windows 98, reboot your system, and retry this option. You also can run the Add New Hardware Wizard from the Control Panel and add the new port using that wizard. ▪

5. Plug in the cable to the port you specified in step 4.

6. Click Next. If you set up your PC as the guest computer, skip to step 15. Otherwise, continue to step 7.

7. You now must specify if you want to enable the guest PC to share printer and file resources on the host machine. To do this, click the File and Print Sharing button to start the Network Control Panel. If you've already configured this for a network connection, you don't have to set this up now.

8. In the Network dialog box, click File and Print Sharing. Select this option so that your PC can share files and a printer with another PC.

9. In the File and Print Sharing dialog box, you can choose to have the guest computer share only the host's printer, the host's files, or both. Click OK. If you are prompted to restart Windows, do so.

10. Click OK in the Network dialog box.

11. Click Next in the Direct Cable Connection Wizard.

   If you do not enable file or printer sharing, a warning screen appears. Click OK and then click Next again to go to the following wizard screen. If file and print sharing is enabled, this screen is bypassed.

12. The host computer is now configured. To add a layer of security to the connection, you can require that the guest computer input a password to access the host system. To do this, enable the Use Password Protection check box and then click Set Password (see Figure 2.13).

FIG. 2.13
Use a password to help keep intruders from accessing the host computer from the guest computer.

 Be sure to share this password with other users if they are accessing the host computer via Direct Cable Connection.

13. In the Direct Cable Connection Password dialog box, enter the password and re-enter it to confirm the spelling of it. Click OK.

14. If you have not done so already, configure the other computer as the guest system. Otherwise, click Finish to initialize the host machine.

15. To configure the guest computer, make sure the Direct Cable Connection Wizard is running (see step 1) on the guest machine and click Guest. Then click Next.

   N O T E If your PC has previously been configured as a host computer, click Change after the Direct Cable Connection Wizard starts to change the configuration. You also can change from guest to host by clicking the same Change button. ▪

16. Select the port to which you want to connect. Remember, the port on the guest computer must match the port on the host machine.

17. Plug in the cable and click Next.

18. Click Finish to start using the Direct Cable Connection.

N O T E See Que's *Special Edition Using Windows 98, Platinum Edition* for information on using Windows 98 Direct Cable Connection application. ■

Configuring Windows 98's PCMCIA Support

Windows 98 supports many *Personal Computer Memory Card International Association* (PCMCIA) cards (also known as *PC cards*), including modems, network adapters, SCSI cards, and others. Windows 98 PCMCIA drivers are 32-bit, dynamically loadable virtual device drivers and consume no conventional memory. Windows 98 enables you to plug in your PCMCIA card in your computer and start using the card immediately. You are not required to shut down and restart your PC for it to recognize the PCMCIA card. (You must have Plug and Play–compliant drivers for this feature to work properly.) If you have a PCMCIA network card, for example, you can plug it into your computer and Windows 98 does the rest: It detects the network card, loads the drivers, and connects to the network.

PCMCIA card installation is performed automatically by Plug and Play if Windows 98 includes supporting drivers for your PCMCIA card and socket. If your card is not configured by Windows 98, you'll need to start the PCMCIA Wizard and set up the card manually. When you run the PCMCIA Wizard, Windows 98 modifies your AUTOEXEC.BAT and CONFIG.SYS files by removing the lines that start the real-mode driver and adds a line that enables the PCMCIA socket.

To see whether your PCMCIA socket is detected by Windows 98, do the following:

1. In the Control Panel, double-click the System icon. In the System Properties dialog box, select the Device Manager tab.

2. Select View Devices By Type and see whether the PCMCIA Socket listing is included with the list of devices. If it's not, you must run the Add New Hardware Wizard from the Control Panel (see Chapter 5, "Installing and Configuring New Hardware and Software," for details on setting up hardware). If the listing is included, you should be able to use your PCMCIA device.

N O T E Some legacy PCMCIA cards are not supported "out of the box" with Windows 98. If your PCMCIA card is not included on the list of supported cards, contact the card's manufacturer for updated installation disks for Windows 98. ■

Once you get your PCMCIA device working, you can display the PC Card (PCMCIA) Properties dialog box (see Figure 2.14). Here, you can remove a PC card, control the way in which the Properties dialog box displays, and have Windows 98 display a warning if you remove a PC card before stopping it. On the Global Settings tab, you can set the way the PC card uses memory and specify whether you want to disable PC card sound effects.

FIG. 2.14
Use the PC Card
(PCMCIA) Properties
dialog box to control
your PC cards.

Configuring Windows 98's Infrared Support

Infrared devices are wireless transmitters and receivers that use infrared signals to transmit information. Some common devices include network adapters and printers. You can use Windows 98's Infrared Monitor to keep track of the infrared activity on your PC. You can find out, for example, when a device is outside the range of your computer. Infrared Monitor also can tell you the status of your device, set the identification of your device, and set infrared device options.

To display Infrared Monitor, you need to install an infrared device using the Add New Hardware Wizard, as described in Chapter 5. After a device is installed, open the Control Panel and double-click the Infrared icon. Or, double-click the Infrared Monitor icon on the taskbar. The Infrared Monitor dialog box appears (see Figure 2.15).

FIG. 2.15
You use Infrared
Monitor to control the
way your infrared
devices operate.

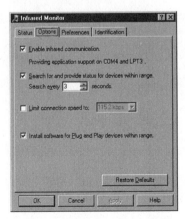

On the Status page, you see the status of your devices.

On the Options page, you can choose from the following options:

- *Enable Infrared Communication.* Turns on infrared support and shows the ports used by infrared devices.

- *Search for and Provide Status for Devices within Range.* Searches for infrared devices that are within the range of your computer. You also can set the time frame Windows uses to search for these devices.

- *Limit Connection Speed To.* To limit the maximum speed at which your infrared devices communicate, enable this option and set a speed. You might find it best to lower this number to reduce the number of retries a device makes.

- *Install Software for Plug and Play Devices within Range.* Specifies that Windows automatically loads Plug and Play software for devices when another device comes into range. For times when you're working in areas in which infrared devices are nearby and you don't want Windows automatically loading software for these devices (because you don't plan on using those devices, for example), disable this option.

On the Preferences tab, you can set the following options for controlling the behavior of Infrared Monitor (see Figure 2.16):

- *Display the Infrared Monitor Icon on the Taskbar.* Specifies whether the Infrared Monitor icon is available on the taskbar.

- *Open Infrared Monitor When Communication Is Interrupted.* Tells you when communications are interrupted between your infrared device and another. After the communication between the devices is restored, Infrared Monitor closes.

- *Play Sounds…* Specifies that a sound plays when a device comes within range of your device or when communications are occurring between your device and another.

FIG. 2.16

Set Infrared Monitor properties from the Preferences tab.

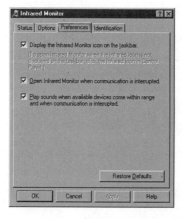

Finally, you can enter a name and description of your computer on the Identification tab (see Figure 2.17). If you have a network already set up on your system, the Computer Name and Computer Description fields are filled in with the computer's name. Any changes you make here are also reflected on the Network Properties Identification tab.

FIG. 2.17
Establish a name and description of your computer.

Part
I

Ch
2

Configuring Power-Saving Devices

Windows 98 provides power-management control over monitors and hard disks to help conserve energy and battery power (on laptops) when these devices are not being used. You can set up power schemes that let you quickly change between power-management settings if you change locations often.

Open the Control Panel and double-click the Power Management icon. The Power Management Properties dialog box appears (see Figure 2.18).

FIG. 2.18
Windows includes settings for turning off idle monitors and hard disks.

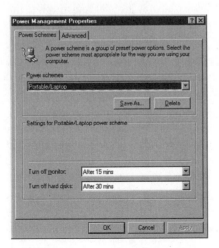

To change to a different preset power scheme, select a scheme from the Power Schemes drop-down list box. You can select Portable/Laptop, Home/Office Desk, or Always On. You also can save your own setting by changing the Turn Off Monitor and Turn Off Hard Disks settings and then clicking Save As. Give your new scheme a name and click OK. Your new scheme is available in the Power Schemes drop-down list box.

 TIP Delete a scheme by selecting it in the Power Schemes drop-down list box and clicking Delete. Click Yes when asked whether you're sure you want to delete the scheme.

To show the power meter on the taskbar, select the Advanced tab and select the Show Power Meter on Taskbar option. You then can double-click the Power Meter icon to display the Power Management Properties dialog box.

Using Windows 98 in Safe Mode

With luck, your computer starts and you have no problems running your new Windows 98 installation. Many times, however, Windows 98 encounters a problem (such as a Registry setting missing or corrupted) during startup that it cannot fix. When this happens, you need to run Windows in Safe mode from the Startup menu. You can display the Startup menu by pressing F8 during the boot process. Press F8 when the instruction Starting Windows appears. This usually appears after your system checks the internal RAM on your system. Windows 98 also starts Safe mode automatically if it detects a problem with the startup files.

The Startup menu has the following options from which to choose. Depending on your specific setup, you may or may not have the same settings:

- *Normal*. Enables you to start Windows 98 in its normal startup manner, loading all device drivers and Registry settings. If Windows 98 automatically displays the Startup menu, choosing this selection probably just will return you to the Startup menu. Choose this option only if you want to watch what happens onscreen during the failed startup.

- *Logged (\BOOTLOG.TXT)*. Creates a file called BOOTLOG.TXT in your root directory that contains a record of the current startup process. This file is created during Setup and shows the Windows 98 components and drivers loaded and initialized, along with the status of each. You can view this file in Notepad.

- *Safe mode*. Starts Windows 98 but bypasses startup files and uses only basic system drivers. In Safe mode, many devices in Windows 98 are not available, such as the Add New Hardware utility in the Control Panel. Safe mode is intended to diagnose and fix problems in the Windows 98 environment. You also can start Safe mode by pressing F5 during bootup or typing **WIN /D:M** at the command prompt.

- *Safe Mode with Network Support*. Starts Windows 98 but bypasses startup files and uses only basic system drivers, including basic networking. You also can start this option by pressing F6 or typing **WIN /D:N** at the command prompt.

- *Step-By-Step Confirmation*. Enables you to confirm each line in your startup files, including AUTOEXEC.BAT and CONFIG.SYS. Answer **Y** to lines you want to run; answer **N** to lines you want to bypass. You also can start this option by pressing F8 after the Startup menu appears.

- *Command prompt only*. Starts MS-DOS (Windows 98 version) with startup files and Registry settings, displaying only the MS-DOS command prompt.

- *Safe mode command prompt only*. Starts MS-DOS (Windows 98 version) in Safe mode and displays only the command prompt, bypassing startup files. This is the same as pressing Shift+F5.

- *Previous version of MS-DOS*. Starts your previous version of MS-DOS if you have a multiboot configuration. You must install Windows 98 into a different directory during Setup for this option to be available. You also can start this option by pressing F4 during startup. This option is available only if BootMulti=1 is in the MSDOS.SYS file.

When Safe Mode is selected from the Startup menu, it bypasses startup files, including the Registry, CONFIG.SYS, AUTOEXEC.BAT, and the [Boot] and [386Enh] sections of SYSTEM.INI. Table 2.1 shows the files that the three most common Safe Mode options bypass and initiate. As the table shows, Safe mode does not load all the Windows drivers. In fact, during Safe mode, only the mouse, keyboard, and standard Windows VGA device drivers are loaded. If you are using other drivers, such as a Super VGA video driver, they are not available in Safe mode.

Part

I

Ch

2

Table 2.1   Files Loaded During Startup Menu Options

Action	Safe Mode	Safe Mode, Command Prompt Only	Network Support
Process CONFIG.SYS and AUTOEXEC.BAT	No	No	No
Process Registry information	No	Yes	No
Load COMMAND.COM	No	Yes	Yes
Run Windows 98 WIN.COM	Yes	Yes	No
Load HIMEM.SYS and IFSHLP.SYS	Yes	Yes	No
Load DoubleSpace or DriveSpace if present	Yes	Yes	Loaded if Safe Mode Command Prompt Only option is selected

continues

Table 2.1 Continued

Action	Safe Mode	Safe Mode, Command Prompt Only	Network Support
Load all Windows drivers	No	No	No
Load network drivers	No	Yes	No
Run NETSTART.BAT	No	Yes	No

After Windows 98 starts in Safe mode, you can access the configuration files, modify configuration settings, and then restart Windows 98 normally.

Creating and Using the Startup Disk

Setup lets you create a startup disk. Regardless of how well you think the Windows 98 Setup program is going, *always* choose to make a startup disk. The startup disk is your life preserver in case you experience problems with Windows 98 after it's installed. By taking a few minutes now and using one floppy disk, you insure yourself against potential problems.

You'll need one floppy disk to reformat when the startup disk is created. Because you will lose all the data on this disk, make sure it does not contain anything important. Your PC must be able to boot the floppy disk from the floppy disk drive, which is the A: drive.

N O T E Many older PCs have 5 1/4-inch floppy disk drives as the A: drive. Many users, however, have abandoned the use of 5 1/4-inch floppy disks. If your A: drive is the 5 1/4-inch drive, you must use this size floppy disk as your startup disk. You cannot change Setup to create a startup disk on the B: drive. ■

The startup disk is a bootable floppy disk that stores several system files (more than 1.2MB). In case you need to use the startup disk, place it in your floppy drive and reboot your machine. You are presented with an MS-DOS command line that provides utilities and maintenance instructions to help you recover your installation.

N O T E The startup disk has limitations. It cannot be used to provide access to a network connection, for example. You need to fix any problems associated with your installation to recover from a network problem. ■

Table 2.2 lists the files Setup copies to the startup disk.

Table 2.2 Startup Disk Files

File	Description
ASPI*.*	A collection of real-mode Adaptec CD-ROM drivers
ATTRIB.EXE	Sets file attributes, such as hidden and read-only
BTCDROM/BTDOSM.SYST	Real-mode Mylex/BusLogic CD-ROM drivers
CHKDSK.EXE	Checks a disk and displays a status report
COMMAND.COM	Starts a new copy of the Windows Command Interpreter, which is the primary operating system file for MS-DOS
DEBUG.EXE	Runs Debug, a testing- and editing-tool program
DRVSPACE.BIN	DriveSpace disk-compression utility
EBD.CAB	CAB file that includes extraction utilities
EBD.SYS	Utility for the startup disk
EDIT.COM	Text editor in MS-DOS
EXTRACT.EXE	Extraction utility for extracting CAB files
FDISK.EXE	Configures a hard disk for use with MS-DOS
FINDRAMD.EXE	RAM drive utility that locates the RAM drive during startup
FLASHPT.SYS	Real-mode Mylex/BusLogic CD-ROM driver
FORMAT.COM	Formats a hard disk or floppy disk for use with MS-DOS
HIMEM.SYS	*Extended Memory Specification* (XMS) memory manager
IO.SYS	Core operating-system file
MSCDEX	Microsoft CD-ROM file extension for the MS-DOS environment
MSDOS.SYS	Core operating-system file
OAKCDROM.SYS	Real-mode ATAPI CD-ROM driver
RAMDRIVE.SYS	Utility for creating a RAM drive during startup
REGEDIT.EXE	Starts the Registry Editor
SCANDISK.EXE	Starts ScanDisk
SCANDISK.INI	Stores system configuration settings for ScanDisk
SETRAMD.EXE	Locates the first drive that can be configured as a RAM drive
SYS.COM	Copies MS-DOS system files and Command Interpreter to a disk you specify
UNINSTAL.EXE	Starts utility for recovering deleted files

Part

I

Ch

2

A few other files that you might want to copy to the startup disk after Windows 98 is installed include AUTOEXEC.BAT, CONFIG.SYS, WIN.INI, and SYSTEM.INI. Other INI files also might come in handy. These files are ones you already should have backed up in Chapter 1, "Preparing to Install Windows 98."

To instruct Setup to create a startup disk, make sure the Yes, I Want a Startup Disk (Recommended) choice in the Startup Disk screen is selected and click Next.

The startup disk available in Windows 98 is different than the one in Windows 95 and provides a much more powerful tool for getting your Windows 98 installation up and running. To see how the Windows 98 version works, place the disk in the A: drive and reboot your computer. The Microsoft Windows 98 Startup menu appears. You can choose from one of the following options:

- Start Computer with CD-ROM Support
- Start Computer without CD-ROM Support
- View the Help File

As you can see, one major change is that the Windows 98 startup disk now includes a multiconfiguration menu that enables you to load common CD-ROM drivers. You also can perform a clean boot (no CD-ROM support) from this menu.

If you select to load the CD-ROM drivers, the startup disk creates a 2MB RAM driver in which the diagnostic tools for troubleshooting your system are installed. The RAM drive emulates a hard drive so that all the system tools can be installed. After the startup disk finishes, the RAM drive is deleted.

N O T E The RAM drive may use the drive letter usually set up for your CD-ROM drive. The RAM drive will be the D: drive, for example, and your CD-ROM drive will be the E: drive. ■

After the tools are loaded (and CD-ROM drivers are loaded, if selected), you're presented with the A:/ prompt. From here, you can switch to the RAM drive (such as the D: drive) and run one of the following utilities:

- ATTRIB.EXE
- CHKDSK.EXE
- DEBUG.EXE
- EDIT.COM
- EXTRACT.EXE
- FORMAT.COM
- MSCDEX.EXE
- RESTART.COM
- SCANDISK.EXE
- SYS.COM
- UNINSTAL.EXE

Run the HELP.BAT file to get a description of each of these tools.

After you run the troubleshooting tool(s), restart your PC with the RESTART utility.

N O T E   If you did not create a startup disk during setup, you can create one using a single floppy disk. In the Add/Remove Programs Properties dialog box from the Control Panel, select the Startup Disk tab. Then click the Create Disk button and follow the instructions onscreen. You should do this even if you are not having problems starting Windows 98. In the future, you might experience a problem that only the startup disk can remedy. ■

Uninstalling Windows 98

If you've changed your mind about Windows 98, you can uninstall it to return to a previously installed version of Windows 95 or Windows 3.1. Windows 98 provides a way to uninstall itself to let you return to a previous Windows installation. If you elected to keep your previous operating system intact during Windows 98 Setup, the Uninstall Windows 98 option on the Add/Remove Programs Properties dialog box will be available.

To uninstall Windows 98, use the following steps:

1. Choose Start, Settings, Control Panel, Add/Remove Programs.
2. In the Add-Remove Programs Properties dialog box, select the Install/Uninstall tab.
3. In the list of software that can be removed by Windows, click Uninstall Windows 98.
4. Click Add/Remove, and then follow the directions on your screen. The Uninstall program removes all long filename entries from your hard disk and then runs an MS-DOS–based program to remove Windows 98 and restore your previous MS-DOS and Windows 3.x files.

TROUBLESHOOTING

I uninstalled Windows 98, but I still have some files left on my machine from Windows 98. Why?
These are long filenames that Windows 98 installs. If you uninstall Windows 98 using a method other than uninstalling it from Windows 98, you are left with these long filenames. You can remove them by running Windows 3.x File Manager and deleting them one at a time.

CHAPTER 3

Selecting Windows 98 Components

by Rob Tidrow

In this chapter

Adding and Removing Windows Components

Chapter 2 walked you through installing Windows 98 using the Windows 98 Setup program. During this installation, you had an opportunity to select the type of installation you wanted and to choose several components that were to be installed under Windows 98. If you upgraded from Windows 95, however, your old system settings were maintained, and you didn't have an opportunity to change or add to the Components list. If you want to add additional components or remove some, you can use the Add/Remove Programs applet.

To use the Add/Remove Programs applet to install or remove Windows components, do the following:

1. Choose Start, Settings, Control Panel, and double-click the Add/Remove Programs icon. The Add/Remove Programs Properties dialog box appears.

2. Select the Windows Setup tab (see Figure 3.1). Components are divided into 12 categories (see the following section, "Reviewing Windows Components"). Check marks indicate entire categories that are installed on your system. Shaded check marks indicate that only part of the category's Components list is installed. A clear check box shows categories in which no components are installed.

FIG. 3.1

Use the Windows Setup tab to install or remove Windows components.

3. Select a component category, such as Accessories, and click Details. A dialog box with individual components under that category appears (see Figure 3.2).

   If a component includes subcomponents, such as the Screen Savers component, the Details button becomes available. Click it to customize which subcomponents you want to install. Click OK.

FIG. 3.2
You can select individual components from this dialog box.

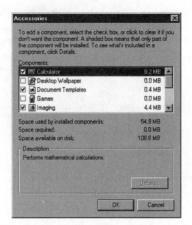

 T I P To install all the components of a category, click the category's check box until an unshaded check mark appears. Conversely, clear the check box to uninstall all components of a category.

Part

I

Ch

3

4. Select or clear check boxes next to those components you want to install or remove. You can see the space requirements for each component on the right side of the Components list.

5. Click OK. The Windows Setup tab appears.

6. Continue adding or removing components.

7. Click OK. You'll be prompted to insert the Windows 98 Setup CD-ROM or floppy disks.

Windows installs or uninstalls components as specified. Depending on the component you select, you might be prompted to restart Windows before you can start using the component.

Reviewing Windows Components

The Windows Components list is broken down into 12 categories. The following list includes the required hard disk space to install all the components for that category on your computer:

Accessibility (4.9MB)

Accessories (17.6MB)

Broadcast Data Services (0.8MB)

Communications (11.8MB)

Desktop Themes (30.5MB)

Internet Tools (15.5MB)

Microsoft Outlook Express (5.4MB)

Multilanguage Support (12.1MB)

Multimedia (14.4MB)

Online Services (1.2MB)

System Tools (8.2MB)

WebTV for Windows

N O T E The hard disk requirements in the preceding list are based on the latest available software at the time of this writing. The final version of Windows 98 might have different components and sizes. Check the Windows Setup tab on your system for actual components and hard disk requirements. ▨

Each of these categories with their hard disk space requirements is explained in detail in the following sections.

Accessibility (4.9MB)

Windows 98 includes several utilities that enable users who have hearing, movement, or vision impairments to use Windows 98 more easily. These utilities include keyboard-, sound-, display-, and mouse-behavior modifications, such as high-contrast color schemes, StickyKeys, and SoundSentry. It also includes the Magnifier tool, Accessibility Wizard, and high-visibility cursors. By default, Windows 98 installs the Accessibility options, which you can access from the Accessibility Options icon in the Control Panel (see Figure 3.3).

FIG. 3.3
By default, the
Accessibility item is
installed.

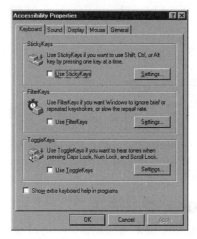

Table 3.1 lists and briefly describes the utilities available when you install the Accessibility options.

Table 3.1 Accessibility Options

Type of Option	Option	Description
Keyboard		Control the way in which the keyboard operates.
	StickyKeys	Enables you to use the Ctrl, Shift, and Alt keys by pressing one key at a time, instead of holding down both at the same time.

Type of Option	Option	Description
	FilterKeys	Instructs Windows 98 to ignore brief or repeated keystrokes. You also can slow down the repeat rate of keystrokes.
	ToggleKeys	Assigns a sound to beep when you press Caps Lock, Num Lock, or Scroll Lock.
Sound		Display visual cues when your computer generates a sound.
	SoundSentry	Instructs Windows 98 to display visual warnings when your system makes a sound. Some of these actions include flashing the active caption bar or desktop when a sound occurs.
	ShowSounds	Configures your applications to display captions for the speech and sound they make.
Display		Controls how your monitor displays information.
	High Contrast	Directs Windows 98 to use colors and fonts that are easy to read, such as white on black, black on white, or a custom combination that you provide.
Mouse		Replaces the mouse with keyboard actions.
	MouseKeys	Enables you to control the pointer by using the numeric keypad on your keyboard. You also can change the pointer speed and choose to use MouseKeys with Num Lock on or off.
General Settings		Configure Accessibility options.
	Automatic Reset	Turns off Accessibility features if they are idle for a specific amount of time. The default is 5 minutes.
	Notification	Prompts you when an Accessibility feature is turned on or off.
	SerialKeys	Enables you to access keyboard and mouse features by using alternative input devices, such as head pointers and eye-gaze systems.
Accessibility Wizard		Walks you through configuring vision, hearing, and mobility settings.
Magnifier		Enlarges sections of the screen to make text and images easier to see.

Part
I
Ch
3

Accessories (17.6MB)

Windows accessories include the Calculator, screen savers, games, wallpaper, and other add-ons. In Windows 98, some of the accessories are improved and have been replaced by other applications. WordPad, for example, is a more powerful word processor that replaces Microsoft Write, which was available in Windows 3.x. The Windows Scripting Host is a new applet that enables you to write scripts to automate Windows tasks.

The following lists summarizes each of the accessories components:

- *Calculator (0.2MB)*. Enables you to perform calculations. Installed by default.

- *Desktop Wallpaper (0.7MB)*. Includes background pictures for your Windows desktop.

- *Document Templates (0.4MB)*. Enables you to easily create new documents for your most common programs. You can see these file types after you install Windows 98 and right-click the Windows desktop. From the context-sensitive menu, choose New and the file type you want to create. Installed by default.

- *Games (0.6MB)*. Entertainment for your entire family! Includes Minesweeper, Hearts, and FreeCell games.

- *Imaging*. Provides the Kodak Image Viewer, ActiveX Controls, and TWAIN support (for scanning). You can use Imaging for viewing faxes.

- *Mouse Pointers (0.4MB)*. Installs easy-to-see pointers for your mouse (see Figure 3.4).

FIG. 3.4
You can select the type of pointers that your mouse uses by choosing different schemes in the Mouse Properties dialog box.

- *Paint (2.5MB)*. Replaces Windows 3.x's Paintbrush application. Paint is used to create, modify, or view bitmap graphics.

- *Quick View (4.7MB)*. Displays a preview of a document without opening it in its native application. On CD-ROM only.

- *Screen Savers (1.1MB)*. Includes several screen savers, including Flying Windows and OpenGL screen savers, which display three-dimensional objects on your screen.

- *Windows Scripting Host (1.2B)*. Provides a script editor that supports JavaScript and Visual Basic Scripting (VBScript) that you can use to write your own scripts to automate Windows tasks.

- *WordPad (1.7MB)*. An accessory in Windows worth using. WordPad replaces Windows Write, which came bundled with Windows 3.x, and is a full-featured, OLE 2.0–compliant word processor. You can create and edit documents in WordPad. It reads and saves files in the Microsoft Word DOC format by default. WordPad can read Word 6.x and 7 DOC files, Windows Write (WRI), Word 97, Unicode text files, rich text format (RTF), and text files (TXT).

Broadcast Data Services (0.8MB)

Broadcast Data Services installs the Announcement Listener, Webcast Client, and TV enhancements, which enable you to receive broadcast television signals on your PC.

Communications (11.8MB)

The Communications components include options for connecting to other computers through the Internet, online services, direct modem-to-modem connections, and serial and parallel cable connections.

The options available follow:

- *Dial-Up Networking (1.2MB)*. Enables you to connect to other computers and to the Internet by using your modem.

- *Dial-Up Server (0.1MB)*. Turns your PC into a dial-up server, enabling you or others to connect to it to upload or download files.

- *Direct Cable Connection (0.5MB)*. Enables you to connect to another computer by using the parallel or serial ports and a cable (see Figure 3.5).

FIG. 3.5
Use Direct Cable Connection when you don't have a LAN set up but need to share files between two PCs.

- *HyperTerminal (0.8MB)*. Replaces Terminal in Windows 3.x and is a full-featured communications package that enables you to connect to other computers and online services. HyperTerminal is a superior product if you need a general communications package.

■ *Microsoft Chat 2.0 (4.5MB)*. Enables you to chat with other users over the Internet or over a LAN that has a chat server.

■ *Microsoft NetMeeting (4.7MB)*. Enables you to call people over the Internet or LAN and conduct online conferences (see Figure 3.6). You can share files, mark up an electronic whiteboard, share applications, and talk to someone.

FIG. 3.6

You can use NetMeeting to conduct online conferences.

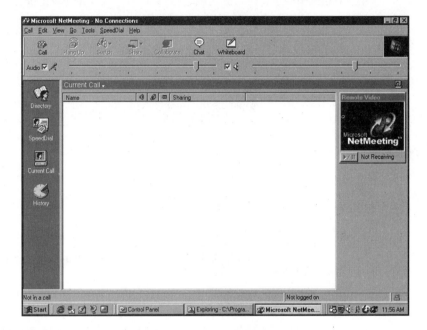

■ *Phone Dialer (0.2MB)*. Enables you to use your computer to dial a phone number by using your modem. After your computer dials, you can pick up the receiver and start talking (assuming that someone picks up on the other end).

■ *Virtual Private Networking (0.1MB)*. Enables you to set up *virtual private network* (VPN) support to have a secure connection to an intranet across the Internet or other public networks.

Desktop Themes (30.5MB)

Desktop themes are collections of files that help dress up your Windows environment. These collections are based on themes and include full-color wallpaper bitmaps, icons, sounds, and mouse pointers. Some of these themes were available as an add-on package (Microsoft Plus!) under Windows 95.

The following is a list of the desktop themes available:

Baseball (2.6MB)   Science (1.4MB)

Dangerous Creatures (1.5MB)   Space (2.2MB)

Inside Your Computer (1.6MB)   Sports (1.6MB)

Jungle (2.1MB)   The 60s USA (1.5MB)

Leonardo da Vinci (2.3MB)   The Golden Era (1.6MB)

More Windows (0.8MB)   Travel (1.5MB)

Mystery (1.9MB)   Underwater (2.7MB)

Nature (1.8MB)   Windows 98 (1.6MB)

To use the desktop themes, you also need to install the Desktop Themes support utility (2.4MB), as shown in Figure 3.7.

FIG. 3.7

The Desktop Themes support utility enables you to configure desktop themes, such as the Baseball theme.

Internet Tools (15.5MB)

The Internet Tools category includes a set of Internet components new to Windows 98. Among other tasks, you can use these tools to create HTML documents (Web pages), view *Virtual Reality Modeling Language* (VRML) content, and publish Web pages to a Web server.

The following list describes each of the components in the Internet Tools category:

■ *Microsoft FrontPad (2.8MB)*. A stripped-down version of Microsoft Frontpage, FrontPad enables you to create and edit HTML pages.

■ *Microsoft FrontPage Express (4.4MB)*. An HTML page editor.

■ *Microsoft VRML 2.0 Viewer (3.7MB)*. Enables you to view VRML images and environments. VRML is a language that is used to create virtual reality environments on the Internet.

- *Microsoft Wallet (1.0MB)*. An application that stores credit-card information you use to purchase items over the Internet.

- *Personal Web Server (0.2MB)*. Provides a Web server you can set up on your Windows 98 computer.

- *Real Audio Player 4.0 (2.5MB)*. Enables you to play Real Audio streaming video, audio, and animation files that you receive across the Internet.

- *Web Publishing Wizard (1.1MB)*. Enables you to upload Web server content to a Web server.

- *Web-Based Enterprise Mgmt (0.2MB)*. Enables system administrators to conduct remote tracking and system administration of your system.

Microsoft Outlook Express (5.4MB)

Outlook Express is an email program, newsgroup reader, and contact manager (see Figure 3.8). You can use Outlook Express to send and retrieve Internet email, as well as participate in Internet newsgroup discussions. You'll learn more about Outlook Express in Chapter 21, "Configuring Outlook Express."

FIG. 3.8
Use Outlook Express for your messaging needs.

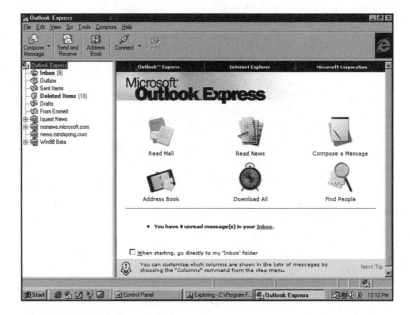

Multilanguage Support (12.1MB)

Windows 98 provides support for multiple languages. To write documents in different languages, select the Multilanguage Support component and select from the following options:

- *Baltic Language Support (2.4MB)*. Includes support for Estonian, Latvian, and Lithuanian languages.

- *Central European Language Support (2.6MB).* Includes support for Albanian, Czech, Croatian, Hungarian, Polish, Romanian, Slovak, and Slovenian languages.

- *Cyrillic Language Support (2.5MB).* Includes support for Bulgarian, Belarussian, Russian, Serbian, and Ukrainian languages.

- *Greek Language Support (2.4MB).* Includes support for the Greek language.

- *Turkish Language Support (2.3MB).* Includes support for the Turkish language.

Multimedia (14.4MB)

The Multimedia component includes programs for playing sound, animation (including Macromedia Shockwave and Flash files), and video. You also can get support for *Digital Versatile Discs* (DVD) players. To select the Multimedia components to install, you must have a multimedia-compliant computer, such as one with a CD-ROM and sound card installed. The following list summarizes each component:

- *Audio Compression (0.2MB).* Compresses audio for playback or recording on your computer.

- *CD Player (0.2MB).* Enables you to play audio CDs on your computer's CD-ROM drive.

- *DVD Player (0.3MB).* Enables you to play DVD movies on your PC.

- *Macromedia Shockwave Director (1.7MB).* Enables you to play Macromedia Director animation files. You can find many of these file types on the Internet.

- *Macromedia Shockwave Flash (0.2MB).* Enables you to play Macromedia Flash files, many of which can be downloaded from the Internet.

- *Media Player (0.3MB).* Plays audio and video clips (see Figure 3.9). Media Player plays the following file formats: Video for Windows (AVI), Wave (WAV), MIDI (MID and RMI), and CD Audio. Installed by default.

FIG. 3.9
In Media Player, you can play back that cool Video for Windows video clip that you've been dying to watch.

- *Microsoft NetShow Player 2.0 (4.0MB)*. Enables you to view NetShow streaming multimedia files across the Internet or LAN.

- *Multimedia Sound Schemes (6.5MB)*. Provides different sound schemes you can associate with different Windows 98 events, such as starting Windows 98 or maximizing a window.

- *Sample Sounds (0.6MB)*. Provides sample sounds you can use to play back on your system or assign to Windows events.

- *Sound Recorder (0.2MB)*. Enables you to record and play sounds on your PC if you have a sound card and microphone. Installed by default.

- *Video Compression (0.5MB)*. Compresses video for multimedia playback or recording on your computer.

- *Volume Control (0.2MB)*. Enables you to adjust the volume of the sound from your sound card (see Figure 3.10). Installed by default if Windows 98 detects a sound card.

FIG. 3.10
You can adjust the volume of your speakers by using the Volume Control utility.

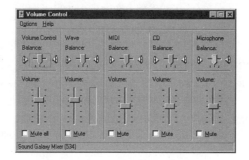

Online Services (1.2MB)

The Online Services category installs the software you need to connect to various online services. Through these services, you can send email, connect to newsgroups, and navigate the Internet.

The online services from which you can choose include the following:

- America Online (0.2MB)
- AT&T WorldNet Service (0.2MB)
- CompuServe (0.1MB)
- Prodigy Internet (0.8MB)
- The Microsoft Network (0.1MB)

System Tools (8.2MB)

The System Tools category provides utilities you can use to maintain your system, view Clipboard contents, convert your system to a FAT32 file system, perform other system tasks, and compress your disks.

The following summarizes each utility:

- *Backup (5.1MB)*. Enables you to back up and restore backed-up files from your hard drive to tape, floppy disks, or hard drives. It also can back up files to a network drive.
- *Character Map (0.1MB)*. Inserts symbols and characters into your documents.
- *Clipboard Viewer (0.1MB)*. Displays the Clipboard's contents.
- *Disk Compression Tools (2.2MB)*. Compress your disks using DriveSpace after Windows 98 is installed. Enable you to pack more files onto your hard disk. Installed by default.
- *Drive Converter (0.4MB)*. Enables you to convert your FAT16 file system to the FAT32 file system to improve performance and yield more usable space on a large hard drive.
- *Group Policies (0.1MB)*. Enables you to set up group system policies.
- *Net Watcher (0.2MB)*. Enables you to monitor your network server and connections. Installed by default.
- *System Monitor (0.2MB)*. Enables you to monitor your system performance. Not to be confused with the System Resource Meter.
- *System Resource Meter (0.1MB)*. Although this option is not selected by default, you might want to install it. It's a helpful utility that lets you view system-resource levels, including *Graphics Device Interface* (GDI) and user resources. As you work, the Resource Meter appears on the far left side of the Windows taskbar. To see the System Meter in more detail, double-click the meter to display the screen shown in Figure 3.11.

FIG. 3.11
Use the Resource Meter to see how your system resources are being used by Windows 98.

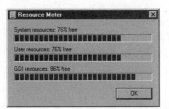

- *WinPopup (0.1MB)*. On a network, enables you to send and receive pop-up messages to and from other users.

WebTV for Windows

WebTV for Windows enables you to subscribe to content that is broadcast over LANs, direct-broadcast satellites, and local TV stations. To use WebTV, you need to have a video card that supports TV reception. See Chapter 17, "Configuring PC TV Devices," for more information. ●

Installing Windows 98 From a Network Server

by Rob Tidrow

Windows 98 provides a batch program—Batch 98—that helps you automate the installation of Windows 98 from a server-based install. Batch 98 can help you install Windows to any number of computers on the network, whether you have five or 500 network users. This chapter teaches you how to plan for and take advantage of Batch 98 to successfully deliver Windows 98 to every desktop in your organization.

NOTE Unlike Windows 95, Windows 98 cannot be run from a diskless, floppy boot, or RIPL workstation over a network.

Also, the NETSETUP.EXE utility is no longer available for Windows 98 (as it was for Windows 95). ■

A *server-based install* provides a central storage location of the files necessary to set up Windows 98. Server-based installations provide control over the distribution of Windows 98 to network clients.

To perform a server-based install, install Windows 98 on the network server and ensure that your network works. A Windows 98 server is a computer that is running Windows 98 with file and printer sharing enabled and that is networked to other machines. This can be two computers or several computers connected together. You just need to be running File and Printer Sharing for Microsoft Networks on the drive (a hard drive or CD-ROM drive, for example) on which the Windows 98 Setup disk resides.

You can copy the Windows 98 Setup files to a Windows 98 network server. You also can install from the Windows 98 Setup CD-ROM by using the CD-ROM drive housed on the Windows 98 server. Installing Windows in this manner can be much faster than installing it from floppy disks, because the network transfers the files quickly.

If you want to set up identical workstations, you can use Batch 98. Batch 98 enables you to easily create a script file with setup parameters for each of the machines on which you install Windows 98.

 TIP Installing from a network to a workstation is an excellent method of installation to use when only the server contains a CD-ROM drive.

Creating Batch Scripts

If you plan to use batch scripts to automate your server-based install, use the Batch 98 utility. Batch 98 is an easy-to-use tool that builds an INF file that Window 98 Setup references for the options and components you want installed. This way, Windows does not prompt you for information to install.

Batch 98 is provided on the Windows 98 CD-ROM in the \Tools\Reskit\Batch folder. Install Batch 98 by running the SETUP.EXE program. After Batch 98 is installed, launch it. The main window appears (see Figure 4.1).

There are a couple of ways to use Batch 98. The following sections describe these ways.

FIG. 4.1
The Batch 98 main window.

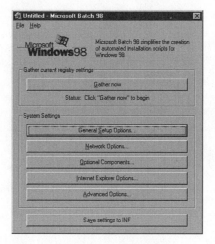

Using Gather Now

One way to use Batch 98 is to set up the current Windows 98 machine exactly the way you want other computer set up. Use the following steps:

1. Click the Gather Now button to create an INF file of the current computer. Batch 98 uses the settings from the local Registry to create this INF file. The following items are collected for this INF file:

   - Video and resolution settings
   - User-level security settings
   - Installed components
   - Network interface card settings
   - Time-zone setting
   - Installed printers
   - 32-bit Microsoft networking services, protocols, and clients and their settings
   - *Most recently used* (MRU) locations
   - Current user name and description
   - Current machine name and description
   - Location of Windows folder

N O T E   The Gather Now feature cannot determine 16-bit networking clients, protocols, and services; or uninstall options. ▦

2. Click the General Setup Options button. The General Setup Options dialog box appears (see Figure 4.2).

3. Select the User Info tab (see Figure 4.3).

Part
I

Ch
4

FIG. 4.2

The General Setup Options dialog box includes several tabs for modifying your INF file.

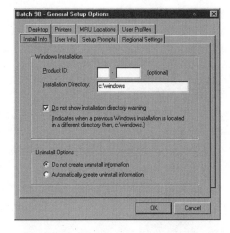

FIG. 4.3

Use the User Info tab to fill out user and network information.

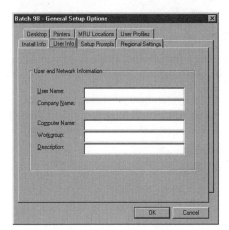

4. Fill out the user and network information fields. If you plan to run this script on many machines that use different machine names, see the section "Creating a Multiple Machine-Name File," later in this chapter.

5. Choose File, Save As to save the file to disk.

Here is a sample of an automatically created INF file:

```
; MSBATCH.INF
;
; Copyright (c) 1995-1998 Microsoft Corporation.
; All rights reserved.
;
[BatchSetup]
Version=3.0 (32-bit)
SaveDate=03/10/98
[Version]
Signature = "$CHICAGO$"

[Setup]
Express=1
```

```
InstallDir="C:\WINDOWS"
InstallType=3
EBD=0
ShowEula=0
ChangeDir=0
OptionalComponents=1
Network=1
System=0
CCP=0
CleanBoot=0
Display=0
DevicePath=0
NoDirWarn=1
TimeZone="US Eastern"
Uninstall=0
VRC=0
NoPrompt2Boot=1
…
```

When you're ready to install Windows, use the following setup command:

```
SETUP drive:\MSBATCH.INF
```

In the preceding syntax, *drive* is the drive (such as C:) on which the installation files reside. Also, MSBATCH.INF is the default name given to the INF file created using Gather Now. If you've given the file a different name than this, be sure to update the syntax with that name.

Choosing System Settings with Batch 98

Another way to use Batch 98 is to choose the individual components and system settings from the Batch 98 System Settings options. You can run Gather Now to create an INF file, and then modify the file using the System Settings options. Or, you can create a batch script from scratch by modifying the System Settings options and saving the settings as an INF file.

Part

I

Ch

4

The System Settings options are described in the following sections.

General Setup Options From the General Setup Options dialog box, you can choose installation options that relate to the basic Windows 98 system setup. This dialog box includes eight tabs.

On the Install Info tab, you can set the following parameters:

- *Product ID.* Enter your product ID number.
- *Installation Directory.* Provide the folder in which you want Windows installed. If you leave this field blank and are installing to a system that doesn't have Windows currently installed, you are prompted to insert a folder name during the installation process. If you leave this field blank on an upgrade machine, the current Windows folder is used, and the current Windows setup is installed over.
- *Do Not Show Installation Directory Warning.* Choose this option when you're performing a Windows system upgrade and you don't want to be shown a warning that a previous installation is in a folder other than C:\Windows.
- *Uninstall Options.* Choose whether to create uninstall information. If you opt to create uninstall information, you'll need another 100MB or so of free space on the hard disk to store the old system's files. You can use the uninstall information to remove Windows 98 at a later date, if necessary.

On the User Info tab, fill out the user and company name for the computer on which Windows will be installed. For many installations, the User Name field is usually filled out with a generic name, such as the name of the company or division. In the Computer Name field, enter the computer name for the computer on which Windows will be installed. You can use up to 15 characters, including these:

```
! . @ $ ^ ( ) { } _ ~
```

TIP Leave the Computer Name field blank if you want Windows Setup to prompt you for a computer name for each computer. You also can use Multiple Machine-Name Save to create a list of computer names for your organization. See "Creating a Multiple Machine-Name File," later in this chapter.

Fill out the Workgroup field with the computer's workgroup name using up to 15 characters. Also, enter a short (up to 48 characters) description of the computer in the Description field.

On the Setup Prompts tab, you can select unattended installation options that bypass prompts issued by Windows 98 Setup (see Figure 4.4). This makes the installation process more automatic (you might be prompted for some information, depending on your configuration, such as the install folder location).

FIG. 4.4
The Setup Prompts tab includes settings for bypassing prompts during installation.

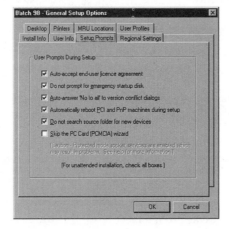

The following list summarizes these options:

- *Auto-Accept End-User Licence [sic] Agreement.* Does not display the EULA screen when Windows 98 first starts installing.

- *Do Not Prompt for Emergency Startup Disk.* Setup does not ask whether you want to create an emergency startup disk. You can make one startup disk that can be used across the organization if all your machines are set up the same. If this check box is disabled, you'll be prompted to install a floppy disk in the boot floppy disk drive. Don't clear this option unless you want to be running around creating startup disks on your machines.

- *Auto-Answer 'No to all' to Version Conflict Dialogs.* If this option is selected, Setup assumes you do not want to overwrite older files. If you clear this option, Windows automatically overwrites existing files. This is usually for DLL and device-driver files.

- *Automatically Reboot PCI and PnP Machines During Setup.* Setup will reboot PCI and PnP computers without user interaction. Clear this option if you want to have Setup wait for a user to manually reboot the machine.

- *Do Not Search Source Folder for New Devices.* Setup will not look in the source folder for new devices and INF files. The source folder is usually on the network. If you want all computers to receive the new supported devices and INF files, clear this option.

- *Skip the PC Card (PCMCIA) Wizard.* Keep this option cleared unless you know that none of your installed PC cards (on laptop installs) are not running real-mode device drivers. During Setup, some protected-mode socket services may cause problems if you select this option.

If you need to set time, keyboard layout, and regional-language settings, click the Regional Settings tab.

From the User Profiles tab, you can specify whether all users on the PC you're upgrading will use the same settings. Or, you can specify whether users can customize their settings and logon to Windows to always use these settings (called *user profiles*). Be sure to indicate the User Profile settings if you choose to let users customize their preferences. These settings include allowing desktop icons, Network Neighborhood, Start menu, and program groups in user profiles.

N O T E   There are times when you will not want to include the Start menu and other items in a user profile. You might want to disable the Start menu so that users cannot easily access the Control Panel and other items, for example. Or, you might want to create a kiosk environment in which all the applications and files a user needs are on the desktop. ■

On the MRU Locations tab, you can specify the most-recently-used file location (see Figure 4.5). The MRU list appears in drop-down lists during Setup when users are prompted for a location to install files. You can add up to 26 MRU locations. To add one, enter the path in the top field and click Add MRU. Click Remove MRU to remove an MRU setting; click Clear MRUs to remove all MRUs at once.

You can specify printers to set up during the batch install from the Printers tab. Fill out the Printer Name, Printer Type, and Printer Port fields with appropriate information. For the Printer Port field, you can enter the LPT port value or the UNC path to the printer. Click Add to add the printer.

The Desktop tab includes a number of options for specifying whether certain desktop icons and other Windows elements should be installed (see Figure 4.6).

Part
I

Ch
4

FIG. 4.5

You can specify where users can install files from during a setup routine from the MRU Locations tab.

FIG. 4.6

Use the Desktop tab to indicate which icons and miscellaneous settings Windows Setup should install.

The following list explains what happens if you clear an option's check box:

■ *My Documents.* Specifies that the My Documents folder should be installed on the desktop. Clear this to remove the icon from the desktop. The folder, however, remains as a \Windows subfolder.

■ *Internet Explorer.* Removes the Internet Explorer icon from the desktop. It does not uninstall IE.

■ *Network Neighborhood.* Removes the Network Neighborhood icon from the desktop. It does not remove Network Neighborhood functionality from the computer.

■ *Outlook Express.* Removes the Outlook Express icon from the desktop. It does not uninstall Outlook Express. This option is dimmed (unavailable) if Outlook Express is not selected on the Optional Components dialog box (see "Optional Components," later in this chapter).

- *Recycle Bin*. Removes the Recycle Bin icon from the desktop. It does not remove the Recycle Bin functionality from the computer.
- *Setup the Microsoft Network*. Removes the Upgrade the Microsoft Network icon from the desktop. It does not remove the Microsoft Network setup routine from the computer.

The options in the Miscellaneous area are self-explanatory.

Click OK to return to the Microsoft Batch 98 main window.

Network Options   As you create a batch file, you can specify which, if any, network options to install. These options include protocols, services, clients, and access control.

Click the Network Options button to display the Network Options dialog box (see Figure 4.7). On the Protocols tab, specify the protocol or set of protocols you want each computer to have installed.

FIG. 4.7
Batch 98 makes it easy to specify the network options you want to install.

Part
I

Ch
4

Most of these options are self-explanatory. However, if you select TCP/IP, you need to click the TCP/IP Settings button and fill out the TCP/IP Options dialog box with IP and subnet mask information (see Figure 4.8). If the computer will obtain an IP address automatically, such as from a WINS or DHCP server, select Obtain an IP Address Automatically.

 TIP   If you select two or more protocols to install on the Protocols tab, select the Default Protocol drop-down list and choose the protocol you want to set as the computer's default.

On the Services tab, you choose the networking services you want to install. Click No File and Printer Sharing Services if the computer will not be sharing resources (drives, files, printers, and CD-ROMs). If the computer is to run over a Microsoft Network and share resources, click the File and Printer Sharing for Microsoft Networks option. This enables you to specify browse master settings and whether LAN Manager announcing is to be used (check LM Announce if you have older LAN Manager servers on the network).

FIG. 4.8

You need to fill out IP and subnet mask addresses if your computer is to have a static IP address.

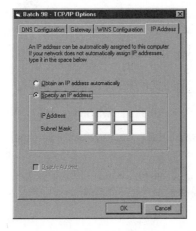

If the computers will run across a Novell network and share resources, click the File and Printer Sharing for NetWare Networks option. You can set *Server Advertising Protocol* (SAP) browsing for the computer, as well as workgroup advertising browsing.

To set up network clients on the computer, select the Clients tab (see Figure 4.9). Select the client(s) you want to install, including Client for Microsoft Networks (for Windows 98, Windows 95, Windows for Workgroups, or Windows NT networks) and Client for NetWare 3x/4x Networks. You also can enable NetWare Directory Service if available on your LAN. You can read more about Windows NT domains and NetWare logon scripts in Chapter 22, "Configuring Windows 98 as a Network Client."

FIG. 4.9

To run a network on the computer, you must install at least one client from the Clients tab.

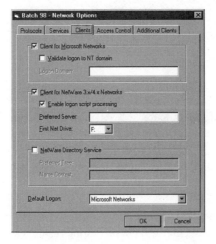

 Specify the type of logon you want to establish as the default logon by selecting a type from the Default Logon drop-down list box.

You can specify the type of access control for the computer by selecting the Access Control tab. Select Share-Level Access Control for share-level access or User-Level Access Control for user- and group-level access. If you're running File and Print Sharing for NetWare Networks or File and Print Sharing for Microsoft Networks, you can use share-level access.

To enable user-level access control, you must specify File and Print Sharing for Microsoft Networks, and you must specify a Windows NT domain or workstation from which to download a list of users to authenticate users.

If you have additional network clients for which you have drivers, select the Additional Clients tab and fill out the information for them (see Figure 4.10).

FIG. 4.10
Windows does not provide the drivers for the network clients listed on the Additional Clients tab; you must provide them.

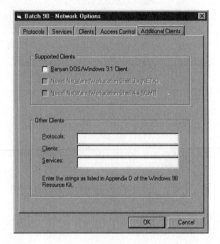

Part
I

Ch
4

You can specify the following clients:

- Banyan DOS/Windows 3.1 clients
- NetWare 3.x (NETX)
- NetWare 4.x (VLM)

You also can specify other protocols, clients, and services in the Other Clients area.

Click OK to save your Network Options settings.

Optional Components   Click the Optional Components button from the Microsoft Batch 98 dialog box to access the Optional Components dialog box (see Figure 4.11). Here, you can specify which Windows components you want to install. To select a component from the Optional Components dialog box, select an item from the Available Areas list box and choose the item to install in the Available Components list box. Click Select All to select all components. Click Clear All to deselect all components.

FIG. 4.11

Optional components include games, accessories, communications, Internet tools, and other utilities.

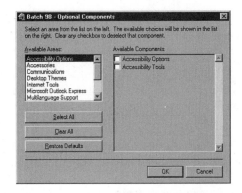

 T I P Click Restore Defaults if you want to return to the default setup that Windows installs.

Click OK to save your optional components settings.

These components are discussed in Chapter 3, "Selecting Windows 98 Components." See that chapter also for component file sizes.

Internet Explorer Options   The Internet Explorer Options dialog box includes settings for items ranging from the desktop to proxy settings (see Figure 4.12).

FIG. 4.12

The Internet Explorer dialog box includes more than just the IE browser.

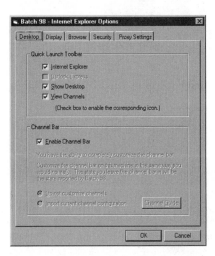

On the Desktop tab, you can specify which, if any, icon should appear on the Quick Launch toolbar. Do this by selecting Internet Explorer, Outlook Express (if selected from the Optional Components dialog box), Show Desktop, or View Channels in the Quick Launch Toolbar area.

You also can specify whether you want to enable the Channel bar on the computers you set up.

Select the Display tab to set up the way in which you want certain Windows elements to behave. You can set up the following items:

- *Active Desktop.* Choose between the Web-enabled desktop or the classic desktop.
- *Browse Folders as Follows.* You can choose to have folders that users select appear in the same window as the previous folder. Or, have folders open new windows when you navigate to them.
- *View Web Content in Folders.* Choose the way you want to view Web pages (such as HTML files) in folders.
- *Click Items as Follows.* You can choose to have single clicks open items, such as when you single click a hyperlink. Or, choose to have double clicks open items, which is the default Windows action.

To set which Web pages display for certain IE actions, select the Browser tab (see Figure 4.13). You can set URLs for the default home page, post-setup page (when IE is first launched), search pane, and online support.

FIG. 4.13

The Browser tab includes settings for default URLs in IE.

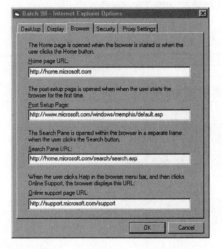

On the Security tab, you can set IE security-zone information (see Figure 4.14). Zones distinguish the security level for the type of zone you're in, including local intranet zone, trusted sites zone, Internet zone, and restricted zone. You can learn more about setting zones in Chapter 20, "Configuring Microsoft Internet Explorer 4.0."

Finally, you can set proxy-server settings on the Proxy Settings tab (see Figure 4.15). A proxy server enables you to access the Internet through a LAN firewall. The fields on this tab are self-explanatory, but you can read a description of each in Chapter 20.

Click OK to save your settings.

FIG. 4.14

Specify zone settings on
the Security tab.

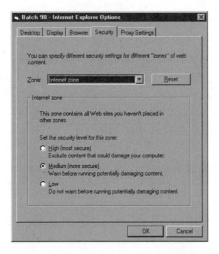

FIG. 4.15

Configure proxy settings
for your computer on the
Proxy Settings tab.

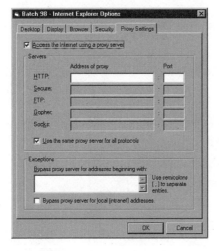

Advanced Options   Back at the Microsoft Batch 98 dialog box, you can click Advanced Options to access the Advanced Options dialog box (see Figure 4.16). Here, you can configure Batch 98 to import Registry files from a location you specify. You can specify multiple Registry files.

If you want to specify system-policy files that the computer should use, enter the policy file and its location. If you don't enter a location, the default location is used; this is the NETLOGON folder in Windows NT and the PUBLIC folder in NetWare.

Finally, select the Windows Update tab (see Figure 4.17). Place an x in the Disable Windows Update check box if you do not want Windows to use the Windows Update feature to retrieve updated drivers and software from the Internet via the Update Wizard.

Click OK to save your settings.

FIG. 4.16
Use the Advanced
Options dialog box to
specify Registry and
system-policy files, and
to control how Windows
Update works.

FIG. 4.17
Windows Update is
used to automatically
download and install
Windows 98 system
updates from the
Internet.

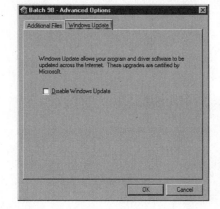

Part

I

Ch

4

Saving *INF* Settings

After you specify the options you want install, click the Save Settings to INF button in the Batch
98 dialog box. You now can start Windows Setup and specify your new INF file by using this
syntax:

```
SETUP drive:\MSBATCH.INF
```

This is the same command that was discussed in "Using Gather Now," earlier in this chapter.

Creating a Multiple Machine-Name File

Batch 98 supports running Setup on multiple machines by specifying a Multiple Machine-
Name file. You create this file to specify computer names and IP addresses for all the machines
to which you plan to install Windows 98.

To set up a Multiple Machine-Name file, use the following steps:

1. Open a text editor, such as Notepad, and create a Machine Name file. On each line in the file, enter the computer name for a single computer and press Enter. If you want to include an IP address, place a comma after a computer name and enter the address. Here is an example:

```
Peart, 126.3.2.2
Lifeson, 126.3.2.1
Lee
Bytor
Snowdog, 126.3.2.5
```

> **CAUTION**
>
> Do not insert a blank line between names. When Batch sees a blank line, it interprets it as the end of the machine names and stops there when creating Multiple Machine-Name files.

2. Save the file as a TXT file.
3. From Batch 98, choose File, Multiple Machine Name-Save. The Multiple Machine-Name Save dialog box appears (see Figure 4.18).

FIG. 4.18

Use the Multiple Machine-Name Save dialog box to set up a file so that you can install Windows to multiple machines simultaneously.

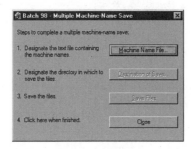

4. Click the Machine Name File button. The Open File dialog box opens.
5. Specify the Multiple Machine-Name file you created in step 1.
6. Click Open.
7. Click OK after Windows tells you how many names were read.
8. Click the Destination of Save button. The Select a Target Directory dialog box opens (see Figure 4.19).
9. Select a folder in which to store the Multiple Machine-Name Save file.
10. Click Open.
11. Click Save Files. Batch 98 creates an INF file for each machine name you've specified.
12. Click OK after Windows tells you how many files it created.
13. Click Close.

FIG. 4.19

The Select a Target
Directory dialog box.

After you create Multiple Machine-Name files, you can run Windows 98 Setup using these files
to automate the setup process. ●

Installing and Configuring New Hardware and Software

by Rob Tidrow

In this chapter

Installing New Hardware on Your Machine

In the past, installing new hardware on a PC was often a harrying and time-consuming task, even for those who considered themselves experienced users. With the Plug and Play specification release with Windows 95 and supported in Windows 98, much of the work of adding new hardware has been simplified, albeit not perfected. Not only can Windows find and install Plug and Play-compatible devices (more on Plug and Play in the next section), but Windows also does a good job of locating and automatically installing support for legacy devices (those that do not meet the Plug and Play specification).

Windows 98 doesn't differ from Windows 95 too much in the way it detects hardware and supports devices. One noticeable difference is that this release includes support for more devices and more types of devices. The new types of devices Windows now supports include the following:

- Television tuners
- DVD devices
- Multiple displays
- Global positioning devices
- Human-interface devices
- Tape-drive devices

Understanding Plug and Play

The Plug and Play specification released with Windows 95 and supported in Windows 98 eliminated, or at least decreased, the number of problems associated with hardware upgrades and installations. Plug and Play is a hardware and software specification supported by Microsoft, Compaq, Intel, and many other manufacturers that frees the user from manually configuring hardware components. The purpose of Plug and Play is to provide a tight integration between the operating system and the hardware device, such as a sound card, CD-ROM device, or mouse. In many cases, system settings, memory access, and other configuration settings now are handled by Windows 98 and the device, not by the user.

If you've upgraded your Windows 3.x system or have added hardware to it, you know the frustrations of configuring device drivers, updating INI settings, figuring out the correct IRQ and DMA channels, and determining other details of setup. Each time you upgrade your system, you have to make sure that the newest device drivers are on your system to run with your software. Many times, the device driver has to be obtained from the manufacturer through a technical-support system or downloaded from the Internet.

NOTE   Downloading device drivers is not eliminated with Plug and Play. You still might need to download an updated driver for a hardware device to increase the device's performance, or even to enable some of its features in Windows 98. If you notice a device that worked fine under Windows 95 but is not functioning correctly under Windows 98, contact the manufacturer or visit its Web site (if it has one). If the problem is known by the manufacturer, you might be able to download an updated driver for it or read instructions on how to correct the problem. ■

When you first install Windows 98, Windows hunts down and configures any Plug and Play device you have on your system. You are not required to memorize IRQs and DMA settings just to get a piece of hardware working. Plug and Play takes care of all this when Windows 98 is set up.

N O T E   Windows 98 snoops out the hardware on your system and attempts to set it up during Setup. If Windows 98 can't figure out what to do with your hardware device and doesn't set it up during install, you can use the Add New Hardware utility in the Windows Control Panel after you have Windows 98 up and running. This utility is examined in more detail in each of the chapters in Part VI, "Configuring Windows 98 in a Networked Environment."

When upgrading from Windows 95, however, Windows 98 does not perform an entire hardware check. This greatly speeds up installation time. Also, if you have legacy hardware installed, which are not Plug and Play devices, Windows 98 detects and sets them up during the Windows 98 first boot after all Plug and Play devices are set up. ■

A major component of Windows is the inclusion of the Registry. The *Registry* is a centralized database of your system settings. The Registry is a hierarchical structure that stores text or binary value information to maintain all the configuration parameters that were stored in INI files in Windows 3.x. See Figure 5.1. The Windows 98 Registry is identical to the one introduced in Windows 95.

FIG. 5.1

Plug and Play relies on the Windows 98 Registry to determine system information.

Part

I

Ch

5

One role of the Registry is to enable the Plug and Play system components to access the hardware-specific information. As new hardware devices are added to your system, Windows 98 checks your Registry settings for hardware-resource allocations, such as IRQs, I/O addresses, and DMA channels, and determines the settings for the new hardware device. With Plug and Play devices, all these configuration settings are performed at the software level, not the hardware level as before. This (virtually) eliminates the need to adjust settings on the hardware itself prior to installation. You can install the hardware and let Windows 98 do the rest.

You activate Plug and Play in one of five ways:

■ During the Windows 98 installation process, which already has been discussed.

■ When you start the Add New Hardware Wizard in the Windows 98 Control Panel. Unlike in Windows 95, the Add New Hardware Wizard in Windows 98 prompts you at the beginning of the Add New Hardware Wizard that your system will be scanned for any new hardware devices. See the section, "Configuring Your Hardware in Windows 98," for more information on the Add New Hardware Wizard.

■ During the normal boot process of Windows 98. As Windows 98 boots, it builds the Registry database (from the USER.DAT and SYSTEM.DAT files) according to the user information and system information on your computer. If the bootup process locates a new device (for example, a sound card), the Plug and Play system sets it up. On hardware devices that are not Plug and Play–compatible, Windows 98 reports that a new device has been detected and that the Add New Hardware Wizard should be run to configure it.

■ During a warm- or hot-docking situation. *Hot docking* refers to inserting a computer in a docking station while the computer is running at full power. (You also can *undock* a computer, or remove a computer from a docking station.) *Warm docking* refers to docking or undocking a computer while it is in *suspended mode*, a state in which the computer is "put to sleep" but not shut off completely. Laptop or portable computers that include a Plug and Play *basic input/output system* (BIOS) and are part of a docking station PC can be hot or warm docked and undocked.

■ Windows supports hot swapping because of PnP. With hot swapping, certain types of devices can be added or removed while the system is running, and Windows automatically can detect the change. You're not required to shut down and restart Windows with hot-swappable devices. Some of the hot-swappable devices available include PC cards, such as modems, network cards, and so on, and some serial and parallel port devices, such as scanners, some printers, and backup devices that hook into your parallel port.

Configuring Your Hardware in Windows 98

It goes without saying (but I'll say it anyway) that you need to install your hardware device in your computer before Windows can detect it and set it. With any device, including Plug and Play devices, follow the manufacturer's instructions for the installation of the card.

Read the documentation that accompanies your new device to learn how to change the *interrupt request* (IRQ) and *input/output* (I/O) settings. If your device automatically resets to the settings imposed by Windows 98, you do not have to manually set the IRQ and I/O settings.

Also, you might need to run any setup programs provided by your hardware manufacturer to finish setting up your device after the Add New Hardware Wizard runs. For older non–Plug and Play devices, these setup programs configure resource settings on the device.

N O T E If there are default positions for any settings on a device, you should leave the settings at their defaults. In general, Windows 98 first looks for devices at the default settings for that card. The only time you need to change the settings from their defaults is if there is a conflict with some other device in your system. ▪

After the hardware has been installed on your computer, you are ready to turn your computer back on and begin the process of telling Windows 98 about the new device. In many situations, just turning on your computer and starting Windows 98 is enough. Windows searches for devices each time it launches and compares each device installed with the device settings from the last time you launched Windows. If a new device appears, Windows attempts to install the correct drivers for the device. You might be prompted to provide the Windows Setup CD-ROM or floppy disks, or any setup disks that came with the device.

If a new device cannot be set up automatically by Windows during the launch stage, you're instructed to run the Add New Hardware Wizard after Windows starts. Also, if Windows doesn't even detect a new device during the startup stage, which is usually the case for legacy devices, you need to manually start the Add New Hardware Wizard.

Follow these steps to start the Add New Hardware Wizard:

1. Choose Start, Settings, Control Panel, and double-click the Add New Hardware Wizard icon. The Add New Hardware Wizard screen shown in Figure 5.2 appears.

FIG. 5.2

The first Add New Hardware Wizard screen tells you what the wizard does and gives you the opportunity to cancel it.

Part

I

Ch

5

2. Click Next. The next wizard screen tells you that Windows 98 will now look for any new Plug and Play devices on your system.

3. Click Next. Windows 98 searches and installs any Plug and Play devices (your screen might go blank for a few seconds) and presents you with the Add New Hardware Wizard screen shown in Figure 5.3. Here, you can see the devices Windows 98 has detected that need to be installed. If your new hardware device is included in the list, select the Yes, the Device Is in the List option. Click Next, and Windows informs you of which drivers and devices are set up. Click Finish to complete the installation stage.

FIG. 5.3

This Add New Hardware Wizard screen list all the Plug and Play devices installed on your computer.

N O T E   Sometimes, devices appear in the Devices list (see step 3) because they are detected but Windows 98 has a problem installing them. If this happens, click the Finish button on the Upgrade Device Driver Wizard to view the properties of the device. ▪

If your device is not in the list of devices to install, select the No, the Device Isn't in the List option.

4. Click Next. If you want Windows 98 to search for your new device, select the Yes (Recommended) option. Click Next to display another Add New Hardware Wizard screen telling you that Windows 98 now will search for your non–Plug and Play device. This process might take several minutes, during which you cannot use your computer. Click Next to start this search.

    If, however, you do not want Windows 98 to look for your hardware, select No, I Want to Select the Hardware From a List. If you know the manufacturer and model of your device, this is the quickest route to take. The following steps assume that you select this option.

5. Click Next. The Add New Hardware Wizard screen shown in Figure 5.4 appears. From this screen, you select the device you want to install from the Hardware Types list box.

FIG. 5.4

From this wizard screen, you can select the type of hardware device you want to install.

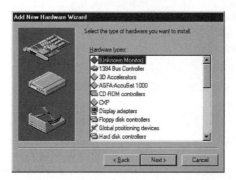

6. Click Next. The hardware Manufacturers and Models lists appear for the type of device you selected. Select the device's manufacturer from the Manufacturers list. Then select the model of the device from the Models list, as shown in Figure 5.5.

FIG. 5.5

Select the device's manufacturer and model you want to install from this wizard screen.

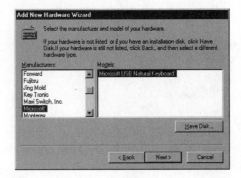

7. Click Next. Or, if you have an installation disk for your new device or your device is not listed, follow steps 9 through 11. If you don't need to install from a floppy disk, jump to step 12.

8. In the Add New Hardware Wizard screen, click Have Disk. The Install From Disk dialog box appears.

9. Specify the disk drive and folder where the manufacturer's installation files should be copied from.

10. Click OK. The Install From Disk window disappears, and you return to the Add New Hardware Wizard.

CAUTION

Not all hardware vendors support Windows 98. As a result, some software drivers might not work properly with Windows 98. Check with the hardware manufacturer for updates to its device drivers. Also look for updated drivers on your manufacturer's World Wide Web site, if available.

11. Click Next to install the new device. Your screen might go blank for a few seconds as Windows installs your device's software. Click Finish to complete the installation.

An Add New Hardware Wizard screen appears if the new device conflicts with another hardware device on your system. Click Cancel to cancel the device installation, or click Next to install the device so that you can troubleshoot the device conflict later.

12. Click Next. Your screen might go blank for a few seconds as Windows installs your device's software. Another Add New Hardware Wizard screen appears.

Part
I

Ch
5

13. Click Finish to see the problem associated with your device. An example is shown in Figure 5.6, which shows a MIDI card properties sheet. Click the Enable Device button. If this doesn't correct the problem, Windows might provide a Hardware Troubleshooter to walk you through correcting the device. In many cases, you might need to remove any other device that is conflicting with your new hardware before the new device will work.

FIG. 5.6

You can use the a device's Properties sheet to resolve some device conflicts.

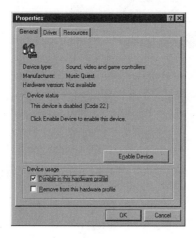

Changing Default Hardware Settings

Sometimes the Add New Hardware Wizard runs fine, but your device might not work properly. If you receive an error message that your device is not working properly, use the following steps to change the default settings that were set up during the Add New Hardware Wizard to the ones configured on your card:

1. Choose Start, Settings, Control Panel, and double-click the Settings icon.

2. Select the Device Manager page.

3. Double-click the item with which you're having a problem. It will have a yellow icon on it denoting that it has a problem associated with it. The Properties dialog box for that device appears.

4. Select the Resources page, as shown in Figure 5.7. Read the conflict message before continuing to see which setting is in conflict and what needs to be changed. Click the Change Setting button.

5. In the Edit Input/Output Range dialog box, change the Value entry to the I/O setting of the device, as shown in Figure 5.8. In the Conflict Information area, watch to see whether the I/O setting you select reads No devices are conflicting. If there are no conflicts, you can keep this setting. If, however, another device currently is using this I/O setting, select another setting that the device supports (make sure that it doesn't conflict with another device) and click OK. You then need to set your device (using the device's setup program software) to this new I/O setting.

You also can perform the same troubleshooting for problems arising from conflicts with IRQ settings.

FIG. 5.7

You use the Resources page for a device to change default settings.

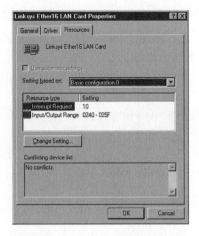

FIG. 5.8

Use the Edit Input/ Output Range dialog box to change the I/O setting for your new NIC.

6. Click OK and restart Windows 98.

Updating Device Drivers

For a hardware device, such as a keyboard, to work with the operating system controlling the computer, you need a sort of intermediary between the two. This is essentially what software device drivers do. Every piece of hardware attached to a computer requires some sort of software driver to tell the operating system what the hardware wants to do. Without the correctly installed driver, a hardware device and the operating system basically will be speaking in different languages to each other, not communicating properly, and essentially bringing the system to a standstill.

Adding or changing device drivers is substantially easier in Windows 98 than in the previous DOS/Windows combination. With Windows 98, you can add or change device drivers easily by using Device Manager, because Device Manager keeps track of assigned system resources.

Part

I

Ch

5

To change the driver for a device (in this example, a standard 101/102-key keyboard), follow these steps:

1. Choose Start, Settings, Control Panel, and double-click the System icon. The System Properties dialog box appears.

2. Select the Device Manager page.

3. Along the left edge are plus signs. Click the plus sign that corresponds to the device you want to change—in this case, Keyboard.

4. Double-click the specific device you want to change. The Properties dialog box for the device appears, such as the keyboard sheet shown in Figure 5.9.

FIG. 5.9

The keyboard properties dialog box.

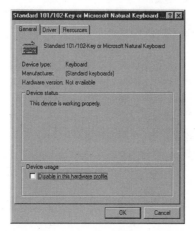

5. Select the Driver tab, as shown in Figure 5.10.

FIG. 5.10

The Driver tab for the Standard 101/102-Key or Microsoft Natural Keyboard enables you to change drivers.

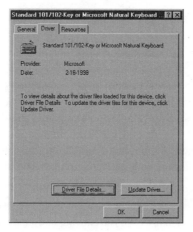

6. Click Upgrade Driver. The Upgrade Device Driver Wizard starts.

7. Click Next. The next Upgrade Device Driver Wizard screen appears, showing two options. Search for a Better Driver Than the One Your Device is Using Now (Recommended) instructs Windows to look for a driver newer than the one currently installed. Click Next to see a list of locations where Windows will look for new drivers, including local floppy disk drives, your CD-ROM drive, the Internet, and a specific location. See Figure 5.11. Clear the check box for location(s) you don't want Windows to search. If you instruct Windows to search the Internet for drivers, you need a dial-up or direct link to the Internet. Click Next to begin your search and follow specific instructions when Windows locates a new driver.

FIG. 5.11
Windows 98 will look for a new driver in various locations, including the Internet.

NOTE If Windows locates a driver that matches the one already installed for your device, you'll see a wizard screen recommending that you keep the current location. You can click Next to finish the Upgrade Device Driver Wizard, or click Back to install a specific driver, as discussed in the following procedure. ■

Part
I

Ch
5

If you want to manually select a new keyboard driver, select the bottom option, which instructs Windows to create a list of drivers from which you can select the new keyboard driver. The following steps assume that you have selected this option.

8. Click Next. The Upgrade Device Driver Wizard screen shown in Figure 5.12 appears. In the Models list, select the model that matches your keyboard. If your model is not listed and you have a new driver on a disk, click Have Disk and specify where this new driver is located.

 TIP A Models list details the keyboard models compatible with your hardware. Make sure the Show Compatible Devices option is selected. If the keyboard you want to set up is not on the list, you should select the Show All Hardware option. The list changes to show all such keyboards.

9. Click Next. You are prompted to insert the disk that contains the new driver. Click OK after you insert the disk, or click OK if the disk already is inserted (such as a CD-ROM or hard drive). After the driver is installed, you are returned to the Upgrade Device Driver Wizard. Click Finish. You are prompted to restart Windows 98 to finish the driver update. Click Yes to restart your computer.

FIG. 5.12
Windows 98 shows a list of manufacturers and models that might match your installed device.

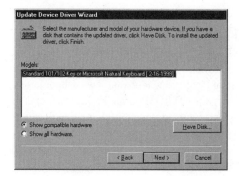

Installing and Uninstalling Windows 98 Applications

Windows 98 applications are designed to be installed in an easy and painless method. Applications distributed on CD-ROM, for example, use the Windows 98 AutoRun feature to automatically launch their setup wizard to guide users through the installation process. The AutoRun feature is activated automatically when a CD-ROM is inserted into a user's computer.

 You can temporarily turn off the AutoRun feature by pressing Shift while inserting a CD-ROM. To permanently turn off the feature, display the Device Manager and open the Properties dialog box for your CD-ROM. Select the Settings page and uncheck the Auto Insert Notification option. Click OK.

If an application you acquire is not on CD-ROM, or it is on CD-ROM and you turn off the AutoRun feature in Windows 98, you can start the installation process by following these steps:

1. Choose Start, Settings, Control Panel.
2. Double-click the Add/Remove Programs icon to display the Add/Remove Programs Properties dialog box, as shown in Figure 5.13.

FIG. 5.13
Use the Add/Remove Programs Properties dialog box to install and uninstall applications under Windows 98.

3. Click Install to start the Install Program Wizard. This wizard locates the setup program on your new application's CD-ROM or floppy disk.

4. Click Next. Windows displays the Run Installation Program dialog box when it locates the setup program. See Figure 5.14. If Windows 98 cannot locate the setup program file, enter the path and filename in the Command Line for Installation Program field.

FIG. 5.14
The Run Installation Program dialog box shows the name of the install program for the application you're installing.

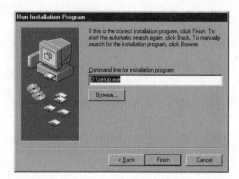

5. Click Finish to start the install process. To complete the application's installation, follow the onscreen instructions and wizards.

 TIP You also can use the Run command from the Start menu to launch an application's setup program. To do this, choose Start, Run, and fill in the path to the setup program in the Open field. Click OK to launch the program.

Uninstalling Software in Windows 98

Windows 98 applications include uninstall features that enable you to remove the program and its associated configuration and Registry settings from Windows 98. To remove an application from Windows 98, use these steps:

1. Choose Start, Settings, Control Panel.
2. Double-click the Add/Remove Programs icon to display the Add/Remove Programs Properties dialog box.
3. In the area at the bottom of the Install/Uninstall page, select the program you want to uninstall. Only those applications that have an uninstall program appear in this list. (Some older Windows 3.x applications include uninstall programs, but you must launch them from the application's program group or folder.)
4. Click Add/Remove to start the Install/Shield Wizard, which walks you through the uninstall process. Follow your application's onscreen instructions to complete the removal process.

NOTE You also can click the Add/Remove button to reinstall an application or to add additional components to an application. ▪

Configuring and Customizing the Windows 98 Desktop

CHAPTER 6

Configuring Windows 98 Classic and Web View Desktops

by Christopher Gagnon

In this chapter

The Classic Desktop Interface

The classic desktop interface was introduced with Windows 95. See Figure 6.1. This section discusses the elements of the interface. You'll also learn about customizing the interface according to your preferences.

FIG. 6.1

The Windows 98 classic-view desktop.

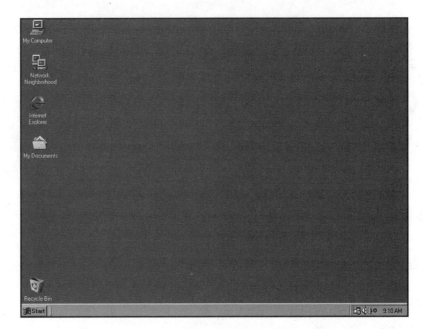

The Taskbar

One of the most significant and noticeable changes in the Windows 98 interface is the taskbar. Instead of restricting you to a single taskbar with limited functionality, Windows 98 allows you to add mini-taskbars called *toolbars*.

Several toolbars are included with Windows 98 designed to help you move more efficiently through your system.

TIP You can activate as many of the toolbars as you want. If you are using screen resolutions of 1024×768 or higher, you might want to expand the taskbar by grabbing the top edge and dragging it up. This way, you can arrange multiple toolbars on your taskbar.

Address   The Address toolbar allows you to quickly access a Web page right from your desktop. See Figure 6.2. It works just like the Address bar in your browser. To use this toolbar, just type in the URL to your favorite site. Windows 98 launches Internet Explorer and connects to the site.

The Classic Desktop Interface

FIG. 6.2
The Windows 98
Address toolbar gives
you a quick way to
jump to a Web site.

Links The Links toolbar is another quick way to get to your favorite Web sites. See Figure 6.3. The default links point to various areas on Microsoft's Web site. You can add links by using the Organize Favorites dialog box in Internet Explorer. Links keep you from having to type the URL every time you want to visit a particular site.

FIG. 6.3
The Links toolbar allows
you to keep buttons to
your favorite Web sites
on the taskbar.

Desktop The Desktop toolbar takes everything on the desktop and displays it on the toolbar. See Figure 6.4. Because the desktop is usually just as accessible as the toolbar, you don't gain much from using this toolbar. It is handy, though, for those times when you have several windows open and the desktop is covered.

FIG. 6.4
The Desktop toolbar
places your desktop
icons on the taskbar.

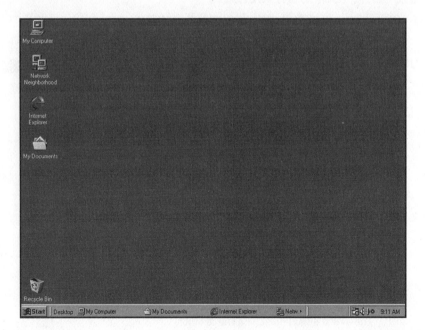

Quick Launch   The Quick Launch toolbar allows you to place shortcuts to your favorite programs on the taskbar. See Figure 6.5. The functionality is very similar to the Microsoft Office shortcut bar. The advantage to Quick Launch is that the shortcuts are kept on the taskbar. This helps you keep your screen organized and free of clutter.

FIG. 6.5

The Quick Launch toolbar lets you keep shortcuts to any program on your taskbar.

To add your favorite items to the Quick Launch toolbar, follow these easy steps:

1. Locate the program executable by using Windows Explorer.
2. Right-click the program file and drag it to the Quick Launch area.
3. Release the right mouse button.
4. Select Create Shortcut Here from the dialog box.

The Quick Launch toolbar gives you an organized place to store your shortcuts. This helps keep your desktop clear and uncluttered.

Creating Your Own Toolbars

If the built-in toolbars don't seem that attractive to you, don't worry! Windows 98 has a way for you to create your own. See Figure 6.6.

FIG. 6.6

You can custom build a toolbar from any directory.

You can create your own toolbar from a folder or a URL. The following example describes how to create a new toolbar called Games:

1. Create a new folder on your machine called Games.
2. Create shortcuts to each of your games in the new folder.
3. Right-click on the taskbar.
4. Choose Toolbars from the shortcut menu.
5. Choose New Toolbar.
6. In the New Toolbar dialog box, browse your system to find the folder you created and click OK.

The new toolbar appears on the taskbar.

You can create a toolbar for any folder you want. It's a great way to organize your programs and increase your productivity.

TIP As with most of the elements in Windows 98, the toolbars can be customized to meet your personal tastes. To access the general properties for the toolbar, right-click on the bar itself. Be careful not to right-click on any of the buttons. If you right-click on a button, you see a properties list for the shortcut associated with the button. After you right-click on the toolbar area, you see a properties list for the entire bar. This list enables you to perform tasks such as displaying the toolbar name, showing titles for the buttons, and changing the button size. Experiment with these settings to find the look and feel that is right for you.

My Computer

My Computer is a desktop icon that was introduced with Windows 95. It contains links to areas specific to the local machine, such as disk drives, Dial-Up Networking, printers, and the Control Panel. You can use My Computer to browse system settings, manage files, and add and configure printers. This is a required file on the desktop and cannot be deleted without altering the Registry.

 TIP An easy way to remove required desktop elements such as My Computer and Network Neighborhood is with TweakUI. This is a set of free tools from Microsoft that allows you to change Registry settings without having to modify the Registry directly.

Network Neighborhood

Network Neighborhood also was introduced in Windows 95. This application enables you to browse the network if you are on a LAN. After you double-click the Network Neighborhood icon, you are presented with a list of computers that are active on the network. Double-click on a computer to see a list of the shares available on that machine. Network Neighborhood is a handy way to track down resources on the network if you are not exactly sure where they are located.

Recycle Bin

The Recycle Bin is one of the handiest utilities to come out of Windows 95 and has been included in Windows 98. Whenever you delete a file from your system, it is placed in the Recycle Bin. The Recycle Bin is actually a separate area on your hard disk that stores unwanted files. Files are not actually deleted from the machine until you empty the Recycle Bin. This allows you to recover a file if you accidentally delete it.

To restore a file from the Recycle Bin, follow this procedure:

1. Double-click the Recycle Bin icon.
2. Find the file you need to restore by scrolling through the deleted files.
3. Right-click the file you want to restore and choose Restore from shortcut menu.

The file is restored to its original location.

Part

II

Ch

6

Internet Explorer

Internet Explorer is a shortcut to Internet Explorer 4.0, which is included with Windows 98. Unlike the previous three elements, Internet Explorer can be removed easily from the desktop by right-clicking the icon, choosing Delete, and confirming that you want to remove the icon.

My Documents

My Documents is an element new to Windows 98. If you have used Microsoft Office, you are used to the folder called My Documents that is placed in the root of your C: drive. Windows 98 takes the approach that all documents should be placed in a common area regardless of the program used to create them. Thus, you should be able to find a folder called My Documents on your C: drive. This folder is the default save location for any document. Go into Notepad and type a few lines. Choose File, Save As to bring up the Save As dialog box. You will notice that Windows prompts you to save in the My Documents folder. Now go into Paint. If you try to save your work here, you'll also notice that the default save location is My Documents. By creating this default save directory, Windows 98 helps you save time looking for your files.

Shortcuts

Shortcuts are icons that point to a program somewhere on your system. Shortcuts are a handy way of organizing your desktop by function. Instead of worrying about where a program is on your system, you can create shortcuts on your desktop that enable you to launch your programs from the same place. You can tell that an icon is a shortcut by the arrow at the bottom left corner of the icon. Immediately after installing Windows 98 on your system, you will find several shortcuts on your desktop. You can add and delete shortcuts from the desktop at your leisure.

Configuring Your Display Properties

Aside from the basic elements on the desktop, there are several features that enable you to change the way your desktop looks. To change these features, you use the Display Properties dialog box. You can get to this dialog box by double-clicking Display in the Control Panel. The Windows 98 Display Properties dialog box contains six tabs; each tab changes a different element of the desktop interface.

The Background Tab   The Background tab enables you to change the way your desktop looks, as shown in Figure 6.7. You have the option of adding wallpaper or patterns to your background. Wallpaper applies a graphics file to the background so that you can put your favorite picture on your desktop. Wallpaper can be centered or tiled, depending on your taste. Windows 98 comes with several wallpaper samples that you can use. Choosing Patterns applies a design to the background color using a tiled 8×8-pixel pattern. Several patterns are included with Windows 98. You also have the ability to modify any of the patterns to create your own interesting designs.

> **N O T E**   Because wallpaper is stored in memory, you should be careful not to use a huge graphics file for your wallpaper. Using patterns or no background at all generally improves your system's performance. ▪

FIG. 6.7

You use the Background tab to add wallpaper or patterns to your desktop.

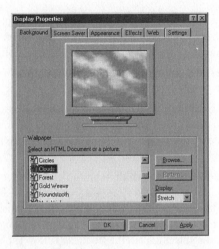

The Screen Saver Tab   Screen savers are an interesting way to personalize your system. See Figure 6.8. They were designed to prevent burn-in on your monitor but have since evolved into a way of expressing yourself. Windows 98 comes with several screen savers that you can use. To enable a screen saver, you simply choose the one you want from the list.

FIG. 6.8

The Screen Saver tab.

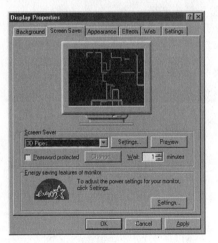

The following list describes the options you have for configuring your screen saver:

- *Settings.* Enables you to change any settings specific to the screen saver you have selected. Some screen savers will not have any specific configuration options, so this button might be grayed out.

- *Preview.* Activates the screen saver. This is a good way to check any configuration changes you applied using the Settings Button.

Part

II

Ch

6

■ *Password Protected.* Checking this box will cause Windows 98 to prompt you for a password before allowing you to stop the screen saver. You can change your screen-saver password by clicking Change and entering your new password.

■ *Wait xx Minutes.* Enables you to set the amount of inactive time Windows will wait before activating the screen saver. The maximum is 60 minutes.

■ *Energy Saving Features of Monitor.* If your monitor is Energy Star–compliant, you can click the Settings button in this area to actually power down the monitor after a preset period of time. This is a particularly handy feature for people who like to leave their computer on all day.

The Appearance Tab   The Appearance tab enables you to change the color scheme used by Windows 98, as shown in Figure 6.9. It also enables you to set window-element sizes and to change the font displayed by the window. You can choose from a number of color schemes, or you can create your own. To change the attributes of a certain window element, you can click the item in the picture, or you can select it from the Item drop-down list box. You then can use the Size, Color, and Font options at the right of the screen to change the attributes. The changes are shown in real-time in the picture at the top of the dialog box, so you will know what the changes will look like before you apply them.

FIG. 6.9
The Appearance tab enables you to change colors and sizes of window elements.

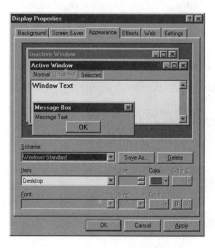

The Effects Tab   The Effects tab will look familiar to anyone who has used the Plus Pack for Windows 95. See Figure 6.10.

FIG. 6.10
You use the Effects tab to apply miscellaneous effects to the interface.

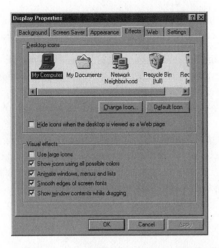

The Effects tab can be broken into two sections. First, it enables you to change the icons of the required desktop items. Second, it gives you a list of the following effects you can activate to further enhance your desktop:

- *Use Large Icons.* Depending on your screen resolution, your icons might be hard to see. Checking this box makes all your desktop icons larger.

- *Show Icons Using all Possible Colors.* Selecting this box enables you to use icons that display more than 16 colors. You won't notice any difference in the standard icons as they were drawn using only 16 colors, but you can find icon sets that contain photo-realistic graphics.

- *Animate Windows, Menus and Lists.* Windows 98 uses more animation when performing tasks than Windows 95. Menus and lists scroll into place rather than just appearing. This provides some pleasing eye-candy, but some people find it annoying. This check box enables you to turn off the animation.

- *Smooth Edges of Screen Fonts.* If you ever zoomed into a document, you probably have seen a phenomenon known as *staircasing*. Staircasing is the jagged-edge effect you see when displaying a curve on a computer screen. This is a phenomenon that occurs because computer screens are made up less prominent by alternating color shades along the edge. This process blurs the edge of the font, which causes the curve to appear smother. Selecting this option activates anti-aliasing for all Windows fonts.

- *Show Window Contents While Dragging.* Enabling this option enables you to see the contents of a window while you drag it. If you deselect this option, Windows only displays an outline of the window when you drag it across the screen. It takes significantly more resources to display the entire window while you drag it, so depending on your machine, you probably will notice that the animation is a little jerky.

The Web Tab   The Web tab enables you to change the way your desktop looks if you are using the Web desktop interface. (See the section, "The Web View Desktop Interface.")

The Settings Tab   The Settings tab enables you to change the physical display settings for your machine, as shown in Figure 6.11. Here, you can change your screen resolution and the maximum display colors on your system. Screen resolution is purely a personal-preference choice. Higher resolutions give you more room on the desktop but display text and icons much smaller than lower resolutions. Color depth defines how many colors your computer is capable of displaying. Choosing this setting might take some thought. If you plan on viewing photo-realistic graphics on your machine, you will not want a setting of 256 colors. If you display a picture containing 16 million colors on a system that is set to display only 256 colors, the picture will look terrible. Most systems can display images at 64,000 colors (high color) without distorting the picture. You will have to test your system to see which color depth is right for you.

FIG. 6.11
The Settings tab.

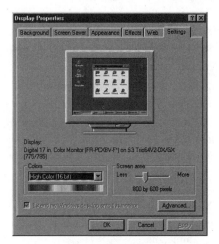

N O T E   Color depth and screen resolution are directly related to the video card you have in your machine. You might find that you can display only certain color depths at certain resolutions. Refer to your system documentation for details. ▪

The Web View Desktop Interface

The most noticeable change in Windows 98 is the integration of the Internet Explorer 4.0 active desktop. This interface enables you to subscribe to your favorite Web channels and to change the way Windows feels so that the entire system acts like a Web browser. In this section, you'll look at some of the most prominent features of the Web interface, including how to set up your favorite Web sites as desktop items that update automatically.

Activating the Web Desktop

You can activate the Web desktop at any time. As with most of the functions in Windows 98, there are several ways of doing this. The quickest method follows:

1. Right-click on the desktop.

2. Choose Active Desktop from the shortcut menu.

3. Choose View as Web Page, as shown in Figure 6.12.

Your system configures the Web interface and returns you to the active desktop. You can use this same method to return to the classic interface.

FIG. 6.12
You can activate the Web interface from the desktop.

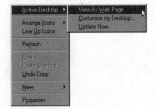

Introducing the Web Desktop

At first glance, the Web desktop doesn't look much different than the classic desktop. The main advantage of the Web desktop is the capability to place active desktop items in the background. See Figure 6.13. This feature enables you to configure areas of your screen to point to different Web sites. These active areas then can be scheduled to update at any given time. This way, you can have your computer download the page when you are not around. Then when you want to view the page, you actually will be viewing it from the local system.

The Web interface also gives you the capability to configure the Windows 98 interface to treat everything as if it were a Web page. This means that file management can be done as if you were viewing the files on the Internet. The standard Internet toolbars are used in every window. You can even set the system to treat icons as hypertext. That way, you don't have to double-click an icon to activate it.

Active Desktop Items

Active desktop items enable you to create an area on your desktop that is linked to a specific URL. You then can keep your favorite Web sites open all the time. Hundreds of active desktop items are floating around the Internet, from stock tickers to news headlines. In this section, you'll look at adding and removing active desktop items, as well as creating your own.

Adding and Removing Active Desktop Items   Active desktop items are controlled from the Web tab in the Display Properties dialog box, as shown in Figure 6.14. The easiest way to add a desktop item is to choose one from Microsoft's Active Desktop gallery.

Part
II

Ch
6

FIG. 6.13
The active desktop fully integrates your desktop with Internet Explorer.

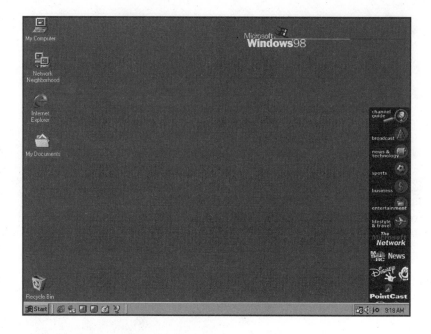

FIG. 6.14
You can control your active desktop items from the Web tab in the Display Properties dialog box.

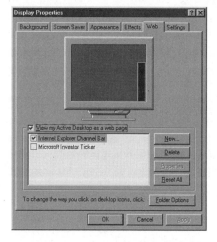

To add a new desktop item, use the following procedure:

1. Select the Web tab in the Display Properties dialog box.
2. Click New.

3. A message box appears asking whether you want to select a desktop item from Microsoft's Active Desktop gallery. Click Yes.

   Internet Explorer launches, and you are taken to the gallery on Microsoft's Web site.

4. Choose the item you want and click the Add to Active Desktop button.

The item then appears on your desktop, as shown in Figure 6.15.

FIG. 6.15
You can find a lot of great active desktop items, like this stock ticker in Microsoft's Active Desktop gallery.

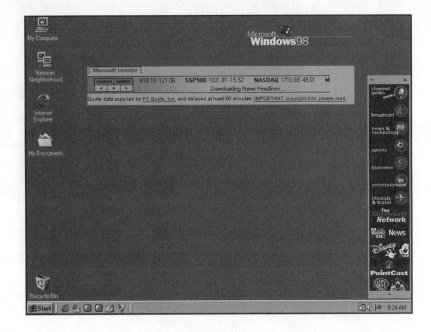

At some point, you might decide that you no longer want a certain item. You have two options for removing unwanted items from your desktop. To disable the item without removing it from the system, you simply uncheck the box next to the item in the Web tab of the Display Properties dialog box. Disabling an active desktop item stops all updates and removes the item from your desktop without actually deleting it. This way, you can re-enable the item later without having to reload it on the system. If you know that you will not use an item again, you can delete it. To delete an active desktop item, select the item in the Web tab of the Display Properties dialog box and click Delete. This permanently removes the item from your system.

Creating Your Own Active Desktop Items Windows 98 also enables you to create your own active desktop items. See Figure 6.16. This feature is handy when you can't find a desktop item that you want or if you just want to put your favorite Web site on your desktop.

Part
II

Ch
6

FIG. 6.16

You can create active desktop items that point to any site on the Internet.

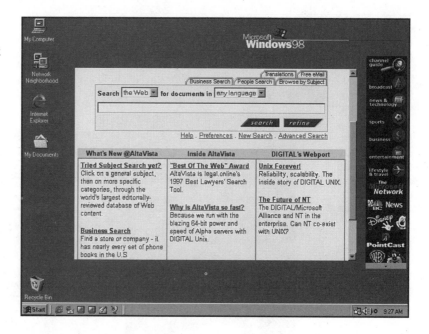

The following procedure walks you through the process of creating your own desktop item:

1. Select the Web tab in the Display Properties dialog box.

2. Click New.

3. A message box appears, asking whether you want to select a desktop item from Microsoft's Active Desktop gallery. Click No.

4. Type the URL to your favorite Web site and click OK.

   It might take a few minutes for Windows 98 to contact the Web site.

5. A confirmation box appears asking you to verify that you want to add the new item to the desktop. Click OK.

The new item appears in the Active Items list.

Manipulating Your Active Desktop Items   You can place active desktop items anywhere on your screen and size them just like any other window. The only noticeable difference between an active desktop item and an ordinary window is that the window border and title bar disappear when not in use. This feature enables the desktop item to blend seamlessly into the background. If you want to move or size your desktop item, hold the mouse over the item for a few seconds. The control bar appears, and you can manipulate the item as if it were a normal window.

Folder Options

Windows 98 enables you to choose whether you want the system to have a classic Windows 95 feel, a Web-browser feel, or a combination of both. You specify these options in the Folder Options dialog box, as shown in Figure 6.17. You can get to this dialog box by clicking Folder Options in the Web tab of the Display Properties dialog box. Each setting offers a number of differences. What you choose comes down to a matter of personal taste.

FIG. 6.17
The Folder Options dialog box.

Web Style   Choosing Web style enables you to interact with your entire system as if it were a Web site. One of the biggest differences is that you no longer will need to double-click icons to activate them. Each icon will be underlined as if it were a hyperlink in a Web document. One of the handiest features of Web view is that your folders will contain a status area on the left side of the window. The status area shows you the properties for the selected file. Depending on the type of file you have selected, you might even get a preview of the file contents.

Classic Style   The Classic Style setting changes your icons and windows to the Windows 95 classic interface. Icons will require a double-click, and Windows will display their contents without the fancy status area. This setting is included for people who are comfortable with the Windows 95 interface and don't want to spend time learning new ways to do the same tasks. If you use the classic interface setting, you will not be able to view any active content on your desktop.

Custom Settings   The Custom, Based on Settings You Choose option enables you to mix features of both interfaces to create the interface you want. You might not want any active content or the single-click option, for example, but you might want the status area in your windows. The Custom Settings dialog box enables you to pick and choose features from each interface type, as shown in Figure 6.18.

Part
II

Ch
6

FIG. 6.18

You use the Custom Settings dialog box to choose your favorite settings from both interfaces.

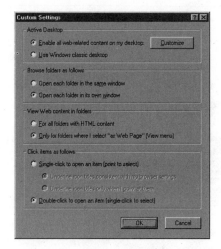

The option areas for Custom Settings follow:

- *Active Desktop*. Enables the active desktop component, which allows you to add active desktop items to your desktop.

- *Browse Folders as Follows*. Enables you to choose between opening each folder in the same window or creating a new window for each folder.

- *View Web Content in Folders*. Enables you to choose between viewing the status area in every folder or in just the folders you designate.

- *Click Items as Follows*. Enables you to activate the single-click option.

CHAPTER 7

Configuring Monitors and Video Cards

by Rod Tidrow

In this chapter

Configuring Your Monitor and Video Card

After your video card has been installed and is configured to work with Windows 98, you can use a few options to configure your display. If you need to install a video card under Windows, see Chapter 5, "Installing and Configuring New Hardware and Software."

Some of the changes you can make include changing the resolution for your display, for example, or choosing the color palette Windows 98 uses to display images on your screen. Depending on the capabilities of your video card, you may have more or fewer choices to select from for each option. If you have a capable video card, for example, you may have a number of resolution settings from which to choose.

TROUBLESHOOTING

When I was installing my video card, I didn't recognize (or I don't know) the manufacturer or model of my video card in the lists that appear in the Add New Hardware Wizard. Also, I couldn't find any disks that might be associated with my video card. What can I do? Windows 98 lets you choose a generic driver for use with your adapter if you are not sure what video adapter is installed in your PC. Choose Standard Display Types from the Manufacturers list box and either Standard Display Adapter (VGA) or Super VGA from the Models list box. If you are not sure whether your monitor is Super VGA capable, choose the VGA option.

You can configure your monitor and video card from the Settings page of the Display Properties dialog box, as shown in Figure 7.1.

FIG. 7.1
You use the Display Properties dialog box to modify the behavior of your monitor and video card.

You can use a few methods to view the Display Properties dialog box:

■ Right-click the desktop to display the desktop context menu. The Display Properties dialog box appears. Select the Settings page.

■ Open the Control Panel and then click the Display icon. The Display Properties dialog box appears. Select the Settings page.

Specifying Resolution Settings

The Screen Area slider on the Settings tab in the Display Properties dialog box enables you to specify the resolution setting for your monitor and video adapter. This setting determines how much information you see onscreen. By dragging the slider to the right, you are able to see more images on your screen, although the images appear smaller.

To change the resolution, follow these steps:

1. Select the Settings page of the Display Properties dialog box.

2. Click and drag the slider in the Screen Area section to the resolution setting you want.

   As the slider stops at the different resolution settings permitted by your video adapter, the image displayed in the sample desktop at the top of the Settings page changes to show you the relative effects of the resolution setting you choose.

3. Click Apply for the resolution setting to take effect immediately and to continue working in the Display Properties dialog box. You also can click OK for your changes to take effect and for the Display Properties dialog box to close.

4. A message box appears, informing you that Windows will resize your desktop and that your screen might flicker for a moment. To continue, click OK.

5. After the screen settings are changed, a message box appears, asking whether you want to keep the new setting. Click Yes to keep the setting. If you don't click Yes or No (to revert to the old setting) within 15 seconds, Windows automatically reverts to the old setting.

CAUTION

Depending on the capabilities of your video adapter, Windows 98 might need to shut itself down and then restart in order for the resolution changes to take effect. This is normal and no reason for worry. You are always warned first, and you have the option of not letting Windows 98 restart itself. If you choose this option, Windows 98 continues to operate normally, but the changes you made to your configuration do not take effect until the next time you start Windows 98.

TROUBLESHOOTING

When I change the resolution of my display, Windows 98 displays a black screen or has a bunch of wavy lines on it. What happened? You probably selected a setting that your video adapter and monitor cannot display. To return to your previous setting, reboot your computer and enter Safe mode by pressing F8 when your system boots and selecting Safe Mode from the Start menu. During Safe mode, the Windows 98 Standard VGA driver is loaded, enabling you to boot into Windows and change the resolution of your monitor.

Part

II

Ch

7

By changing the Screen Area setting, you change the number of pixels used to create the images that appear on your screen. Pixels (*picture ele*ments) are the small units of color that make up the images you see onscreen. The setting that appears below the slider tells you how many pixels will be used to make up the images on the screen. The first number refers to the number of pixels in each row; the second number refers to the number of pixels used in each column. A setting of 640×480 pixels, for example, means that the images on your screen will be made up of 640 rows of 480 pixels each.

The greater the number of pixels used to create the images on your screen, the more clear the resolution. The smaller the size of the pixels, the greater the number of pixels that can be used; hence, the resolution is sharper, and you see more images onscreen.

Generally, the higher the resolution, the slower the display refreshes. Also, as you increase the resolution, the text size, menus, icons, and other screen elements decrease in size. For some users, this might make reading text or locating items on the desktop difficult. With some monitors, as you increase resolution, the monitor hum changes and might unnerve you until you get used to it or change the resolution setting.

TROUBLESHOOTING

I can't seem to move the slider in the Screen Area in any direction. The Less and More labels appear to be dimmed. The points along the slider where you can stop the pointer are determined by the capabilities of your video card and monitor. If your video card and monitor are capable of one setting only, you cannot move the slider in the Screen Area at all. The labels Less and More at each end of the slider appear dimmed if your video adapter and monitor are not capable of multiple resolution settings.

Using the QuickRes Utility

You also can specify resolution settings via the QuickRes utility. This utility enables you to quickly change the screen resolution and bit depth (such as 16 or 24 bit) without going through the Display Properties dialog box. Instead, you access a pop-up menu from the Windows taskbar to select the setting you want.

N O T E   QuickRes originally was available as a Windows 95 PowerToy utility. It now is integrated into Windows 98. If you previously installed QuickRes under Windows 95, it still may appear on your taskbar (next to the clock) and will work fine under Windows 98. You don't have to turn it on using the following steps. ■

To turn on QuickRes, use the following steps:

1. On the Settings page, click A̲dvanced. The General page of your display adapter's Properties dialog box appears, as shown in Figure 7.2.

FIG. 7.2

The General page provides an option to turn on the QuickRes utility.

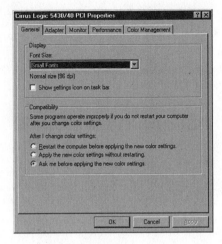

2. Select Show <u>S</u>ettings Icon on Task Bar.

3. Click OK.

4. To change your display setting, click the QuickRes icon, and select a menu setting, such as 640×480 256 Color. See Figure 7.3. The current display setting is denoted by a check mark next to the setting value.

FIG. 7.3

The QuickRes utility is handy if you need to switch between resolutions several times a day.

When you select a new setting, QuickRes immediately changes the display setting. You are not presented with the Display Properties or Monitor Settings message boxes as you were in steps 4 and 5 in the preceding section.

If you have the QuickRes PowerToy installed from an earlier Windows 95 installation and want to remove it, open the Registry Editor and locate the following subkey:

`HKEY_CURRENT_USER\Software\Microsoft\Windows\CurrentVersion\Run`

Edit the Taskbar Display Controls setting to remove the `,QUICKRES_RUNDLLENTRY item` (including the lead comma). Don't remove any other piece of this entry. Close the Registry Editor, shut down, and restart Windows. You now can complete the preceding steps to turn on the Windows 98 QuickRes utility.

Part

II

Ch

7

You also can access the Display Properties dialog box from the QuickRes menu by double-clicking the QuickRes icon or selecting <u>A</u>djust Display Properties instead of selecting a new setting value.

Setting the Color Palette

You can specify the color palette Windows 98 uses to display colors onscreen. Instead of choosing specific colors, you can specify the scope of the palette Windows use. You might choose the 16-color palette, for example, or you might choose the 256-color palette. The Color drop-down list shows the number of colors and color palette (high-color or true color) that your monitor supports. For many users, 256 Color is appropriate. For artists or users who work with graphics-intensive software, high color or true color is required to achieve professional results.

> **CAUTION**
>
> Although choosing a palette with more colors enhances the images on your screen, more memory is used to display these colors, so overall system performance may suffer.

You choose the color palette from the Colors drop-down list that appears on the Settings page in the Display Properties dialog box, as shown in Figure 7.4. The capabilities of your video adapter determine how many choices are shown in the Colors drop-down list box.

FIG. 7.4

You can choose how many colors are used to paint the images you see on your screen.

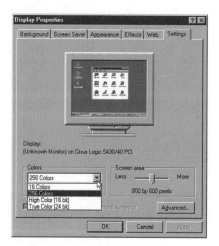

To change the color palette, follow these steps:

1. Select the Settings page of the Display Properties dialog box.

2. Choose the palette from the Colors drop-down list box. After you make a selection, the rectangular area below the drop-down list containing all the colors in the current palette you are using changes to show the palette you chose.

3. Click Apply or OK. Depending on the capabilities of your video adapter, Windows 98 might shut itself down and then restart in order for the resolution changes to take effect.

Some programs might not operate properly after you've changed color settings. You might need to restart your computer to have these color settings take effect (that is, if Windows doesn't restart when completing the preceding steps). You can choose from three compatibility settings to control how Windows reacts when you change color settings. To change these settings, follow these steps:

1. On the Settings page on the Display Properties dialog box, click Advanced.

2. On the General page, set one of the options in the Compatibility section. If you select the Apply the New Color Settings Without Restarting option, you should exit and restart any applications that are running when you change color settings.

3. Click OK.

Setting Font Size

Many users are concerned with screen real estate. That is, they want more of it. Some users like to see more information onscreen even at the expense of the clarity of the onscreen image. You can display more information on your screen by changing the resolution setting, as demonstrated in the "Specifying Resolution Settings" section. Now, you'll learn how to squeeze more information on the screen by changing the font size of the text used in Windows 98. You also can use the change-font-size functionality to enlarge the font size so that text appears larger in Windows 98.

Figure 7.5 shows the Control Panel with the font size enlarged to the Large Fonts setting. Notice how the space between the icons has increased and how you can see less icons in the folder at one time. Figure 7.6 shows the Control Panel folder with the font size decreased with the Small Fonts setting. Notice how the space between icons has been decreased so that you can have many more icons at the same time in the folder.

FIG 7.5
Working with enlarged fonts.

Part
II

Ch
7

FIG 7.6
Working with smaller
fonts.

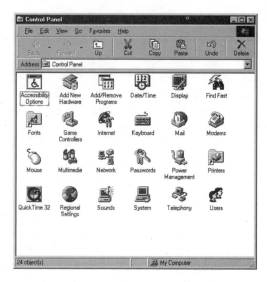

Changing the font size in Windows 98 is easy. You can choose from two predefined sizes, small fonts or large fonts, or you can specify a customized size by supplying a percentage size based on the normal size. You also can increase and decrease the size of the font by maneuvering a graphical ruler.

 TIP Your monitor and video card must be capable of multiple resolution settings in order for you to be able to change the font size. Windows 98 forces users to choose a resolution setting other than 640×480 pixels in order to change the font size.

To change the font size by using one of the predefined settings, follow these steps:

1. Select the Settings page of the Display Properties dialog box.

2. Change the Screen Area setting to something other than 640×480 pixels (see "Specifying Resolution Settings," earlier in this chapter, for help).

3. Click Advanced.

4. Choose Small Fonts or Large Fonts from the Font Size drop-down list. Refer to Figure 7.2. On some systems, you might see the Change System Font message box, as shown in Figure 7.7, which tells you that the font change will not take effect until the fonts are installed and Windows is restarted. Click OK.

FIG. 7.7
The Change System Font
message box informs
you that fonts for the
new display size must
be installed.

5. Click OK. Another Change System Font message box appears, asking whether you're sure you want to change your system fonts. Click Yes.

6. Click OK on the Display Properties dialog box.

7. Depending on the capabilities of your video adapter, Windows 98 might prompt you to shut down and restart in order for the font-size changes to take effect. Click Yes to do this.

   When Windows restarts, the new font setting takes effect.

   Or, click OK for your changes to take effect and for the Display Properties dialog box to close.

To change the font size by specifying a custom size, follow these steps:

1. Select the Settings page of the Display Properties dialog box.

2. Change the Screen Area setting to something other than 640×480 pixels.

3. Click Advanced.

4. Choose Other from the Font Size drop-down list on the General page. The Custom Font Size dialog box appears, as shown in Figure 7.8.

FIG. 7.8
You can specify a custom size for the font used in Windows 98, expressing the size as a percentage of the normal size.

5. Enter the new percentage size in the Scale Fonts To Be edit box. You also can choose from a predefined percentage by clicking the down arrow. Or, click anywhere on the ruler and drag to the left to decrease the size or to the right to increase the size.

6. Click OK.

7. Click Apply for the new font size to take effect immediately and to continue working in the Display Properties dialog box. Or, click OK for your changes to take effect and for the Display Properties dialog box to close. Depending on the capabilities of your video adapter, Windows 98 might shut itself down and then restart in order for the font-size changes to take effect.

Changing Video Drivers

If you obtain a new video driver for your video-adapter card, you can update to it using the Adapter page. This page is available by clicking the Advanced button on the Setting page of the Display Properties dialog box and selecting the Adapter page, as shown in Figure 7.9. This page contains information about the adapter card and the currently installed device driver. You'll see information on the manufacturer, chip set, installed video memory, and other items.

Part
II

Ch
7

FIG. 7.9

The Adapter page includes information about your display adapter, as well as the Change button.

To change a video driver, click Change. The Update Device Driver Wizard starts, as shown in Figure 7.10. Work through this wizard as discussed in Chapter 5.

FIG. 7.10

The Update Device Driver Wizard walks you through updating your video driver.

If your monitor doesn't work right with the drivers included with Windows 98 or with supplied drivers from your manufacturer, you can use Windows 3.x driver. One problem with these drivers, however, is that they don't take advantage of the enhanced graphics support in Windows 98. Windows 3.x drivers do not support changing your monitor resolution on-the-fly, for example.

To install Windows 3.1 display drivers while running the Update Device Driver Wizard, specify the path to the disk or folder containing the Windows 3.1 drivers you want to use. You might need to copy these drivers from floppy disks or a previous Windows 3.1 directory.

N O T E Some Windows 3.1 drivers require the screen resolution to be specified in the
[boot.description] section of SYSTEM.INI, such as in the following example:

```
display.drv=GD5430 v1.22, 800x600x256 ▮
```

You also can set the refresh rate of your monitor. The settings in the Refresh Rate drop-down list depend on the monitor you use. Some monitors don't offer any settings that users can modify. Others offer settings such as 60Hz, 72Hz, and 75Hz. When you install Windows, the Adapter Default option is selected in order to support as many monitors as possible. Change the setting to one your monitor supports.

> **CAUTION**
>
> If you set a refresh rate to a setting not supported by your monitor, you can damage the monitor. Read your monitor's documentation for information on which refresh rates it supports.

Changing Monitor Types

You can set up Windows to recognize the type of monitor you use. In many cases, the monitor type is simply set up as Standard or Super VGA with 640×460, 800×600, 1024×768, or 1280×1024. These monitor types might work fine for you, but your specific monitor might have special features that work only when that particular monitor type is known by Windows.

To set your monitor type, display the Monitor page, as shown in Figure 7.11, by clicking Advanced on the Settings page of the Display Properties dialog box.

FIG. 7.11

The Monitor page lets you set the type of monitor you use, as well as other options for that monitor.

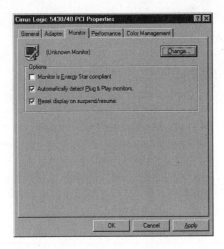

Next, follow these steps:

1. Click Change. The Select Device dialog box appears, as shown in Figure 7.12.
2. Specify the manufacturer and model. If your monitor comes with an installation disk, click Have Disk and specify the drive on which the installation disk resides. Click OK.
3. Click OK to install the monitor type.

Part

II

Ch

7

FIG. 7.12
Use the Select Device dialog box to specify the monitor manufacturer and model.

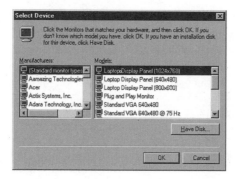

If you want to change monitor options, you can do so from the Monitor page. The following are options that appear on this page:

- *Monitor Is Energy Star Compliant.* Specifies that this monitor adheres to Energy Star standards and can reduce its power usage. Turn off this option if the information on the screen is garbled or irregular when the power-management screen appears.

- *Automatically Detect Plug & Play Monitors.* Instructs Windows to detect whether your monitor is plug and play–compatible.

- *Reset Display on Suspend/Resume.* Specifies that Windows should reset the display after you resume activity once the monitor has been in Suspend mode.

4. Click Apply to save your settings.

Changing Acceleration Setting

You can adjust the acceleration setting of your graphics card by selecting the Performance page of your display adapter's Properties dialog box, as shown in Figure 7.13. Move the Hardware Acceleration slider to the Full setting. If you have problems with the graphics display after setting this to the Full setting, move the setting to the left until the problem abates. You might need to experiment with this setting until you find the best setting for your graphics card.

Setting Default Color Profiles

In Windows 95, Microsoft introduced *Image Color Management* (ICM) technology. ICM attempts to get consistent colors across scanners, displays, and output methods (such as printers, film, and commercial printing presses). Each monitor, scanner, and output device uses different *illuminants* (lighting) and *colorants* (dyes or pigments) to produce colors for you to see. Also, each device uses a different gamut to get a range of colors. A monitor, for example, might have a larger range of colors (gamut) than a commercial printing press. To improve color consistency across all these devices, a color-management system is required.

Windows 98 includes the ICM 2.0 API to provide even greater color management than ICM 1.0. You easily can set up ICM profiles in Windows 98 so that all applications can use the same profile for each input, display, and output device. (Usually, each application must create its own profile for each device.)

FIG. 7.13

The Advanced Properties dialog box enables you to set how Windows 98 uses your graphics hardware.

To select profiles in Windows 98, do the following:

1. Select the Color Management page on your display adapter's Properties dialog box, as shown in Figure 7.14.

FIG. 7.14

You can select a default color profile for your system from the Color Management page.

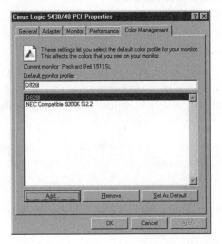

2. Select a profile from the list of profiles and click Set As Default. If a profile is not on this list, or you want to add a new one, click Add. The Add Profile Association dialog box appears, as shown in Figure 7.15.

3. Select a color profile and click Add.

4. From the list of profiles, select one and click Set As Default.

5. Click OK to save your setting.

Part

II

Ch

7

FIG. 7.15

The Add Profile Association dialog box includes ICC and ICM files for managing colors on your system.

 Color management is a complex issue, particularly if you create commercial-quality output on your PC. Visit the Image Color Management Web page at

`http://www.microsoft.com/windows/platform/icmwp.htm`

to read more about this topic. Also, visit the *International Color Consortium* (ICC) Web site at

`http://www.color.org`

Enabling Microsoft Magnifier

For many users who have difficulty seeing onscreen text and images, one welcome feature of Windows 98 is the Microsoft Magnifier. Magnifier displays a separate window that displays a magnified view of a portion of your screen.

To start Magnifier, choose Start, Programs, Accessories, Accessibility, Microsoft Magnifier. Magnifier starts with the top of the screen changed to show a magnified view of your screen, as shown in Figure 7.16. As you move the mouse pointer, the magnified view follows the mouse pointer to enable you to see your display easier.

By default, Magnifier is set up to magnify your view by two. You can change the magnification by modifying the Magnification Level field. Acceptable levels range from 1 to 9.

You also can specify the following options:

■ *Follow Mouse Cursor.* Shows a magnified view of your display by following the movement of your mouse pointer.

■ *Follow Keyboard Focus.* Shows a magnified view of your display by following keyboard movements, such as when you press the arrow keys and Tab.

■ *Follow Text Editing.* Shows a magnified view of your display by following the insertion point in a document.

■ *Invert Colors.* Inverts the color of the magnification area, which might make it easier for some users to track cursor or mouse movements.

■ *Use High Contrast Scheme.* Changes your display to high-contrast, such as shown in Figure 7.17. This setting affects the entire display, not just the magnification area.

FIG. 7.16
Magnifier shows a
magnified view of a
portion of your desktop.

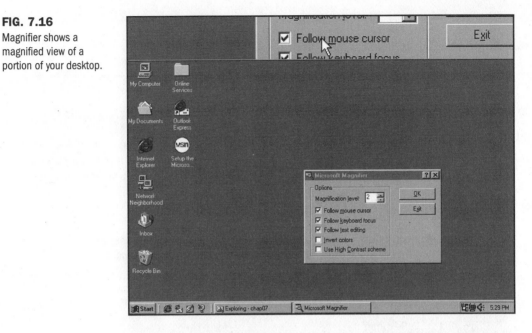

FIG. 7.17
You can set up
Microsoft Magnifier to
use a high-contrast
color scheme.

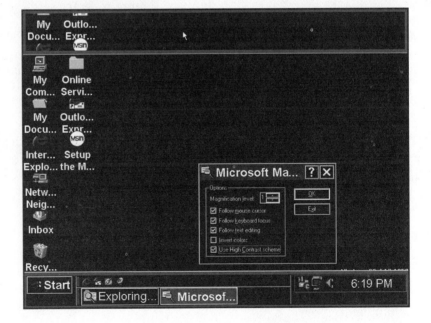

Click QK to save your settings, or click Exit to turn off Microsoft Magnifier.

TIP After you run Microsoft Magnifier with the Use High-Contrast Scheme option turned on and then exit Magnifier, you might need to readjust your taskbar so that the Quick Launch toolbar is inline with the rest of the taskbar.

Setting Up Multiple Monitors Under Windows 98

Windows 98 enables you to install and use up to nine monitors on the same PC. These monitors can run at different resolutions to help you get more virtual screen real estate, as well as to create livelier environments for games and online interactions. You can use multiple monitors to display desktop-publishing documents so that you can see multiple pages at the same time, for example.

NOTE Many applications are not yet designed to support multiple monitors. In the near future, you'll be able to find applications that take full advantage of this new feature. ▓

To set up multiple monitors under Windows 98, your monitors and computers must be *Peripheral Computer Interconnect* (PCI) or *Advanced Graphics Port* (AGP) compliant.

To install multiple monitors under Windows 98, perform these steps:

1. Shut down your computer and insert the second video adapter card into your PC.

2. Restart your PC. Upon startup, Windows should detect your second monitor. You might be prompted to insert the Windows installation disk.

3. During setup, you might be asked whether you want to restart Windows. Click No until you are prompted that you must restart Windows. Then, click Yes to restart.

Upon startup, the monitor that shows your desktop icons and items is your primary monitor. Also, you can tell which is your primary monitor by running a full-screen MS-DOS window. The window appears in the primary monitor. If you want to change which monitor is the primary one, shut down Windows and plug the monitor you want as the primary one into the primary adapter. Plug the other monitor into the secondary adapter card. Restart Windows. ●

CHAPTER 8

Configuring Your Desktop and Fonts

by Rob Tidrow

In this chapter

Creating Shortcuts

Windows 98 enables you to create shortcuts. A *shortcut* is a link to an object that enables you to access that object more quickly. Shortcuts are similar to program icons in Windows 3.x, but shortcuts differ in that you can create them for any object on your system, including programs, files, documents, networked objects, and even hardware devices. You might provide a shortcut to your spreadsheet application, such as Excel for Windows, that you can double-click to start the application, for example. You also might create a shortcut to a specific document, such as a Word 97 document (see Figure 8.1). If Word is not open when you double-click the document shortcut, the shortcut opens Word and loads your linked spreadsheet.

You can distinguish shortcuts from other items on the desktop, such as folders, by the small, arcing arrow on the icon. This denotes that the icon is linked to an object that you can start or open by double-clicking the icon.

FIG. 8.1

Shortcuts can be to folders, applications, devices (such as hard drives), files, or other objects.

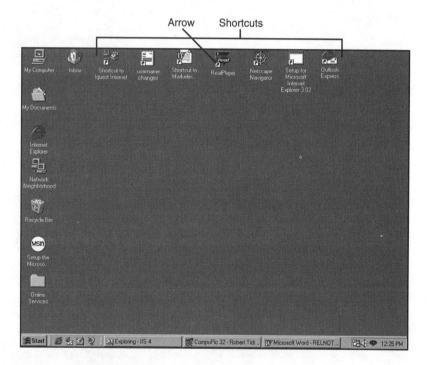

TIP

Another place where you can embed shortcuts is inside a document or email message. When the recipient opens the document or message, he or she can double-click the shortcut to open the associated object.

You can add shortcuts to your desktop, on the Quick Launch toolbar, or in a folder so that you can quickly access them as you work. The next two sections show you how to add and delete shortcuts to and from your desktop.

TROUBLESHOOTING

One of my shortcuts lost its link. How can I reestablish it? For the most part, Windows 98
automatically updates a shortcut when you move the object's file. If Windows cannot find the filename,
however, you can right-click the shortcut and choose Properties. Select the Shortcuts page on the
Shortcuts Properties dialog box. In the Target box, enter the full path of the filename to which the
shortcut is linked.

Adding Shortcuts to Your Desktop

Windows 98 provides a few ways to add shortcuts to your desktop. You can stay on the desktop
to create a shortcut, or you can use Explorer or My Computer to drag and drop objects to the
desktop.

To create a shortcut using the desktop context-sensitive menu, follow these steps:

1. Right-click anywhere on your desktop. The context-sensitive menu appears (see Figure
   8.2).

FIG. 8.2
Use the context-
sensitive menu on the
desktop to create a
shortcut.

2. Choose New, Shortcut. The Create Shortcut Wizard appears, as shown in Figure 8.3.

FIG. 8.3
The Create Shortcut
Wizard enables you to
add shortcuts to your
desktop.

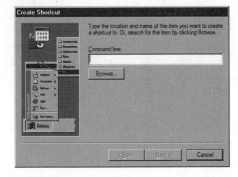

3. In the Command Line field, type the path and filename of the object for which you want
   to create a shortcut.

T I P   Click <u>B</u>rowse to navigate your system for a specific object name and location. By default, Windows 98 displays only programs. You can locate any file or object by selecting All Files from the <u>F</u>iles of Type drop-down listbox. Select the object you want, and click <u>O</u>pen.

4. Click Ne<u>x</u>t. The Select a Title for the Program dialog box appears.

5. In the <u>S</u>elect a Name for the Shortcut field, enter a name for the new shortcut. Windows 98 provides a default name that is the same as the filename of the object. You can use this name or type over it to create your own. Changing the shortcut name does not alter the original filename.

N O T E   When you create a shortcut name, you can use up to 256 characters. ■

6. Click Finish.

Windows places your new shortcut on the desktop. You can move the icon on the desktop, rename it, or delete it (see "Deleting Shortcuts," later in this chapter).

Another way to create a shortcut is to use Explorer or My Computer to drag objects onto the desktop. This is the quickest way to create several shortcuts at once. Use the following steps to create a shortcut using Explorer:

1. Open Explorer to the folder that contains the file or object you want to set up as a shortcut.

2. Right-click the item you want as a shortcut and drag the item to the desktop. Press Shift while clicking items to select multiple items; press Ctrl while clicking items to select multiple, noncontiguous items. Release the mouse button and choose Create <u>S</u>hortcut Here from the context-sensitive menu (see Figure 8.4).

Windows creates a shortcut to the object you selected.

CAUTION

If you drag an item from Explorer to the desktop using the left mouse button, Windows 98 automatically moves that item to the Desktop folder. This occurs for any object except applications. If you drag an application using the left mouse button, Windows 98 automatically creates a shortcut to that application without moving the application file.

N O T E   After you create a shortcut, you can quickly rename it by clicking the shortcut name and typing a new name. Press Enter. You also can right-click the shortcut and choose Rena<u>me</u> from the context-sensitive menu. Type the new name and press Enter. ■

As mentioned earlier, you can quickly create several shortcuts at once by dragging several objects from Explorer. To do this, press Ctrl while right-clicking objects in Explorer, and then release both Ctrl and the mouse button after you drop the objects on the desktop. You then can rename the shortcuts.

FIG. 8.4
Right-click an object
and drag it to the
desktop so that you
can create a shortcut
for the object.

Dragging a shortcut from
Windows Explorer

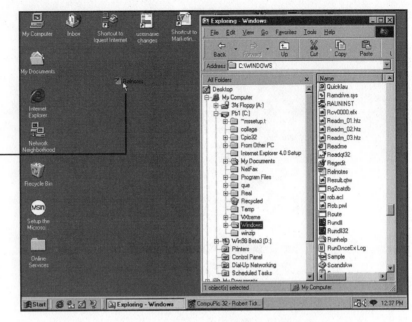

N O T E To create a shortcut to a printer, choose Start, Settings, Printers. In the Printers folder, right-
click the printer to which you want to create a shortcut and drag the printer icon onto the
desktop. Then choose Create Shortcut(s) Here. Now you can drag files from Explorer or the desktop on
top of the printer shortcut to print your documents. ■

Changing Shortcut Properties

You can view or change the properties of a shortcut by right-clicking the shortcut and choosing Properties. In the Shortcut Properties dialog box that appears, select the Shortcut page
(see Figure 8.5). Here, you can change the icon, what kind of window it appears in, or the key
combinations used to start it.

The icon that appears when you create a shortcut might not suit your needs. Or you might
have a difficult time seeing it against the desktop wallpaper. You can change the icon by clicking Change Icon in the Shortcut Properties dialog box and scrolling through the Current Icon
list in the Change Icon dialog box until you find an icon you like (see Figure 8.6). Click the icon
and click OK. In the Shortcut Properties dialog box, click Apply. The shortcut's icon changes
to the one you selected.

TIP Click the Browse button to find other icons on your computer. One file that contains additional icons is
the MORICONS.DLL file in the \Windows folder.

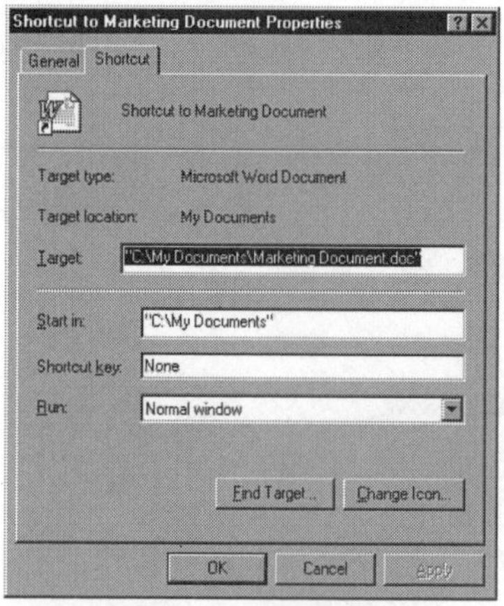

FIG. 8.5

The Shortcut Properties dialog box enables you to customize your shortcut.

FIG. 8.6

Tired of that drabby icon for your shortcut? Change it by modifying the shortcut's properties.

Another setting you can change for your shortcuts is the keyboard combination that activates or switches to the shortcut. In the Shortcut Key box in the Shortcut Properties dialog box, enter the keyboard shortcut you want to use. You can use this key combination in any Windows application to start or switch to the shortcut's application. You might want to assign Ctrl+Shift+W to start Word for Windows, for example.

CAUTION

You cannot use the key combination you set up with the preceding instructions in any other application or feature in Windows 98. The Windows 98 shortcut key combination overrules all other settings you already have set.

N O T E The Shortcut Properties settings also include an option to set the way in which the shortcut item opens. In the Run drop-down listbox, you can select Normal, Minimized, or Maximized. Normal displays the window sized as you last used it, Minimized opens the object and places it on the taskbar in a minimized state, and Maximized displays the object in a maximized window. ∎

Deleting Shortcuts

Shortcuts placed on the desktop are a handy way to start items you use frequently. Through the course of a week, if you add a shortcut for each file, application, or device you use, your desktop might start getting cluttered. Even though the resource requirements of shortcuts are minimal, they can add up after a while. If you find yourself being hampered by the number of shortcuts you have set up, delete a few.

You can delete shortcuts in several ways. The quickest way is to click the shortcut and press Delete. Answer Yes to the confirmation box that appears. Another way to delete a shortcut is to right-click a shortcut and choose Delete. Again, answer Yes to confirm the operation.

TROUBLESHOOTING

How do I remove the Network Neighborhood icon from my desktop? The Network Neighborhood icon appears on your desktop automatically when you install network resources (including an Internet connection) under Windows 98. You cannot drag the Network Neighborhood icon to the Recycle Bin or right-click it and choose Delete to remove it. You must use the System Policy Editor to delete it. The System Policy Editor should be used only by advanced users who feel comfortable making system changes to their computers. Also, before you start the System Policy Editor, be sure that your system is backed up in case you encounter problems and lose data. The System Policy Editor is available on the Windows 98 installation CD-ROM in the \ADMIN\APPTOOLS\POLEDIT\ folder. Double-click the Poledit application to start the System Policy Editor. Choose File, Open Registry. Then, open Local User (or your user ID), switch to \User\Shell\Restrictions, and enable the Hide Network Neighborhood check box. Click OK, close the System Policy Editor, and restart Windows 98.

Adding Folders to Your Desktop

Although you can add a shortcut to a folder on the desktop, you also can create a folder that exists on the desktop. You might want to place a folder on the desktop that contains all your business-related documents—memos, faxes, spreadsheets, and databases—so that you can open one folder to access all of them (see Figure 8.7).

FIG. 8.7
Create folders on your desktop to hold all your important—or not so important—files and documents.

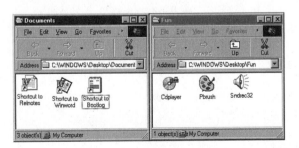

In fact, when you install Windows 98, a few common folders are placed on your desktop automatically, including the following:

- My Computer
- Network Neighborhood (if a network or Internet connection is installed)
- Recycle Bin
- My Briefcase (if installed)
- Inbox (if installed)
- My Documents
- Online Services

N O T E Windows 98 places a shortcut to the My Documents folder on your desktop. The My Documents folder, which was introduced in Microsoft Office 95 and other Windows 95 applications, provides a common data-storage area for your files, documents, and other key objects. Applications that are configured to save documents and files in the My Documents folder will place them into this new My Documents folder. You can delete the My Documents shortcut, move it to another folder (such as onto the Start menu), or leave it on the desktop. ■

To add a folder to the desktop, follow these steps:

1. Right-click anywhere on the desktop.
2. From the context-sensitive menu, choose New, Folder. A new folder appears on the desktop.
3. Name the folder and double-click it to add items to it.
4. In the new folder, choose File, New, Shortcut to add shortcuts to the folder. Or, choose File, New, Folder to add a folder within the folder.

 You also can drag files, folders, and other objects from Explorer or My Computer into your new folders to store them. For added convenience, the folder does not have to be open for you to drag an object to it. Just drag and drop the object over the closed folder.

Setting Background and Wallpaper Properties

On your wall or desk in your office, you probably have family pictures, awards, Post-it notes, photographs of the ocean, and other items that help you escape the pressures of the day. Not to be outdone, Windows 98 enables you to jazz up your desktop by adding color to it. You can change the background patterns and wallpaper and even create your own wallpaper. The following sections show you how.

Changing Patterns and Wallpaper

When Windows 98 installs, it loads a standard Windows desktop theme and wallpaper. You can experiment with the background patterns and wallpaper to suit your tastes. To change the desktop settings, you modify the desktop properties, which you can access by right-clicking anywhere on the desktop and choosing P<u>r</u>operties from the context-sensitive menu. The Display Properties dialog box appears (see Figure 8.8).

FIG. 8.8
You change the way your desktop looks by using the Display Properties dialog box.

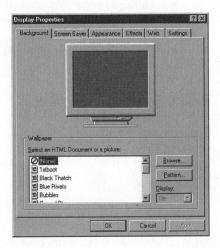

 TIP You also can open the Display Properties dialog box by double-clicking the Display icon in the Control Panel. Or you can choose Start, <u>S</u>ettings, A<u>c</u>tive Desktop, <u>C</u>ustomize My Desktop, Background.

To change the wallpaper, scroll down the Wallpaper listbox. The names of wallpaper from which you can choose include Black Thatch, Blue Rivets, Circles, Houndstooth, Setup, and more.

N O T E By default, only a few wallpaper files are installed during Windows Setup. To add wallpaper files, double-click the Add/Remove Programs icon in the Control Panel. Then select the Windows Setup page and select the Accessories item in the <u>C</u>omponents list. Click <u>D</u>etails, select Desktop Wallpaper, and click OK twice. Make sure that you have your Windows 98 installation disks or CD-ROM handy when you do this. ▄

After you select the wallpaper, you can preview it in the preview monitor in the Display Properties dialog box. Click <u>A</u>pply to place the wallpaper on your desktop.

You can set the way wallpaper displays on the desktop by selecting one of these options in the <u>D</u>isplay drop-down listbox:

- ▄ *Center.* Displays the wallpaper in the center of your screen.
- ▄ *Tile.* Displays the wallpaper over the entire screen, repeating the wallpaper image as necessary to fill the desktop.
- ▄ *Stretch.* Stretches the wallpaper to fill the entire desktop.

To change the desktop pattern, click Pattern to display the Pattern dialog box (see Figure 8.9). You must have the (None) choice in the Wallpaper list selected for the Pattern button to be active. You can choose from a number of patterns to display on your desktop. These range from Bricks and Buttons to Triangles and Waffle's Revenge. You also can choose (None), which places no pattern on the desktop. Scroll through the list of patterns and click one to view an example of how it looks in the Preview area on the Pattern dialog box. Click OK to place the pattern on your desktop and to return to the Background page of the Display Properties dialog box.

FIG. 8.9

Use the Pattern dialog box to select a desktop pattern.

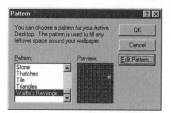

You can change the way the pattern looks or create your own pattern by choosing a pattern in the Pattern dialog box and clicking Edit Pattern. In the Pattern Editor dialog box, click the pattern box to edit or create a new pattern (see Figure 8.10). If it is a new pattern, type a new name in the Name drop-down listbox. Click Done when you finish, and then click OK.

FIG. 8.10

Use the Pattern Editor to modify the way your desktop pattern looks.

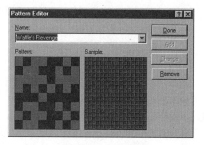

You can remove a pattern when you are in the Pattern Editor by selecting its name from the Name drop-down listbox and clicking Remove.

After you select a pattern, it fills the entire background. The color of the pattern is determined by the color you have set up for your background, which is set on the Appearance tab of the Display Properties dialog box and is discussed later in this chapter in "Specifying Desktop Colors."

Choose OK when you have the pattern or wallpaper you like. Your desktop displays your selections, as shown in the example in Figure 8.11.

FIG. 8.11

The Pinstripe wallpaper is added to the Windows 98 desktop.

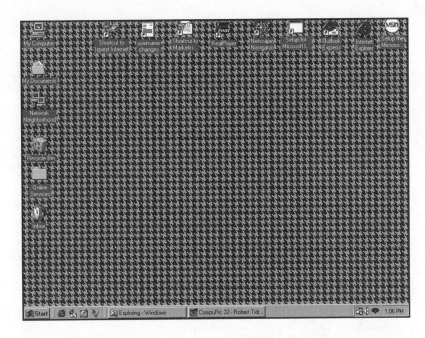

 TIP Another way to change the wallpaper on your desktop is to use an image you are viewing in Internet Explorer as your wallpaper. To do this, display a Web page in Internet Explorer that contains an image. Next, right-click the image and choose Set As Wallpaper. (If the image is hyperlinked, be sure to right-click the image and not left-click it. Otherwise, you jump to the resource linked to the image.) The image you selected as your desktop wallpaper is displayed with the name of Internet Explorer Wallpaper.

Creating Your Own Wallpaper

If you don't like the ready-made images Windows gives you for wallpaper, you can do one of three things. First, you can elect not to have wallpaper. Second, you can purchase wallpaper files or download them from the Internet (they're just BMP picture files).

Third, you can create your own wallpaper image. To do this, all you need is a bitmap image saved as a BMP file. If you have a graphic that you've saved on your computer, such as from the World Wide Web or a CD-ROM loaded with pretty pictures, you can convert it to BMP format using graphics converters. If the file is already in BMP format, you don't need to worry about converting it.

N O T E An excellent graphics utility that enables you to convert graphics formats is Paint Shop Pro, a shareware utility from Jasc Software, Inc. You can find it on the Web at

`http://www.jasc.com`

Paint Shop Pro reads several file formats, including PCX, JPG, TIF, and GIF, and enables you to convert files to BMP. ▨

Place the BMP file in any folder on your system and then open the Display Properties dialog box. On the Background page, click Browse and locate the file on your system. Click OK after you select the file, and then click OK again to place your custom-made wallpaper on the desktop. Again, you can tile, stretch, or center the image to your liking.

Setting Up Screen Savers

Another way to set up the way your desktop behaves is to use a screen saver that starts when your computer is inactive for a specified time. When you set up a screen saver, you need to specify the screen-saver name, the time to wait for it to start, and whether it will be password protected. The following sections discuss these items.

Choosing a New Screen Saver

To choose a screen saver, right-click the desktop and choose Properties from the context-sensitive menu. In the Display Properties dialog box, select the Screen Saver page (see Figure 8.12). A list of installed screen savers appears in the Screen Saver drop-down listbox. Select a screen saver from this list and look at a preview of it in the preview monitor on the Screen Saver page. Click Apply when you locate the screen saver of your choice.

FIG. 8.12
Select a screen saver from the Screen Saver tab in the Display Properties dialog box.

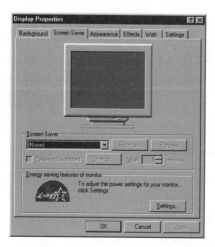

TIP Click Preview to get a full-screen view of a screen saver. Move the mouse to stop the preview.

Part
II

Ch

8

You can configure the behavior of the screen saver by clicking Settings. This displays a property sheet or dialog box for the screen saver, in which you can adjust specific settings for each screen saver.

Not all screen savers have the same dialog box settings. The 3D Flower Box screen saver, for example, has options that enable you to set your screen saver's color, spin, shape, complexity, and size. On the other hand, the 3D Text screen saver includes options for displaying custom text, the time, what the surface texture of the text looks like, and the size.

After you configure the screen saver's settings, click OK and click Apply in the Display Properties dialog box. On the Screen Saver tab, you can adjust the time for the screen saver to wait before it starts. Set this time in the Wait box. You can select between 1 and 99 minutes. After your display is inactive for the selected number of minutes, the screen saver starts.

Setting Screen-Saver Passwords

You can use your screen saver to ward off sinister snoopers who want to use your computer when you are away from your desk. To do this, set a password that users must type to stop the screen saver. The following steps show you how to set up a password:

1. On the Screen Saver page in the Display Properties dialog box, enable the Password Protected check box.
2. Click Change to set the password. The Change Password dialog box appears.
3. Type a password in the New Password box. Retype the password in the Confirm New Password box.
4. Click OK to set the password.

To disable the password, disable the Password Protected check box on the Screen Saver tab.

 TIP Remember your password. If you forget your password, you can restart your computer and boot Windows 98. Before your screen saver starts, go in and disable the password option for that screen saver or click Change and create a new password.

Specifying Desktop Colors

Earlier in this chapter, you saw how to change the background and wallpaper on your computer. You also can select the colors of your desktop, including the colors of the menu bars, dialog boxes, and other elements. Windows 98 provides more than two dozen predefined color schemes that you can choose from, or you can create your own scheme. Another way is to use a predefined scheme and then modify it to suit your tastes.

Using Predefined Color Schemes

In the Display Properties dialog box, select the Appearance page to access the different color schemes available to you (see Figure 8.13). In the Scheme drop-down listbox, select from the various choices, including Eggplant, Pumpkin, Brick, Rose, and others.

FIG. 8.13
Color schemes are a
nice way to add some
color to your life.

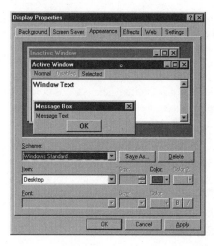

The best way to decide whether you like a scheme is to click it and look at it in the preview window. Some color schemes have interesting names (such as Rainy Day and Marine), but their schemes are somewhat hard on the eyes. Pick the one that's best for you and your display.

After you select a scheme, click OK to change your display to the selected scheme.

Customizing Color Schemes

If you get tired of looking at the built-in schemes Windows 98 provides, create your own. To do this, return to the Appearance page in the Display Properties dialog box. In the Item drop-down listbox, click the name of an item you want to change, such as Active Title Bar. Depending on the item you choose, you can modify the color, font size, font characteristic (bold or italic), and font.

The following list describes the options you can modify:

- *Size.* Sets the size of the selected item. This may be the size of the window and its borders, for example.
- *Color.* Selects the color of the item.
- *Font.* Sets the font of the item. You can choose from all the fonts you currently have installed on your system.
- *Size.* Sets the font size for the selected item.
- *Color.* Sets the color of the font for the selected item.
- *Bold, Italic.* Displays the selected item's text in bold or italic.

After you create a new color scheme, you can save it and name it. Click the Save As button and type a name in the Save This Color Scheme As dialog box. Click OK. To delete a color scheme, select it in the Scheme drop-down listbox and click Delete.

Adding Fonts to Your System

Windows 98 includes an enhanced way to manage and view fonts on your system. The Windows 98 Fonts folder stores all the fonts on your system. When you open the Fonts folder, a window similar to the one shown in Figure 8.14 appears. You can view a sample of the way a font looks by double-clicking one of the font icons. This displays a window that contains sample text of the font and includes details of other font properties, including the font name, file size, version number, and manufacturer of the font.

FIG. 8.14
You use the Fonts folder to store and manage all the fonts on your system.

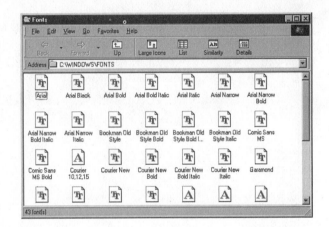

To access the Fonts folder, choose Start, Settings, Control Panel. Double-click the Fonts folder in the Control Panel. You also can access this folder by navigating to the \Fonts folder in your Windows 98 folder, such as \Windows\Fonts. After the folder appears, you can view, delete, print, and install fonts.

You can display a toolbar on the Fonts folder by choosing View, Toolbar. A submenu appears, from which you can select the following Toolbar options:

- *Standard Buttons.* Displays the standard toolbar buttons, including Back, Forward, Up, Large Icons, List, Similarity, and Details.
- *Address Bar.* Displays the Folder and URL Address toolbar.
- *Links.* Displays Web links from the Internet Explorer Links toolbar. See Chapter 20, "Configuring Microsoft Internet Explorer 4.0," for more information on the Links toolbar.
- *Text Labels.* Displays the name of the toolbar button below each button icon.

On the toolbar, you can reconfigure the way the fonts appear in the Fonts folder by clicking the different toolbar buttons. The following list describes how the Fonts folder appears after you select these buttons:

- *Large icons.* Displays icons of each font. Each icon includes the font name and type of font, such as TrueType (TT) and screen and printer fonts (A).

■ *List.* Displays a list of the icons on your system, with small icons representing the type of font installed.

■ *Similarity.* Sorts each font to show fonts according to their similarity with one another (see Figure 8.15). You can select a font from the List Fonts By Similarity To drop-down listbox, and Windows sorts the fonts by similarity to the chosen font. You might want to know how similar other fonts are to the Times New Roman family of fonts, for example.

■ *Details.* Displays all the details of the font file, including the font name, filename, file size, and last modification date.

FIG. 8.15
You can find fonts that are similar to each other by clicking the Similarity button on the toolbar.

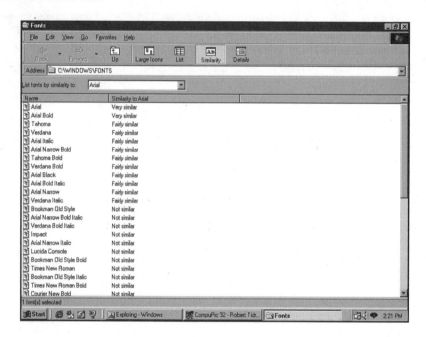

 Use the Details view to get the filename of a font you want to copy or delete from your system.

Installing New Fonts

Simply copying a font file to the \Windows\Fonts folder does not install the font for use with your Windows applications. You must install the font by choosing File, Install New Font in the Fonts folder. When you install a new font, Windows 98 places a setting in the Windows Registry to make it available for your applications.

To install a new font, follow these steps:

1. Choose File, Install New Font from the Fonts folder to display the Add Fonts dialog box (see Figure 8.16).

FIG. 8.16
Use the Add Fonts
dialog box to install
new fonts on your
system.

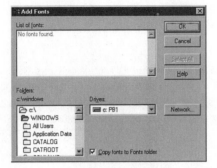

2. Select the font name(s) in the List of Fonts box.

 TIP To select more than one font name in the List of Fonts box, press Shift as you select contiguous fonts, or press Ctrl as you select noncontiguous fonts. To select all the listed fonts, click Select All in the Add Fonts dialog box.

3. If the font is in another folder, locate the folder in which the font is stored in the Folders listbox. You also can change the drive by clicking the Drives drop-down listbox and selecting the appropriate drive.

4. Enable the Copy Fonts to Fonts Folder check box to instruct Windows to copy the selected font(s) to your \Windows\Fonts folder. This places a copy of the font file in the Fonts folder on your system, effectively duplicating the font file on your system. If you leave this check box clear, the font files remain in the original source location, but the Windows 98 Registry includes references to these locations. This still enables you to use those fonts in your applications, even when they are not in your \Windows\Fonts folder.

 TIP When you operate in a network environment, you might want to leave your font files on the network server to conserve space on your local machine. You can install fonts from the network by clicking Network in the Add Fonts dialog box and locating the font file names on your server. Make sure that the Copy Fonts to Fonts Folder check box is not checked.

5. Choose OK to finish the installation steps and to install the fonts on your system.

Removing Fonts

You can remove a font from your system by opening the Fonts folder in the Control Panel and then clicking the font(s) you want to delete. Next, press Delete or choose File, Delete. Then click Yes when Windows asks whether you are sure you want to delete these fonts. This deletes the font file and places the font file in the Recycle Bin.

 TIP Windows 3.x had a problem of using up a lot of memory when you installed numerous fonts on your system. Windows 98 does not have this same problem, even though you might want to reduce the number of font files on your system if you need to clean up some disk space.

TROUBLESHOOTING

How do I view only TrueType fonts in my applications? If you use only TrueType fonts in your applications, such as Word 97, you can instruct Windows 98 to display only TrueType fonts when you are working. In the Fonts folder, choose View, Folders Options and select the TrueType page. Enable the Show Only TrueType Fonts in the Programs on My Computer check box. Click OK.

Configuring the Taskbar and Start Button

by Rob Tidrow

In this chapter

Setting Taskbar Options

The taskbar was one of the most fundamental changes to Windows 95 (see Figure 9.1). The taskbar sits at the bottom of the screen (by default, but you can move it to other screen positions) and enables you to switch between open applications, displays the time, and provides access to other items. The taskbar is intended to make 95 percent of what you want to do in Windows 98 easy to accomplish. In Windows 98, the taskbar is still relatively the same as it was in Windows 95, but it does include a few new features.

FIG. 9.1

The taskbar is a simple yet powerful tool.

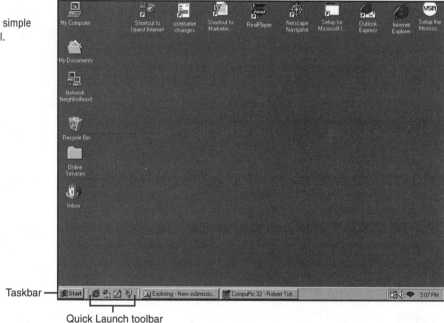

Taskbar

Quick Launch toolbar

The taskbar includes a few items of interest—namely, the Start button, toolbars, and task buttons. The Start button is discussed in detail in "Setting Start Button Options," later in this chapter. *Toolbars*, which are new to Windows 98, sit on the taskbar and give you quick access to folders, Internet URLs, and other tasks. *Task buttons* represent all the open applications you are using in Windows 98 (see Figure 9.2). Task buttons appear on the taskbar even when an application is not minimized, giving you a quick way to switch between tasks.

Items that appear on the far right side of the taskbar are in the *tray area*. In this area, you can find the clock and the applications running in the background, such as the Task Scheduler, modems, printers, and volume controls. You can quickly modify the configurations of these items by right-clicking their icons. Next, choose an item from the context-sensitive menu, such as Adjust Audio Properties to set the properties associated with your sound card (see Figure 9.3). This brings up the Properties dialog box of that device.

FIG. 9.2

Task buttons, such as the Exploring, CompuPic 32, and Microsoft Word buttons, make it easy to switch between open applications.

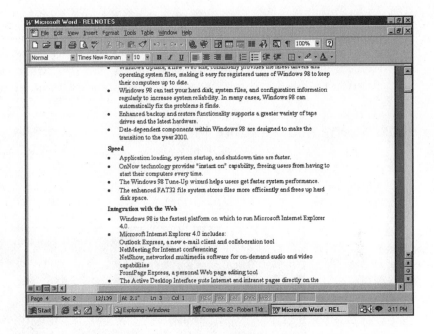

T I P Move the mouse pointer over the clock to see the day and the date.

FIG. 9.3

Use the taskbar to access properties of the devices running in the background, such as your sound card.

Some of the ways to customize the taskbar follow:

- Reposition and resize the taskbar.
- Specify the way the taskbar will be displayed.
- Show the clock.
- Add or remove toolbars.

These items are discussed in the following sections.

TROUBLESHOOTING

I changed the time in Windows 98, but my system clock displays a different time. Can you help?
On some systems, you must start your system startup utility during the boot process to change the

system time and date on your computer. To do this, refer to the manual that came with your computer to see how you can start the system utility. On some computers, you can press Ctrl+Alt+Esc or a function key assigned to the utility. After you are in the system settings screen, use the navigational commands, such as the arrow keys and Page Up and Page Down, to navigate the screen and make changes to the system time and date. The way you make changes depends on your system.

Repositioning and Resizing the Taskbar

If you don't like the taskbar at the bottom of your screen, grab it with your mouse pointer and drag it to another location on your desktop. Don't try to put the taskbar in the middle of the screen; it only sits on the edges of the desktop—on the left, right, top, or bottom. Figures 9.4 and 9.5 show how the taskbar looks on the top and right sides of the desktop.

FIG. 9.4

Having the taskbar at the top of the screen is not a bad option.

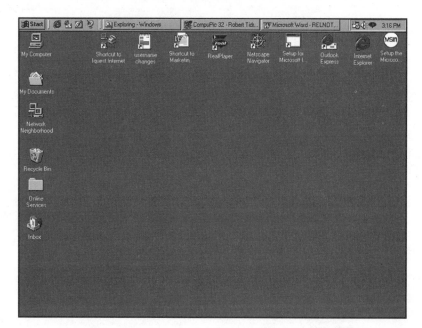

CAUTION

Depending on the width of the taskbar, you might see only the application icon and its first two letters when you move the taskbar to the side of your desktop. This can make it difficult to recognize your open applications.

To see the full description of a button, place the mouse pointer over the button. A ToolTip appears with the name of the button.

FIG. 9.5
But having the taskbar on the side requires you to get familiar with your application icons to understand which application is which, because you can't see the words describing each icon.

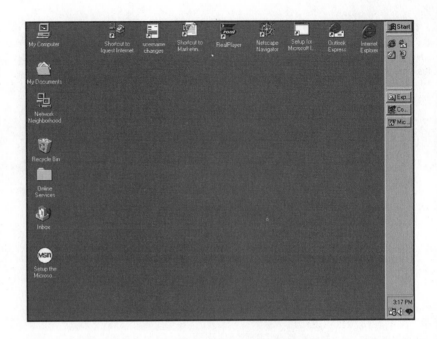

Another way to customize your taskbar is to resize it. Move your mouse pointer over the exposed edge of the taskbar—the side that is closest to the desktop, such as the top edge if the taskbar is at the bottom of the screen. After the mouse pointer changes to a double-sided arrow, press and hold your left mouse button and drag the taskbar to the size you want. Figure 9.6 shows a taskbar diagnosed with elephantiasis!

 You can resize the taskbar to at least half the size of your desktop by dragging it with your mouse.

Setting Display Options

By default, the taskbar always appears. Even when you maximize an application, the taskbar still is visible at the bottom of the screen. Microsoft refers to this state as being *always on top*, and this is probably the most efficient way to use the taskbar. When the taskbar is on top, you can quickly see which other applications are open, the time of day, and the status of your printer or modem; and, you can readily access any of these items.

You can make the taskbar disappear when you are not using it. To do so, you need to set the Auto Hide feature, as shown in the following steps:

1. Right-click any exposed part of the taskbar.

CAUTION
Don't right-click a task button, or you will display a context-sensitive menu for that button.

FIG. 9.6

Do you get frustrated when you can't find the taskbar? Just make it a little bigger.

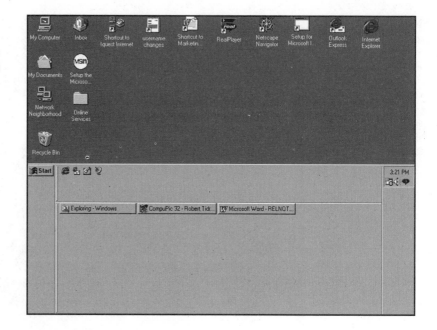

2. Choose Properties to display the Taskbar Properties dialog box (see Figure 9.7).

FIG. 9.7

You can choose how the taskbar behaves by changing its properties.

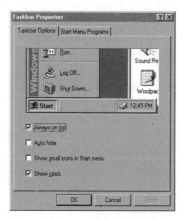

3. On the Taskbar Options page, enable the Auto Hide check box, and (as an option) disable the Always on Top check box.

4. Click OK.

Now when you move the mouse pointer off the taskbar, the taskbar disappears by "sliding" off the edge of the screen. To make it reappear, move the mouse down to the bottom of the screen (or wherever you have the taskbar). The taskbar automatically "slides" back into view, unless you have an application covering that part of the screen. If you disabled the Always on Top check box in step 3, the taskbar does not appear on top of the open application. You must move or resize the application's window to see the taskbar. Use this option when your real estate is limited and you want to use the entire screen for your applications. Otherwise, leave the default as is.

N O T E Generally, if you run in 800×600 or higher resolution, and you use the taskbar or Start button a great deal, you should have no problem keeping the taskbar visible at all times. ■

Setting Clock Options

You can change the time the clock displays by double-clicking the clock on the taskbar. This displays the Date/Time Properties dialog box (see Figure 9.8).

FIG. 9.8
Set the time, date, and time zone by double-clicking the clock on the taskbar.

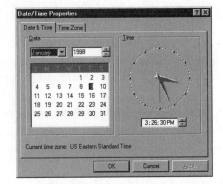

On the Date & Time page, you can adjust the following properties:

■ *Date*. Use the drop-down listbox to select the month, and set the year in the option box next to it. On the calendar, click the correct day of the month. The highlighted day is the current day.

■ *Time*. Set the time you want Windows to display in the Time option box. The large analog clock displays the time. Note that this box does not reset your system clock. You must do this by using the system utilities that come with your computer.

On the Time Zone page, you can specify the time zone in which you live or work. Use the drop-down listbox to choose the time zone. If you live in an area with Daylight Savings Time, click the option at the bottom of the screen to have Windows automatically update your clock during these time changes. Click OK after you configure these options.

If you don't want the clock to show at all, follow these steps:

1. Right-click any exposed part of the taskbar.

2. Choose Properties to display the Taskbar Properties dialog box.

3. Disable the Show Clock check box and click OK.

Adding and Removing Toolbars

With Windows 98, you can add or remove toolbars from the taskbar. These toolbars provide quick ways to launch applications, open folders, show desktop items, and access an Internet or Web resource. When you first install Windows 98, the Quick Launch toolbar is displayed by default. The Quick Launch toolbar includes the following four buttons:

- *Launch Internet Explorer Browser.* Launches Internet Explorer 4.0.

- *Launch Outlook Express.* Launches Outlook Express.

- *Show Desktop.* Minimizes all windows so that you can see the Windows 98 desktop. Click Show Desktop again to return the windows to their previous states.

- *View Channels.* Launches Internet Explorer 4.0 and views Web channels. See Chapters 20, "Configuring Microsoft Internet Explorer 4.0," and 8, "Configuring Your Desktop and Fonts," for more information on viewing channels.

To turn on or off taskbar toolbars, follow these steps:

1. Right-click on the taskbar.

2. Choose Toolbars from the context menu and select the toolbar name from the pop-up menu. A check mark appears next to the toolbars that currently appear onscreen. You can choose from the following toolbars:

- *Address.* Provides an address location for entering URLs to locate resources on the Internet, Web, or intranet.

- *Links.* Places task buttons for the link buttons set up on your Links toolbar in Internet Explorer 4.0.

- *Desktop.* Places task buttons for all the items on your desktop.

- *Quick Launch.* Places the Quick Launch toolbar on the taskbar.

- *New Toolbar.* Enables you to create your own custom toolbar.

Figure 9.9 shows an exaggerated view of all the toolbars displayed on the taskbar. Although this is probably not the way you will display your toolbars, you can get an idea of how they look on the taskbar.

To remove a toolbar from the taskbar, repeat the preceding steps and click the toolbar you want to remove to hide it.

To create your own toolbar, use the following steps:

1. Right-click the taskbar and choose Toolbars, New Toolbar. The New Toolbar dialog box appears (see Figure 9.10).

2. Select the folder that contains the items you want to display on the toolbar. The name of the folder becomes the toolbar name. Also, all items within the folder you select are displayed on the toolbar. You might want to remove items from the folder (using Explorer or My Computer) that you don't want to display on the toolbar. It's a good idea to keep the toolbar items to a minimum, such as three to five items.

FIG. 9.9
Windows 98's taskbar toolbars make it easy to access folders, Internet resources, and desktop items.

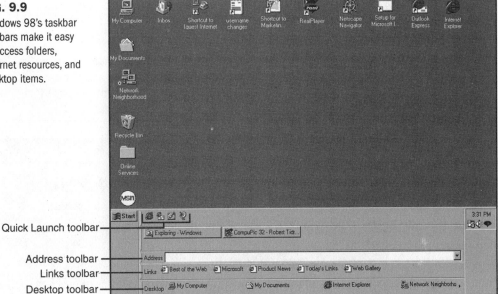

Quick Launch toolbar

Address toolbar
Links toolbar
Desktop toolbar

Part
II

Ch
9

FIG. 9.10
The New Toolbar dialog box enables you to create your own toolbar.

 TIP To quickly add items to a toolbar, drag the items onto the toolbar. Shortcuts will be created for these items. Also, if you add a shortcut to a Web address on a custom toolbar instead of a folder, an image of the Web page appears. Finally, the Address toolbar can be incredibly useful. You can type Internet addresses to launch Internet Explorer, but you can also type a path to open a folder, document, or application, such as C:/My Documents.

If you want to include an Internet address (URL) as a toolbar item, enter the complete URL in the field at the top of the New Toolbar dialog box. Then you can click that URL on the toolbar to access the associated Internet resource.

3. Click OK.

You can delete a custom toolbar by turning it off. You cannot turn off a custom toolbar and turn it back on, though, as you can the built-in toolbars. When you turn off the custom toolbar, you delete it and must re-create it to display it again.

Also, you can resize toolbars by pressing the left mouse button while grabbing the vertical line on the left side of the toolbar. When you do this, a double-sided resizing arrow appears. Slide the toolbar to the new size you want and release the mouse button. Notice in Figure 9.11 how the Quick Launch toolbar has been enlarged compared to the one in Figure 9.10.

FIG. 9.11
You can resize taskbar toolbars.

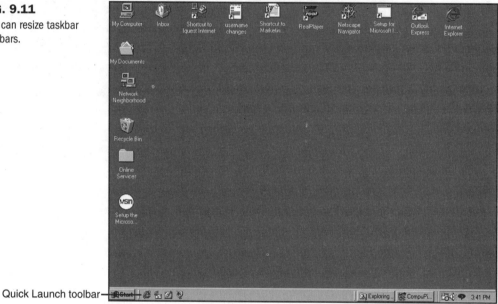

Quick Launch toolbar

Each toolbar has a context menu you can access by right-clicking the toolbar (see Figure 9.12).

FIG. 9.12
You can configure a toolbar by right-clicking it and choosing commands from its context menu.

The context menu contains the following menu choices:

■ *View.* Displays the toolbar icons in a large or small size.

- *Show Text.* Turns on or off the name of the toolbar button. By default, the name is turned off, but you can see a ToolTip of the name by placing the mouse pointer over the toolbar button.

- *Refresh.* Updates the toolbar with any changes made to the folder that contains the toolbar items.

- *Show Title.* Turns on or off the name of the toolbar. By default, the name is turned off.

- *Toolbars.* Displays a list of the toolbars.

- *Properties.* Displays the Taskbar Properties dialog box.

- *Close.* Turns off the toolbar.

Setting Start Button Options

By default, the Start button resides on the far left of the taskbar. The Start button's purpose is to give you a leg up on getting your work done. After you click the Start button, a menu pops up that contains several items (see Figure 9.13). You can use the Start button to launch programs, start Help, shut down Windows 98, and find files. You also can access the Control Panel to configure many of your system settings and devices.

FIG. 9.13
The Start button's menu gives you access to all your files, applications, and settings.

TIP You can quickly display the Start button on the taskbar by pressing Alt+S or by pressing the Windows key found on some newer keyboards.

Windows 98 gives you several Start button options to customize according to your tastes. You can set up the Start button menu with the programs or files you use most often to give you one-button access to them. You might use WinCIM to dial into the CompuServe Information Service, for example. Place WinCIM on the Start button to quickly start it each time you want to dial CompuServe.

N O T E Windows 98 places items in the Programs folder in alphanumeric order. If you want to
change the order of an item on the Programs folder, you can change the name of that item
so that it appears in the order you want. Or you can rename the item and include a numerical value in
front of the name. If you want an item named Zipper to come first in the folder, for example, rename
the item 1. Zipper.

Another way to take advantage of the Start button menu is to add documents or specific files
that you use all the time. This may be a daily spreadsheet you fill out or a document template in
Word for Windows.

By default, the Start menu shows large icons and a Windows 98 logo. You can reduce the size
of the menu by using the Show Small Icons option on the Taskbar tab, as shown in the following steps:

1. Right-click any exposed part of the taskbar.

2. Choose Properties to display the Taskbar Properties dialog box. Make sure that the
   Taskbar Options tab is selected.

3. Select the Show Small Icons in Start Menu option and click OK. Figure 9.14 shows the
   reduced Start menu.

FIG. 9.14
You can configure the
Start menu to use small
icons to reduce the
amount of space the
menu uses.

Adding and Removing Start Menu Items

The Start menu contains programs that are placed there during the Windows 98 installation. If
you install Windows 98 over your existing Windows 3.x or Windows 95 setup, Windows 98
automatically places all your installed applications on the Start menu. As you use Windows 98
and install new applications, you can add these programs to the Programs folder on the Start
menu, much like you can add program groups to Program Manager in Windows 3.x.

If you upgrade your system from Windows 3.x to Windows 98, Windows 98 automatically converts your old program groups to folders. You can locate these programs by choosing Start,
Programs and looking at the folders that appear.

Another way to see the contents of the Programs folder is to view it in Windows Explorer. You
can view the Programs folder by opening the folder in which Windows 98 is stored and then
choosing Start, Programs. You then can view items, delete items, and drag and drop other
items to the Programs folder.

TIP You can use Windows 3.x's version of Program Manager from within Windows 98 if you installed Windows 98 to its own directory (for dual booting). Launch the PROGMAN.EXE file from the Windows 3.x directory to start Program Manager. The only difference you might notice is that the groups are not arranged in the same fashion on the desktop as they were when running under your previous Windows 3.x configuration.

You can add items to the Start menu by following these steps:

1. Right-click any exposed part of the taskbar.
2. Choose Properties to display the Taskbar Properties dialog box.
3. Select the Start Menu Programs tab (see Figure 9.15).

FIG. 9.15
Use the Start Menu Programs page to add new programs and program folders to the Start menu.

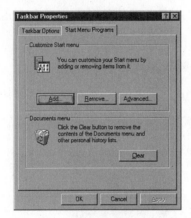

4. Click Add to display the Create Shortcut Wizard.
5. In the Command Line textbox, enter the full path to the program or file shortcut you want to add to the Start menu.

TIP Click the Browse button to search for the program or file you are trying to find.

6. Click Next.
7. In the Select Program Folder dialog box, click the folder in which you want to place the program or file shortcut (see Figure 9.16). Generally, you'll add the program to the Programs folder or create a new folder by clicking New Folder and entering a new folder name.

N O T E To add a program or shortcut to the Start menu, add the program or shortcut to the Start Menu folder in the Select Folder To Place Shortcut In listbox. ■

FIG. 9.16
Specify the folder in
which you want to place
the program or shortcut.

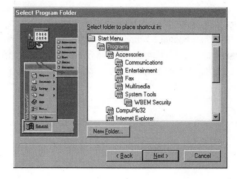

8. Click Next.

9. In the Select a Title for the Program dialog box, enter a name for the program in the Select a Name for the Shortcut box (see Figure 9.17).

FIG. 9.17
Accept the default
name or change it
according to your
tastes.

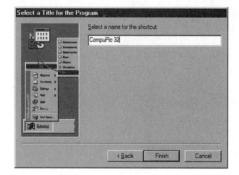

10. Click Finish.

If you want to add more programs or shortcuts, click the Add button on the Start Menu Programs tab. If you are finished, click OK to close the Taskbar Properties dialog box.

 Like in Windows 95, you also can add a shortcut to the Start menu by dragging the item onto the Start button. With Windows 98, however, if you drag an item onto the Start button but do not release your mouse button, the Start menu will open up. You then can continue dragging the item to any location in the Start menu—even subfolders.

You also can rearrange your Start menu this way. Click the Start button and drag any item on the menu to a new location with your left mouse button.

 Click the plus sign (+) next to a folder to expand it.

You can remove a program, file, or folder shortcut by clicking the Remove button on the Taskbar Properties dialog box and following these steps:

1. Scroll down the list of items in the Remove Shortcuts/Folders dialog box (see Figure 9.18).

FIG. 9.18
You can remove a program or shortcut from the Start menu as quickly as you add one.

2. Click the item to remove.
3. Click Remove.
4. Continue selecting and removing items, as needed. When finished, click Close.
5. Click OK.

N O T E You can click the Advanced button on the Taskbar Properties dialog box to see your Start menu in Explorer view. You can add items to the Start menu using this view by clicking the Advanced button and then opening another session of Explorer. Next, from the Explorer view that contains all your directories, drag items into the Start Menu Explorer view.

You also can remove items from your Start menu using this view. To do so, click the item you want to remove and press Delete. After the Confirm File Delete message appears, click Yes to send the item to the Recycle Bin. ▪

Clearing the Documents Folder

Another feature available on the Start menu is the Documents folder. This folder contains shortcuts to the last 15 files that you worked with in Windows 98, giving you quick access to these files for editing or reviewing. You can click on a document name to launch the application associated with that document and display the document.

To remove the items from the Documents folder, use these steps:

1. Right-click any exposed part of the taskbar.
2. Choose Properties to display the Taskbar Properties dialog box. Select the Start Menu Programs page.
3. In the Documents Menu area, click Clear.

Configuring Storage Devices

CHAPTER 10

Installing and Configuring Hard Disk Drives

by Rob Tidrow

In this chapter

Identifying Types of Hard Disk Drives Supported

The majority of users interested in adding a hard drive to their computer already have Windows 98 installed. If you do not have Windows 98 installed and you want to add a new hard drive to your system, you need to install the new hard drive and then install Windows 98 on it using the Windows 98 Setup routine. You'll need the full version of Windows 98 to do so. Consult Chapters 1 and 2 when installing Windows 98 on your blank, freshly formatted hard drive.

▶ **See** "Hard Drive Requirements," **p. 19**

▶ **See** "Using Windows 98 Setup," **p. 30**

N O T E A valuable resource when you install a new hard drive is your system documentation. In this manual, you'll find specific information that relates to your system, such as interrupt settings and CMOS settings.

Also, if you need more information on how to install a hard drive on your system, refer to *Upgrading and Repairing PCs, Sixth Edition*, published by Que. ▪

For this chapter, it is assumed that you are adding another hard drive to your PC to use with your current Windows 98 installation. Some users opt for a second hard drive if their first hard drive becomes full or if they have a need to separate their data and programs from their operating system. This is the case in many situations when you use a removable hard drive that you carry with you or store in a secure place.

Before you rush in and start installing a hard drive, you first should examine the types of hard drives you can install in Windows 98. The following types of hard disk drives are supported under Windows 98:

> ESDI
> Hardcards
> IDE
> IDE LBA
> MFM

Windows 98 supports the following types of bus adapters:

EISA	RLL
ISAMCA	SCSI
PCI	SCSI 2
PCMCIA	VL bus

Although Windows 98 supports other types of drives, the following two sections discuss IDE and SCSI devices in more detail. IDE and SCSI devices are the most prevalent devices available on current computers.

IDE Drives

Windows 98 supports *Integrated Drive Electronics* (IDE) drives, which are the most popular hard drive interfaces used in computers. If you have a computer that was manufactured in the last several years, it more than likely includes an IDE drive.

One of the improvements Windows 98 has with IDE drives is its support for large IDE disk drives. New IDE drives support the *logical block addressing* (LBA) scheme, which enables them to exceed the 528MB size limitation. These new drives sometimes are referred to as *Enhanced IDE drives*. Running the FAT16 file system, Windows 98 can support primary partition sizes of 2GB, with support of multiple 2GB logical drives in extended partitions. Running the FAT32 file system, however, Windows 98 supports primary partitions that are larger than 2GB, with the additional benefit of smaller cluster sizes. Also, versions of Windows prior to Windows 95 support large hard drives in real mode, but Windows 95 and Windows 98 support large IDE drives using a protected-mode disk driver included with Windows 98.

Windows 98 includes an updated IDE hard disk driver that supports the following technologies:

- Compaq's *Self-Monitoring Analysis and Reporting Technology* (SMART), which is a hard drive fault-prediction system. SMART also is supported by other third-party hard disk drive manufacturers.
- IDE tape backup drives.
- ATAPI CD-ROM changers that have up to seven CD-ROM slots.
- Bus-mastering chipsets, including the Opti Viper M and Intel Triton chipsets.

Another feature of Windows 98 is its support of a second IDE controller in your computer, if your computer can support it. You need to refer to your computer's documentation to determine how to set up your CMOS configuration to handle this second IDE controller. If you use a laptop, you can use a combination of an IDE controller and a controller in a docking station, if you use a docking station with your laptop.

Part
III

Ch
10

> **N O T E** A hard disk *controller* acts as a "middleman" between the hard drive and your computer. A controller is needed because a PC cannot use a hard drive directly. It needs something to communicate instructions to and from the hard drive. In many cases, the BIOS is used to pass hard drive requests from the PC to the hard drive controller. The controller then accesses the hard drive. ■

SCSI Drives

Windows 98 includes 32-bit disk device drivers for several *Small Computer System Interface* (SCSI) controllers. Some of these controllers include Adaptec, Future Domain, Trantor, and UltraStor. The SCSI interface is a sub-bus to which you can connect up to seven peripherals. The SCSI supports up to eight units, but one of the units is used to connect the adapter card to the PC, leaving seven open units. You can attach hard drives, CD-ROM drives, scanners, and other devices to a SCSI adapter.

Installing a Hard Disk Drive

When you install a hard drive, you need to be aware of several factors that help lead you to a successful installation. Because each computer, hard drive, and Windows 98 installation is different, this section shows you some of the general steps to help you physically install your hard drive. You should use this section as an overview and reference another resource for hardware-specific questions you might have.

Before you begin ripping open your computer and stuffing a new hard drive inside it, be sure your computer supports the type of hard drive you are installing. You should be able to find this information on the computer specification you received with your PC. If you are the type of user who is not comfortable installing hardware, this chapter probably will not make you more comfortable doing so. It will show you how to configure your hard drive after it's installed, however. You can get this information later in this chapter in the section "Configuring Your Hard Disk Drive."

 TIP Before you turn off your computer to add the new hard drive, you should back up your system in case you lose any data on your existing hard drive.

Plug and Play and Legacy Hard Drives

In Chapter 5, "Installing and Configuring New Hardware and Software," you learn about Plug and Play and how it helps you set up your devices quickly and easily under Windows 98. Another term you might hear is *legacy*. Legacy refers to devices that do not support the Plug and Play specification. Many of the troubleshooting problems you'll run into under Windows 98 are related to legacy devices, because they are older devices.

The Plug and Play feature requires cooperation among BIOS manufacturers, device manufacturers, and the software developers. Therefore, in order to use this feature, you need a BIOS that supports Plug and Play, a hard disk drive that is Plug and Play–compliant, and Windows 98, which has the support to recognize a new Plug and Play–compliant device and perform an automatic installation of it. This makes the addition of new hardware a simple and painless operation. In some cases, you don't even need to turn off the power to the PC to install a Plug and Play device (although it's recommended that you power down your computer anytime you remove its case).

Disk Drive Addressing

To access a hard disk drive, the address of the disk must be specified. The *address* is a single, alphabetic character followed by a colon. If the colon is omitted, Windows 98 interprets the drive letter as a filename consisting of a single letter instead of a disk drive address.

NOTE The addressing scheme can become complicated. If you are connected to a network, each disk you want to have on the network also will have an alphabetic character assigned to it. To further complicate the issue, you can use the DOS command SUBST to substitute one disk address for another. Schemes such as these are beyond the scope of this book. ▪

In addition, Windows 98 has specific addresses it uses for the disk devices and CD-ROMs. The addresses of the floppy-disk and hard-disk drives are determined by the cables attached to them. To simplify this discussion, you can use a standard form of addressing. You safely can assume the following for this discussion:

- An installed CD-ROM has an address of K:
- Any network disks have an address starting with L:
- The DOS command SUBST is not to be used

When Windows 98 is started, the existing disks are assigned an address based on the following scheme:

- The first floppy disk drive is A:
- The second floppy disk drive is B:
- The first hard disk drive is C:
- The second hard disk drive is D:
- The third hard disk drive is E:
- The fourth hard disk drive is F:
- The CD-ROM address is specified during installation. If it is not specified, its address is the next alphabetic character after the last hard drive character.

TIP If your CD-ROM drive allows you to, always assign the address for a CD-ROM drive to a letter that is a few letters after your last hard disk drive. If, for example, your hard drives are C: and D:, make your CD-ROM F: or G:. That way, if you add more hard disk drives, the address of your CD-ROM does not change and you do not have to change any links to files on a CD-ROM. See Chapter 12, "Installing and Configuring CD-ROM and DVD Drives," for information on installing a CD-ROM drive.

Sometimes, however, Windows sets up a CD-ROM drive with a specific drive letter that you might not be able to change even after installing a new hard drive. This might make the CD-ROM drive letter higher than the new hard drive.

Referencing the Windows 98 Device Manager

The Windows 98 Device Manager is used to display and change the parameters associated with your system's hardware, including hard disk drives. In most instances, the default settings selected by Windows 98 are the correct ones. Sometimes, however, you might encounter a problem after you install your hard drive, and you'll need to access the Device Manager to fix the problem. For this reason, you should become familiar with the Device Manager, even before you install a new hard drive. To access the Device Manager, use the following procedure:

1. Choose Start, Settings, Control Panel, and double-click the System icon.
2. After the System Properties dialog box appears, select the Device Manager page, as shown in Figure 10.1.

FIG 10.1

You can view your system's hard disk drive(s) properties by using the Device Manager.

To view your hard drive properties, you need to look at both the Disk Drives setting and the Hard Disk Controllers setting. Click the plus sign (+) next to each of these settings to reveal the type of drives and controllers you have installed.

Figure 10.1 shows two drives under Disk Drives. The drive named GENERIC IDE DISK TYPE01 is the hard drive on the system. The other drive is the floppy disk drive installed. Under Hard Disk Controllers, two controllers are listed, both named Standard Bus Mastering IDE Hard Disk Controller.

Installing a Hard Drive

As pointed out earlier, this chapter assumes that you already have one hard drive installed on your system with Windows 98 running on it. Unless you piece together your own computer, the first hard drive is always installed when you purchase your computer. Today's computers usually can support at least two hard disk drives.

> **CAUTION**
>
> Static electricity can be discharged from your body and can cause permanent damage to the chips in your computer. If you do not use an antistatic strip, always touch something metal, such as the case, before touching any components inside the computer.

To install a new hard drive, use the following steps:

1. Turn off the power to the computer. You should leave the power cord plugged in to keep the electrical ground established.

2. Disconnect all cables from the computer and note their locations with a piece of masking tape.

3. Remove the case by unscrewing the six or eight screws holding it to the frame.

You now are ready to install your second hard disk drive. Because each hard drive and computer is different, this is where you need to read and follow the instructions provided by the hard drive manufacturer to install the hard disk drive. Some generalized guidelines follow:

1. Locate an available bay in which to install the hard drive. Many hard drives come with a drive kit, usually at an additional charge, with all the necessary hardware to mount the drive in the bay. You might need an adapter if your bay is for a 5 1/4-inch hard disk drive and you are installing a 3 1/2-inch hard disk drive. In addition, rails, which are attached to the side of the hard disk drive, also may be needed. You now can install the drive with the appropriate screws (usually four 6/32×1/4-inch screws).

 T I P It might be easier to connect the power connector and hard disk drive cable before sliding the hard disk drive into the bay.

2. Next, locate an available power-supply connection. If none is available, you have to purchase a Y–cable. The Y–cable enables you to share an existing power connector with two devices. To install it, locate a device near the empty bay that has a power connection plugged into it. Then disconnect that plug, and then plug the female end of the Y–cable into it. Now, one of the male ends is for the device you just unplugged, and the other male end is for your new hard disk drive. Because a hard disk drive uses more electricity than most other devices, you should use a Y–cable of 18 gauge or heavier.

3. You now are ready to attach the hard disk drive cables between the hard disk controller and the hard disk drive. These are two flat, wide ribbon cables, with a red or blue stripe along one edge. This colored edge should be next to pin number 1 when it is connected to the hard disk drive and the hard disk controller. You can locate the pin number by referring to your computer's documentation and looking at the schematic drawing of the motherboard.

   Most disk drives have a single cable that combines the functions of the data cable and the control cable. Also, to help ensure that the cable is connected properly, a plastic key might be placed between a row of pins in the connector. With this plastic key, the connector can be attached only to the disk drive.

After the hard disk drive is secured to the bay and the drive cable and power cable are connected, you are ready to close the computer and begin configuring Windows 98 for your new hard disk drive.

N O T E Because Windows 98 supports up to two IDE disk controllers, you can install a second controller if you install a third or fourth hard drive in your system. Again, consult your hardware documentation for the placement of the new controller on your PC's motherboard. Some motherboards include a set of golden pins labeled to identify them for the second controller, such as Secondary IDE. ■

Closing the Computer

With all the new hardware installed, you now can close the computer to complete the configuration of the new hardware.

 TIP If you're like me, you like to make sure everything is working before you go through all the trouble of refastening all those screws on your computer. You might want to bypass this section for now and go to the "Configuring Your Hard Disk Drive" section to make sure that your hard drive works. Of course, you need to attach all the cables and power cords before booting up your computer, but you might save time if the hard drive doesn't work and you need to check loose cables and the like by keeping the case off for now.

These are the general steps to close your computer:

1. Refasten the case by reversing the procedure used to remove it. Namely, place the case back over the frame of the computer and insert the removed screws to refasten the case to the frame. Ensure that all cables and wires are placed neatly inside the computer, in a position where they aren't pinched by other components or trapped between the case and the frame of the computer.

2. All cables now can be plugged into their proper ports, according to the labels on each cable.

After you install a new hard drive in your computer, you need to configure it to work properly with your specific computer. To do this, reboot your computer and run your computer's setup program to enable you to make changes to your CMOS settings. On some machines, you can start the setup program by pressing F1 during bootup. Refer to your computer's and hard disk drive's documentation at this point to configure your machine to work with the new hard drive. You might need to run specific software provided by your hard drive manufacturer, for example, before partitioning and eventually installing Windows 95 and Windows 98 on your new drive. After you make these changes, be sure to save them and then reboot your computer.

Partitioning Your New Hard Disk Drive

Before you use your new hard drive with Windows 98, you can partition it using the FDISK command. Some hard drives come prepartitioned and preformatted, so you might not have to partition your drive. When you *partition* a hard drive, you define the areas of the disk for Windows 98 (or any other operating system, for that matter) to recognize as a volume. To Windows 98, a *volume* is the part of the disk that is specified as the drive letter, such as C or D.

When you partition a drive, you set it up in one of the following partition types:

- *Primary.* A primary partition is the partition on which the bootable operating system resides. If you have two partitions, one of them must contain the operating system.

- *Extended.* Extended partitions usually don't contain operating system files but can be divided into logical drives (with letters D through Z).

After you set up partitions, you need to specify the active partition, which your PC uses to boot to. If you elect to place Windows 98 on one partition and Windows NT on another, for example, you need to specify the Windows 98 partition as the active one to run Windows 98. Likewise, when you want to boot Windows NT, you need to switch the active partition to the partition on which NT is installed.

Partitioning Requirements for Installing Windows 98

To install Windows on your new hard drive, you must create a FAT partition on your new hard drive. You cannot install Windows 98 on a computer that has only *Hewlett-Packard file system* (HPFS) or *Windows NT file system* (NTFS) partitions.

> **N O T E** For information on setting up your hard drive as a FAT32 partition, read "Using FAT32" in Chapter 14, "Configuring Memory, Disks, and Devices." ▪

Part
III

Ch
10

The following list describes how Windows 98 Setup handles different types of disk partitions:

- *MS-DOS Partition.* Windows 98 Setup recognizes and begins installation over existing MS-DOS FAT partitions. Windows 98 supports MS-DOS FDISK partitions on removable media drives, such as the Iomega Bernoulli Box drives.

- *Windows NT.* Windows 98 Setup cannot recognize information on an NTFS partition on the local computer. You can install Windows 98 on a Windows NT multiple-boot system if enough disk space is available on a FAT partition. On a Windows NT multiple-boot system, you must install Windows 98 on an existing FAT partition with MS-DOS, MS-DOS and Windows 3.x, or Windows 95. Another way to install Windows 98 is to partition and format free space on the hard drive in a FAT partition, and then perform a new installation onto this new FAT partition.

> **N O T E** With Windows NT 4.0, you can use long filenames like you can with Windows 98. This enables you to install Windows 98 (as an upgrade to an existing Windows 95 installation) and Windows NT 4.0 on the same partition using the FAT file system. If you want to use NTFS with Windows NT 4.0, be sure to install Windows 98 on a separate partition. ▪

- *OS/2.* Again, a DOS partition must be available from which to install Windows 98. You cannot install Windows 98 straight from OS/2.

Using *FDISK*

When you use the FDISK command, you can partition your hard drive into one or several partitions. You might want to partition your new hard drive into two partitions if you want to install a different operating system, such as OS/2 Warp, on your computer. This way, you can have both Windows 98 (as an upgrade to an existing Windows 95 installation) and OS/2 residing on the same computer but occupying different hard drives.

CAUTION

Running FDISK destroys all data on the partitions you change or create. Do not use FDISK if you are not comfortable making these changes and if you have not backed up all the data on your drive. If you are in a company, consult your MIS or help-desk person before continuing.

Another time when you can partition a hard drive is when you already have set up a hard drive, and you want to *repartition* it. If you want to repartition a hard drive with several logical drives into one drive, you first must use FDISK to delete all existing partitions and logical drives, and then create a new primary partition and make it active. The *active partition* is the partition in which your system boots. For this chapter, your active partition already is set up and is not modified. This is the partition on the hard drive that contains Windows 98. You don't need to worry about partitioning that hard drive. In fact, if you repartitioned that drive, you would lose all the date on it, including Windows 98.

As you just read, when you partition a hard drive, you lose all data on it. When repartition an existing hard drive, be sure to back up all your data onto another hard drive or tape backup. You cannot recover the data after you partitioned the drive.

FDISK is an MS-DOS–based application that you can run from the DOS command prompt. You also can run it in a DOS window in Windows 95 or Windows 98. As you use FDISK, each FDISK screen displays a Current Fixed Disk Drive line, followed by a number. This number is the number of the current drive that is selected. Computers with only one hard disk drive use the label 1. Computers with more than one hard disk drive label the drives in this way: the first hard disk drive on the computer is 1, the second is 2, and so on. The Current Fixed Disk Drive line refers only to physical disk drives, not logical drives.

To configure a hard drive by using FDISK, use the following steps:

1. At the DOS command prompt, type **FDISK**. The FDISK Options screen displays the following:

```
1. Create a partition or logical drive
2. Set the active partition
3. Delete a partition or logical drive
4. Display partition information
5. Change current fixed disk drive
   Enter choice [1]
   Press Esc to exit FDISK
```

 You can press Esc anytime to exit FDISK.

2. In the preceding options list, the fifth option is not available when you have only one hard drive installed on your computer. Because you have two hard drives installed now, select 5 to switch to the second hard drive to partition it and press Enter.

3. Now that your new drive is selected, choose option 1 and press Enter. This creates a partition on your drive. When you are prompted to set the size of the partition, the default is to use the entire drive. Select Yes in most cases.

4. Return to the FDISK menu and be sure to select your primary fixed disk (usually, the C: drive) by selecting option 5 before you exit FDISK. Otherwise, when you reboot your system, your computer will try to boot from your new drive.

N O T E If you installed a disk-compression program from Microsoft or another vendor, FDISK displays the uncompressed size of the drives, not the compressed size. Depending on the software, FDISK may not be able to display information about all the drives used by a disk-compression program from another vendor. You should obtain information from the software vendor if you are having difficulties. ■

TROUBLESHOOTING

What do I do when I get an error that Windows 98 Setup can't find a valid boot partition? This error might be a result of your disk-compression software or network components mapping over the boot drive. This can occur if you are mapping a network drive to H, but H is the hidden host drive for your disk-compression software. To resolve the invalid partition error, make sure the drive is not mapped over or logically remapped. You also should verify a valid, active partition using the FDISK command. If no active partition exists, use FDISK to mark an appropriate partition as active. Also, make sure the disk-compression software's host drive does not conflict with a mapped network drive.

Windows and Partitioning Software

For hard drives that already are installed, you should not repartition the hard drive by using FDISK if the partitions were created using Disk Manager, Storage Dimension's SpeedStor, Priam, or Everex partitioning programs. When these programs are used, they replace the existing PC's BIOS in interactions between MS-DOS and the hard disk controller. For these cases, you must use the same disk-partitioning program that was used to partition the disk in the first place. For example, if you use SpeedStor on a computer that has more than 1,024 cylinders, do not use FDISK to partition your hard drive. Use SpeedStor instead.

You can tell which type of program created the partition by searching for these files on your system: HARDRIVE.SYS for Priam, SSTOR.SYS for SpeedStor, DMDRVR.BIN for Disk Manager, and EVDISK.SYS for Everex. Usually, you find device= entries for these files in CONFIG.SYS. If you need help repartitioning the hard drive or are unsure whether the BIOS is being replaced, contact the manufacturer of the original disk-partitioning program.

Configuring Your Hard Disk Drive

After your hard drive is installed and the cables are reattached to your computer, boot your computer and start Windows 98. During the boot process, Windows 98 looks at your system and, if everything goes as planned, it detects your new hard drive. It configures the new hard drive and controller to work under Windows.

One of the problems with Plug and Play is that your computer's BIOS also needs to support Plug and Play devices. Most computers being used do not have a BIOS that supports this new specification. For this reason, Windows 98 also includes the auto-detect feature for legacy systems. If Windows 98 finds your new hard drive during bootup but cannot automatically configure it, you are presented with a screen asking whether you want to set up the device now. The best response is to answer Yes to this screen and let Windows 98 try to set it up for you.

If Windows 98 does not automatically detect your new hard drive, use the Add New Hardware Wizard to set up your hard drive. You'll find a discussion of this wizard in Chapter 5.

Formatting a Hard Disk Drive

Now that your hard drive is partitioned, and Windows 98 can recognize it, you need a way to access it. To do this, you need to perform a high-level format on it. Another reason to format a hard drive is if you want to clean up the hard drive by removing all its files and folders. Of course, you cannot do this on hard drives that currently contain data that you are using, including Windows 98.

You can format a hard drive in Windows 98 using a graphical approach with Explorer or using the FORMAT command at the MS-DOS prompt.

> **CAUTION**
>
> Before using the FORMAT command or utility on a drive that already contains data, make sure that your hard drive does not contain valuable data that is not backed up. When you format a hard drive, all data is erased from the disk, and you cannot recover it.

To format a hard disk drive using Explorer, use the following steps:

1. In Windows Explorer, right-click the drive icon for your hard disk drive, and then choose Format from the context-sensitive menu.

2. In the Format dialog box, set the appropriate options for the type of format you want to perform. If your hard drive is new, you need to select the Full option in the Format Type section. In the Capacity drop-down list, select the size of your hard disk drive.

3. In the Other Options area, type a label for the hard drive in the Label box. The *label* is the name you want to identify this drive with; don't confuse this with the drive letter.

4. Click Start. Windows 98 formats the hard drive and, if you selected the Display Summary When Finished option in the Other Options area, a summary sheet appears that shows the amount of space available on the disk and how much space is taken up by system files and bad sectors, if any are found.

5. Click OK when you finish reading the report.

6. Click Close to close the Format dialog box.

TROUBLESHOOTING

I've used the Format utility in Explorer and the FORMAT command in MS-DOS, but I still can't format my hard drive. If the disk was compressed by using DriveSpace 3, you must use the Format option in DriveSpace 3 to format the compressed drive. Choose Drive, Format to start the format process in DriveSpace 3.

If you need to format a drive at the DOS command line, use the following syntax:

```
FORMAT driveletter
```

The `driveletter` parameter is the letter used to denote the hard drive you are formatting. To include a label for the drive, use the following syntax, with the label name replacing *label*:

```
FORMAT driveletter V:label
```

Your new hard drive now is ready for use.

Testing Hard Disk Drives Under Windows 98

Testing the hard disk drive is simple. All you have to do is use it. Before using it, however, you can ask Windows 98 to show you which drives are present. If you have two drives, they are shown as your C: drive and D: drive. The third one is the E: drive, and the fourth one is the F: drive. Some ways to see these drives follow:

- Double-click My Computer and see which drives are shown.

- From Explorer, go to the top of the list and see which hard disk drives are listed.

To make sure that your new hard drive functions properly, copy a file from your old hard drive to the new hard drive. When finished, compare the two files to see whether the file was copied successfully. Likewise, copy the file you just copied to the new hard drive back to the old hard drive and change the name. Now compare the two files on the old hard disk drive to see whether they still are identical.

▶ **See** "Improving Hard Drive Performance," **p. 243**

TROUBLESHOOTING

How do I configure my Syquest removable IDE drive for Windows 98? For a Syquest IDE drive to work properly under Windows 98, be sure to configure the drive's Properties dialog box to enable it as a removable drive. If this doesn't work, add the entry `RemovableIDE=true` to the `[386enh]` section of your `SYSTEM.INI` file.

I do a lot of work with large files (several megabytes in size), and transferring them to other machines not on the local area network is difficult. What is the easiest way to move these files around using hard drive technology? There are several solutions you can use. One of the most commonly used technologies is tape backup, which you can read about in Chapter 13, "Setting Up Backup Systems."

Another solution is to use a Syquest drive or similar technology that uses tape cartridges to store data. Probably one of the most popular technologies being used today is the removable hard drive or portable hard drive system. Iomega, for example, manufactures the Iomega Zip and Iomega Jaz drives, which you can use as portable and removable hard drives. You can attach these units to your system using a SCSI II host or parallel port (in the case of Zip drives). The Zip drive supports cartridges the size of 3 1/2-inch disks that hold 100MB, whereas the Jaz drive uses 1GB cartridges to enable you to store and access files.

One advantage of the Zip and Jaz drives over backup systems is that the Zip and Jaz drives act like regular hard drives. In fact, the Jaz drive has seek times as fast as 10ms to 12ms, making them faster than most hard drives found on PCs.

Troubleshooting Hard Disk Drives Under Windows 98

At times, you'll experience problems with your hard disk drive. Some of these problems are discussed in this section. You might encounter one of these problems during bootup. If your computer stalls because of the new hard drive, you might have a problem with where your hard disk drivers are installed. The I/O Supervisor requires the hard disk driver files with the extensions PDR, MPD, VXD, and 386 to be located in the SYSTEM\IOSUBSYS subfolder in your Windows 98 folder. The I/O Supervisor is responsible for loading these hard disk device drivers.

If your computer locks up during startup or hardware detection, use the following troubleshooting steps to fix the problem:

1. Look for SYS files in the IOSUBSYS folder. These are Windows NT miniport drivers that detect the I/O ports and may cause your computer to stop. (These appear only on hard drives with previous versions of Windows NT installed on them.) Replace the Windows NT driver with a Windows 98 miniport or a real-mode driver.

2. Check your IOS.INI file for real-mode drivers not replaced by protected-mode drivers.

3. When loading protected-mode drivers, the real-mode driver generally remains loaded in memory, even though the protected-mode driver is running. In CONFIG.SYS, type **REM** at the beginning of the line that calls the real-mode driver.

4. Some systems might encounter problems with devices that use ASPI drivers, such as tape backup units. Try using only real-mode drivers, and then try using only protected-mode drivers.

The section "Closing the Computer," earlier in this chapter, suggested that you might not want to replace the computer case just yet. Well, now is when you'll appreciate this advise. If your device does not work, and it's not because of the preceding failure, the problem might be hardware-related. You need to take a look at the physical connections your new hard drive has inside the computer. Sometimes, a loose connection can create huge problems during setup.

Some possible areas to investigate follow:

■ *Hard disk drive cable is defective.* Replace the cable with another one to see whether the problem is resolved.

■ *Hard disk drive cable is installed improperly for a single hard disk drive system.* Ensure that the hard drive cable has the twist in the center of the cable near the connector to your disk drive. This is how hard disk drive C: is identified. The remaining connector is attached to the hard disk drive controller.

■ *Hard disk drive cable is installed improperly for a dual hard disk drive system.* Ensure that the hard drive cable has the twist in the center of the cable near the connector to your disk drive. This is how hard disk drive C: is identified. The connector at the center of the cable is for hard disk drive D:. The remaining connector is attached to the hard disk drive controller.

■ *Hard drive device is defective.* If the hard disk drive cable is connected properly and the hard disk drive is not working properly, then the fault might be with the hard disk drive itself. Install a different hard disk drive and see whether the problem is resolved.

■ *Hard disk controller is defective.* If the hard disk drive cable is connected properly and the hard disk drive is working properly (it was tested on another computer), then the fault might be with the hard disk drive controller. Install a different hard disk drive controller and see whether the problem is resolved.

N O T E   In the following list, the term *hard disk drive cable* is used to mean the controller cable and/or the data cable, depending on which system you have. ■

After adjusting the cables and/or replacing the hard drive, reboot the computer and walk through the Add New Hardware Wizard again. If none of these solutions help, call the technical-support number included with your hard drive. New drivers for Windows 98 might be available that they can send to you.

Part
III

Ch
10

Using Bus Mastering

A problem you might encounter is if bus mastering is enabled on a hard drive that is not specifically certified to work with a Windows bus master driver. To know whether your hard drive supports bus mastering, perform the following steps:

1. Choose Start, Settings, Control Panel, and double-click the System icon.

2. In the System Properties dialog box, select the Device Manager tab.

3. Double-click the hard drive you want to examine. Do not double-click the drive's controller.

4. Select Properties.

5. Select the Settings tab. Look for DMA appears under the Int 13 unit option. Keep the DMA option unchecked unless your hard drive specifically supports bus mastering. If there is no check box, your motherboard chipset does not support a compatible bus master interface.

CHAPTER 11

Installing and Configuring Floppy Disk Drives

by Rob Tidrow

In this chapter

Installing Floppy Disk Drives in Your Computer

If your floppy disk drives work with Windows 95, you won't need to do anything to get Windows 98 to recognize them. If you're adding a new floppy drive or having problems with a current drive, however, this chapter can help you troubleshoot many common disk drive problems and show you how to install a new drive.

N O T E   Along with the information covered in this chapter, you should follow specific instructions provided with your floppy disk drive. ■

To install a new floppy disk drive into your computer, follow these steps:

1. If the floppy disk drive is still in its box, check to make sure that it has the installation screws (usually four to eight or more) and a cable, if necessary (if you already have a floppy disk drive installed, you can use the existing cable). Because you'll be working near very sensitive electronic parts, wear an antistatic wristband.

2. Turn off and unplug the computer.

3. Find the location on the front panel where you'll be installing the drive. Note the direction of the opening (vertical or horizontal).

4. Open the computer's case.

5. You should see the space in the front of the chassis where the drive will fit. Slide it into place. Most new cases have what looks like a 3 1/2-inch-wide metal box beside the drive bays. This looks like a perfect place for a 3 1/2-inch floppy disk drive, but it's made for a hard drive. There is no corresponding opening in the front of the computer's case.

   Lightly attach the installation screws, tightening them only when you're sure the drive's face will be flush with the front of the PC (if possible, use an existing drive as a guide). Some cases require the addition of plastic or metal rails on the sides of the drive before you can slide it in place.

 T I P   You'll be attaching two cables to the back of the drive. If it looks like you won't be able to get your fingers behind the drive when it's secured, leave the installation screws off until you've attached the cables.

6. The two cables you need to attach are a ribbon cable and a power cable. If you're adding a second floppy disk drive or replacing one, you see the ribbon cable running into the back of the original drive. A few inches from the drive end of the cable, you should see another connector, which you use for the second drive (the B: drive) in the system. The end of the ribbon cable always goes to the A: drive. Slide the connector into place on the back of the floppy disk drive.

   You might need an adapter to hook the ribbon cable connector to your floppy disk drive. If you want to make a 3 1/2-inch floppy disk drive (with a pin connector), for example, you need to get an edge-to-pin adapter, because the A: drive and the end of the ribbon cable are for a 5 1/4-inch drive (edge connector).

N O T E   Even though the cables are set up for your A: and your B: drive, you have to make sure that the CMOS is set up the same way. ■

7. Find a power lead from the computer's power supply for your drive. You should see leads going to the motherboard and any drives you already have installed, all from the same location. Find a lead that is not yet connected to a drive. If no leads are available, get a Y connector from a computer supply store to split one of the existing leads. Connect the power lead to the back of the drive.

N O T E   You might need an adapter for the power-supply lead. If the only available leads are the larger type (about 3/4-inch wide in a D shape) and you're installing a drive with a small, square power socket (like most 3 1/2-inch drives), you need an adapter. Some drives include this adapter with the mounting kit, but if you don't have this adapter, you should be able to get one at a computer supply store. ■

Before you replace the cover on your PC, you might want to test the new floppy drive. This way, you don't have to remove the case if you need access to the drive again. Reconnect the computer's power cable and any other cables you disconnected earlier, and then turn it back on to complete the next steps in the process.

Getting the PC to Recognize the New Floppy Disk Drive

When you turn on your computer after installing a new floppy disk drive, it might squawk, beep, and/or display error messages on the screen. This is perfectly normal; the PC doesn't know how to handle the new device until you tell it manually.

The PC's device configuration is stored in the Setup or CMOS section of the computer. The information in the Setup or CMOS sections includes the types of drives you have, the time of day, the video-controller type, and some more arcane settings. The CMOS has its own battery, which is how it retains these settings (and keeps your computer's clock running) when the computer is turned off or unplugged. When you add a new *basic* device (a floppy drive, hard drive, or video card, as opposed to a nonessential device, such as a sound card or CD-ROM drive), the CMOS needs to find out about the device's settings before it will work.

If the computer halts during startup after you install the new drive, it might display a message like Press Enter to run setup or Press Ctrl+Alt+Insert now (or some other keyboard sequence). If it just tells you Incorrect CMOS setup and continues to boot up normally, you'll have to turn the computer off and on to get back to the start of the boot sequence. In the early stages of the boot process, you should see a message on your screen telling you what you have to do to start the CMOS Setup program. The message might say Press Delete to run Setup (or F2, F12, or almost any other key or key combination). You usually have to press this key sequence *before* you see the Starting Windows 98 message.

TIP   Some systems don't display any message at all, so you might have to refer to your PC's documentation or manufacturer.

When the Setup program appears on your screen, read its instructions carefully. It might offer you a menu of basic and advanced options. Choosing the floppy drive is usually in the `basic` section. When you get to the correct screen, you should see a list of drives—usually two floppy disk drives and two hard drives—and some other information about the date, time, and other devices. Instructions on this screen show how to go from section to section. In some Setup programs, for example, you use the arrow keys to move around and Page Up/Page Down to change the settings, whereas other programs have you use Tab or the space bar for these functions.

Move to the correct section (usually, `Floppy A` or `Floppy B`) and change it until it correctly identifies your new drive. The program should run through a list of standard drive types (both types of 3 1/2-inch drives, both 5 1/4-inch drives, and `None`, which you can use to disable a drive).

After you select the correct drive, exit the CMOS Setup program (usually by pressing Esc, Enter, or F10) and make sure you save the settings. You'll probably see a menu with options to ignore the changes or save them, with Ignore as the first option. The computer should start up normally after you exit Setup.

Installing Floppy Disk Drive Controllers

After you start Windows 98, your new floppy drive should be accessible via My Computer, Explorer, and other disk-accessing programs. If you cannot locate your new floppy drive, however, run the Add New Hardware Wizard to manually install your floppy disk driver controller under Windows 98. Your new floppy disk drive then should work. Chapter 5, "Installing and Configuring New Hardware and Software," covers using the Add New Hardware Wizard to install new hardware.

N O T E   Windows 98 includes a new floppy disk drive device driver named Windows 98 `HSFLOP.PDR` designed to improve floppy disk drive performance. This device driver replaces the old `HSFLOP.PDR` file in Windows 95 and is located in the `WINDOWS\SYSTEM\IOSUBSYS` folder. You should not have to ever change this driver unless Microsoft releases a newer version at a later date. ■

Understanding Floppy Disk Drive Installation

After you have the floppy disk drive controller installed under Windows 98, the only place Windows 98 really has an effect on floppy disk drive installation is in diagnosis. It can't change the drive's settings (at least not in legacy drives); it can tell you only whether the drive works properly.

To make sure the drive is properly installed and identified in the CMOS setup, follow these steps:

1. Choose Start, Settings, Control Panel, and double-click the System icon. The System Properties dialog box appears.

2. Select the Device Manager page.

3. Click the plus sign next to the Disk Drives icon, as shown in Figure 11.1. The available drives are displayed under it.

FIG. 11.1

You can use the Device Manager to view the available drives on your system.

Part
III

Ch
11

4. Double-click the drive you want to check. The General page of the Properties dialog box tells you whether the drive is working properly or whether Windows 98 has detected a problem. See Figure 11.2.

FIG. 11.2

The General page lets you see the working status of your floppy disk drive.

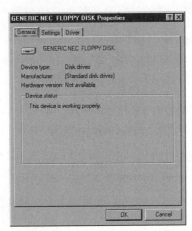

N O T E   If you select the Settings page and you have a legacy drive, you'll see most of the options
grayed out, as shown in Figure 11.3. Current Drive Letter Assignment is one option that
looks changeable but isn't. To change the drive assignment, you'd have to switch the cable connections
between the floppy drives and then rerun the CMOS setup. ▣

FIG. 11.3

The Settings page
includes handy options
if your floppy disk drive
is Plug and Play–
compatible; otherwise,
most options are not
available.

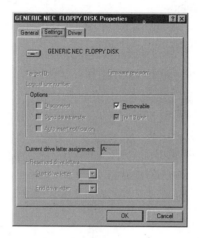

5. Click OK twice to exit the Device Manager.

Testing and Troubleshooting Floppy Disk Drive Installation

Before you put the cover back on your computer, make sure the floppy disk drive works properly. Because the medium is notoriously susceptible to dust and other contaminants (specifically because of its "open air" design), testing floppy disk drives can be a little taxing. It's all too
easy to believe that the newly installed drive isn't working when the real problem is a dusty
disk—or a stray strand of hair in the drive. So, before you count out your floppy disk drive, test
it thoroughly.

The cardinal rule when testing floppy disk drives is to test the drive on an *entire* disk. This
assures you that the drive heads can access the entire disk's surface, not just part of it. Viewing
a directory of the disk in Windows Explorer, for example, isn't a reliable test, because the
directory is stored on a very small section of the disk. To verify the drive's operation across the
entire disk, try any of these tests:

- ▪ Format a blank floppy disk. (Double-click the My Computer icon, select the drive, and
  choose File, Format.)

- ▪ Run ScanDisk by choosing Start, Programs, Accessories, System Tools. After the
  ScanDisk window appears, select the floppy disk drive (make sure that a floppy disk is
  inserted into your drive) you want to test in the Select the Drive(s) You Want to Check
  for Errors box. Make sure you choose Thorough in the Type of Test area before you
  click Start. See Figure 11.4.

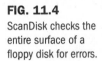
FIG. 11.4
ScanDisk checks the
entire surface of a
floppy disk for errors.

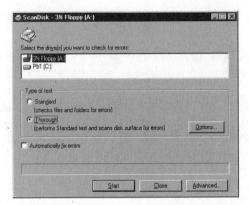

If your drive can successfully complete one or both of these tests, it's a pretty safe bet that the drive is installed correctly. If your drive fails these tests, you can do several things to track down the problem.

First, find the *general* location of the problem. It could be any of the following:

- Disk
- Drive
- Ribbon cable
- Power cable
- Drive controller

If the drive doesn't appear in the My Computer or ScanDisk window, for example, the problem is probably not the disk itself. If the drive shows up in these windows, you know the power cable is connected; Windows wouldn't know the drive was there if it didn't have power. This process often is called the *long-knife approach*, because each question eliminates a large chunk of the problem.

When you have shortened the list of suspects enough, eliminate each variable until you find the culprit.

TROUBLESHOOTING

When I launch My Computer or Windows Explorer, my floppy disk drive always checks to see whether a disk is inserted. How can I turn this off? Choose Start, Settings, Control Panel, and double-click the System icon. Select the Performance page on the System Properties dialog box. Click File System to display the File System Properties dialog box and select the Floppy Disk page. Clear the Search for New Floppy Disk Drives Each Time Your Computer Starts check box.

Checking for a Faulty Disk

If the disk itself could be the problem, try to read it in another computer. If the disk works in other computers, the disk probably is not at fault. Verify this by trying other disks in the problem drive. If other disks work, the first disk might be incompatible with the drive (the wrong size, for example).

 TIP   If you have access to CompuServe, the Internet, or another online source, look for the freeware program DRIVTY or DRIVTYPS. When you run it from the MS-DOS command line, it tells you whether your disk drive(s) can accept high-density disks.

In rare cases, the alignment of a drive's heads allows it to read and write disks that can't be used on other computers. If you need to share disks with other computers and no one else seems to be able to use disks from your computer, try a different drive.

Checking for Faulty Cables

When you turn on the computer, watch the light on the drive. It should light up for about one second, and you should hear the drive's motor spinning or "cranking." If it doesn't light up at all (or if it stays lit all the time), you probably have a problem with your cables.

If your drive does nothing, check the power cable. Disconnect it and reconnect it to make sure it's seated correctly. If that doesn't work, check another of your power supply's leads.

If the drive light is always on, the culprit is probably the ribbon cable. Although most drives only allow you to put the cable on one way, some can be connected upside-down (especially edge connectors). See whether you can flip the ribbon cable's connection, either on the drive end or the card end—but not both. If the connectors will only go one way, check the pin connectors for folded (bent) or broken pins.

If all the connectors look to be in working order, the problem might be a short in the ribbon cable itself. Try a different cable. If possible, try the ribbon cable on a different computer to see whether it works. This could point to a faulty drive or controller.

Checking for a Faulty Drive

If all the cables and disks check out, the problem could be in the drive. If you can, try the drive in another computer with a working disk drive of the same type. If you don't have a spare computer for testing, see whether you can try another drive in its place. You might have to take the computer in to a computer repair shop for testing.

Before you give up on the drive, try a commercial drive-cleaning kit (about $10 to $15 from any computer store), which can help eliminate dust and other contaminants from the drive heads.

Checking for a Problem in the Controller

If you've eliminated every other possibility, the controller could be at fault. If possible, try a different controller in its place, or try it on a different machine. Even if your disk controller is on the motherboard, you should be able to disable it and try a different controller—but only after you've disabled the onboard controller. To disable it, you'll probably have to reset a jumper on the motherboard. Some motherboards clearly label the jumper you'll need to switch, such as FDD or FD CNTRL (Intel motherboards are a good example), but others have cryptic labels that you'll need a manual or technical support person to decode.

 T I P Some jumper settings for drives and motherboards are available online. Check the manufacturer's World Wide Web site. You also can visit an online search engine (such as Yahoo! at http://www.yahoo.com) to search keywords related to your disk drive's company (such as Intel or Sony) or device type or topic (such as disk controller or CD-ROM drive).

If you've installed a new drive controller on a PC that already has a controller installed (either on the motherboard or on another card), you might run into a conflict (as viewed in the Device Manager) if the earlier controller isn't properly disabled. Check the jumpers and documentation for the card to make sure it's disabled.

TROUBLESHOOTING

I receive a disk-write error when I try to copy some files to a 360KB floppy disk. What can I do to make Windows 98 copy files to my disk? Disable the 32-bit protected-mode disk drivers by choosing Start, Settings, Control Panel, and double-clicking the System icon. Select the Performance page on the System Properties dialog box. Click File System to display the File System Properties dialog box and select the Troubleshooting page. Click the Disable All 32-Bit Protected-Mode Disk Drivers option. Then click OK twice.

CHAPTER 12

Installing and Configuring CD-ROM and DVD Drives

by Serdar Yegulap

In this chapter

Setting Up Your CD-ROM for Network Use

CD-ROMs are most often used to provide files for a single workstation or server, but it's also common practice to serve out a CD-ROM for network use. A shared CD-ROM will allow other users in your workgroup to access your CD-ROM drive freely as if it were a drive installed on their own systems.

In order to share out a CD, you need to have File and Print Sharing installed on both your Windows 98 machine and whatever other machines will be sharing your CD-ROM. In addition, you both need to have the same network protocols installed as well. LANs traditionally use NetBEUI for file sharing, but TCP/IP also works. Generally, a shared CD-ROM drive will be designated to share out a particular CD-ROM disc, but the disc can be swapped out when no one is connected to the host system.

To enable File and Print Sharing, go to the section entitled "Configuring Network Properties" in Chapter 24, "Setting Up Windows 98 on a Peer-to-Peer Network."

Sharing Out the CD-ROM

Once you have File and Print Sharing enabled, follow these steps to share out a CD-ROM drive to other users on the network.

1. From the Desktop of the computer that has the CD-ROM, double-click the My Computer icon to open it. Note that if you have Active Desktop turned on, or are viewing your desktop and folders as Web pages, Windows 98 will open icons with a single click.

2. Right-click the icon that represents the CD-ROM. Select Sharing. This brings up the Sharing tab of the CD-ROM's Properties sheet (see Figure 12.1).

FIG. 12.1
The CD-ROM Properties sheet.

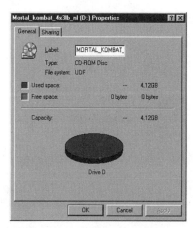

3. Click the Shared As radio button to enable sharing.

4. Click the Share Name text box and type a one-word name to describe the shared CD-ROM. This could be something as simple as the CD-ROM drive letter, which is what the Share Name box is set to by default.

5. Select the Comment field by clicking it and type a descriptive comment for the shared CD-ROM. For instance, you may want to describe which computer that particular CD-ROM belongs to, or the contents of the CD-ROM drive.

6. The Access Type radio button should be set to Read-Only if you want to allow anyone on the network to be able to read the CD-ROM. If you want to enable password protection for access to the CD-ROM (see Figure 12.2), click the Depends on Password radio button.

FIG. 12.2

Setting up sharing on the CD-ROM's Properties page.

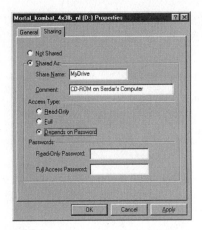

7. To specify a password for the CD-ROM, click in the Read-Only Password box and type in a password. The password will only be echoed to the screen as a series of asterisks.

8. Click OK or Apply to continue.

9. If you have specified a password, you will be prompted to retype the password to confirm it. Retype the password and click OK to continue. If you don't give the right password, you'll be given a "Password you typed is incorrect" message and be asked to retype the password. You can back out by hitting Cancel, which will take you back to the Shared properties sheet.

10. The shared CD-ROM will appear in My Computer with the "shared" symbol on it. This is usually a hand "offering" the CD-ROM to be shared (see Figure 12.3).

Removing a Share on a CD-ROM

Removing a share on a CD-ROM is simple enough. Right-click the CD-ROM icon in Explorer, select Sharing, and then click the Not Shared radio button in the Sharing tab of the Properties sheet.

> **CAUTION**
>
> Removing a share on a CD-ROM drive will delete all share names, comments, and passwords associated with that CD-ROM drive. If you place a new share on the drive, you will have to manually re-enter all of that information.

Part

III

Ch

12

Sharing a CD-ROM can slow your system down enormously. If you are planning to serve the same files to many different computers at once, you may fare better by copying the contents of the CD-ROM to a shared hard drive, if you can spare the room.

Another important issue is copyright and licensing. Many software programs are licensed to be used by one user at a time only, and are not supposed to be accessed by multiple users through a share. Check your software's licensing agreement before sharing it out on a CD-ROM.

FIG. 12.3
The shared CD-ROM.

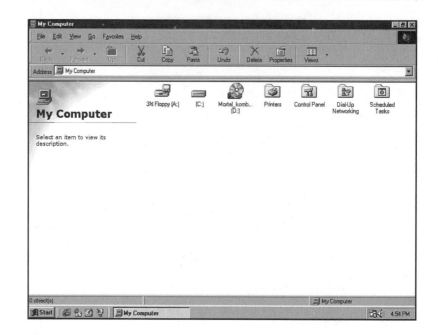

CD-ROM Features

CD-ROMs are generally designed to run without much maintenance or adjustment. However, there are options that can be changed which may enhance performance, especially for SCSI CD-ROMs.

CD-ROM Options

To view the options available for a CD-ROM device, open the System Properties sheet from the Control Panel. You can also do this by right-clicking My Computer and selecting Properties.

In the Device Manager, open up the subtree that contains your CD-ROM device, right-click the device, and select Properties. Choose the Settings tab (see Figure 12.4).

FIG. 12.4
The options available
for a CD-ROM device.

N O T E Not all the options may be available for all CD-ROM drives. Some IDE CD-ROMs do not support all the options that some SCSI CD-ROMs do, for instance. ■

The options available on the Settings page are the following:

■ *Disconnect*. This is generally only supported on SCSI CD-ROMs, and allows the SCSI chain to operate more flexibly and rapidly with the CD-ROM. If this option is checked by default, don't change it or it may degrade performance. Some IDE CD-ROMs also support this option. If this isn't checked and you know your CD-ROM supports it, turn it on, as it will enhance performance on device chains where there are a number of devices that have high data rates.

■ *Sync data transfer*. This option is generally not enabled for CD-ROMs, but is enabled for hard drives and some types of optical discs.

■ *Auto insert notification*. Checking this box enables the CD-ROM to use AutoPlay when there has been a change of disc. (This allows programs that automatically run upon the insert of a CD-ROM to be enabled.)

■ *Removable/Int 13 Unit*. These options are not enabled for CD-ROMs and are reserved for hard drives. They should be grayed out—but if they aren't, don't enable them.

Changing CD-ROM Drive Letters

A CD-ROM gets assigned a drive letter at boot time, depending on what other drives are in the system. If you are adding and removing other fixed or removable drives and want the CD-ROM drive letter to remain fixed—for instance, if you're using applications that require the CD-ROM be assigned a consistent drive letter—you can force a drive-letter assignment.

1. Open the System Properties sheet from either the Control Panel or by right-clicking My Computer and selecting Properties. In the Device Manager, open up the subtree that

Part

III

Ch

12

contains your CD-ROM device. (To expand a subtree, click the "+" symbols in the list next to the CD-ROM.) Right-click the device, and select Properties. Choose the Settings tab (see Figure 12.5).

FIG. 12.5

The settings for a CD-ROM device, with no drive letters assigned.

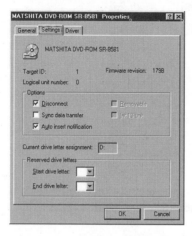

2. The Start Drive Letter and End Drive Letter drop-down lists at the bottom of the Properties sheet (see Figure 12.6) let you choose the first and last valid drive letters you want to allow the CD-ROM to be assigned at boot time. If you want to lock the CD-ROM to a particular drive letter, choose the same letter for both Start and End.

FIG. 12.6

Setting drive letters for a CD-ROM.

3. When you are done, click OK on the Properties sheet for the CD-ROM drive, and then click OK on the System Properties sheet. Reboot to make the changes take effect.

Troubleshooting CD-ROM Drives

CD-ROM drives are designed to need little maintenance or upkeep to work correctly. Like hard drives, they should work reliably once plugged in, configured, and turned on. A good number of the problems inherent in CD-ROM drives have been ironed out thanks to the introduction of CD-ROM drives with consistent, industry-standard interfaces, such as ATAPI/IDE or SCSI. Many of the original problems with CD-ROM drives stemmed from the proprietary interface cards that came with the drives. The hardware or drivers for some often conflicted with other hardware present in the system, or wasn't being loaded properly.

Many of the problems users have with CD-ROM drives can be traced to an incorrect configuration of the CD-ROM drive's interface, whether ATAPI/IDE or SCSI, and all of those possibilities should be exhausted before considering that the drive itself is damaged. Some of the common symptoms of CD-ROM trouble are the following:

- No CD-ROM is readable, or certain CD-ROMs cannot be read reliably.
- Data from the CD-ROM is corrupted.
- CD-ROMs refuse to load and are ejected.
- CD-ROMs spin wildly but do not transfer any data.

Common CD-ROM Problems and Solutions

Many of the problems that arise with CD-ROMs are totally independent of the type of CD-ROM (SCSI, IDE, internal, external). Here is a list of some of the most common reasons for problems and some suggested solutions.

- Make sure the device is getting power. If the CD-ROM is internal, make sure the power connector plugged into the CD-ROM is actually delivering power by plugging into another device, like a hard drive that you know is functional. The same goes for external drives, which frequently use standard three-prong power cords. The cord itself may be damaged or not plugged in properly.
- The pins on both the CD-ROM data connector and the motherboard (or controller card) should not be bent or broken. Pull out the connector on both ends and check it to make sure that no pins are damaged. Bent pins can be put back into position by unbending them *gently and slowly* with a pair of needle-nosed pliers.
- Make sure the signal cable for the CD-ROM is not damaged. Folds or creases in a CD-ROM cable are a possible sign of a break in the cable's internal wiring. If the cable has been crimped or folded for a long time, it should be considered faulty and discarded.
- Make sure you are using the correct width cable. An unkeyed internal IDE cable (see later in this chapter for more about keyed and unkeyed cables) does not have as many wires as an internal SCSI cable, and can be plugged by accident into a SCSI controller. (The reverse can't happen, of course, since SCSI cables are too big to fit into IDE sockets.)

Part
III

Ch
12

■ Over time, the lens of a CD-ROM can accumulate dust and dirt that can cause discs to be misread or appear to be defective. Some drives are equipped with a built-in brush to clean the lens, but many cheaper models don't. However, many computer accessory stores sell a special cleaning disc that comes with a built-in brush or felt pad for this purpose.

CAUTION

Cleaning discs should be used sparingly—more often if the user smokes or works in an environment with a great deal of dust. Too much cleaning can damage the lens irreparably.

■ Make sure the data cable to the CD-ROM is not disconnected or connected backwards. Most CD-ROM data cables are "keyed"—they have a small nub on the side that matches a slot in the CD-ROM cable connector or on the motherboard, preventing the cable from being connected incorrectly.

 Some cables aren't keyed and can be mistakenly connected backwards on the motherboard, controller card, or the CD-ROM. In such cases, the cable will have one of its edges marked in red to indicate which wire goes to pin 1 on both ends. Pin 1 is usually marked with a number or an arrow on both the motherboard and the drive.

Troubleshooting for ATAPI/IDE CD-ROMs

One of the biggest steps towards the acceptance of CD-ROMs as a standard-issue piece of PC equipment was the creation of the ATAPI standard, which allowed CD-ROMs to be plugged into the same controllers that normally handled high-capacity hard drives. This created opportunities for a great many problems as well as conveniences.

ATAPI/IDE CD-ROMs have a host of possible problems that can arise because of their particular design and construction. Following is a list of possible problems and recommended solutions.

■ If you're using the CD-ROM with another device on the same device chain, either as a master or a slave, make sure both devices are properly designated as master and slave. If that doesn't work, try installing the CD-ROM on its own device chain. Some cheaper brands of CD-ROMs or hard drives do not cooperate well with other devices on the same chain, whether or not they are configured according to specifications. In order to cut corners, some manufacturers write firmware for the devices that don't completely comply with proper standards. This saves some cost, and the drive generally works properly by itself, but can sometimes malfunction in conjunction with other drives.

■ If you are using an on-board IDE controller, make sure that it supports CD-ROM drives in the controller's BIOS. Generally, the BIOS will contain a section that governs which devices are booted and in what order (A:, C:, network, and so on) If a CD-ROM isn't one of those choices, there's a good chance the controller doesn't support CD-ROMs at all. The best bet to figure out what's supported is to set the controller to autodetect what devices are plugged into it. If it doesn't support CD-ROMs, the controller will report back that nothing's plugged in.

■ Be wary of IDE controllers that are installed on sound cards, or that come on their own standalone adapters. They are generally of very low quality, and often conflict with other hardware installed in the system, including any on-board IDE adapters. If you can use an existing IDE adapter for an IDE CD-ROM, do so, and disable any auxiliary IDE controllers.

Troubleshooting for SCSI CD-ROMs

SCSI CD-ROMs are a little more flexible than IDE CD-ROMs. They can be set up externally far more easily than IDE CD-ROMs, can be configured far more flexibly and in conjunction with many more devices than IDE CD-ROMs, and can theoretically support much higher transfer rates. That doesn't make them immune to trouble—if anything, it makes them susceptible to a whole slew of unique problems.

Here's a list of common troubleshooting checkpoints to go through if you encounter problems with SCSI CD-ROMs, plus some possible solutions.

■ Check the termination of the SCSI chain. The devices on either end of a SCSI chain should be terminated, with all other devices in between un-terminated. Termination of a CD-ROM is usually controlled by setting a jumper, or by adding or removing resistor packs from the CD-ROM's on-board circuitry.

■ Make sure the cable for the CD-ROM is not inordinately long. The total length of any CD-ROM chain should never be more than 15 feet, and even that may be too long for chains with several high-speed devices. The longer the chain, the greater the noise and interference problems that arise in longer SCSI chains.

■ External drive users: If you're using a series of cables dovetailed together with adapters, get a single, shorter cable with the proper connectors on each end. Spliced cables are prone to errors and noise.

■ Make sure the correct driver is being loaded for the correct SCSI controller. Some manufacturers, such as Adaptec or BusLogic, have many different controllers with slightly different names, and it is possible to get them confused. Some may even successfully load and be identified as the right driver, but may not operate correctly with hardware.

■ Check the device number of the CD-ROM to make sure it is not conflicting with other hardware in the device chain or the controller itself. The device number is either set with a jumper (for internal drives), or a dial or selector switch (for external drives). Look on the back or the underside of the unit for the jumpers or selector for setting the device number. Take inventory of all SCSI devices, *including the controller itself (which is usually set to device #7)*, and make sure you're not using a conflicting device number.

■ A good way to check if the CD-ROM is being located on the device chain at all is to use the setup BIOS on board the SCSI controller, if the controller has one. This is usually accessed by pressing a control key during system startup; consult your controller's documentation for details. Within the setup BIOS, you can scan the SCSI chain to get a list of all currently attached devices. If the CD-ROM doesn't show up, there may be a connectivity problem.

Installing DVD-ROM Support in Windows 98

Windows 98 adds rudimentary DVD-ROM support "out of the box," meaning that it's possible to pop in a DVD-ROM drive and read data from discs. Installing the DVD-ROM drive itself follows the same pattern as installing a conventional CD-ROM. once connected to its host adapter, IDE or SCSI, Windows 98 detects it automatically and installs basic support for the DVD-ROM drive directly from its repository of drivers on the Windows 98 CD-ROM.

N O T E The name of the device driver on the DVD-ROM should not be "CD-ROM"; if it is, the system has misdetected the device and a proper DVD-ROM driver should be installed, as detailed later. ■

DVD-ROM support for Windows 98 is divided into two separate classes of drivers: support for the drive itself, which is mostly automatic, and support for the audio/video decoder card that is frequently sold with the drive. (Buying a DVD-ROM drive alone does not give you the ability to play back DVD-based movies; the decoder card handles that job.)

The decoder board is installed in much the same manner as a sound or video capture board. Each board has its own peculiar setup procedure, provided by the manufacturer, but there are some common elements: the drive for the decoder card can be found in the "Sound, video and game controllers" branch of the Device Manager (see Figure 12.7), and from there it's possible to update the driver, change its settings, or remove it entirely.

FIG. 12.7
A DVD-ROM decoder board as listed in Device Manager.

N O T E Unless you're specifically instructed to do so by your DVD-ROM drive's documentation, or if you are attempting to use the DVD-ROM in conjunction with a decoder card, don't try replacing the default DVD-ROM driver. The default driver is designed to support all the basic functions of a DVD-ROM drive built to specification. ▉

Installing Support for DVD-ROM Decoder Boards in Windows 98

Once the drive itself has been installed in your computer, the next step is to install the DVD-ROM decoder board, if one has been provided with the drive. The board allows you to decode DVD-ROM discs that have multimedia on them—video, audio, or both—and play them back on your computer, or on a TV. Since the decoding is handled entirely in hardware, the load on the CPU is minimal, and the computer can be used for other, processor-intensive activities without degrading playback performance.

The components used in the decoder board to perform the image and sound decompression are the same ones used in commercial-quality DVD-ROM players, and afford the same kinds of features for titles that support them: multiple audio channels, subtitles, multiple camera angles, menuing, chapter stops, supplementary materials, and so on. Many decoder boards also support Dolby Digital 5.1 sound decoding, but this can only be played back through a stereo amplifier that supports discrete 5.1 sound.

Types of Decoder Boards

Decoder cards come in two basic varieties: pass-through and substitution. A pass-through decoder card takes the output from the system's existing graphics adapter, whatever it may be, and uses a "chroma-key" system to layer in the output from the DVD-ROM board. This is done by using a specific color on the display—usually a bright pink—as an indicator to the DVD-ROM decoder board where to layer in the video playback window. A cable from the video card plugs into the decoder board, and the monitor plugs into an outgoing port on the decoder board as well.

Pass-through boards have a number of advantages. If they malfunction, the main graphics system in the computer will still continue to work, because they don't replace the functionality of the graphics card, just add to it.

Pass-through boards can also be used in a slightly wider variety of computers. They are usually sold as ISA cards, not PCI, and therefore can be used in machines that do not have anything more sophisticated than a 16-bit ISA bus.

On the downside, the quality of the layered video is strongly dependent on the quality of the board's manufacture and its isolation potential, because the image is being converted to analog before being layered in and can pick up noise and distortions along the way.

A substitution card uses a decoder card that is also a graphics board, and substitutes for the existing graphics board in the computer. The graphics hardware and the decoder hardware work far more closely together, and the result is usually cleaner and of higher quality than a pass-through board. Also, a substitution card only takes one slot instead of two.

There are drawbacks to substitution boards. Because most of them are PCI, not ISA, they will not work in older systems at all. Also, their construction often prevents them from being used in Windows NT—not the most critical drawback for Windows 98 users, but people who are planning to upgrade or put a symmetrical install of Windows NT on the same computer should be aware of this, and make sure the hardware they will be using can support NT if they need it.

Decoder Board Installation Issues

There are some other basic issues with installing a DVD-ROM decoder board that should be observed:

- Place the decoder board as far away from other boards as possible. If you're using a pass-through board, place it in either the far-left or far-right slot, with the display board as far from it and other boards as possible. This is to minimize crosstalk and noise from other boards, especially high-frequency boards like network cards.

- Don't use any cabling other than the type provided by the manufacturer to connect a pass-through board to the video card. Some varieties are specially grounded and shielded to reduce noise, and some are custom-designed connectors. Don't attempt to wire your own connector.

- Some decoder boards feature an RCA output that sends a high-frequency digital signal to a Dolby Digital decoder. This connector should not be confused with the RCA output for a TV. If you attempt to connect a TV or VCR to this port, you may damage the TV.

- Some decoder boards have an RCA output for connecting to a TV or a VCR. For the best possible results, use high-grade, videophile-style RCA cable, such as Monster brand. These cables use much stronger shielding and higher-quality components than the low-end type that are often sold with decoder boards. A well-shielded RCA cable will reduce noise and distortion from the computer itself.

- Also use high-quality cables to connect the decoder board's output to your sound card, especially if you're using an external connection (for example, routing a cable from the outside of the board to the sound card's auxiliary-in jack).

Installing Plug and Play Decoder Boards

This is a basic set of instructions for installing Plug and Play compatible decoder boards under Windows 98.

1. Check the instructions and ensure that you have enough IRQs, memory addresses, and DMAs free. Plug and Play hardware generally does not have extremely rigid require-ments, but will require that you have one of a set or IRQs free, such as 3,5,7,9 or 11. The Plug and Play subsystem cannot assign addresses already in use by non-Plug and Play

hardware, or which has been reserved for other system functions. If the needed address or IRQ is being used by another piece of Plug and Play hardware, it will be reassigned.

 TIP One easy way to determine what IRQs are free is to open up the Device Manager, double-click the Computer icon in the hardware list, and then look at the View Resources tab. You can view available resources by IRQ, DMA, I/O port and memory address (see Figure 12.8).

FIG. 12.8

The resources list in Device Manager.

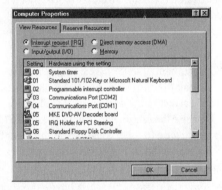

2. Install the decoder board in your system. Follow the product documentation for the details on this procedure. You may need to set a jumper on the board that tells the board to use Plug and Play standards for IRQ/memory address assignments. Also make sure that the video connections are set up correctly for a pass-through board. If you are using a non-pass-through board on a machine with integrated video, check to make sure that the integrated video subsystem does not need to be disabled through a jumper or BIOS setting. Some systems have a jumper or BIOS setting that reserves an IRQ for the on-board video system; disabling this allows the new video card to use the IRQ freely.

3. Power up the system and observe the boot process carefully. Plug and Play-compatible systems will usually provide a quick list of Plug and Play devices at boot-time, along with the IRQs and memory addresses of them. PCI devices generally have far less trouble being assigned a proper IRQ and memory space than ISA devices.

4. If the decoder board isn't being assigned an address or IRQ, you may need to reset the Plug and Play configurator. This is generally done through BIOS. Most BIOSes have a setting in the subpage of the BIOS that handles Plug and Play devices which reads "Reset Plug-and-Play settings" or "Reset device settings." When this is reset, the computer is forced to re-poll all Plug and Play devices and assign them fresh IRQs and memory addresses.

5. Once the decoder board is successfully assigned an address and IRQ, Windows 98 should bring up a dialog box during the boot process that informs the user of the new device, and attempts to install a driver from either the Windows 98 CD-ROM or a provided disk. Insert the disk that contains the decoder card's drivers and type A:\ as the pathname for the needed drivers.

Part

III

Ch

12

6. You may need to reboot before the changes take effect. Check the Device Manager to make sure the decoder card's driver is loaded and running without problems. If the device loads properly but still does not work, you may need to contact the manufacturer for an updated or Windows 98-specific driver.

Installing Non-Plug and Play Decoder Boards

Non-Plug and Play decoder boards need to supervised far more closely during installation than Plug and Play boards. The following instructions are meant as a general guideline for installing non-Plug and Play decoders. Follow the documentation for your board for details not provided here.

1. Check the decoder card's documentation for which IRQs, DMAs, and memory addresses will be needed to install the card, and then verify that the same addresses and ports are free. As described earlier, in the section on installing Plug and Play decoder boards, you can use the Device Manager to verify what is and isn't in use in your system. You may need to reassign hardware to other locations in the meantime by changing the hardware's jumpers (if it's a plug-in board) or BIOS settings (if it's a piece of integrated hardware, like a COM: port).

2. Set the board to the appropriate addresses and then power the system down and install the decoder board. Follow the board's documentation for properly connecting the speakers and video cabling.

3. Power up the system. If during boot you get a "Configuration error" message or "Device conflict" message or something similar, continue booting the system, but pay attention to any additional error messages that may indicate with what the device may be conflicting. Also check the Device Manager for additional details. If the system doesn't boot at all, the decoder board is probably conflicting with something critical to the system—such as the timer or keyboard IRQ—and needs to be set to another memory address or IRQ.

4. Go to the Add New Hardware Wizard, which is available through the Control Panel. Activate it and click Next to allow the wizard to search for Plug and Play devices. Your decoder card will probably not be found during this stage, but if it is, supply the appropriate drivers from the manufacturer's disks.

5. The next stage of the wizard allows you to supply drives for non-Plug and Play devices. The fastest way to proceed is to supply the needed driver and let Windows automatically attempt to activate the driver. Click No, I Want To Select the Hardware From a List, and then click Next.

6. Select Sound, Video and Game Controllers from the Hardware Types list, and then click Next.

7. Click Have Disk and then supply a path to the disk that contains your drivers (usually A:\).

8. Select the device you are installing from the Models list. If your disk has drivers for more than one piece of hardware, make sure you select the correct one down to the letter. Click OK. Windows 98 will then copy the driver from the disk and install it.

9. Reboot to start the driver. Check the Device Manager to ensure that it's working correctly.

> **N O T E** These instructions also apply to boards being used in machines that don't have Plug and Play support, or for boards that have Plug and Play support disabled. Most ISA Plug and Play boards allow you to disable Plug and Play and hard-assign an address through jumpers or software. ■

DVD-ROM Playback and Device Issues

When you install the DVD-ROM decoder board in your computer, the installation software will also place one or more MCI (Media Control Interface) drivers into the Multimedia Devices list. You can see this list by double-clicking the Multimedia icon in the Control Panel and then selecting the Devices tab. If you expand the Media Control Devices subtree, you should see drivers that relate to your DVD-ROM playback hardware.

The exact types of driver vary, but generally there will be one driver for the DVD-ROM system itself and another driver to interface with the decoder card for MPEG decoding.

Adjusting DVD-ROM Device Settings

If you want to edit the driver's settings, there is generally a utility provided by the manufacturer for this, but you also can usually make changes to the driver's settings by selecting the driver from the Multimedia Devices list, clicking Properties, and then clicking Settings in the driver's property sheet. The adjustments you can make will vary enormously from one driver to another, but an example of what you may see can be seen in Figure 12.9. This example is taken from the Creative Labs DVD-ROM kit.

Part

III

Ch

12

FIG. 12.9

Sample settings for the DVD-ROM decoder hardware.

DVD-ROM Issues

DVD-ROMs and conventional CD-ROMs are different in many ways, and some of those differences are worth mentioning here as "dos and don'ts."

■ Don't attempt to play a DVD-ROM in a conventional CD-ROM drive. The CD-ROM drive will not be able to sync up properly and may even damage itself trying out different rotational speeds to force synchronization.

■ Treat DVD-ROMs with greater care than conventional CD-ROMs. The information is packed approximately four times more densely on the average DVD-ROM than it is on the average CD-ROM. Scratches, dust, and dirt will make playback much more difficult. If you need to clean a DVD-ROM, wipe from center to edge with a chamois cloth, and use only chemical cleaners marketed specifically for CD-ROMs or DVD-ROMs. Do not use soap as this will leave a film on the DVD-ROM surface.

■ The information on a multimedia DVD-ROM title can be seen through Explorer, and it may even be possible to copy the files off onto another drive. Don't do it. You'll be violating copyright laws, and you may also discover that the copied files won't play back correctly. There are numerous copy-protection safeguards built into the DVD-ROM and decoder hardware to prevent this.

■ Most DVD-ROM multimedia titles, such as movies, come with a "region code" that tells the DVD-ROM player whether or not it's legal to be played in certain areas of the world. For instance, titles marketed in North America are marked as region 1, and cannot be played on players sold in Europe or Asia. The same applies for discs sold in Europe or Asia and played here. The reason for this is to properly enforce copyright restrictions, since software is generally licensed and not sold. If you are having trouble playing back a particular title and receiving error codes to the effect that the "region isn't valid," or something similar, check to make sure you're not playing a disc that's marked for another region. Most DVD-ROM drives and decoders sold in the U.S. are hard-wired to only play region 1 or regionless discs. To determine what region the disc is sold for, look on the packaging for a small globe icon with a number superimposed on it and a text description of the region.

N O T E Many titles sold in Hong Kong or Japan are now being coded without region markers and will play anywhere. Some American titles are also regionless, but they are generally few and far between, and are usually sold by smaller independent companies that are trying to maximize profits. Generally, any title from a major company (especially a major movie company) will have region coding. ■

■ DVD-ROM drives and CD-ROM discs don't mix. DVD-ROM drives use a markedly different laser diode than conventional CD-ROM drives. The wavelength of the beam emitted by this diode makes it difficult for them to read CD-ROMs, and in fact can damage CD-ROMs or make them unuseable. As a rule of thumb, don't use CD-ROMs in DVD-ROM drives.

CHAPTER 13

Setting Up Backup Systems

by Rob Tidrow

In this chapter

Installing Microsoft Backup

Microsoft has included a backup application along with Windows 98 that allows excellent integration with the operating system. This backup software works with the following media:

- Hard and floppy disk drives
- Network drives
- Various parallel, SCSI, and IDE/ATAPI devices, including QIC-40, QIC-80, QIC-80 Wide, QIC-3010, QIC-3010 Wide, QIC-3020, QIC-3020 Wide, TR1, TR2, TR3, TR4, DAT (DDS1&2), DC 600, 8MM, and DLT.

Several backup drives and media are available that Microsoft Backup does not support—notably, some DAT tape backup systems (Backup supports DDS1&2 DAT media). Although Microsoft Backup for Windows doesn't support these drives, manufacturers will provide Windows backup software that works with their drives. Usually, this software comes bundled with the drive or can be obtained from the manufacturer for an additional cost or the cost of downloading it from the World Wide Web.

After you install your internal tape backup drive by following the manufacturer's instructions or connect the external tape drive to the parallel port, you are ready to load the backup software. Windows' default installation does not load Microsoft Backup for Windows. However, you easily can install this accessory by using the following steps:

1. Choose Start, Settings, Control Panel.
2. Double-click the Add/Remove Programs icon.
3. In the Add/Remove Programs Properties dialog box, select the Windows Setup page.
4. Select System Tools from the Components list box.
5. Click Details to display a list of the default Windows 98 system tools. The tools you currently have installed are marked with a check.
6. Check the box next to Backup to mark it for installation, as shown in Figure 13.1.

FIG. 13.1

Marking Backup for installation.

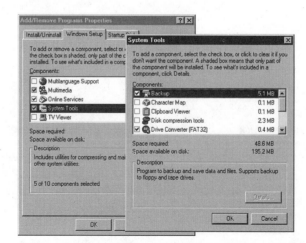

7. Click OK twice. Windows prompts you to insert the appropriate disk or CD-ROM to load the Microsoft Backup for Windows software.

After the backup software is loaded, you can proceed to the next step by letting Microsoft Backup auto-detect your tape-drive system.

Letting Microsoft Backup Detect Tape Hardware

When you run Microsoft Backup for Windows the first time, it attempts to detect the type of backup system you have. Microsoft Backup for Windows supports those media devices listed earlier in the "Installing Microsoft Backup" section.

If your drive type is not listed there, see the next section, "Working with Legacy Backup Systems."

If your tape drive was detected, skip to the section later in this chapter, "Configuring Windows Backup."

Working with Legacy Backup Systems

Some legacy backup systems might not be supported by Microsoft Backup. Many vendors have their own backup software that works with their tape backup systems. Some of the systems listed here do not have Windows backup software, while others do. Check with your tape-drive manufacturer to see whether it has a Windows 98 backup solution or whether its current DOS or Windows backup software works with Windows 98.

DAT Tape Syatems   Most DAT tape backup systems connect to a SCSI interface board in the computer. Microsoft Backup supports DAT DDS1&2 media, but other DAT media devices are available. Windows 98 can detect and install drivers for many SCSI controllers; however, the manufacturer's Windows tape backup software still is required to perform the backup.

If you are using DOS-based tape backup software, Windows 98 prompts you with a warning message telling you to restart Windows 98 in a command-prompt only mode. This action enables older DOS programs that may communicate directly with the hardware to work properly. After you complete a backup using DOS backup software, you can reboot your system back to Windows mode.

Additionally, even if your program does run, you can back up only files and directories that match the DOS format FILENAME.EXT naming convention. While Windows 98 does a good job of shortening long directory names like Data Files down to DATAFI~1, you will not be able to restore the original directory to Data Files after you have backed it up.

Part

III

Ch

13

> **CAUTION**
>
> If you ignore the warnings Windows displays and run your DOS tape backup software in a command-prompt box, you might cause Windows to lock up. In the worst case, your software might appear to work properly, but
>
> *continues*

continued

you might actually be losing data as it writes to the tape. If you run your software in this way, you need to verify every tape you write to ensure that no data has been lost. This is not recommended!

QIC-02 Tape Drives   Many companies have older tape backup hardware that is in its seventh year of active use or is gathering dust on a shelf in the storage room. In either case, you might want to use such a backup system under Windows 98.

QIC-02 tapes run off an interface board that is provided with the tape drive unit. These units typically are external, because the drive mechanism is about the size of a lunch box. It's unlikely that Windows 98 will recognize the QIC-02 adapter card in your system, so you should take care to verify that the settings of the tape drive adapter do not interfere with the settings of the other cards installed in your system.

After you install your hardware, you need to run the software supplied with the tape drive. Because these units typically are pre-Windows, you most likely will use DOS backup software. In addition to the fact that the programs were written in DOS, you should be aware that the backup programs were written for DOS versions that date back 10 years. The programmers did not have to worry about extended memory management or disk-compression software like DriveSpace. Your software may or may not run under Windows running in command-prompt mode.

Additionally, even if your program does run, you can back up only files and directories that match the DOS format FILENAME.EXT naming convention. Although Windows 98 does a good job of shorting long directory names like Data Files down to DATAFI~1, you cannot restore the original directory to Data Files after you have backed it up.

CAUTION

Using tape backup software built before 1990 might not work or might result in strange or unexpected results.

Other Tape Drives   Many other tape drives exist that may or may not have Windows backup software available. In all cases, you should contact the manufacturer to see whether it has a Windows 95 backup solution for your system. This way, you'll know that your system has been tested with Windows 98. If your manufacturer is not working on a Windows 95 version, ask whether it has a Windows 3.1 version that has been tested with Windows 98. Often, Windows 3.1 software works the same under Windows 98.

As the earlier sections on DAT and QIC-02 tape systems mentioned, if you have DOS-based software, run it only in Windows command-prompt mode. Also, remember that long filenames are shortened to fit DOS filename structures.

Configuring Windows Backup

Microsoft Backup can be configured with many options to suit your particular needs. This section shows you how to configure and run Microsoft Backup. The examples used in the following sections are based on a Ditto Easy 800 QIC-WIDE tape device. The actual screens you will see may differ slightly. However, the general information here should closely match your experience.

Creating Backup Jobs

You can back up files to the tape system in several ways. Your backup needs often determine which option you choose. Look at the Properties dialog box in Microsoft Backup to see what these options are. To start Backup, follow these steps:

1. Choose Start, Programs, Accessories, System Tools, Backup. The Microsoft Backup screen appears, as shown in Figure 13.2.

FIG. 13.2
The Welcome screen appears when you start Microsoft Backup.

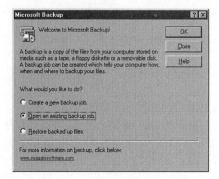

2. From this screen, you can choose one of the following options:
   - *Create a New Backup Job.* Enables you to back up an entire drive or select files you want to back up.
   - *Open an Existing Backup Job.* Enables you to examine an existing backup job you've created in the past. This is the default option.
   - *Restore Backed Up Files.* Enables you to copy backed up files to your PC.
3. These steps show what happens when you select the Create a New Backup Job option. This runs the Backup Wizard.
4. Click OK. The Backup Wizard starts, as shown in Figure 13.3.
5. Select one of the following options:
   - *Back Up My Computer.* Microsoft Backup backs up all files located on your PC's local drive. See the following tip.
   - *Back Up Selected Files, Folders, and Drives.* Microsoft Backup backs up only those files, folders, or drives you specify. After you make a computer back up, this option is probably your best bet for daily or weekly backups. You can set up Backup to

Part
III

Ch

13

back up only those folders or drives on which dynamic data (such as daily reports, spreadsheets, and email) are saved. That way, you always have a backup of your most critical and important data.

FIG. 13.3
The Backup Wizard walks you through the process of backing up your files.

 TIP It's recommended that you back up your entire PC at least once. That way, if you encounter a total system failure at some point, you can use these archived files to restore your PC.

The following steps show how to select specific files, folders, and drives to back up.

6. Click Next. You now need to specify those files, folders, or drives you want to back up. In the What To Back Up window, click the check box next to the item you want to back up, as shown in Figure 13.4. To display the contents of a drive or folder, click the plus (+) sign next to the drive or folder. The contents of a folder are shown in the right window.

 TIP Click the Name, Size, Type, and Modified column headers in the right window to sort files by name, size, type, or modification date.

7. Select the items you want to back up. If you place a check mark next to a drive, the entire drive is selected. However, you can deselect specific folders or files by removing the check mark next to the items you want Backup to specifically ignore.

8. Click Next. A Backup Wizard screen asks what files to back up, as shown in Figure 13.5. This might sound redundant (see step 7), but it's not. This screen asks whether you want to back up all files you've selected, regardless of whether you previously backed them up. Or, do you want to back up only new files and those files that have changed since your last backup session? The idea behind this is to avoid wasting time backing up files that haven't changed since your last backup.

9. Select All Selected Files or New and Changed Files, depending on your needs.

10. Click Next. In the Where to Back Up drop-down list, select the destination of the back up job, as shown in Figure 13.6. Your backup device is listed in this drop-down list, along with File. If your device is not listed, install it using the general steps for installing

hardware devices in Chapter 5, "Installing and Configuring New Hardware and Software." If you have multiple devices installed, they all show up on the Where to Back Up drop-down list.

FIG. 13.4
You need to specify the drives, folders, or files you want to back up by placing a check mark next to them.

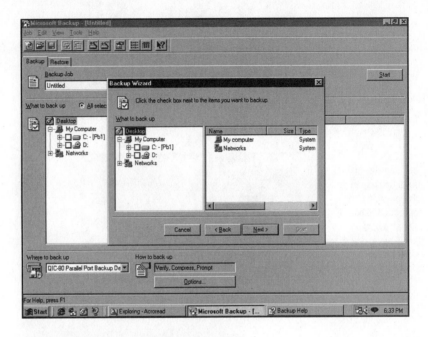

FIG. 13.5
Sometimes you'll want to back up all files, regardless of whether these files already are included in a backup set.

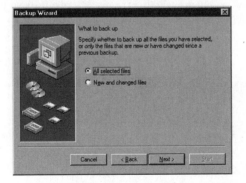

Part
III

Ch
13

N O T E The File option on the Where to Back Up drop-down list enables you to back up items to a file stored on a local, floppy, or network drive (even an Internet drive, if you have access to one). If you select this option, another drop-down list appears in which you need to enter a filename for the backup file. See Figure 13.7. The default extension is `.qic`, but you can add your own extension if desired. The following steps assume that you select a backup destination other than the File option. ▪

FIG. 13.6

Select the destination of your backup job from this screen.

FIG. 13.7

Selecting File enables you to back up to a drive or device that is not formatted specifically as a backup media, such as a shared network drive or a removable hard drive.

11. Click Next. You now can choose whether to have Microsoft Backup compare original files with backed up files to ensure that they back up properly. See Figure 13.8. You also can choose to compress backup files to reduce the amount of space the backup files consume. By default, both these options are selected.

FIG. 13.8

You should keep the two options shown on this dialog box enabled for most of your backup jobs.

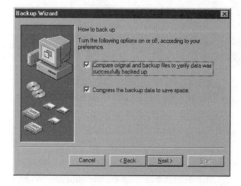

Both of the preceding options are good ideas to select. By verifying backed up data as the backup set is being created, you can have some assurance that your files will not be corrupted on the backup set.

The downside to enabling one or both of these options is the time it takes to create the backup job. In some cases, the time is doubled or even tripled, depending on the size of individual files and the drive's I/O capabilities. Likewise, the time it takes to restore a compressed backup job usually is doubled, because Backup first must uncompress the data before copying it to your local drive.

CAUTION

Data compression can be estimated only over a broad range of file types. For average users, this will approximate the 2:1 compression that most tape-system manufacturers advertise. However, you might not get a high compression ratio if you back up these types of files:

- Graphics files with the GIF or JPEG formats
- Compressed archives, such as ZIP, LZH, PAK, and ARJ files
- Large numbers of EXE files

12. Click Next. Name the backup job, or select a name from the drop-down list, as shown in Figure 13.9. Backup jobs can have up to 130 characters in their names, including spaces. If you choose a name from the drop-down list, the previous backup job will be overwritten if a job by that same name appears on the storage media (such as a tape) you're now using.

FIG. 13.9

Be sure to specify a new name or use a different storage media if you do not want to overwrite old backup jobs.

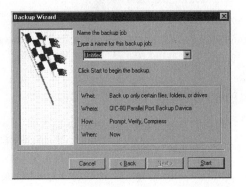

Part III Ch 13

N O T E Be descriptive when naming files. If you have a data folder named Accounting Data, for example, you might want to name your set **Accounting Data - Full Backup** if you are performing a full backup. Try to avoid set names such as Data, Tape Backup, Stuff, or Files, because these are not very descriptive.

13. Click Start to begin the backup process. The Backup Progress dialog box opens to show you the status of the backup job, as shown in Figure 13.10. If you need to insert a storage media into your backup device, Windows prompts you to do so now, as shown in Figure 13.11.

FIG. 13.10

Watch the Backup Progress dialog box to see the status of your backup job.

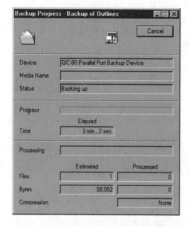

FIG. 13.11

If a storage media is not in your backup device, you are prompted to insert one.

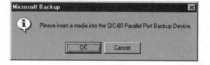

When your backup job completes, you receive a message telling you the job is finished. Click OK. Click OK again to remove the Backup Progress dialog box.

If you want to create another backup job but not use the Backup Wizard as shown in the preceding steps, perform the following steps:

1. Choose Job, New.
2. Select All Selected Files or New and Changed Files on the Backup tab (see Figure 13.12).
3. Select the drives, folders, or files you want to add to the new backup job.
4. From the Where to Backup Up drop-down list (it's located at the bottom of the Backup tab), select the destination (such as a tape backup media) for the backup job.
5. Choose Job, Options to display the Backup Job Options dialog box, as shown in Figure 13.13. From here, you can set options that affect your new backup job. Some of these options are available when running the Backup Wizard. Others, however, can be set only through this dialog box. Set options for your new job. The following section, "Setting Backup Job Options," describes each of these options in more detail.

FIG. 13.12
You use the Backup tab to set up new backup jobs.

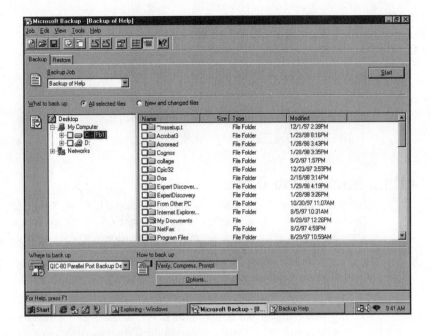

FIG. 13.13
You can configure backup job options using this dialog box.

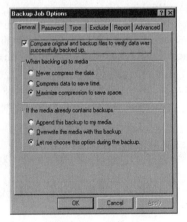

6. Click OK to close the Backup Job Options dialog box.

7. Choose Job, Save, to display the Save Backup Job As dialog box, as shown in Figure 13.14.

8. Name the new backup job (up to 130 characters) in the Job Name field. By default, the job's name is Untitled.

9. Click Save. The new name now appears in the Backup Job drop-down list on the Backup tab.

10. Click Start to run the new backup job.

Part
III

Ch
13

FIG. 13.14
Enter a new job name in
the Save Backup Job As
dialog box.

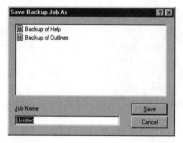

Setting Backup Job Options

All backup jobs can use the same backup job settings. However, if you plan to create full
backup sets on a weekly or monthly basis, and make daily backups of new or changed files, you
might want to have different job settings for these different types of jobs.

You can specify job options by choosing Job, Options (or clicking the Job Options toolbar
button). The Backup Job Options dialog box appears. Refer to Figure 13.14. On the General
tab, you can change the following settings:

- *Compare Original and Backup Files to Verify Data Was Successfully Backed Up.* This
  option commonly is used to make sure that the files copied to the tape match the files on
  the hard drive. Of course, you would think that they always would, because you just
  finished the backup operation; however flaws in the tape media might go undetected
  when you are saving the files. Select this option if you are uncertain about the quality of
  your tape media or if you are using a tape cartridge for the first time.

 TIP You always should choose to verify your backups after you have completed a full backup of your
system. Although it will take twice as long to complete the entire operation, you can rely on the integrity
of your system backup.

- *When Backing Up to Media.* Use these options to specify whether you want to compress
  backed up data:
  - *Never Compress the Data.* Tells Microsoft Backup not to compress data in the
    selected job.
  - *Compress Data to Save Time.* Compresses files, but not to their maximum com-
    pression rate. By choosing this option, you can partially compress files to save
    media space.
  - *Maximize Compression to Save Space.* Compresses files to their maximum com-
    pression rate. When you choose this option, your backup job will take longer to
    create than if you choose the preceding two options.
- *If the Media Already Contains Backups.* This set of options tells Microsoft Backup how to
  handle media that already contains backup jobs:
  - *Append This Backup to My Media.* The new backup job is appended to the media
    after the last backup job on the media.

- *Overwrite the Media with This Backup.* The new backup job replaces the existing backup job on the media. This option is handy if you have to recycle tape media for daily backup jobs. If you don't plan your backup jobs carefully, however, you might overwrite archived data that is no longer on your local drive. If this happens, the data is lost forever.
- *Let Me Choose This Option During the Backup.* Enables you to select one of the preceding two options when you run the backup job.

On the Password tab, you can password-protect your backup jobs, as shown in Figure 13.15. This is handy if the data you're backing is sensitive and there is a possibility that others may have access to your media. If you don't password-protect your backup jobs, there is no barrier for another user to use Microsoft Backup to restore your files on their systems.

FIG. 13.15
Be sure to remember the password you create for your backup jobs, or you will not be able to restore files copied to the backup set.

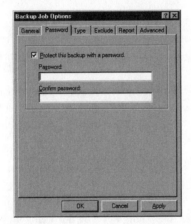

To set a password, enable the Protect This Backup with a Password check box. Enter a password in the Password field, and type it again in the Confirm Password field.

On the Type tab, you can specify the type of backup to make, as shown in Figure 13.16.

FIG. 13.16
You can specify the type of backup job to create using the Type tab.

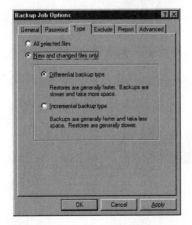

Part
III

Ch
13

The options on the Type page follow:

- *All Selected Files.* Copies all selected files during the backup job, regardless of whether they have changed since the last time you backed up your system. This option can take a snapshot of your system as it is right now.

- *New and Changed Files Only.* Use this option to specify a differential or incremental backup type:

  - *Differential Backup Type.* Specifies that only the files that have changed since the last All Selected Files backup operation should be backed up.

  - *Incremental Backup Type.* Specifies that only the files that have changed since the last backup operation are copied to tape. This makes the backup go much faster, because few files are changed from week to week under typical circumstances.

N O T E Windows keeps track of which files you have modified since the last backup by using the Archive flag on each file. You can see how Windows stores this by right-clicking a file in Explorer and choosing Properties. The Archive check box indicates whether the file has been changed since the last backup.

When you perform a full backup, the Archive flag for every file is turned off when it is copied to tape. When you perform an incremental backup, the backup software searches your files for the Archive flag and copies only those files with that flag turned on. After the changed files have been saved on the tape, the Archive flag is turned off.

On the Exclude tab, you can specify the file types you want to exclude from the backup job, as shown in Figure 13.17. This is handy if you don't want to back up a specific type of file, such as Windows system files, in a backup job. If you back up all your data files, for example, you might not want to include .sys files or similar files. This way, you don't clog up your backup sets with file types you don't want to archive.

FIG. 13.17

You might want to exclude certain file types from your backup job using the Exclude tab.

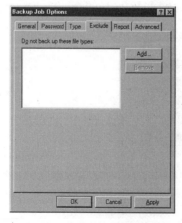

Click Add to display the Add Exclude dialog box, as shown in Figure 13.18. From this dialog box, select a file type in the Registered Type window and click OK. You also can enter a type not shown in the Registered Type window in the Custom Type field and click OK. The file types selected are displayed in the Do Not Back Up These File Types window on the Exclude tab. Click Remove to delete a file type from the Exclude tab.

FIG. 13.18

Use the Add Exclude dialog box to specify those files you do not want backed up.

On the Report tab, you can choose items to be included in a backup job report, as shown in Figure 13.19. These reports can be viewed or printed by choosing Tools, Report from the Microsoft Backup menu bar. The items available on this tab are straightforward enough that they do not need to be explained in detail.

FIG. 13.19

The Report tab enables you to specify the items you want included in the backup jobs report.

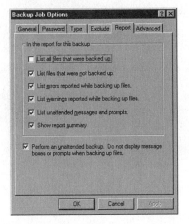

On the Advanced tab, you can select whether to have the Windows Registry backed up with your backup job, as shown in Figure 13.20. When you enable the Back Up Windows Registry check box, the Registry is backed up automatically when the Windows folder is selected to be backed up.

FIG. 13.20

You should back up the Registry if you need to restore your entire system at some point.

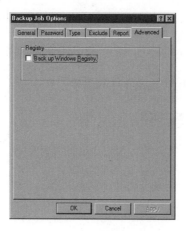

N O T E When you create a Full System Backup set, Microsoft Backup automatically includes a copy of your Registry files. *Registry files* include detailed information that holds the configuration data for running Windows. ▦

After you select the options for your backup, click OK to save your settings.

Restore Options

After you create a backup job, you might need to restore the files on that backup set. To access the Restore option settings, follow these steps:

1. Select the Restore tab in Microsoft Backup, as shown in Figure 13.21.

FIG. 13.21

The Restore tab shows the backup jobs contained on a selected media type.

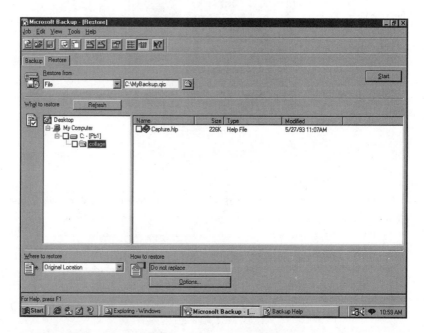

2. Select the media type from which you want to restore a back job from the <u>R</u>estore From drop-down list.

3. Choose <u>V</u>iew, <u>R</u>efresh (or click the Refresh button) to refresh the Restore tab view.

4. Click <u>Y</u>es when asked whether you want to refresh the current view. The backup jobs for the selected media appear in the Wh<u>a</u>t to Restore area.

5. Select the drives, folders, or files you want to restore.

6. From the <u>W</u>here to Restore drop-down list, select the destination for the restored files.

7. Click <u>O</u>ptions to modify restore options. These options are described in the following section, "Setting Restore Options."

8. Click OK to save your option settings.

9. Click <u>S</u>tart to restore the selected files. You are requested to insert the media required to restore the backed up files.

When the restore finishes, a message displays reporting that the operation was completed. Click OK. Click OK again to close the Restore Progress dialog box.

TROUBLESHOOTING

I can't see the tape drive from within Microsoft Backup for Windows. You might not be using a supported tape drive unit. Check the list of supported media in the "Installing Microsoft Backup" section. If you have some other tape drive, you need to use the manufacturer's backup software.

Setting Restore Options

You can modify the restore options by choosing <u>J</u>ob, <u>O</u>ptions or clicking the <u>O</u>ptions button on the Restore tab. The Restore Options dialog box appears, as shown in Figure 13.22.

FIG. 13.22

The Restore Options dialog box includes a few options for restoring backup jobs.

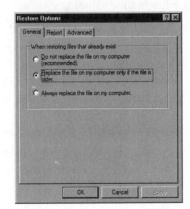

On the General tab, choose one of the following options:

- *Do Not Replace the File on My Computer.* Enables you to protect any data that you have on your hard drive from being overwritten by the files being restored from media.

- *Replace the File on My Computer Only If the File Is Older.* Overwrites files on your hard drive only if they are older than the files that are being restored from media.

- *Always Replace the File On My Computer.* Overwrites files on your hard drive with files on the restored media.

The Report and Advanced tabs include settings identical to those discussed in the "Setting Backup Job Options" section, earlier in this chapter.

Click OK to save the backup job's restore options.

Setting Microsoft Backup Preferences

Along with the options you can set for backup and restore jobs, you also can set three preferences for Microsoft Backup. You can display the Preferences dialog box by choosing Tools, Preferences, as shown in Figure 13.23.

FIG. 13.23

You can set Microsoft Backup options from the Preferences dialog box.

From the Preferences dialog box, you can select the following options:

- *Show Startup Dialog When Microsoft Backup Is Started.* Displays the Microsoft Backup screen each time Microsoft Backup starts. Refer to Figure 13.2.

- *Back Up or Restore the Registry When Backing Up or Restoring the Windows Directory.* Instructs Microsoft Backup to automatically back up your computer's Registry when you select to back up the Windows folder. You can modify this setting for each backup job by using the Backup Job Options dialog box. Refer to Figure 13.20.

- *Show the Number and Size of Files Before Backing Up, Restoring and Comparing Data.* Displays a message box showing you the estimated number of files that will be backed up or restored, as well as the estimated time that a job may take.

Creating Routines for Backing Up Standalone Computers and Networks

When choosing to back up your local workstation, you should set up a rotation of tapes to handle both full-system backups as well as incremental file backups. If you can afford it (in terms of time and economics), you should perform a full backup each time you run Microsoft Backup. However, if this is not a possibility, you should perform full backups on a periodic basis. A full system backup might occur only once per month or possibly as frequently as once per week. Incremental file backups can occur weekly (if you are performing full backups monthly) or daily (if your full backups are performed weekly).

The frequency of your backups depends on the usage of your machine to store data. If you store most of your data on a network server that is backed up by a computer-operations staff, you might find that your backups can occur quarterly. If you store your company's critical data on your computer, you might find that daily backups are essential. In either case, it is important that you actually do the backups when you've planned them.

 TIP You should perform a full-system backup at least twice a year or once each quarter. Even if you don't think your files change much in that time period, you will want to have a backup in case of emergencies.

You don't need to back up applications as frequently as the data files that you use on a day-to-day basis. Because applications can readily be reinstalled from the original disks or CD-ROMs, you should be most concerned about saving your data files, which might be difficult to reconstruct if you lose them. Additionally, backing up your applications will take a long time and a lot of room on your tape.

 TIP The My Documents folder, created when you install Windows 98, is intended to store all the files you create on your system. Whether or not you use this folder for this purpose, you should create a special folder in which you store all your data files. Not only does this make finding your data easier, but it also makes the job of backing it up all that much easier.

If your computer is used as a network server for other Windows workstations, or if you want to centralize the backup operations for all the workstations in your workgroup, you will want to set up a procedure for backing up your network. Microsoft Backup can back up other workstations on the network if the computer with the tape-backup drive can access the data on the other systems. You might want to set up some policies (either formally or informally) to ensure that network data can be accessed for backup during the specified times. It could even be as simple as keeping the read-only share password on everyone's local hard drive the same so that the person performing the backup can access the data to be saved to the tape.

 TIP Try to elect (or appoint) someone to maintain the backup rotation for your network. This person might be you, if your computer hosts the tape-backup system.

You should decide on a schedule for when the backups occur. Ideally, backup should happen after business hours when network traffic is light and the computers are not being used. If you plan on scheduling an after-hours backup, set up Task Scheduler to run unattended backups.

If your network data does not fit on one tape, however, you might need to switch tapes when they fill up. If you suspect that your network backups will fill up more than one tape, you might want to stagger which workstations are backed up each night or consider purchasing a larger tape-backup system to handle the larger volume of data.

TROUBLESHOOTING

The tape system I use is supposed to hold 2.5GB on a tape, but sometimes I can only get 1.5GB on one tape. Why? The tape-drive manufacturers often inflate their capacity claims to match an estimated 2:1 compression ratio. Your tape probably can hold only 1.5GB of uncompressed data. If you are experiencing less than a 2:1 compression ratio with the particular files you are backing up, your actual tape capacity is less. Or, the files you are backing up cannot be compressed, such as some graphics files that already are compressed (JPEG/JPG, for example).

You also will want to create a backup set that includes the data directories of the computers on you network. A backup set is essential if you are performing unattended backups and are extremely helpful even if you manually start the backup operation before you leave work.

> ### CAUTION
> If someone is using a file on the network or the file is left open during a network backup, that file will not be saved to tape, because the contents of that file are not accessible to another user while the file is open.

You probably will not want to make a full-system backup of every computer on the network onto a single medium (if the medium is large enough to hold several drives' worth of data). It would be much wiser to make individual full-system backups that you can identify easily if a problem occurs. Your schedule should be a weekly backup of all the data files and a daily backup of only the changed data files. You should have at least one tape for each day of the week and two tapes for alternating full backups. Make sure you buy enough tapes to handle this sort of rotation.

> ### CAUTION
> Do not store all your backup tapes near your computers. If you have a fire and all the tapes are destroyed, what good is your backup system? Keep at least the alternating weekly data backups off-site. If that means that you bring them home with you, then do it. You might save your company by performing this simple procedure.

Getting Your System Back on its Feet with System Recovery

Despite your best maintenance efforts, your system may crash hard enough that a simple recovery becomes impossible. In that case, you have no alternative but to format (or replace) your hard drive and start from scratch. However, that doesn't mean you have to laboriously reinstall Windows 98 and your applications. With some advance planning, you can use the new System Recovery utility to both reinstall Windows 98 and return your hard drive to its pre-crash state.

System Recovery consists of three pieces:

PCRESTOR.BAT: After you format your hard drive, you boot from your startup disk and then run this batch file. PCRESTOR.BAT performs several chores, but its main task is to start the Windows 98 Setup program with various switches and parameters.

MSBATCH.INF: This is an information file that specifies a number of settings and parameters used by Setup. In particular, this file tells Setup to run the System Recover Wizard (see below). When PCRESTOR.BAT starts Setup, it tells the program to use MSBATCH.INF.

System Recovery Wizard: After Windows 98 is reinstalled, this Wizard loads automatically to take you through the rest of the recovery process, including restoring the files from your system backup.

N O T E HOW DOES IT WORK?

How is Setup able to run the System Recovery Wizard automatically? The key (literally!) can be found inside MSBATCH.INF, where you'll find the following settings:

```
[RegistrySettings]
HKLM,%KEY_RUN%,BatchReg1,,"%11%\srw.exe"

[Strings]
KEY_RUN="SOFTWARE\Microsoft\Windows\CurrentVersion\Run"
```

These settings modify the following Registry key:

```
HKEY_LOCAL_MACHINE\Software\Microsoft\Windows\CurrentVersion\Run
```

This key is used to specify programs that run automatically at startup. In this case, the program SRW.EXE—the System Recovery Wizard—is added to the key. ■

Part
III

Ch
13

To use System Recovery successfully, you must assume your machine will crash one day and so make the necessary preparations. Specifically, you must follow these guidelines:

- Create a Windows 98 startup disk.
- Perform a full backup of the hard disk that contains the Windows system files.
- Your main Windows 98 folder must be C:\WINDOWS.

Running System Recovery

System Recovery is one of those tools that you hope you never use. However, if the day does come when your system needs to be recovered, you'll be glad to know that doing so takes just a few steps:

1. Boot your system using the startup disk. Make sure you enable CD-ROM support.

2. Format drive C if you haven't done so already.

3. Insert your Windows 98 CD-ROM.

4. Create a folder named WIN98 on your hard disk and then copy the Windows 98 Setup files (that is, all the files in the WIN98 folder of your Windows 98 CD-ROM) into that folder.

5. In your Windows 98 CD-ROM, head for the folder named \TOOLS\SYSREC and copy PCRESTOR.BAT and MSBATCH.INF to the root folder of the *same* hard disk that you used to create the WIN98 folder in Step 4.

6. In the root folder of your hard disk, run PCRESTOR.BAT and, once you've read the welcome message, press any key. The Windows 98 Setup begins.

7. Once Setup is complete, the System Recovery Wizard loads, as shown in Figure 13.24. The initial dialog box offers an overview of the process, so click Next >. System Recovery prompts you to enter your name and company name.

FIG. 13.24

The System Recovery Wizard takes you through the process of restoring your system to its pre-crash state.

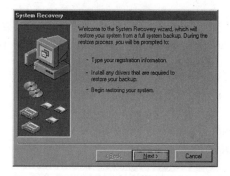

8. Enter your name and (optionally) your company name, and then click Next >. System Recovery lets you know that it is about to restore your system.

9. Insert the backup media that contains your full system backup.

10. In the final Wizard dialog box, click Finish. System Recovery launches Microsoft Backup.

11. Use Backup to restore your files. (Make sure you choose to overwrite all files.) When Backup asks if you want to restore the Registry and the hardware and software settings within the Registry, make sure you select Yes.

12. When the restore process is done, Backup will ask if you want to restart. Click Yes and, when Windows 98 restarts, your system will be completely recovered.

Making System Recovery More Flexible

As you've seen, System Recovery is quite rigid about a few things. For example, it will only reinstall Windows 98 into `C:\WINDOWS`, and it will only install from a hard disk. System Recovery would be a much more useful tool if it enabled you to overcome these and other limitations. However, although Microsoft does not recommend or support customized System Recovery procedures, it *is* possible to improve upon the basic process.

The reason System Recovery is so inflexible is that most of its options are set in advance within the `PCRESTOR.BAT` and `MSBATCH.INF` files. These are just text files, however, and text files can be edited, albeit with a modicum of caution and a nod to common sense. Here are a few techniques you can try:

To reinstall Windows into a different directory: The installation directory is governed by the `InstallDir` setting within the `[Setup]` section of `MSBATCH.INF`. If you prefer to install Windows 98 on drive D, for example, you must modify this setting as follows:

```
InstallDir="D:\Windows"
```

Customizing the network logon: If you're on a network, Setup prompts you to log on to the network during the reinstall. However, System Recovery uses a generic username of "System Recovery" and a generic workgroup name of "WORKGROUP," which is also used as the logon domain. System Recovery also sets up a generic computer name of "Windows 98 User." You can customize all four values using the following settings in `MSBATCH.INF` (note that these values assume a Microsoft Networking login):

```
[NameAndOrg]
Name="System Recovery"

[Network]
ComputerName="Windows 98 User"
Workgroup="WORKGROUP"

[VREDIR]
LogonDomain="WORKGROUP"
```

To reinstall Windows from the CD-ROM: The reason you must reinstall Windows from a hard drive is that `PCRESTOR.BAT` launches Setup from a `WIN98` directory that's in the same drive as `PCRESTOR.BAT`:

```
cd\
cd win98
setup.exe c:\restore\msbatch.inf /is /id /iq /im /id /ie /IW
```

To start Setup from another location, you must modify the first two lines. For example, if you want to run Setup from the Windows 98 CD-ROM in drive D, modify the first two lines as follows:

```
d:
cd\win98
```

Part
III

Ch
13

Configuring Memory, Disks, and Devices

by Rob Tidrow

In this chapter

Modifying Virtual Memory Options

As Windows 98 executes programs (especially when executing several programs at once), it performs better when it possesses more memory. To achieve better performance, Windows 98 uses spare room on your hard drive as additional memory. This is called *virtual memory*. The room on your hard drive that is used by Windows 98 as virtual memory is called the *swap file*. This file grows and shrinks as you use your computer. The more programs you run at once, the larger the swap file grows. As you close programs, the swap file shrinks. Normally, you won't need to adjust the default settings for virtual memory. However, if your hard drive doesn't have much spare room on it, you might want to control how Windows 98 grows and shrinks the swap file.

> **CAUTION**
>
> In most cases, it is best to leave the swap-file allocation setting at its default to let Windows manage the swap file. Most of the time, unless indicated by Microsoft or by a specific application, Windows can manage swap-file allocation better than users.

To change the virtual memory settings, use the Virtual Memory dialog box. To open the Virtual Memory dialog box, follow these steps:

1. Choose Start, Settings, Control Panel.

2. Double-click the System icon to open the System Properties dialog box.

 You also can get to the System Properties dialog box by right-clicking the My Computer icon on the desktop. This brings up a context menu. Choose Properties, and the System Properties dialog box opens.

3. Select the Performance tab in the System Properties dialog box.

4. Click Virtual Memory.

The Virtual Memory dialog box opens, as shown in Figure 14.1.

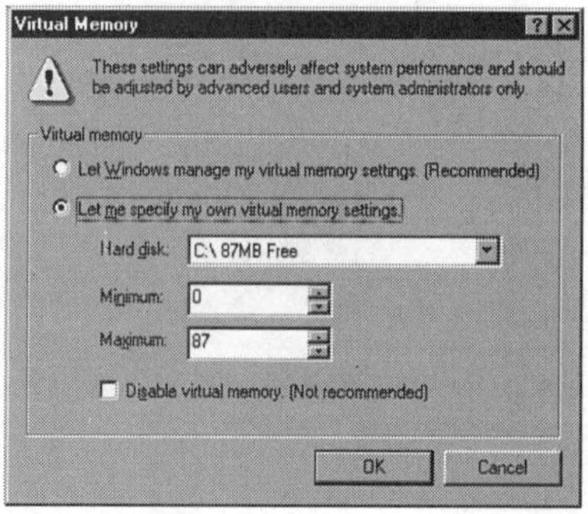

FIG. 14.1

You can change virtual-memory settings using the Virtual Memory dialog box.

Virtual Memory	? X
⚠ These settings can adversely affect system performance and should be adjusted by advanced users and system administrators only.	

Virtual memory
- ○ Let Windows manage my virtual memory settings. (Recommended)
- ● Let me specify my own virtual memory settings.
  - Hard disk: C:\ 87MB Free
  - Minimum: 0
  - Maximum: 87
  - ☐ Disable virtual memory. (Not recommended)

[OK] [Cancel]

You have two main choices when dealing with virtual memory. You can let Windows decide how to manage the virtual memory, or you can specify your settings. If you need to specify your settings, there are three parameters to set:

■ Where (on what drive) Windows should create the swap file.

■ What's the smallest size the swap file should shrink to.

■ What's the largest size the swap file can grow to.

> **CAUTION**
>
> If you have 16 or more megabytes of RAM, you are given the option of turning off virtual memory. Don't do this. If you do turn off virtual memory, you might not be able to run more than a few, small programs simultaneously, or you might not be able to work with large amounts of data. Microsoft (and I) recommend that you don't disable virtual memory.

Specifying the Hard Drive on Which the Swap Exists

Normally, Windows creates the virtual-memory swap file on the same drive on which Windows 98 is installed. However, you can have Windows 98 create the swap file on a different drive. You might want to use a different drive because it has more free space (allowing you to have more virtual memory), or you might want to use another drive because it is a faster disk drive (improving performance). All the available drives, as well as the amount of free disk space on each drive, are listed in the drop-down list box.

To change the default location for the swap file, follow these steps:

1. Select the Let Me Specify My Own Virtual Memory Settings option on the Virtual Memory dialog box. Refer to Figure 14.1.

2. View the list of available drives by clicking the down arrow at the right of the Hard Disk drop-down text box.

3. Click the drive you want to use for the swap file.

4. Click OK.

N O T E Windows 98 constantly reads and writes to the swap file. Reading and writing to a compressed drive is slower than reading and writing to a noncompressed drive. This is because you have the overhead of compressing and uncompressing data when you read and write to it. So, for the best performance, you shouldn't locate the swap file on a compressed drive.

However, if you need more virtual memory than you can fit on any noncompressed drive, you can use a compressed drive. Although it works more slowly, you will be able to run more programs simultaneously. If you run large programs, such as Word and Excel, for example, and you are using *object linking and embedding* (OLE) to share data between them, you will need a lot of memory. If you run out of memory using the default swap file, your only option to get everything to work might be to put the virtual-memory swap file on a compressed drive. ■

Part
III

Ch
14

Setting the Minimum Swap File Size

You can specify the smallest swap file that Windows 98 creates. If you know that you are going to be needing a lot of memory (because you are running several programs or manipulating a large amount of data), you can have Windows 98 preallocate the memory. If you don't, you might notice an additional delay as you load new programs or data and Windows 98 has to grow the swap file to increase the amount of virtual memory.

TIP Swap files can become fragmented, which hurts the performance of your system. It's a good idea to make the minimum swap file as large as you can afford to in order to help alleviate that problem.

Another way to improve a swap file's performance is to have it created on a drive or partition separate from the one used for system and application files. This way, the drive or partition is not fragmented as much as it would be on a drive with all your files.

To specify the minimum size for the swap file, follow these steps:

1. Select the Let Me Specify My Own Virtual Memory Settings option on the Virtual Memory dialog box. Refer to Figure 14.1.

2. In the Minimum edit field, type in the size for the smallest swap file (in megabytes).

3. Click OK.

> **CAUTION**
>
> Windows 98 will not let you set the minimum memory less than 12MB (the total of your physical RAM and virtual memory). However, if you do set your total memory to 12MB, you might have problems trying to run additional programs, work with OLE documents, and so on. If you plan to run any large program or work with OLE objects, keep the minimum memory to at least 16MB.

Setting the Maximum Swap File Size

Windows 98 grows the swap file for virtual memory as large as it needs to, unless you set a maximum size. Windows 98 also shrinks the swap file to accommodate disk drive shortage and offers to clean up your drive for you if it runs out of space. If you don't need a certain amount of space left over, you don't need to set a maximum. However, if you know that you need a certain amount of space available for an application to run, you need to set the maximum value. If you have 20MB left on your hard drive, for example, and you know that you will need 5MB free for downloading a file, limit the swap file to 15MB.

To set the maximum size of the swap file, follow these steps:

1. Select the Let Me Specify My Own Virtual Memory Settings option on the Virtual Memory dialog box. Refer to Figure 14.1.

2. In the Maximum edit field, type in the size for the largest swap file (in megabytes).

3. Click OK.

Improving Hard Drive Performance

The performance of your hard drive affects the performance of your system under Windows 98. This happens for several reasons. First, the time it takes to load programs and data files affects performance. Second, because Windows 98 uses the hard drive as virtual memory, maintaining your hard drive's efficiency affects overall performance. Windows 98 provides five tools to help you maintain your hard drive:

- *ScanDisk*. Provides error checking and correction.
- *Disk Defragmenter*. Organizes files into contiguous files.
- *Backup*. Makes backup copies of files on your hard drive.
- *Disk Cleanup*. Locates files you can remove from your system to increase free drive space.
- *Maintenance Wizard*. Provides a regular maintenance schedule to improve system performance.

Given the object-oriented nature of Windows 98, you easily can keep your hard drive in top condition by working from the Properties dialog box of the hard drive itself. The individual Properties pages provide you with information about the drive and ways to easily access the tools you'll use to maintain the drive.

To access the properties of a drive, follow these steps:

1. Open the My Computer folder by double-clicking the My Computer icon on the desktop.
2. Right-click the drive to bring up its context menu.
3. Choose Properties.

The Properties dialog box normally contains three pages, as shown in Figure 14.2.

FIG. 14.2
The Properties dialog box for the C: drive.

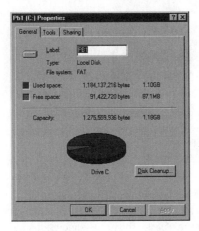

Part III
Ch
14

Here are the three Properties pages:

■ *General*. Displays drive information, such as drive label, drive type, and drive usage.

■ *Tools*. Provides easy access to ScanDisk, Disk Defragmenter, and Backup. Also informs you of how many days ago you last ran these tools. See Figure 14.3.

FIG. 14.3
The Tools page provides access to disk drive utilities.

■ *Sharing*. Allows you to specify whether and control how to share this drive with other networked users. This option is available only when you have set up your computer with File and Print Sharing for Microsoft (or NetWare) Networks. See Figure 14.4.

FIG. 14.4
The Sharing tab shows the status of a shared drive.

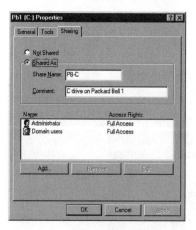

Although you can start ScanDisk, Disk Defragmenter, and Backup from the Tools tab, the examples in the remainder of this chapter run the disk drive maintenance tools from the Start menu. But remember, by selecting the *object*—the drive—and choosing its properties, you can access all the tools from one location.

Using ScanDisk

Although Windows 98 is a much more robust operating system than previous Windows operating systems, including the DOS–Windows 3.1x combination and Windows 95, the files on your computer are still vulnerable to application errors. When an application crashes (or worse, your entire system crashes), your files and folders might become a bit scrambled. Left unfixed, these scrambled files and folders can produce a domino effect, causing more crashes and further scrambling your drive. Fortunately, Windows 98 comes with ScanDisk, a tool that unscrambles your files and folders.

N O T E   If you did not install ScanDisk, refer to Chapter 3, "Selecting Windows 98 Components," for information on how to install individual components. ■

ScanDisk checks your hard drive(s) for any problems. ScanDisk can perform one of two types of tests: *Standard* and *Thorough*. A Standard test checks the file system for errors—such as fragments of files or cross-linked files. A Thorough test adds a surface scan test to the Standard test, which helps to detect when a portion of the hard drive is beginning to malfunction.

N O T E   A Thorough test takes much longer to complete than a Standard test. Depending on the size and speed of your hard drive and your computer's speed, a Thorough test can take a long time to complete. You should perform a Thorough test on a monthly basis or if you suspect a problem. ■

Performing a Standard ScanDisk Test   To run a standard ScanDisk test on a drive, follow these steps:

1. Choose Start, Programs, Accessories, System Tools, ScanDisk. The ScanDisk dialog box appears, as shown in Figure 14.5.

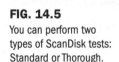
FIG. 14.5
You can perform two types of ScanDisk tests: Standard or Thorough.

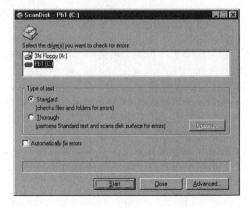

Part
III

Ch
14

2. Select the drive you want ScanDisk to check for errors.

3. Select Standard.

4. Click Start.

TIP You can select several drives at once on which to run ScanDisk. To do this, press Ctrl while clicking each drive you want to check for errors.

You can customize the behavior of ScanDisk by clicking the Advanced button in the ScanDisk main window. The ScanDisk Advanced Options dialog box appears, as shown in Figure 14.6.

FIG. 14.6

Set advanced options for ScanDisk in the ScanDisk Advanced Options dialog box.

From this dialog box, you can set the following options:

■ *Display Summary.* After ScanDisk finishes testing the drive, it can display a summary of the test. You can choose to always have the results displayed if you want to verify any of the hard drive statistics—size, number of files, allocation unit size, and so on. You can choose to never display the results if you automatically run ScanDisk during startup. Your third option is to display the results only if an error was detected.

■ *Log File.* You can choose to have ScanDisk create a log file. This file contains detailed results of the test. The file is created in the root folder of each drive that is tested and is called—you guessed it—SCANDISK.LOG. You have three choices: always create a new log file (Replace Log), add on to the existing log file (Append to Log), or never create a log file (No log).

■ *Cross-Linked Files.* Cross-linked files occur when two (or more) files use the same part of the drive. When ScanDisk detects a cross-linked file, you can have ScanDisk perform one of three actions. First, you can select Delete to have ScanDisk delete all files containing the cross-link. Second, you can select Make Copies to have ScanDisk make copies of the cross-linked information for each file. Third, you simply can select Ignore to have ScanDisk ignore the cross-link and continue. Probably the best option is to make copies of cross-linked files. This way, after ScanDisk runs, you can examine these files to see which ones, if any, can be deleted without hurting any other files. By deleting all cross-linked files, you might corrupt a file associated with the cross-link.

■ *Lost File Fragments.* ScanDisk might encounter pieces of data that are no longer contained in any file. You can have ScanDisk free the data and reclaim that portion of the drive as free space, or you can have ScanDisk convert the data into a file. If you select Convert to Files, the file is saved in the root folder of the drive and is given names such as File0000 or Dir0000 (if the data was part of a folder).

- *Check Files For.* ScanDisk also can check files to make sure that filenames, file dates, duplicate filenames, and file times are all valid. ScanDisk checks the creation and modification dates and times of each file to see whether any invalid dates or times are found. These could cause the files to sort incorrectly, as well as hamper backup and restore procedures. If any invalid information is discovered, ScanDisk prompts you and asks whether it should fix the problem.

- *Check Host Drive First.* If the drive you want ScanDisk to check is compressed with DoubleSpace or DriveSpace, you can specify whether ScanDisk first should check the uncompressed host drive for errors. Deselect this option only if you already checked the host drive for errors.

- *Report MS-DOS Mode Name Length Errors.* If ScanDisk finds MS-DOS name-length errors, you receive a report about them.

N O T E Here are the default settings for the ScanDisk Advanced Options dialog box:

Display Summary	Always
Log File	Replace log
Cross-Linked Files	Make Copies
Lost File Fragments	Convert to Files
Check Files For	Invalid file names
Check Host Drive First	Enabled
Report MS-DOS Mode Name Length Errors	Enabled

Performing a Thorough ScanDisk Test   To run a Thorough ScanDisk on a drive, follow these steps:

1. Choose Start, Programs, Accessories, System Tools, ScanDisk.
2. Select the drive you want ScanDisk to check for errors.
3. Select Thorough.
4. Click Start.

If you want ScanDisk to perform a Thorough test, you can set several options by clicking the Options button. These options enable you to customize how ScanDisk performs the surface-scan portion of the test. As Figure 14.7 shows, these options enable you to do the following:

- Select the areas of the drive to scan.
- Restrict ScanDisk to reading only from the drive.
- Restrict the types of files ScanDisk repairs.

Part

III

Ch

14

FIG. 14.7

Set ScanDisk to scan both the system and data areas of the drive.

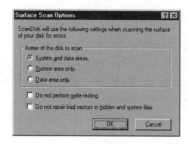

ScanDisk enables you to control three aspects of its Thorough disk drive test:

- *Areas of the Disk to Scan.* You can specify that ScanDisk scan your entire drive, only the system portion of your drive, or only the data portion of your drive. If you select only the system area, ScanDisk checks the system area for physical damage and usually cannot correct any errors that it finds. If errors are found, you might need to replace the drive. If you select Data Area Only, ScanDisk checks the data area for physical damage and usually can relocate data to areas on the drive that are not damaged. ScanDisk then marks the area as bad; data stored in damaged areas might not be recoverable, however.

- *Do Not Perform Write-Testing.* Normally, to perform the surface test on a drive, ScanDisk reads and writes to the drive. This ensures that your drive can be read from and written to correctly. You can disable the writing to the drive by selecting this option. By disabling this option, you can decrease the amount of time ScanDisk takes to complete its test. However, your drive will not be tested on how it reads and writes data.

- *Do Not Repair Bad Sectors in Hidden and System Files.* If ScanDisk finds errors, it moves the information to another location on the drive. Normally, you should allow ScanDisk to repair these errors. However, a few older programs require that certain hidden files not be moved. If they are moved, the programs might not work properly. If you run older programs that use this technique as a copy-protection scheme, disable this type of repair.

Setting ScanDisk to Automatically Fix Errors   You can have ScanDisk automatically repair errors that it discovers. To set this option, enable the Automatically Fix Errors check box on the main ScanDisk window. Refer to Figure 14.5.

If you choose to have ScanDisk automatically fix errors, set the advanced options so that you can do the following:

- Make copies of cross-linked files.
- Convert lost fragments into files.
- Append new information to your existing log file.

By setting these options, you prevent ScanDisk from removing information from your drive without your approval. You need to review the log file periodically to see what ScanDisk has done. At that time, you can delete or recover any files ScanDisk created.

 You can automate the running of ScanDisk by setting the Maintenance Wizard to run ScanDisk at a specific time.

TROUBLESHOOTING

I've tried to run ScanDisk, but it says it can't fix a problem it found. ScanDisk might be unable to repair errors for files that are in use while ScanDisk runs. Because Windows 98 itself has many files in use, ScanDisk might not be able to completely repair all the errors it finds. To fix these errors, choose Start, Sh<u>u</u>t Down and select Restart the Computer in <u>M</u>S-DOS mode. Then, run the DOS version of ScanDisk. This file is located in the WINDOWS\COMMAND folder.

Performing Backup

The Microsoft Backup tool provided with Windows 98 copies the files on your computer to floppy disks or supported tape drives. There are two main ways to use Backup. First, the application can be used in a manual mode. In this mode, the Backup program looks and behaves very much like Explorer. You manually select the folders and files you want to back up. In the second method, you can use the Backup program by creating backup sets. With backup sets, you can back up files using a simple drag-and-drop operation.

Because an entire chapter is devoted to Microsoft Backup, this chapter does not go into detail on creating backup sets. You can learn more about this topic in Chapter 13, "Setting Up Backup Systems."

Defragmenting Your Hard Drive

Over time, as a hard drive is used (as files are saved, edited, resaved, and deleted), the files become fragmented into pieces scattered on the drive. Then, when a file needs to be loaded, it takes longer to load the file because it is not in one piece. A badly fragmented drive does not perform as well as a drive on which all the files are neatly organized. The Disk Defragmenter tool supplied with Windows 98 helps keep files on your drive organized into contiguous pieces.

NOTE The Maintenance Wizard schedules and runs Disk Defragmenter automatically for you. ■

You can control how Disk Defragmenter works by changing the Disk Defragmenter Settings, as shown in Figure 14.8. You can change these by clicking the <u>S</u>ettings button in the Select Drive dialog box. See Figure 14.9.

FIG. 14.8
You can set the Disk Defragmenter to perform a full defragmentation.

Part
III

Ch
14

You may select the following settings:

- *Rearrange Program Files So My Programs Start Faster.* Arranges your most frequently used program files so that they start up faster. It rearranges your files so that each file is contiguous and you have one large contiguous free space available. This is the best method of defragmenting your drive; it also takes the most time to complete.

- *Check the Drive for Errors.* Checks your folders and files for errors prior to defragmenting your drive.

- *I Want to Use These Options.* You can set these options to be used every time you run ScanDisk, or just use these settings for this particular ScanDisk activity.

Click OK to save your settings.

 TIP By default, Disk Defragmenter checks a drive for errors before it attempts to defragment the drive. However, you can disable this error-checking by deselecting Check the Drive for Errors on the Disk Defragmenter Settings dialog box. Disable this feature only if you are positive that the drive doesn't have any errors. If you have just run ScanDisk on the drive, for example, you could disable the error-checking.

To defragment your hard drive, follow these steps:

1. Choose Start, Programs, Accessories, System Tools, Disk Defragmenter. The Select Drive dialog box appears, as shown in Figure 14.9.

FIG. 14.9
Use the Select Drive dialog box to select the drive you want to defragment.

2. Select the drive you want defragmented by choosing the drive from the drop-down list box.

3. Click OK, or press Enter.

4. Click Start.

As Disk Defragmenter runs, you see a dialog box like the one shown in Figure 14.10. To see a graphical representation of the defragmentation process, click Show Details. See Figure 14.11.

FIG. 14.10
Disk Defragmenter usually takes some time to finish.

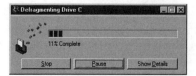

FIG. 14.11
This is a popular way to view Disk Defragmenter in action.

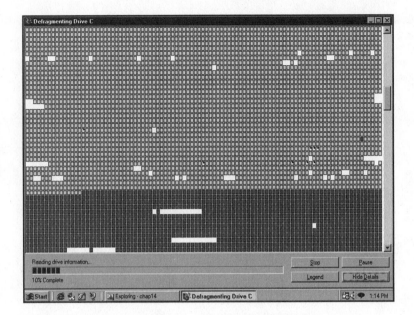

Disk Cleanup

You can use the Disk Cleanup utility to systematically go through your disk drives (it cannot clean up CD-ROM drives, of course) to delete unneeded files. This frees up drive space for other files to be stored.

To run Disk Cleanup, perform these steps:

1. Choose Start, Programs, Accessories, System Utilities, Disk Cleanup. The Disk Cleanup dialog box appears.
2. From the Drives drop-down list, select the drive you want to clean up.
3. Click OK.

Disk Cleanup returns a list of the types of files you can delete to free up disk drive space, as shown in Figure 14.12.

The Files to Delete list includes the following types of files:

- Temporary Internet Files
- Downloaded Program Files
- Recycle Bin
- Temporary Files
- Delete Windows 98 Uninstall Information

Part
III

Ch

14

FIG. 14.12
Select the types of files
you want Disk Cleanup
to remove from your
system.

Select the types of files you want to remove. If you select the Temporary Files option, Disk
Cleanup deletes only those temporary files that have not been modified for more than a week.
It does not delete temporary files created during your current session, which could be prob-
lematic for your system and any open data files.

 To view individual files that are selected to be removed by the Temporary Internet Files, Downloaded
Program Files, and Recycle Bin options, click View Files. This displays an Explorer view of the files found
by Disk Cleanup that will be deleted.

Click the More Options tab to see other ways to free additional space on your system. These
ways include removing Windows components you no longer use, uninstalling applications, and
converting your drive to use FAT32.

Finally, the Settings tab includes an option that automatically launches Disk Cleanup any time
your drive gets low on space. By default, this option is enabled.

Using Maintenance Wizard

You can use the Windows Maintenance Wizard to set up a maintenance schedule to the following performance-improving utilities:

- Disk Defragmenter
- ScanDisk
- Disk Cleanup

To set up a schedule for running these utilities, follow these steps:

1. Choose Start, Programs, Accessories, System Tools, Maintenance Wizard. The Maintenance Wizard appears, as shown in Figure 14.13.

FIG. 14.13

Use the Maintenance Wizard to set up a schedule to run disk drive maintenance tools.

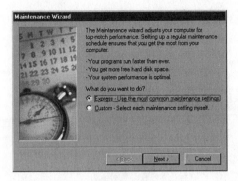

2. Select one of the following options:

   - *Express*. Sets the Maintenance Wizard to run all three utilities at night, during the day, or in the evening. This option does not provide a way to deselect any tools or to make modifications to the times when the tools can run.

   - *Custom*. Enables you to select each tool you want to schedule, as well as when you want each tool to run. You can set a detailed schedule for each tool or just keep the settings established by default.

   The Maintenance Wizard displays different screens, depending on the preceding option you select. The following steps assume that you select the Custom option.

3. Click Next. Select a maintenance schedule to specify when you want the Maintenance Wizard to run your disk drive utilities. You can select Nights, Days, Evenings, and Custom. The following steps assume that you choose Custom.

4. Click Next. On the Speed Up Programs dialog box, you can set up the Disk Deframenter utility. If you do not want to schedule this tool, select No, Do Not Defragment My Disk.

5. Click Reschedule to change the schedule for the Disk Defragmenter. The Reschedule dialog box appears, as shown in Figure 14.14. Set the schedule for the utility. In Figure 14.14, for example, Disk Defragmenter is set to run weekly, every Monday, Wednesday, and Friday at 6:00 A.M.

To create multiple schedules for a utility, enable the Show Multiple Schedules check box. This lets you create or delete different schedules that the Maintenance Wizard can use to run disk drive utilities.

6. Click OK to save your schedule settings.

7. Click Settings to display the Disk Defragmenter utility, so you can set runtime options for Defragmenter. See the "Defragmenting Your Hard Drive" section, earlier in this chapter, for information on setting up Defragmenter. Click OK to return to the Maintenance Wizard.

Part

III

Ch

14

FIG. 14.14

You can set customized schedules for the disk drive tools using the Reschedule dialog box.

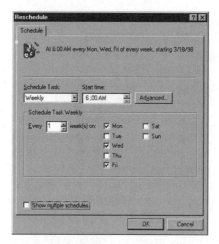

8. Click Next. Set scheduling and runtime options for ScanDisk from this screen. Or, select No, Do Not Scan My Hard Disk for Errors if you don't want to run ScanDisk with Maintenance Wizard. Clicking the Reschedule button displays the Reschedule dialog box, which is the same as the one described in step 5. In addition, the Settings button displays the ScanDisk utility to set runtime options.

9. Click Next. From the Delete Unnecessary Files dialog box, you can select which types of files you want Disk Cleanup to remove when the Maintenance Wizard runs. Or, you can select No, Do Not Scan My Hard Disk for Errors if you don't want to run Disk Cleanup with Maintenance Wizard. The Reschedule and Settings buttons work the same as the ones you use when setting the Disk Defragmenter and ScanDisk tools.

10. Click Next to see a listing of your Maintenance Wizard schedule.

 If you want to run the scheduled utilities now, click the When I Click Finish, Perform Each Scheduled Task for the First Time option.

11. Click Finish to save your settings.

Maintenance Wizard now is set up to run the scheduled utilities.

If you run Maintenance Wizard from the System Tools folder, you are asked whether you want to run your schedule now or change the maintenance settings or schedule.

Using the Device Manager

Although Windows 98 supports Plug and Play hardware devices, many of the devices still in use are not Plug and Play devices. Windows 98 consolidates the management of all of these different devices into one central spot—the Device Manager. With the Device Manager, you quickly can see all the devices in your system and change the setting for any device.

Changing Device Properties

To change the properties of a device using the Device Manager, follow these steps:

1. Right-click My Computer.
2. Choose Properties. The System Properties dialog box opens.
3. Select the Device Manager tab in the System Properties dialog box, as shown in Figure. 14.15. All devices with errors are marked in the list. An X denotes devices that are disabled. An exclamation point (!) denotes devices that have problems.

FIG. 14.15

The Device Manager page enables you to change the properties of a device.

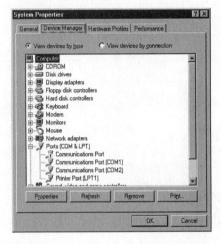

4. Click the plus sign in the small rectangle to the left of the type of device you want. This expands the item, showing all the devices of that type in your system. By clicking the DISK DRIVES folder, for example, the tree expands to show all physical drives in the system.
5. Click the device you want to modify or examine.
6. Choose Properties.

Although the Properties dialog box for each device is unique, you will see standard pages. All devices have a General page. The General page lists the following information:

- Device name
- Device type
- Manufacturer
- Hardware version
- Device status
- Device usage

Part
III

Ch
14

Changing Device Resources

Some devices will have only the General page. However, if the device uses system resources (such as DMA and IRQ settings), the device also will have a Resources page.

To change the resources for a device, follow these steps:

1. From Device Manager, select the device you want to modify or examine.
2. Click Properties.
3. Select the Resources tab, as shown in Figure 14.16.

FIG. 14.16
You can change the resources used by a modem on this page.

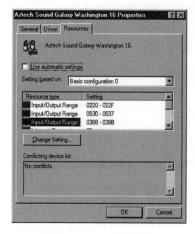

4. If the Use Automatic Settings check box is marked, deselect it.
5. Click the resource type you want to change in the Resource Type box.
6. Click Change Setting. A dialog box appears, enabling you to edit the specific resource settings.

TROUBLESHOOTING

I changed the resource for one of my devices, and now Windows 98 won't restart. If you can't restart Windows 98, restart your computer. When the words Starting Windows 98... appear on your monitor, press F8. The Windows 98 Startup menu appears. Select Safe mode to restart Windows as a default configuration. You should be able to go back and undo your changes using Device Manager.

Changing Device Drivers

Some devices will have drivers associated with them. If a device does have a device driver, there will be a Driver page. This page displays the following information:

- Device name
- Driver files—the files used by the driver
- File details—information about the driver, such as the company that wrote the driver and version of the driver

To change the driver for a device, follow these steps:

1. From Device Manager, select the device you want to modify or examine.
2. Click Properties.
3. Select the Driver tab, as shown in Figure 14.17.

FIG. 14.17
You can change a device driver to a display device.

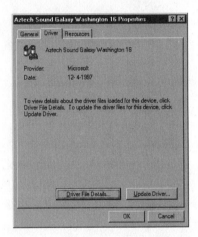

4. Click Update Driver. The Update Device Driver Wizard appears, enabling you to install a new device driver, as shown in Figure 14.18. You can learn more about this wizard in Chapter 5, "Installing and Configuring New Hardware and Software."

FIG. 14.18
Use the Update Device Driver Wizard to help you update a device's driver file.

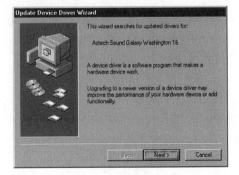

Part
III

Ch
14

IV

Configuring Multimedia for Windows 98

CHAPTER 15

Installing Sound and MIDI Cards

by Rob Tidrow

In this chapter

Examining the Windows 98 Multimedia Environment

Microsoft markets Windows 98 as the premiere operating system for handling multimedia files and applications. Although this is probably an overstatement, Windows 98's multimedia support improves upon several multimedia features first introduced in Windows 95 and is a tremendous improvement over the way in which MS-DOS and Windows 3.1 ran multimedia applications.

Windows 98 includes the following multimedia features:

- *Built-in support for Microsoft* AVI *video files.* AVI files commonly are available on the Internet and are used by many applications and games to provide video clips. AVI files also can contain audio and text elements. You learn more about video in Chapter 16, "Configuring Full-Motion Video Capabilities."

- *Built-in recorder, editor, and player for audio files.* If you have a supported sound card and microphone, you can use Windows 98's Sound Recorder application to record and edit sound files. Use the Volume Control application to set the volume of audio files during playback.

- *Media Control Interface (MCI).* MCI runs multimedia devices separately. This enables you to run sound cards, digital video files, and animation devices simultaneously in separate memory spaces.

- *CD-ROM sharing.* This enables you to share CD-ROM devices on a network. This capability is handy if you have a limited number of CD-ROM drives in your company, or if you have a multidisk CD-ROM device you want to share with a workgroup or team.

- *DirectX.* Windows 98 includes DirectX 5, which is an enhanced programming environment for multimedia applications and hardware, including 3D audio hardware.

To take advantage of these capabilities, you need to make sure that your computer is equipped with the right multimedia hardware devices.

Purchasing a Multimedia System

Many of the personal computers you purchase at retail outlets and computer stores and through mail-order catalogs are fully equipped to handle much of your multimedia needs. You should look for a computer that passes the *Multimedia Personal Computer* (MPC 3) specification devised by the Multimedia PC Marketing Group. By following the MPC 3 specification, you can feel comfortable that your PC can run most multimedia applications and games available on the market.

▶ **See** The MPC Home Page at http://www.spa.org/mpc/default.htm

If you want to run applications and files that include sound, video, and animation, you need the following to pass the MPC 3 specification:

- *75 MHz Pentium processor or higher.* Many systems you can purchase now include 166 MHz or higher Pentium processors.

- *16MB of RAM or higher.* Systems usually come with 16MB of RAM installed, but many systems now include 32MB to accommodate higher application demands.

- *16-bit sound card,* with multivoice synthesizer supporting six simultaneous voice tracks and two percussion tracks. You also should look for a sound card that is Sound Blaster compatible (Sound Blaster is a product manufactured by Creative Labs).

- *4- to 10-watt speakers* that also have built-in amplification. Some PCs come with speakers that hook to your monitor. Be sure the monitor you purchase has the same type of connections as these speakers. 4-watt speakers generally are acceptable for desktop audio, and 10-watt are acceptable for situations when you want to conduct a presentation in a small room or office.

- *A graphics board* that supports 30 frames per second of video at 352×240 pixels. It also should be MPEG-1 compliant. Your graphics card should have 2MB of graphics RAM and should be PCI compliant (*Peripheral Component Interconnect* is a bus type that many new PCs have).

- *A 4X CD-ROM with 250ms seek.* For most games and applications that must access the CD-ROM periodically, you should purchase a 6X (200ms seek) or 8X (150ms seek) CD-ROM that is multisession capable. Most multimedia PCs you purchase today have 24x or above CD-ROMs installed.

- *A 540MB hard drive.* Probably the most common hard drive size on new computers is more than 2GB. Because most video and graphics files already are compressed when you use them, you don't get any benefit from compressing a hard drive that has these types of files on it. Get the largest hard drive you can find and afford.

N O T E As an optional component for your multimedia computer, you also might want to invest in a joystick. This is true especially if you purchase games such as Flight Simulator. Two affordable yet advanced joysticks are the Microsoft SideWinder Pro 3D and Sidewinder Force Feedback Pro joysticks. ▧

As technologies expand and new capabilities are added to applications and games, you might look to upgrade your system to meet the needs of the newer programs. One example of this is with the type of processor you purchase. Although MPC 3 specifies a Pentium 75, you should look for a system that has a Pentium 266 or higher to play back high-end MPEG video and 3D animations.

What to look for in sound cards for your PC is determined by your needs and your budget. In general, the better the sound quality you need, the higher the price of the sound card and speaker system. For situations in which you want to listen to simple sound events in education or general software titles, sound files you download from the Internet, or other situations in which sound quality is not a major concern, you usually can find sound systems that cost less than $100 to satisfy your needs. In many cases, when you purchase a new PC, it comes equipped with a low-end sound card and speakers. This type of system is ideal for most end users.

If you want high-quality sound cards and speakers, your investment will be higher. A typical sound card that is considered high quality is 16-bit, offers CD-quality audio (that is, it sounds like a CD you play back using an audio CD player), provides 3D wraparound sound, and supports Windows 98 Plug-and-Play features. It also has high-quality speakers, which usually are rated at 10 to 40 watts per channel and have separate volume, bass, and treble controls.

The following are some general points to consider when purchasing a sound system for Windows 98:

- *16-bit is better than 8-bit.* If possible, purchase a 16-bit sound card instead of an 8-bit card. Or, if you have a legacy card that is 8-bit, consider upgrading to 16-bit. The number of bits refers to the amount of sound data is delivered through the sound card. The higher, the better. Also, look for sound cards that take advantage Microsoft's DirectSound 5 API specification. DirectSound 5 handles audio messages between a sound-capable application (such as a game) and your sound card's device driver. This provides a rich environment for audio, including recording, mixing, and 3D audio. With 3D audio, for example, audio emanating from your speakers sound as if it is coming from all directions, not just from your two speakers.

- *Look for Sound Blaster compatible.* Creative Lab's Sound Blaster line of sound cards is usually the de facto standard for audio devices. Most hardware (such as CD-ROM devices) and software are compatible with Sound Blaster cards. Most sound cards you find today that support Windows 98 are Sound Blaster compatible. However, look for information on the packaging or marketing data of the sound card you buy to make sure it tells you whether it is Sound Blaster compatible.

- *Buy a Plug-and-Play sound device.* Plug and Play makes installing and configuring sound cards a breeze. All you do is physically install the card and then boot Windows 98. During the boot process, Windows notices the new device and sets it up automatically. Also, the goal of Microsoft is to eventually have its entire line of Windows operating systems (including Windows 95, Windows 98, Windows NT 5, and Windows CE) support Plug-and-Play hardware devices. This means that you can invest in these types of devices and feel comfortable that they will be supported in future releases of Windows.

- *Wavetable lookup sounds better than FM synthesis.* For *Musical Instrument Digital Interface* (MIDI) sounds, there are two ways sound cards generate the tones. Wavetable lookup contains samples of actual musical sounds stored in *read-only memory* (ROM). This enables the playback of MIDI sounds to sound more life-like. FM synthesis, however, plays back sounds by using tones that are artificially created, causing the sound to be less life-like. As you can imagine, wavetable lookup devices generally cost more than FM synthesis.

As you purchase a multimedia system, you also might want to look for devices that support Microsoft's DirectX technology, which is discussed in the following section.

Reviewing Windows 98's DirectX 5 Features

Microsoft's DirectX technology is an API that provides applications (such as games) with direct access to your computer's hardware. This enables the application to take advantage of hardware accelerators. If hardware accelerators are not available, DirectX can emulate hardware accelerators to provide a robust multimedia environment. Windows 95 was the first platform to support DirectX.

N O T E Initially, DirectX was distributed as part of the Microsoft Games *Software Development Kit* (SDK) to programmers interested in designing advanced games and animation titles. With the release of DirectX version 2 in mid-1996, DirectX is was being distributed as its own SDK by Microsoft. Recently, Microsoft released DirectX 5. ∎

The components of DirectX are described in the following list:

- *DirectSound.* Enables Windows 98 to handle audio files more efficiently and enhances the quality of audio files. DirectSound gives games programmers the capability to use high-quality audio in their games, for example.

- *DirectDraw.* Provides an environment for very fast graphics displays for 2D, 3D, video, and animation graphics. This capability enables Windows to support fast-action games and full-motion video. One example of where DirectDraw is being used heavily is on the World Wide Web. Many Web sites incorporate video files as part of their content, requiring visitors to have a platform such as Windows 95 or Windows 98 to take full advantage of the site. DirectDraw replaces the *Display Control Interface* (DCI) technology that Microsoft and Intel jointly created for Windows 3.1 (and include as a core technology in Windows 95 and Windows 98) for games and digital video.

- *DirectVideo.* Provides advanced video playback capabilities. DirectVideo works with DirectDraw to create an environment capable of displaying full-motion video on computers that have Pentium processors. One way Windows users display video is by using a compression format called *Moving Picture Experts Group* (MPEG) and by installing a dedicated MPEG adapter card. Having an MPEG card installed is probably the best way to get excellent video on your PC, but DirectVideo can handle MPEG files very well even without an MPEG adapter installed. See Chapter 16, "Configuring Full-Motion Video Capabilities," for information on configuring video settings.

- *Direct3D.* Enables Windows to render real-time 3D graphics and animation. Direct3D handles 3D objects and 3D scenes to create life-like images and video. Direct3D applications, such as games, combined with a 3D accelerator card, can make Windows 98 an above-average 3D platform with which to create and view 3D files.

- *DirectInput.* Increases Windows 98's built-in support for input devices, such as joysticks, virtual-reality headgear, head-mounted displays, and other devices.

- *DirectSetup.* New with DirectX 3, DirectSetup helps DirectX applications make Registry entries during installation.

- *DirectPlay.* DirectPlay enables multiple users to interact with the same game or application simultaneously over a LAN, modem, or other connectivity device. DirectPlay is designed to allow users to connect to the game or application with mixed connections; this means that users can connect in a variety of ways, such as by using high-speed LAN access, 28.8Kbps modem connections, and ISDN connections, without suffering performance losses.

- *DirectShow 2.0.* Provides an environment in which streams of multimedia data, such as video and audio, are played. Windows 98 includes the runtime version of DirectShow 2.0, so you can play AVI or Apple QuickTime (MOV) movies.

To take advantage of DirectX technologies, you need to purchase or acquire applications that support DirectX. One way to see whether you have DirectX components installed on your system is to search for these *dynamic link libraries* (DLLs) in your Windows\System folder: DVIDEO.DLL, DDRAW.DLL, and DSOUND.DLL.

Adding a Sound Card

If your PC comes equipped with a sound card that is functioning properly under Windows 95, the card should work under Windows 98. If you need to add a new sound card or replace the one currently installed, you'll need to install it using the Add New Hardware Wizard or let Windows auto-detect it if the card is Plug and Play compatible. To learn how to install a sound card, read Chapter 5, "Installing and Configuring New Hardware and Software."

Updating Sound Card Drivers

At times, you might need to update or change the device driver installed for your sound card. To do this, you can use the Device Manager.

N O T E Windows 98 doesn't work with all the different sound cards on the market. If you have drivers that come from the component manufacturer, the Device Manager might not properly recognize the board. ■

To update a sound card driver, follow these steps:

1. Choose Start, Settings, Control Panel and double-click the System icon. The System Properties dialog box appears.
2. Select the Device Manager tab.
3. Click plus sign (+) next to Sound, Video, and Game Controllers.
4. Double-click the sound card you want to modify. The Properties dialog box for the sound card appears.
5. Select the Driver page, as shown in Figure 15.1.

FIG. 15.1
Use the Driver page to update sound card drivers.

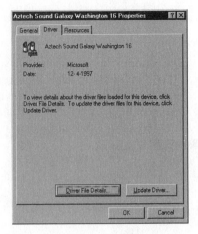

6. Click Update Driver. The Update Device Driver Wizard appears, as shown in Figure 15.2. Work through this wizard as explained in Chapter 5, "Installing and Configuring New Hardware and Software."

FIG. 15.2
The Update Device Driver Wizard walks you through installing a new sound card driver.

Setting System Sounds

When using Windows, you might want to assign sounds to specific events. Or, you might want to use a predefined set of sounds that were placed on your system when you installed Windows 98. If you've made a personalized group of event sounds, you might want to save the configuration or delete an old set of sounds you don't use anymore. In the next few sections, you'll learn how to perform these tasks confidently.

Specifying Event Sounds

Windows knows when certain events occur while you use your computer. It knows when you open or close a program, for example. You can specify a sound to play when these events occur.

To begin configuring event sounds, do the following:

1. Choose Start, Settings, Control Panel.

2. Double-click the Sounds icon. The Sounds Properties dialog box appears, containing the Sounds page, as shown in Figure 15.3. In the upper half of the screen, you see the list of events to which you can assign sounds. You can tell whether an event has a sound assigned to it, because it has a speaker icon to the left of the event name.

FIG. 15.3

The Sounds Properties dialog box enables you to assign sounds to an event.

The speaker icon indicates that the event has an assigned sound.

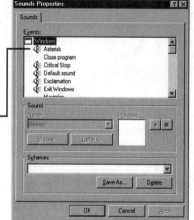

N O T E   When you installed Windows, a default set of sounds and events was chosen for you. ■

3. Choose an event from the list—the Asterisk event, for example. You'll notice that several things happen, as shown in Figure 15.4. Working from left to right, the name of the sound (Chord, in this example) is placed in the Name drop-down list box, the Browse and Details buttons are enabled, the Preview window shows the sound's icon, and the Play button is enabled (it looks like the Play button on a VCR remote control).

4. To listen to this sound, click the Play button. If you like the sound, play it again! Then, select other events in the list and listen to their assigned sounds until you find one you want to change.

5. You can assign a WAV file to the selected event in three ways. First, you can click the down arrow at the end of the Name drop-down list box to display a list of available sounds. Scroll through the list and select one of the sounds. To preview what your current selection sounds like, click the Play button again.

N O T E   The sounds in the Name drop-down list reside in the WINDOWS\MEDIA folder. ■

FIG. 15.4
If you've selected an event with a sound, the controls in the middle of the window become enabled.

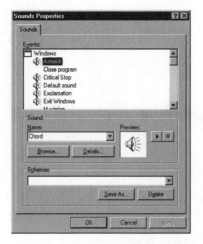

The second method requires using the <u>B</u>rowse button to assign a sound. After you click the button, the Browse dialog box appears, as shown in Figure 15.5. The title of the dialog box matches the name of the event with which you're working. By default, browsing begins in the WINDOWS\MEDIA folder. If you find the name of a sound interesting, highlight it (don't double-click). If you double-click the name of the sound, it is assigned immediately to the event. Because you can't undo this change unless you cancel all the changes you've made so far, just select the name of the sound.

Notice the set of preview buttons at the bottom of the Browse dialog box. These buttons enable you to preview the sounds while you browse. After you highlight the sound you want to use, click OK. The name of the sound is placed in the <u>N</u>ame drop-down list box of the Sounds Properties dialog box.

FIG. 15.5
You can preview a sound in the Browse dialog box by clicking the preview buttons at the bottom of the window.

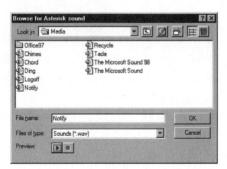

The third method is to type the exact location and file name of the sound in the <u>N</u>ame drop-down list box.

6. Sometimes, sounds have extra information that provides useful details. If you like a particular set of sounds and want more, these details sometimes contain the name and address of who to contact to obtain similarly styled sounds. You can view these details for the current sound by clicking <u>D</u>etails.

Figure 15.6 shows the copyright, media-length, and audio-format data in the Properties dialog box. If more detailed information is available, the Other Information group box becomes visible at the bottom of the dialog box. Select an item in the lefthand box to display its details in the right-hand box. Click OK to close the sound file's Properties dialog box.

FIG. 15.6

You can view the copyright, media length, audio format, and other details of a sound file.

7. To immediately apply the change you made to the event, click Apply in the Sounds Properties dialog box.

NOTE You *can* repeat the preceding steps to change other events' sounds without clicking Apply between each change. Windows temporarily remembers all your changes until you're ready to save them. ▉

8. If you decide you like the new combination of sounds, click OK to save them and close the Sounds Control Panel. If you aren't sure what changes you've made or don't like what you created, click Cancel to restore the event sounds to the state they were in the last time you clicked Apply.

When you install other programs, more events are listed as those programs make their events known to Windows, giving you an even more personalized audio environment.

Selecting Sound Schemes

Sometimes, setting individual sounds for each Windows event can take more time than you have to spend. Or, you might have taken the time to carefully craft a set of event sounds you want to preserve for special occasions or holidays. But right now, you don't want sounds for a national holiday every day of the year. With Windows 98, you can pick a predefined sound scheme. You also can find schemes from various online sources.

To begin working with sound schemes, follow these steps:

1. Open the Sounds Properties dialog box. Here, you can use the Schemes drop-down list box to select, save, and delete sound schemes.

2. Open the Schemes drop-down list.

3. Pick an intriguing, favorite, or personal scheme name.

NOTE If a dialog box pops up asking whether you want to save the previous scheme, you should choose Yes to save your current sound scheme, No to not save your scheme, or Cancel to stop selecting a new sound scheme. If you choose Yes, name the scheme so that it can appear in the Schemes drop-down list box. ■

4. Click OK in the Sound Properties dialog box.

Saving Sound Schemes

If you created your own set of event sound settings or modified an existing one, you should save it for future use. You can do this by following these steps:

1. Display the Sounds Properties dialog box and click Save As in the Schemes group box. The Save Scheme As dialog box appears, as shown in Figure 15.7.

FIG. 15.7
The Save Scheme As
dialog box enables you
to name your group of
event sounds.

2. Enter a name for the scheme of event sounds defined in the Sound Properties Events list. If you use the same name as an existing scheme, a dialog box appears, asking you to confirm your decision to replace the existing scheme.

 TIP You cannot use the name Windows Default for a new sound scheme. This name is reserved for the default scheme installed under Windows.

After you complete these steps, you can click OK to close the Sound Properties dialog box.

Deleting a Sound Scheme

If you want to delete a configuration of event sounds, you can do so by following these steps:

1. Display the Sounds Properties dialog box and locate the scheme you want to remove by opening the Schemes drop-down list box.

2. Click Delete in the Schemes group box. A confirmation box appears, asking you to confirm your decision to replace the existing scheme.

N O T E Deleting the scheme does not delete the actual WAV file; it just deletes the connection between the event and the sound it plays. ■

After you complete these steps, you can click OK to close the Sound Properties dialog box.

Using Desktop Themes

One of the optional components you can install under Windows 98 is the Desktop Themes component. Desktop Themes is a set of pointers, sound events, wallpaper, and other items you can use to dress up Windows. To use Desktop Themes, you need to run the Add/Remove Programs applet and install the Desktop Themes components. You then double-click the Desktop Themes icon in the Control Panel to display the Desktop Themes window, as shown in Figure 15.8.

FIG. 15.8
Use Desktop Themes to add additional sound events to Windows.

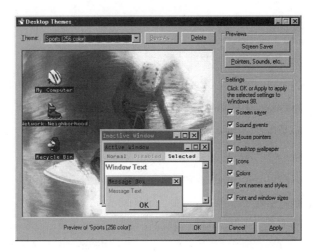

In the Desktop Themes window, select a theme from the Theme drop-down list box. Next, click Pointers, Sounds, and so on... to display the Preview window for the theme you choose. Select the Sounds tab to preview the sound associated with a Windows event. Select the event and click the Play button next to the icon at the bottom of the tab. Click OK.

If you don't want to use the sound events for this theme, deselect the Sound Events check box in the Settings area of the Desktop Themes window.

Click OK to set up the desktop theme of your choice. You then can return to the Sounds Properties dialog box to preview or change a system event setting, as you learned in "Specifying Event Sounds," earlier in this chapter.

To remove the theme, open the Desktop Themes window and select Windows Default or another theme from the Theme drop-down list box. Click OK.

Setting Audio Volume Levels

While using your computer, you might notice that your volume is too loud or too soft. Your CD-ROM drive, sound card, and MIDI instrument (usually part of your sound card) are all sources of the sounds and music. It's not unlikely that one of them is much louder or softer than the rest. In the next two sections, you'll look at adjusting the master volume for Windows audio and adjusting each sound source's volume.

Controlling Volume with the Taskbar Volume Control

If you need to adjust the overall volume of sound coming out of your computer, use the taskbar speaker icon for quick and easy volume changes.

If the yellow sound icon does not appear on your taskbar, use the following steps to enable the taskbar speaker icon:

1. Choose Start, Settings, Control Panel.
2. Double-click the Multimedia icon. The Multimedia Properties dialog box appears with the Audio page selected by default, as shown in Figure 15.9. Place a check mark in the Show Volume Control on the Taskbar check box. Selecting this option displays the volume control icon in the taskbar.

FIG. 15.10
The Multimedia Properties dialog box enables you to turn on the taskbar volume control.

3. Click OK to save the new setting and close the Multimedia Properties dialog box.

TROUBLESHOOTING

I can't seem to find the Multimedia Control Panel or the Audio page in the Multimedia Properties dialog box. What's wrong? Either you don't have a sound card installed in your computer, or Windows 98 did not recognize it. Read Chapter 5, "Installing and Configuring New Hardware and Software," for instructions on setting up your sound card in Windows 98.

Now that the speaker icon is visible, you'll be able to learn how to adjust the volume or quickly mute the audio level.

To adjust or mute the master volume, use these steps:

1. Click the speaker icon. The Volume Control Panel appears with a vertical slider, as shown in Figure 15.10.

FIG. 15.10

The taskbar's Volume Control Panel appears after you click the taskbar speaker icon.

2. Drag the slider up or down to adjust the master volume accordingly. If you need to mute the volume, enable the Mute check box to instantly mute every source of audio on your computer.

> **N O T E** If you mute the volume, notice how the speaker icon changes to a speaker icon covered by a red circle with a line through it. ▪

3. To close the Volume Control Panel, click anywhere else on the desktop except on the Volume panel.

TROUBLESHOOTING

I try to play video with sound, and it isn't synchronized. What's wrong? You might have a computer that isn't fast enough. You can try to improve performance and add RAM, but if you have an older, slower processor and a relatively slow hard drive, you might need to think about upgrading to a new PC with fast video capabilities built in. Many new PC lines are including MPEG boards to enhance the playback of digital video and audio.

Controlling Volume with the Volume Control Dialog Box

While using Windows 98, you might have noticed that one source of sound is louder or softer than the rest. Or, a particular sound source might not be producing *any* sound. In this section, you'll learn how to access individual sound source volumes and adjust them by following these steps:

1. Verify that the yellow taskbar speaker icon is visible. If it isn't, see the preceding section, "Controlling Volume with the Taskbar Volume Control."

2. Double-click the speaker icon. The Volume Control dialog box appears, as shown in Figure 15.11. Your Volume Control dialog box might have different controls and features, depending on the capabilities of your sound card. Also, different controls appear, depending on the mixer properties you have selected.

FIG. 15.11

The Volume Control dialog box gives you access to each sound source.

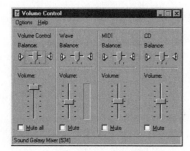

3. Choose Options, Properties to change which mixer properties are displayed. The Properties dialog box appears, as shown in Figure 15.12. In this dialog box, you select the device you want to adjust, such as your sound card or other audio device, from the Mixer Device drop-down list box.

FIG. 15.12

The Properties dialog box enables you to change which controls appear on the Volume Control dialog box.

4. In the Adjust Volume For area, select the type of sound you want to control, including Playback, Recording, and Other. Other includes sound card–specific controls, such as Voice Commands.

5. Select the controls for the type of sound in the Show the Following Volume Controls list box. These controls differ, depending on the type of sound you chose in step 4.

6. Click OK to save your settings. You return to the Volume Control dialog box.

7. On the Volume Control dialog box, the leftmost slider and Mute All check box is the same as the Volume Control Panel that is displayed after you single-click the speaker icon in the taskbar. To the right of this slider, each column is a control dedicated to each sound source. Each column has Balance and Volume sliders and Mute check boxes. If your sound card supports stereo audio, a left-right balance slider appears above each vertical slider that supports stereo. By causing selected pairs of sound sources to play long segments of sound, you can adjust the vertical sliders correspondingly.

8. After you make your adjustments, choose Options, Exit to close the Volume Control dialog box and save your settings.

Changing Audio Device Settings

At times, you might need to change the configuration settings assigned to a multimedia device, such as if you want to shut off an audio device. You can change such device settings via the Multimedia Control Panel. Follow these steps to change settings on your sound card:

1. Choose Start, Settings, Control Panel, and double-click the Multimedia icon. The Multimedia Properties dialog box appears.

2. Select the Devices page, as shown in Figure 15.13.

FIG. 15.13

You can change multimedia device settings by selecting the component from the Multimedia Devices list.

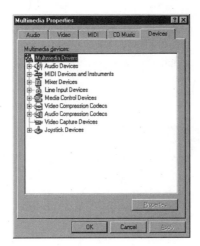

3. Click the plus sign next to the Audio Devices item.

4. Select the device you want from the resulting list and click Properties. The General page of your sound card's Properties dialog box appears, as shown in Figure 15.14. Set the following options:

   - *Use Audio Features on This Device.* Enables your sound card. This is the default setting if your sound card is working properly.

   - *Do Not Use Audio Features on This Device.* Disables your sound card, but leaves its device driver on your hard drive.

   - *Do Not Map Through This Device.* Instructs Windows 98 to not let any applications use the sound card unless the application specifically requests it.

5. Click OK twice.

FIG. 15.14
You can modify device settings for your sound card by using the General page.

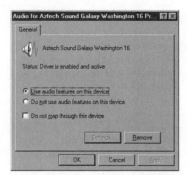

Changing Audio Playback Settings

You can change the playback settings of your sound card by setting advanced properties for it. These properties include selecting the preferred speaker setup for your computer and setting performance controls.

To make these changes, use the following steps:

1. Choose Start, Settings, Control Panel, and double-click the Multimedia icon. The Multimedia Properties dialog box appears.

2. Select the Audio page.

3. In the Playback area, click Advanced Properties. The Advanced Audio Properties dialog box appears, as shown in Figure 15.15.

FIG. 15.15
Use the Advanced Audio Properties dialog box to change speaker and performance settings.

4. From the Speaker Setup drop-down list box, select the speaker or headphone setup that most closely matches yours. If your speakers are part of a laptop PC, for example, select Laptop Mono Speakers or Laptop Stereo Speakers.

5. Select the Performance page, as shown in Figure 15.16.

Part
IV

Ch
15

FIG. 15.16
Use the Performance page to configure how Windows will play audio through your sound card.

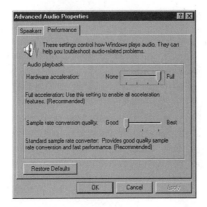

6. Set the following playback performance settings:

- *Hardware Acceleration.* Sets the acceleration rate for your sound mixing. Set this to Full unless you experience computer problems and think the sound card is the problem.

- *Sample Rate Conversion Quality.* Sets the quality of the sound card sampling rate. For the best sampling rate, set this to Best. However, to devote less CPU time to sampling, set this to Good.

- *Restore Defaults.* Switches your customized settings back to those first established when Windows was installed.

7. Click OK.

Changing Sound Quality When Recording

You can change the sound quality of your recording reproduction depending on your needs. A presentation probably will require a better quality sound reproduction than something like a short voice file you would attach to an in-house email message to distribute to coworkers. To change the recording sound quality, do the following:

1. Choose Start, Settings, Control Panel, and double-click the Multimedia icon. The Multimedia Properties dialog box appears.

2. In the Recording area of the Audio page, click Advanced Properties. The Advanced Audio Properties dialog box appears.

3. Set the following recording performance settings:

- *Hardware Acceleration.* Sets the acceleration rate for your recordings. Set this to Full unless you experience computer problems and think the sound card is the problem.

- *Sample Rate Conversion Quality.* Sets the quality of the sound card recording rate. For the best recording rate, set this to Best. However, to devote less CPU time to recording, set this to Good.

- *Restore Defaults.* Switches your recording settings back to those first established when Windows was installed.

4. Click OK twice.

TIP The higher the quality of the sound file you record, the more disk space is required. If you have limited disk storage space, don't select the highest recording quality unless you really need it.

TROUBLESHOOTING

I hear hissing during the playback of a sound file. What's happening? The file might be recording in 8 bits and playing back in 16 bits. The 16-bit board doesn't realize that the 8-bit file isn't the same high quality as a 16-bit file, so playing the file with expectations of higher sound quality emphasizes the lower detail.

Installing and Configuring MIDI Cards in Windows 98

Musical Instrument Digital Interface (MIDI) sound allows your computer to create complex-sounding music without using large amounts of memory like WAV files do. MIDI stores the instructions to play the sounds, not the actual sounds themselves. Very often, computer games require a MIDI-compatible sound card. In order to enjoy the games to their fullest, you need to ensure that your MIDI sounds are configured correctly.

The MIDI card acts as a connection between the MIDI controller, such as a keyboard or guitar, and your PC. Also in that equation is a synthesizer, which actually generates the MIDI sounds. The MIDI can be part of a sound card, which is how most users will come to know about MIDI, or a separate interface card. Either way, without a MIDI, you can make use of an external con-troller for your MIDI recordings. If you have a sound board with a MIDI in the form of the MIDI/joystick port, you won't need a separate MIDI card.

Windows 98 greatly reduces the complexity of configuring MIDI sounds via the Multimedia Control Panel applet.

N O T E This section and the following ones discuss the MPU-401 interface protocol. It is actually the MIDI "language" originally invented by Roland and now is virtually the de facto standard when it comes to MIDI use on the PC. ▪

After you insert your new MIDI card and before you can configure it to use with Windows 98, you have to install it. Chapter 5 covers adding a new device to your computer.

Adding a MIDI Instrument

If you have a MIDI device that Windows 98 doesn't know about yet, you need to add its configuration and capabilities to the list of known MIDI instruments. Before you proceed, you need the instrument definition file (*.IDF) from the hardware manufacturer containing the definition of the device. For some MIDI cards, Windows installs an IDF file(s) when you install the card itself. Follow these steps:

1. Plug the instrument you plan to use with your MIDI card into a MIDI port.

2. Choose Start, Settings, Control Panel, and double-click the Multimedia icon. The Multimedia Properties dialog box appears.

3. Select the MIDI page, as shown in Figure 15.17.

FIG. 15.17

The MIDI page of the Multimedia Properties dialog box provides control over MIDI output and MIDI instruments.

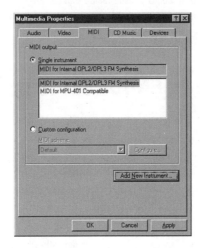

4. Click Add New Instrument. The MIDI Instrument Installation Wizard opens, as shown in Figure 15.18.

FIG. 15.18

The MIDI Instrument Installation Wizard guides you through setting up a new MIDI instrument.

5. Select the MIDI port to which the new instrument is attached.

6. Click Next. Select the type of MIDI instrument you're installing. If the type is not listed in the Instrument Definitions list, click Browse to locate an IDF on a disk.

7. Click Next. Enter a name for the instrument. This name will appear below the MIDI port name on the MIDI page of the Multimedia Properties dialog box. A default name is supplied, but you might want to change it to help you identify the device.

 TIP A good way to identify your new instrument is by its make and model instead of its location. Instruments tend to be moved a lot, but the make and model don't change unless you upgrade your equipment.

8. Click Finish. This adds the new instrument to the MIDI Properties dialog box.

Selecting the MIDI Output Destination

After you define your instrument(s), you need to identify where the MIDI data should go. If you have only one instrument or an internal sound card that can receive MIDI data, follow these steps:

1. Open the Multimedia Properties dialog box and select the MIDI page.

2. Select Single Instrument.

N O T E The Custom Configure option is better left unselected unless you are a professional musician with MIDI experience. Adjusting MIDI channels to various MIDI-in and MIDI-out ports takes careful planning for all MIDI instruments involved. If you are experienced with MIDI, the MIDI Configuration dialog box is easier for you to use than almost any other computer MIDI interface. ■

3. Click OK to save your choice and close the Multimedia Properties dialog box.

Adjusting MIDI Card Volume Settings

Having installed your new MIDI card, you now can adjust its sound. You can adjust your MIDI card volume level via the Audio page in the Multimedia Properties dialog box. To adjust the playback and recording volume level, do the following:

1. Open the Multimedia Properties dialog box; the Audio page should be selected by default.

2. Click the Volume Control button next to the Preferred Device drop-down list. The Volume Control dialog box appears.

3. Adjust the slider control in the MIDI column of the Volume Control dialog box to your desired level.

TROUBLESHOOTING

I can't get MIDI files to play back properly. What can I do? This may happen for a number of reasons. To start with, check the card's resource settings, such as IRQ settings, to make sure they are configured correctly for your specific MIDI board. Then make sure the MIDI board is correctly identified in Device Manager.

Moving a MIDI Instrument to Another Board

You can move MIDI instruments between boards. You might want to do this, for example, if you have a choice of sound boards to output your MIDI playback.

To move an instrument between boards, follow these steps:

1. Open the Multimedia Properties dialog box and select the Devices page.

2. Click the plus sign next to MIDI Devices and Instruments.

3. From the ensuing list, click the plus sign next to the board to which your MIDI instrument is connected. See Figure 15.19.

FIG. 15.19
You use the Device page in Multimedia Properties to specify the MIDI instrument you want to move.

4. Click the instrument you want to move, and click Properties. The Properties dialog box for the selected MIDI instrument appears.

5. From the MIDI instrument Properties dialog box, select the Details page, as shown in Figure 15.20.

FIG. 15.20
Using the External MIDI
Instrument Properties
dialog.

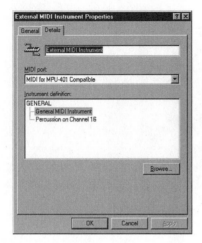

6. From the MIDI Port drop-down list, choose the name of the board to which you want to connect the instrument. If there are no other port choices in the MIDI Port drop-down list, you have only one board set up to which you can connect your instrument.

7. Click OK to save your setting.

8. You return to the Advanced page in Multimedia Properties; click OK.

9. Plug your MIDI instrument into the new board you specify in step 6.

Removing a MIDI Instrument

If you no longer use a MIDI instrument, you can remove it from the MIDI page. To this, use the following steps:

1. Open the Multimedia Properties dialog box and select the Devices page.

2. Click the plus sign next to MIDI Devices and Instruments.

3. From the ensuing list, click the plus sign next to the board to which your MIDI instrument is connected.

4. Click the instrument you want to delete, and click Properties. The Properties dialog box for the selected MIDI instrument appears.

5. From the MIDI Instrument Properties dialog box, select the General page, as shown in Figure 15.21.

6. Click Remove. The instrument is deleted and the Details page returns.

7. Click OK.

FIG. 15.21
You can remove an instrument by using the General page.

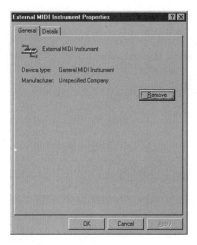

TROUBLESHOOTING

There is hissing and distortion when I play MIDI files. How can I get rid of it? Interference might be coming from the power source or another card installed in your computer. Turn off your PC and move the MIDI board as far away from the power supply and other boards as possible. If you can, leave a few empty expansion slots between the MIDI board and the next card.

TROUBLESHOOTING

I've tried everything and still can't hear anything from my sound card. Could there be a problem with my speakers? How would I know? You can look at some of the following things to check on your speakers to get them to work with your sound card:

- Make sure the speakers are switched on.
- Ensure that power is coming into the speakers. If your speakers are AC powered, make sure the cord is plugged in. If they are DC powered, make sure your batteries are fresh and are inserted.
- Check to see whether the volume on the speakers is turned up.
- Make sure the speakers are connected to your sound card.
- For speakers that are placed close to or are attached to your monitor, make sure that the speakers are shielded. This eliminates electromagnetic interference from the speakers to your monitor. If you suspect interference, move the speakers or purchase ones that are shielded.

CHAPTER 16

Configuring Full-Motion Video Capabilities

by Rob Tidrow

In this chapter

Examining the Windows 98 Video Environment

Over the past three or four years, the availability of digital video clips for PCs has increased dramatically. Many of the clips available are intended for entertainment or marketing purposes. However, a significant number of video files and applications that incorporate video for business, education, and information dissemination (such as news, weather, and sports) are also available.

One way that digital video has found its way onto the desktop of corporate business users, for example, has been the wide-ranging appeal of the World Wide Web. Video clips of news events can be downloaded from USA Today's or MSNBC's Web sites. This way, executives or staff members can easily download news items throughout the day to stay abreast of late-breaking news. Or users who want control over when they listen to and watch the news can access it when they have the time. The Web is not the only source for PC video. Some applications such as games, education programs, and interactive music CD-ROMs include video events.

If you're upgrading from Windows 95, you know that Windows provides a nice environment in which to play back full-motion video and animations. Windows 98 provides the same multimedia architecture as Windows 95 but provides additional features to make Windows 98 a richer platform on which to play and record video.

Video files, like other multimedia files, are very large. A one-minute video clip saved to disk straight from video would take up more than 1GB of hard disk space. To enable PCs to record video efficiently, compression software is used. During playback, decompression software expands the file so that you can view it on your screen. Windows 98's multimedia component architecture includes the Video Compression Manager (VCM), which handles video and image data compression. Within the VCM, the software that handles compression and decompression is known as *codec*. How well a video file plays compared to its original noncompressed format depends on the codec's compression method and compression parameters.

When multimedia developers design video titles to run on Windows 98, they can provide a codec with their titles or use one already installed on Windows. If they provide a codec, it must be installed on your machine prior to running the multimedia title. Usually, this installation is part of the general installation process for the title.

In most cases, multimedia developers rely on the codecs that are preinstalled with Windows 98. They include the following:

- Radius Cinepak
- Intel Indeo R3.1, R3.2, 5.02
- msh261 and msh263
- RLE (run-length encoding)
- Microsoft Video 1

Another important aspect of video files is the file format in which a title is saved. The following points summarize the formats supported by Windows 98:

■ *Video for Windows (AVI)*. Video for Windows format was developed by Microsoft to run under Windows 3.x. With Windows 95 and Windows 98, Video for Windows is now 32 bit and provides an efficient and fast platform to play back video files. In general, AVI movies run in 320×240 resolution (see Figure 16.1), but the actual display of a movie depends on Windows. It determines the best performance setup for the video depending on your display.

FIG. 16.1
This AVI movie is running in 320×240 resolution.

■ *QuickTime for Windows (MOV, QT)*. QuickTime for Windows is the cousin to Apple's QuickTime for Macintosh video and animation file format. Because QuickTime supports multiple platforms (Mac and Windows), and because QuickTime files are a little clearer than AVI files, serious multimedia developers have adopted QuickTime files as the de facto standard. At one time, QuickTime files were the dominant video format available, particularly on the World Wide Web and on CD-ROM. Now, however, the availability of AVI files has grown, but the mindshare is still held by the QuickTime format. Therefore, Windows 98 now supports QuickTime for Windows files natively using the ActiveMovie runtime DLL (dynamic link library). (See the next bullet item for more information on ActiveMovie.) This support is welcome relief for those millions of Windows 3.x and 95 users who had to acquire and install a separate QuickTime for Windows player to view MOV files.

■ *ActiveMovie*. ActiveMovie, which is a streaming architecture created by Microsoft, provides support for several video formats, including AVI, MOV, and MPEG video. The concept of ActiveMovie is to provide a DirectX (see Chapter 15, "Installing Sound and MIDI Cards") control for Microsoft Internet Explorer 4.0 to use when Internet and intranet documents containing multimedia content are viewed. Instead of IE 4.0 relying on separate applications to launch (called *spawning*) to play a video file, the ActiveMovie control spawns to handle the file.

■ *MPEG*. MPEG (Moving Picture Experts Group) provides good quality video in relatively small files, which makes MPEG suitable, if not ideal, for video distributions via CD and the World Wide Web. One downside to MPEG is that it requires a great deal from your system, and it generally performs better on systems with special MPEG hardware devices.

N O T E   A new technology introduced by Microsoft and supported by Windows 98 is Surround Video. Surround Video enables full-screen, interactive multimedia movies to play on PCs. Users can interact with Surround Video titles in a 360-degree "environment," which provides training, game, and other multimedia title developers a rich development tool in which to create breathtaking and realistic-looking video. You can learn more about Surround Video on the Web at http://www.microsoft.com. Search on the word surround. ■

Configuring Video Settings

Windows 98 includes built-in support for AVI, MOV, and MPEG video files. This support enables you to download these file types and play them on your desktop without worrying about downloading and configuring a separate video file player. It also means that you can send files in these formats to other people who use Windows 98 and feel confident that they can play the files you send them.

Depending on the components you install during Windows 98 Setup, you may or may not have video support installed on your system. The Media Player and Video Compression (codecs) components must be installed to play back video on your system. To find out, open the Add/Remove Programs Properties page and click the Windows Setup tab. Click the Multimedia option and then click Details. Make sure the two components just mentioned are installed. If these components are not installed, install them now.

 You also can look in the Start, Programs, Accessories, Multimedia folder for the Media Player applet. However, you cannot easily see whether the Video Compression components are installed.

Using the Video Properties Page

Windows 98 provides two primary tools to use and display information about video files. You can view information about video files by using the Video Properties page. To display this page, locate a video file, such as an AVI file, on your system. If you elected to install all the Help files during the Windows Setup, for example, look in the Windows\Help folder for a collection of AVI files. You also can look on the Windows 98 CD-ROM in \Cdsample\Videos for a few AVI and MPEG files.

Right-click the file in Windows Explorer and select Properties. This action displays the Video Properties page with the name of the file in the title bar of the property page, as shown in Figure 16.2. On the General tab, you can see information about the video file, including size, creation date and time, and its attributes. You can change the attributes of the file to make it read-only, hidden, or archive.

FIG. 16.2

The General tab of the Video Properties page shows information about the selected AVI file.

Part

IV

Ch

16

For AVI files, the Details tab shows information about the contents of the files (see Figure 16.3). This information includes the name of the file, who holds the copyright to the file, the length of the video, and audio and video compression information. At the bottom of the Details tab for some files, you may see the Other Information area. In this area, you can click an item in the left panel to see the description of the item in the right box. The items in the Other Information area vary depending on the file. Some files may show only one item in this area, whereas others may have several items.

FIG. 16.3

The Details tab shows information about the contents of an AVI file.

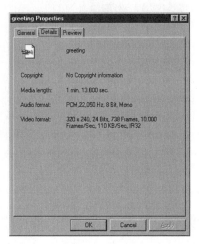

Click the Preview tab (for AVI files only) to see the starting frame of the AVI file. Click the play button to view the entire video (see Figure 16.4). You can click the stop button to pause the AVI.

Click OK after you finish viewing the Video Properties page.

FIG. 16.4
The Preview tab includes a play button to enable you to play back the selected AVI file.

Using the Media Player

The Media Player application is used to play back many multimedia file types, including AVI files, Autodesk Animator files, MIDI, and QuickTime, and video files.

You can launch the Media Player by selecting Start, Programs, Accessories, Multimedia, Media Player. This action displays the Media Player application (see Figure 16.5).

FIG. 16.5
Media Player enables you to play back many types of multimedia file types.

To see which types of multimedia file types are configured for your copy of Media Player, select the Device menu. To run an AVI file, for example, select the Video for Windows option. This action displays the Open dialog box, from which you can select an AVI file to run.

 You also can select File, Open and select the Files of type drop-down list to display the types of files you can play back in Media Player.

After you open a video file, a window appears under the Media Player main window (see Figure 16.6). The buttons on the Media Player window are activated so that you can control the playback of the video. The following list describes each of the VCR-type controls you can use to run and control the video file:

- *Play*. Starts the video playback.
- *Stop*. Stops the video playback.
- *Eject*. Ejects an audio CD-ROM. Not active when you run an AVI file.

- ■ *Previous Mark.* Moves you to the previous beginning or end of a clip or section of a video.

- ■ *Rewind.* Reverses the video.

- ■ *Fast Forward.* Moves the video forward.

- ■ *Next Mark.* Moves you to the beginning or end of a clip or section of a video.

- ■ *Start Selection.* Enables you to mark a place in the video if you want to play only a portion of the video.

- ■ *End Selection.* Enables you to mark the end point of a selection if you want to play only a portion of the video.

Part

IV

Ch

16

FIG. 16.6

Media Player provides controls to let you start, pause, or stop a video, or jump to a specific section of a video.

Although the Media Player does not have many user-configurable options, you can do a few things to change the way Media Player looks. You can, for example, resize the Media Player window by grabbing the window edges and resizing it with your mouse. One problem with this method is that it may distort the image somewhat. To resize the Media Player window more precisely, select Device, Properties (available with AVI files) to display the Video Properties dialog box (see Figure 16.7).

Next, click the drop-down list next to the Window option to choose the size of the window. The default setting is Original size, which is usually 320×240 or 160×120 pixels. You also can select from Double original size, 1/16 of screen size, 1/4 of screen size, 1/2 of screen size, or Maximized. If you don't like any of these choices, exit the drop-down list and click the Full Screen option. This action displays the video in a window that covers the entire Windows 98 desktop, including the taskbar. Click OK to exit and view the AVI file in the window size you select.

You also can set playback options to customize how the video window looks and behaves during playback. Select Edit, Options to display the Options dialog box (see Figure 16.8). The following is a description of each of the options in this dialog box:

- ■ *Auto Rewind.* Automatically rewinds the AVI file after it finishes.

- ■ *Auto Repeat.* Loops the AVI file until you click the stop button.

- *Control Bar On Playback.* Displays controls for starting and stopping, as well as a slider bar, on video files when they are inserted in documents as OLE (Object Linking and Embedding) objects.

- *Caption.* Enables you to enter a caption for the video file when it is embedded as an OLE object.

- *Border around object.* Places a thin box around the embedded icon when a video file is inserted in a document.

- *Play in client document.* Instructs the video file to play inside a document when you insert the file as an OLE object.

- *Dither picture to VGA colors.* Adjusts the colors of the video to VGA setting.

Click OK to exit the Options dialog box and save your settings.

FIG. 16.7
The Video Properties dialog box enables you to set the size of the video window.

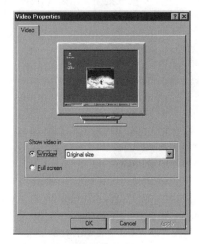

FIG. 16.8
Use the Options dialog box to configure how Media Player looks and plays back AVI files.

Optimizing Video Settings in Windows 98

You may find that optimizing your system in general will provide a better platform on which to run any multimedia file, including video files. You can, however, maximize your environment for video files in some ways.

First, if you plan to work on the World Wide Web, you should prepare your system so that it can use the ActiveMovie control to play AVI, MPEG, and QuickTime files. By default, when you run Internet Explorer 4.0, ActiveMovie is installed. On some systems, ActiveMovie may not run properly due to hardware incompatibilities. Table 16.1 lists a number of common video adapters that currently support ActiveMovie.

Table 16.1   Video Adapters Supporting ActiveMovie

Adapter Manufacturer	Adapter Product Name
ATI Technologies	ATI 8514-Ultra (mach8)
ATI Technologies	ATI Graphics Pro Turbo (mach64)
ATI Technologies	ATI Graphics Pro Turbo PCI (mach64)
ATI Technologies	ATI Graphics Ultra (mach8)
ATI Technologies	ATI Graphics Ultra Pro (mach32)
ATI Technologies	ATI Graphics Ultra Pro EISA (mach32)
ATI Technologies	ATI Graphics Vantage (mach8)
ATI Technologies	ATI Graphics Wonder (mach32)
ATI Technologies	ATI Rage/Rage II PCI (ati_m64)
ATI Technologies	ATI Rage/Rage II+ PCI (ati_m64)
ATI Technologies	ATI VGA Wonder
ATI Technologies	ATI WinTurbo (mach64)
Cardinal Technologies	Cardinal VIDEOcolor (Cirrus Logic)
Cardinal Technologies	Cardinal VIDEOspectrum (Cirrus Logic)
Chips & Technologies	Chips & Technologies Accelerator
Chips & Technologies	Chips & Technologies Super VGA
Chips & Technologies	Chips & Technologies 64310 PCI
Chips & Technologies	Chips & Technologies 65545 PCI
Chips & Technologies	Chips & Technologies 65548 PCI
Chips & Technologies	Chips & Technologies 65550 PCI
Chips & Technologies	Chips & Technologies 65554 PCI
Cirrus Logic	Cirrus Logic
Cirrus Logic	Cirrus Logic 5429/30/34
Cirrus Logic	Cirrus Logic 5430/40 PCI

continues

Table 16.1   Continued

Adapter Manufacturer	Adapter Product Name
Cirrus Logic	Cirrus Logic 5434 PCI
Cirrus Logic	Cirrus Logic 5436 PCI
Cirrus Logic	Cirrus Logic 5446 PCI
Cirrus Logic	Cirrus Logic 5462 PCI
Cirrus Logic	Cirrus Logic 7542 PCI
Cirrus Logic	Cirrus Logic 7543 PCI
Cirrus Logic	Cirrus Logic 7548 PCI
Compaq	Compaq Notebook Display (WD)
DFI	DFI WG-1000 (Cirrus Logic)
DFI	DFI WG-1000VL Plus (Cirrus Logic)
DFI	DFI WG-1000VL/4 Plus (Cirrus Logic)
DFI	DFI WG-3000P (S3)
DFI	DFI WG-5000 (Tseng)
DFI	DFI WG-6000VL (WD)
Diamond Multimedia Systems	Diamond SpeedStar (Tseng)
Diamond Multimedia Systems	Diamond SpeedStar 24 (Tseng)
Diamond Multimedia Systems	Diamond SpeedStar 24X (WD)
Diamond Multimedia Systems	Diamond SpeedStar 64
Diamond Multimedia Systems	Diamond SpeedStar Pro (Cirrus Logic)
Diamond Multimedia Systems	Diamond SpeedStar Pro SE
Diamond Multimedia Systems	Diamond Stealth 24 (S3)
Diamond Multimedia Systems	Diamond Stealth 32 (Tseng)
Diamond Multimedia Systems	Diamond Stealth 64 DRAM PCI
Diamond Multimedia Systems	Diamond Stealth 64 DRAM VLB
Diamond Multimedia Systems	Diamond Stealth 64 PCI
Diamond Multimedia Systems	Diamond Stealth 64 Video VRAM PCI
Diamond Multimedia Systems	Diamond Stealth 64 Video VRAM VLB
Diamond Multimedia Systems	Diamond Stealth 64 VRAM VLB

Adapter Manufacturer	Adapter Product Name
Diamond Multimedia Systems	Diamond Stealth Pro
Diamond Multimedia Systems	Diamond Stealth SE PCI
Diamond Multimedia Systems	Diamond Stealth SE VLB
Diamond Multimedia Systems	Diamond Stealth Video PCI
Diamond Multimedia Systems	Diamond Stealth Video VLB
Diamond Multimedia Systems	Diamond Stealth VRAM (S3)
Digital Equipment Corp.	DEC PC76H-EA (S3)
Digital Equipment Corp.	DEC PC76H-EB (S3)
Digital Equipment Corp.	DEC PC76H-EC (S3)
Digital Equipment Corp.	DEC PCXAG-AJ (S3)
Digital Equipment Corp.	DEC PCXAG-AK (S3)
Digital Equipment Corp.	DEC PCXAG-AN (S3)
ELSA	ELSA WINNER 1000Trio (S3)
ELSA	ELSA WINNER 1280 (C&T)
ELSA	ELSA WINNER 2000 VL (S3)
ELSA	ELSA WINNER 2000PRO (S3)
ELSA	ELSA WINNER/2-1280 (C&T)
Genoa Systems	Genoa Phantom 32I (Tseng)
Genoa Systems	Genoa Phantom 64 (S3)
Genoa Systems	Genoa WindowsVGA 24 Turbo (Cirrus Logic)
Genoa Systems	Genoa WindowsVGA 64 Turbo (Cirrus Logic)
Hercules Computer Technology	Hercules Dynamite (Tseng)
Hercules Computer Technology	Hercules Dynamite Pro (Tseng)
Hercules Computer Technology	Hercules Graphite 64 (S3)
Hercules Computer Technology	Hercules Graphite Terminator 64 (S3)
Hercules Computer Technology	Hercules Graphite Terminator Pro (S3)
IBM	IBM ThinkPad 755cx (WD)

Part
IV

Ch
16

continues

Table 16.1 Continued

Adapter Manufacturer	Adapter Product Name
Matrox Graphics	Matrox MGA Millennium
Matrox Graphics	Matrox MGA Mystique
NeoMagic Corporation	NeoMagic MagicGraph 128V
NeoMagic Corporation	NeoMagic MagicGraph 128ZV
Number Nine Visual Technology	Number Nine 9FX Motion 531 (S3)
Number Nine Visual Technology	Number Nine 9FX Motion 771 (S3)
Number Nine Visual Technology	Number Nine 9FX Vision 330 (S3)
Number Nine Visual Technology	Number Nine FlashPoint 32 (Cirrus Logic)
Number Nine Visual Technology	Number Nine FlashPoint 64 (Cirrus Logic)
Number Nine Visual Technology	Number Nine GXE (S3)
Number Nine Visual Technology	Number Nine GXE64 (S3)
Number Nine Visual Technology	Number Nine GXE64 Pro (S3)
Number Nine Visual Technology	Number Nine Imagine 128
Orchid Technology	Orchid Fahrenheit 1280 Plus (S3)
Orchid Technology	Orchid Fahrenheit Pro 64 (S3)
Orchid Technology	Orchid Fahrenheit VA (S3)
Orchid Technology	Orchid Kelvin 64 (Cirrus Logic)
Orchid Technology	Orchid Kelvin EZ (Cirrus Logic)
Orchid Technology	Orchid ProDesigner II (Tseng)
Paradise	Paradise Accelerator Ports O'Call (WD)
Paradise	Paradise Accelerator VL Plus (WD)
Paradise	Paradise Bahamas (S3)
Paradise	Paradise Barbados 64 (S3)
Paradise	Paradise Super VGA (WD)
Rendition, Inc.	Rendition Verite 1000 PCI
S3	S3 Vision864 PCI
S3	S3 Vision868 PCI
S3	S3 Vision964 PCI
S3	S3 Vision964 PCI

Adapter Manufacturer	Adapter Product Name
S3	S3 Vision968 PCI
Spider Graphics	Spider 32 VLB (Cirrus Logic)
Spider Graphics	Spider 32Plus VLB (Cirrus Logic)
Spider Graphics	Spider 64 (Cirrus Logic)
Spider Graphics	Spider Tarantula 64 (S3)
Trident Microsystems	Trident 9320 PCI (v6.00.20)
Trident Microsystems	Trident 9440 PCI (v6.00.20)
Trident Microsystems	Trident 9685/9680/9682/9385/9382/9385-1 PCI (v6.00.20)
Tseng Labs	Tseng Labs ET4000
Tseng Labs	Tseng Labs ET4000/W32
Tseng Labs	Tseng Labs ET4000/W32 PCI
Tseng Labs	Tseng Labs ET6000 PCI

Part IV

Ch 16

 TIP If your video adapter is not listed in Table 16.1, contact your manufacturer to find out whether an updated driver supporting ActiveMovie is available. Also, visit the Hardware Compatibility List Web site at http://www.microsoft.com/hwtest/hcl and search in the Display Adapter category (see Figure 16.9).

FIG. 16.9
The Hardware Compatibility List is helpful when you want to know whether your video adapter will work with Windows 98 and ActiveMovie.

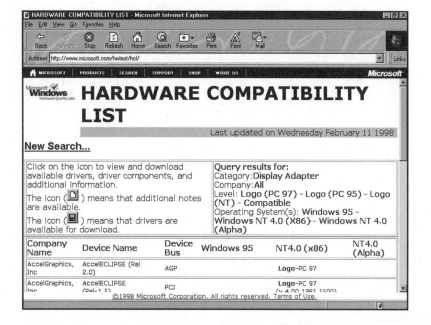

To increase video performance, you shouldn't look only at which adapter you have installed. You also should look at the following optimization items for your adapter and other system components :

- Install more video adapter RAM, if possible. Doing so increases color depth and resolutions.

- Increase the number of colors to above 256. On the Display properties Sheet's Setting tab, click the Colors drop-down list and select High Color (16 bit) or True Color (24 bit). If your card does not support this capability, ask your card's manufacturer if an updated driver will help. If not, you're stuck with 256 colors. If you increase colors, the depth of colors displayed in a video card will be clearer and closer to the actual color of the original video. Although this change will increase the look of items on your screen, your display will take longer to paint items because of the increase in information that must be displayed.

- Turn off the VESA support if a DOS driver must be loaded. Doing so greatly increases the performance of the video during playback.

- Use a generic Windows display driver if your manufacturer does not provide an updated driver. You may need to experiment with a few until you hit on one that works.

- Install at least 32MB of RAM on your computer. Doing so ensures that enough RAM is allocated for processing your video and that an ample portion of the video is stored in RAM during playback. Video playing back from the hard drive or from a CD is much slower than playing back from RAM.

- Open the AUTOEXEC.BAT file and add the SET TEMP = and SET TMP = values to a folder that can temporarily store video files during playback. Make sure that you have sufficient space in this folder for the video files you plan to play back. Save AUTOEXEC.BAT and reboot to have these settings take effect.

- Defragment your hard drive periodically to clean up fragmented files.

- Run ScanDisk to check and fix errors found on your drive(s) and to repair bad sectors on your drive.

- Turn off any application and service you're not using, such as screen savers and network monitoring utilities.

CHAPTER 17

Configuring PC TV Devices

by Dean Andrews

In this chapter

Installing TV Viewer to Work with Windows 98

Windows 98 adds a brand new component called WebTV for Windows to the Windows operating system. It allows you to view both standard and interactive television broadcasts over your computer. You can also browse television program listings, which get regularly updated over the Internet.

Before you enable this feature, you should purchase and install a TV tuner card, if you don't already have one installed. TV tuner cards are hardware boards that fit into an ISA or PCI slot in your PC. These boards receive TV broadcast signals either through a standard antenna or via a cable television service cable that you attach to the back of the card. TV tuners range in price from around $50 to $100 and are manufactured by several different companies including the video board makers Matrox and ATI Technologies.

If you don't own and aren't planning to buy a TV tuner card, you can still use the free TV listings in the WebTV Program Guide to view the schedule for upcoming television broadcasts and cable channel programming.

> **CAUTION**
>
> Be aware that some TV tuner cards work only in conjunction with video boards from the same manufacturer. For example, the Rainbow Runner Television board from Matrox functions only when used with the Mystique 220 and Rainbow Runner Studio daughter card that Matrox manufactures.
>
> In other cases, you may need to update the drivers for your video board to support the viewing of TV broadcasts. If you have difficulty getting a TV tuner card to work properly, check the Web site of your video card manufacturer for the latest drivers.

Use the following steps to install the WebTV for Windows component of Windows 98:

1. Open the Start menu and choose Settings, Control Panel.
2. Choose the Add/Remove Programs object. Then select the Windows Setup tab.
3. Scroll down until you see the WebTV for Windows entry in the Components list. Then put a check in the box next to WebTV for Windows (see Figure 17.1).
4. Click OK to install the WebTV for Windows component.

N O T E Windows 98 refers to a TV tuner board as a *TV Data Adapter* in the dialog boxes during installation. ∎

Windows 98 needs to restart Windows to complete the WebTV component installation process, so click Yes when asked whether you want to restart. In the next boot cycle, Windows automatically finds your TV tuner card and installs drivers for it, if you have one installed. Then Windows needs to restart one more time to complete the installation of this new hardware.

FIG. 17.1
Put a check next to the
WebTV for Windows
component.

Configuring TV Viewer

After WebTV is loaded, you need to download the latest program listings and customize the
viewer to your personal preferences. To launch WebTV, open the Start menu and choose, Programs, Accessories, Entertainment, WebTV for Windows. Alternatively, you can choose the
little TV icon in the system tray of the Windows taskbar.

The first time you launch WebTV, you see a Welcome screen explaining its features. Move
through the overview of WebTV features by clicking the Next button. At the end of the overview tour, you see a Finish button. Click this button to see the main program listings screen.

Retrieving Program Listings

WebTV originally loads with default program listings. To update this list, you need an active
connection to the Internet because the program data is retrieved via the Web.

▶ **See** "Configuring Modems," **p. 309**

To retrieve WebTV's program listings from the Internet, use the following procedure:

1. Choose the TV Configuration channel from the list of channels (see Figure17.2).

2. Click the Watch button on the remote control at the right side of the window.

3. Choose the Guide Plus+ link in the TV Configuration menu. Windows then connects you
   to the Internet using Internet Explorer 4.0 and automatically browses the Program
   Listing site of Starsight Telecast, Inc.

4. Enter your five-digit zip code in the appropriate box by pressing the numeric keys on
   your keyboard.

5. After you've typed your zip code, another box pops up with the message Select your
   cable provider or broadcast region pops up. If you have a cable television hook-up
   that you can connect to your computer, select your cable service provider from the list.
   Otherwise, choose BROADCAST (see Figure 17.3)

FIG. 17.2
Choose the TV
Configuration channel.

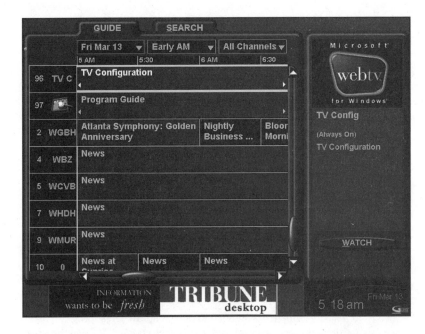

FIG. 17.3
If you have cable TV,
choose your service
provider; otherwise,
choose BROADCAST.

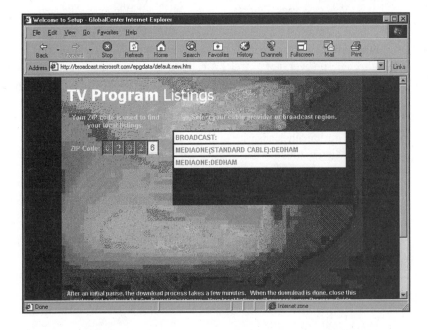

6. When you see the TV Program Listing Data Downloader box, choose Download to begin
   receiving the program listing information (see Figure 17.4)

FIG. 17.4
Choose Download to
begin downloading the
program listings.

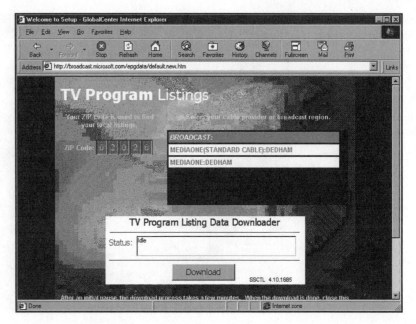

7. The process of downloading the program listings may take several minutes. When the process is complete, you see the message Success! Loader has completed in the Status window of the TV Program Listing Data Downloader box. At this point, you can close the Internet Explorer window by choosing File, Close.

Back in the Program Guide screen of WebTV, you then find an updated list of TV programming in your area. Each download brings you two days' worth of local TV scheduling.

Searching for Channels

In case you want to find a particular show or type of show, but don't know where to find it, WebTV provides two ways to search through the television channels. You can either browse the listings by category or by title.

To search the channels by category, use the following procedure:

1. In WebTV, choose the Search tab to display the search window (see Figure 17.5)

2. Scroll the list of TV show categories (Action, Comedy, Movies, and so on) on the far left of the window.

3. Choose a category to display a list of shows.

To search the channels by title, use the following procedure:

1. In WebTV, choose the Search tab to display the search window.

2. On the lower left of the search window, enter the keyword(s) for which you want to search into the Search For box (see Figure 17.6)

FIG. 17.5
Choose the Search tab to display WebTV's search window.

FIG. 17.6
Enter your keywords in the Search For box.

3. Choose the Search button below the Search For box to display a list of shows matching your keyword(s).

You can also modify the search list by using the Sort by time and All days drop-down boxes at the top of the Search window. These boxes let you sort the list of shows by date and title, as well as, narrow down the number of days you want to search through.

Changing WebTV Options

You can adjust the list of channels that the Program Guide displays by modifying the Settings options of WebTV. The Settings options let you select all the channels in your area or just the ones that you are interested in watching. In Settings, you can also pick whether WebTV should show you which shows have closed captioning.

To adjust the settings for WebTV's Program Guide, use the following procedure:

1. In WebTV's Program Guide, press the Alt key on your keyboard (or move your mouse cursor up to the top of the window) to display the Program Guide toolbar (see Figure 17.7).

FIG. 17.7

Press the Alt key to display the Program Guide toolbar, or just move your mouse cursor to the top of the window.

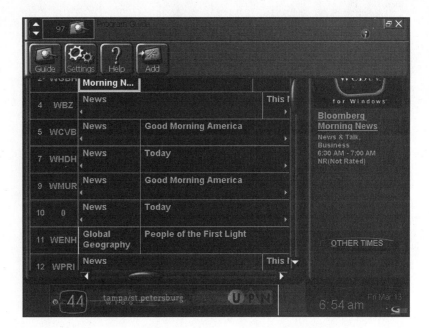

2. Choose the Settings button on the toolbar to display the Settings dialog box (see Figure 17.8)

3. Put a check next to the channels you want displayed in the Program Guide, or choose Show all to display the entire list. Put a check next to Show closed captioning if you want closed caption information displayed in the summary of shows.

4. Click OK to close the Settings dialog box.

FIG. 17.8

Choose the Settings
button on the toolbar to
display the Settings
dialog box.

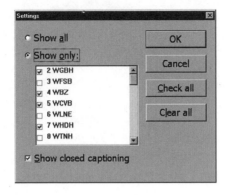

Configuring Windows 98 Communication Capabilities

CHAPTER 18

Configuring Modems

by Rob Tidrow

In this chapter

Choosing a Modem

A modem converts computer signals to telephone signals and back again so that you can use the telephone lines to communicate with other computers. You can use a modem to send email, faxes, and files to and receive them from any other computer with a modem. Also, you can use your modem to connect to online services such as America Online and CompuServe, and even the Internet. Windows 98 includes various programs you can use with a modem, including HyperTerminal, Internet Explorer 4.0, Outlook Express, Phone Dialer, and a handful of online services, such as America Online and the Microsoft Network (MSN).

Windows can autodetect and install any of hundreds of modems by using the Modem Wizard. Alternatively, Windows enables you to install your modem manually by choosing the manufacturer and model from a list.

You can choose from numerous modems, and the one you choose governs how fast your computer communicates over the phone lines. You'll really notice the speed of your modem when you transfer large files to or from another computer. The faster your modem, the more efficiently the data transfers. You can find information about manufacturers of modems by visiting `http://www.yahoo.com/Business_and_Economy/Companies/Computers//Hardware/Peripherals/Modems/`.

N O T E A device that converts from digital (computer signals) to analog (telephone signals) is called a *modulator*; a device that converts from analog to digital is called a *demodulator*. MOdulator-DEModulator is how *modem* got its name. ▨

N O T E When you're deciding whether to use an internal or external modem, keep in mind that an internal modem is generally less expensive and takes up less space on the desktop than the external. Internal modems also do not require you to purchase a separate serial cable, which you must do with external modems.

On the downside, however, internal modems require you to remove the case or cover of your PC and install the modem inside your computer. Although this task is not difficult, it may intimidate some users who have never done this kind of work before. Also, external modems have status indicator lights that provide you with visual cues to what the modem is doing, such as connecting to another modem or transferring data. ▨

Understanding Modem Speeds

The speed of a modem is measured in *bits per second* (*bps*). Make sure that you get the fastest available; today's maximum analog modem speed is 56,000 bps. However, 33,600 bps and 28,800 bps are the most typical type you find on PCs being sold today. Slower modem speeds are 14,400; 9,600; and 2,400 bps. A 14,400 bps modem is also acceptable, but don't use anything slower, or you'll be disappointed with your communications.

N O T E Windows 98 supports both of the 56,000 bps modem "standards." Lucent Technologies and Rockwell Semiconductor are working together on a standard called *K56flex* that will enable modems rated at 56Kbps to interoperate with each other. Other companies supporting this standard include AST Research, Compaq, Hewlett-Packard, and Toshiba. Although 56Kbps modems are available today, many online services and Internet service providers (ISPs) may support only one of the 56K modem types. If you decide to purchase one of these modems and have an account with a service, make sure that you contact your service to find out whether it can support your modem.

On February 6, 1998, a compromise over the 56K modem war was reached. The International Telecommunications Union (ITU) released the V.90 modem standard. This new standard "harmonizes" the two standards and will allow ISPs and online services to support both X2 and K56flex modems. If you have a 56K modem, you should, in many cases, be able get software from your modem manufacturer to make your existing 56K modem compatible with the V.90 standard. For more information, visit `http://www.v90.com.` ■

The two modems must communicate using the same speeds. If your modem is 28,800 bps, and the modem on the other end of the phone lines is only 14,400 bps, for example, your modem slows down to 14,400 to accommodate the other modem.

Understanding ISDN Modems

One of the most recent developments in modems is *ISDN modems,* which you can use to transfer data while connected to an ISDN line. *ISDN,* which stands for *Integrated Services Digital Network,* is a type of high-speed telephone network that offers both voice and data capabilities over the same line. This capability enables you to use your modem and telephone at the same time—a capability that is currently not feasible with normal telephone lines. ISDN lines also provide faster communications than normal phone lines, providing speeds as much as five times faster than what a 28.8Kbps modem can achieve. If you're suffering with slow World Wide Web connections or remote access hookups, ISDN promises a substantial speed increase.

At present, not all areas offer ISDN services. Likewise, if an area is set up to provide ISDN, many ISPs do not offer ISDN connections to the Internet. Another limiting factor to ISDN is that it is usually much more expensive than normal phone lines, and usually includes tariffs for each call you make. Fees range from $30 to $130 per month, plus an initial installation fee of $100 to $600 depending on the phone company that installs the service. In addition to the service, you also need to purchase a modem specifically designed to work on ISDN lines. ISDN modems usually start around $140 to $180. In addition to the phone service charges, ISPs generally charge much more for ISDN service than analog service.

If you are interested in obtaining ISDN service, contact your local telephone company to see whether your area provides the service. If so and its cost is within your budget, you should then call around for ISPs in your area that offer Internet access via ISDN.

Part

V

Ch

18

Understanding Cable Modems

Another fast connection to online resources is through cable modems. These modems are attached to your computer and are then connected to your cable TV wire. This type of connection can be up to 100 times faster than a standard 28.8Kbps modem.

Windows 98 supports cable modems that connect to cable modem services, such as the Time Warner Road Runner service. A true cable modem is not really a modem; it's a network interface card that connects to the fiber-optic or coaxial cable network. Some services use both a network interface card for incoming traffic and a regular modem for outbound traffic (stuff you're uploading). Most cable modem companies require that a service representative install and configure your cable modem service (much like when you order cable television service). For that reason, this chapter does not show how to install cable modems under Windows 98.

The future for cable modems looks positive. Many cable television companies have invested money into providing Internet access to home users via the cable wire. @Home (`http://www.home.net`) is one of the largest cable modem suppliers, with investors from several companies providing funding, including Netscape, TCI, Comcast, Intermedia, Marcus, and Cox.

Time Warner's Road Runner service, mentioned earlier, is available in a number of cities, including San Diego, Tampa Bay, Portland (Maine), Akron, Columbus (Ohio), Memphis, and other cities. To use its service, you must configure your computer with an Ethernet card. To give you an example of the type of hardware you would need for the Road Runner service, look at the following list of cards supported by Road Runner:

- 3Com EtherLink 111 PC Card 3C589C-TP (PCMCIA)
- 3Com EtherLink 111 Card 3C562-TP
- 3Com Parallel Tasking Ethernet Adapters 3C509B-TP (ISA bus)
- Parallel Tasking Ethernet Adapters 3C590-TPO (PCI bus)
- SMC EtherEZ PC Card SMC8020T 10base-T adapter Type 11 (PCMCIA)
- SMC EtherEZ SMC8416T Ethernet Network 10base-T adapter
- Intel EtherExpress Pro/10
- Intel EtherExpress Pro/10 (RJ45) PILA8420

If you want more information about the Road Runner service, visit the Web site at `http://www.pathfinder.com/rdrun`.

Installing Your Modem

Windows includes a wizard that can detect a modem you've added to your system and identify the port, install the appropriate driver, and identify the modem speed. You can let the wizard configure your modem, or you can manually configure your modem.

Install your modem by first turning off your computer and then attaching the cables to the external modem and attaching the phone line. When you're finished, turn on the modem and restart the computer.

Letting Windows Autodetect the Modem

When you use the Modem Wizard to identify your modem, Windows queries the attached modem and ascertains the port, speed, and driver needed for the modem. Windows asks you to confirm its findings and then sets up the modem for you.

To use the Modem Wizard to set up your modem, follow these steps:

1. Open the Control Panel and double-click the Modems icon. The Install New Modem dialog box appears (see Figure 18.1).

FIG. 18.1

After attaching your modem to your computer, you can use the Modem Wizard to configure the modem for you.

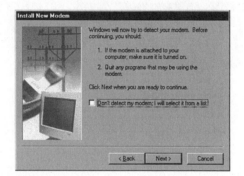

2. Click the Next button to tell Windows to begin checking for your modem. The second wizard dialog box appears. The wizard searches for your modem and identifies the port to which it's connected.

3. When the wizard finishes querying the modem, it displays the Verify Modem dialog box. If the modem is the correct one, choose Next; if you want to change the modem, click the Change button and then refer to the next section, "Manually Specifying a Modem."

   Also if Windows cannot locate your modem, click Next and see step 2 in the following section.

4. Windows sets up your modem and then displays the last wizard dialog box. Choose Finish to close the dialog box.

5. When the Modem Wizard dialog box closes, Windows displays the Modems Properties dialog box, in which you can adjust the modem's settings and troubleshoot modem problems. Click OK to close the dialog box. You can learn more about modem properties in the section "Modifying Modem Properties" later in this chapter.

Manually Specifying a Modem

If you prefer, you can identify your modem instead of letting Windows detect it. You might want, for example, to use the manufacturer's driver with your modem instead of one supplied by Windows. The driver supplied by your manufacturer may be more current than the one included in Windows. If so, always use the most current driver you have.

Windows enables you to specify both the manufacturer and the modem type, as well as to install the driver from a disk.

To manually specify your modem, follow these steps:

1. Open the Control Panel and double-click the Modems icon. The Install New Modem dialog box appears.

2. Choose the Don't detect my modem; I will select it from a list option and then choose Next. The next wizard dialog box appears (see Figure 18.2).

FIG. 18.2

You can choose the manufacturer and model of your modem in this wizard dialog box.

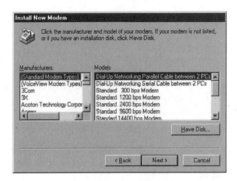

3. In the Manufacturers list, choose the maker of your modem. In the Models list, choose the appropriate model of your modem.

   If you do not see the manufacturer or if you want to load the driver from a disk, choose Have Disk. The Install From Disk dialog box appears. Enter the drive letter in the text box and click OK. Windows installs the driver from the specified disk.

4. Click Next to continue installing the modem. Windows displays the next wizard dialog box.

5. Select the port you want to use with the modem. When you click the Next button, Windows installs the modem.

6. When the wizard is finished, Windows displays the last wizard dialog box, telling you that the installation was successful. Choose Finish to close the dialog box. Windows then displays the Modems Properties dialog box, in which you can adjust the modem's settings and troubleshoot modem problems. Click OK to close the dialog box.

CAUTION

Windows lets you set up any type of modem and assign any port to that modem, regardless of whether it's correct. If you assign the wrong port or model, the modem does not work when you're ready to use it. If you are unsure of the port or the modem model, let Windows autodetect the modem for you, as described in the preceding section.

Modifying Modem Properties

You can adjust the modem settings at any time after you install your modem. For example, you might want to change ports, adjust the speaker volume, or change the designated speed. Additionally, you can set the modem for specific dialing preferences, change the location from which you're dialing, set up the modem to use a calling card, and so on.

Finally, you can adjust the advanced connections settings, such as flow control, error control, modulation type, and so on.

Modifying Dialing Properties

Use the Dialing Properties sheet to modify how calls are dialed and to set options such as dialing with a calling card, specifying various locations from which to call, and using tone or pulse dialing.

To modify dialing properties, follow these steps:

1. Open the Control Panel and double-click the Modems icon. The Modems Properties page appears (see Figure 18.3).

FIG. 18.3

Adjust modem and port settings in the Modems Properties page.

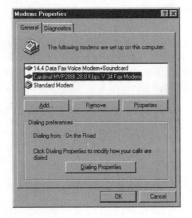

Part

V

Ch

18

2. To set dialing preferences, click the Dialing Properties button in the General tab of the Modems Properties page. The Dialing Properties page appears (see Figure 18.4).

3. Enter information and/or choose options as described in Table 18.1.

TIP The dialing properties you define apply to any program from which you dial on the computer.

FIG. 18.4

Customize the dialing properties to suit your needs.

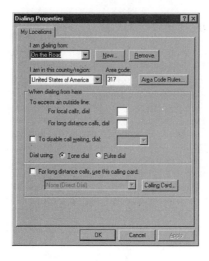

Table 18.1 Dialing Properties

Option	Description
I am dialing from	Choose the first location you want to set up from the list. To set up a new location, choose New and enter a location name in the Create New Location dialog box; then click OK. To remove a location, select it from the list and choose Remove.
I am in this country/region	Choose the country you're in from the drop-down list.
Area code	Enter the area code from which you are dialing.
To access an outside line	Enter the number for local and/or the number for long distance in the appropriate text boxes; if you do not need to access an outside line, leave these text boxes blank.
To disable call waiting, dial	Select the check box and enter code to disable call waiting.
For long distance calls, use this calling card	Select (check) to display the Calling Card dialog box; enter one or more calling card names and numbers. Choose Advanced to enter specific rules for your calling card, such as dialable digits, area code, pauses, second dial tone, and so on.
This location has call waiting	Check if you have call waiting.
Dial using	Choose either Tone dialing or Pulse dialing.

4. Click OK to close the Dialing Properties page.

N O T E   As you fill out the Dialing Properties page, you can click the Area Code Rules button to set up rules on how Windows should dial numbers in your area code. From the Area Code Rules dialog box, click the top New button to add the phone number prefix in your area code that Windows should use. Likewise, click the bottom New button to specify a prefix in your area code that Windows should not use. Click OK to save your settings. ■

TROUBLESHOOTING

I can hear the modem sending tones as it dials, but nothing happens afterward. Check the telephone cables to be sure that they're properly connected to the modem and to the wall jack. On some modems, you may need to plug the modem directly into the telephone line wall jack instead of plugging your telephone into that jack.

Verify that the modem is dialing with pulses or tone by checking the Dialing Properties page.

T I P   One of the Microsoft PowerToys created for Windows 95 that you may want to run under Windows 98 is the Telephony Location Selector utility. You can find this utility at `http://www.microsoft.com/Windows95/info/legacy.htm`. When you run this utility, which sits on the Windows 98 taskbar (next to the clock), it enables you to change your dialing locations quickly. This capability is handy for mobile users who have set up multiple dialing properties for different locations, such as office, home, hotel, or remote office. Also, the Telephony Location Selector includes a menu from which you can display your dialing properties and execute the Phone Dialer application.

Part

V

Ch

18

Modifying Your Modem's Properties

You can have more than one modem attached to your computer, and you can choose each modem and modify its specific properties. Each modem's Property dialog box may contain slightly different options, but the following example gives you an idea of the options you can modify.

To modify a specific modem's properties, follow these steps:

1. In the Modems Properties page, select the specific modem you want to modify and click the Properties button. The modem's Properties page appears (see Figure 18.5).
2. On the General tab, set your choices for the following options:
   - *Port.* Select the serial port to which your modem is connected.
   - *Speaker volume.* Adjust the speaker volume for the modem between Off and High. If your modem does not support this feature, the option is dimmed.
   - *Maximum speed.* Set the maximum speed with which your modem can connect; your modem will connect at that speed and all speeds less than the set speed. The preferred setting for a 28.8 modem is, in fact, 57.6 or 115.2 due to data compression factors.
   - *Only connect at this speed.* Choose this option to limit the modem from connecting at any speed other than the specified one. If your modem does not support this feature, the option is dimmed.

FIG. 18.5

Set the properties of your specific modem in the modem's Properties page.

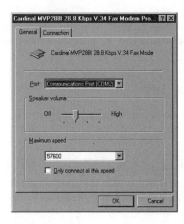

3. On the Connection tab, choose the options you want to modify (see Figure 18.6). Table 18.2 describes the options in the Connection tab.

FIG. 18.6

Set preferences for your connection and dialing for your specific modem.

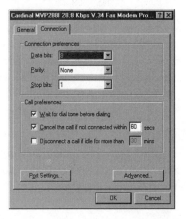

Table 18.2   Connection Preferences

Option	Description
Connection Preferences Area	
Data bits	Set the number of data bits—each data character consists of 7 or 8 bits—specified for your modem.
Parity	Set *parity*—a formula for adding a bit to each byte before sending in data communications—to None, Even, Odd, Mark, or Space.
Stop bits	Set *stop bits*—the last bit in a set of data—specified for your modem.

Option	Description
Call Preferences Area	
Wait for dial tone before dialing	Choose this option unless you must before dialing manually dial the phone for the modem.
Cancel the call if not connected within _ secs	Check this option and enter an amount of time for the modem to continue trying to connect before disconnecting.
Disconnect a call if idle for more than _ mins	Check this option to hang up the phone if no activity occurs within the specified amount of time.

 See the following section for information on port and other advanced settings.

4. Click OK to close the specific modem's Properties page. Click Close to close the Modems Properties page.

Modifying Advanced Settings

Windows enables you to modify specific settings for your modem so that you can control the flow of data between your modem and your computer and between your modem and the modem with which you're communicating. If you have a question about any advanced settings, refer to your modem's documentation. Not all modems support all the following controls.

Port Settings If data sent from the computer to the modem is transferred faster than the modem can move it across the line to the other modem, the FIFO (First In, First Out) data buffers (in conjunction with flow control) keep information from being lost. You can adjust buffers in the Advanced Port Settings dialog box.

To change advanced port settings, follow these steps:

1. In the Control Panel, double-click the Modems icon to open the Modems Properties page.
2. In the General tab, choose the modem from the list and select Properties. The selected modem's Properties page appears.
3. In the Connection tab, select the Port settings button. The Advanced Port Settings page appears (see Figure 18.7).

FIG. 18.7
Set the FIFO buffers for the modem's port.

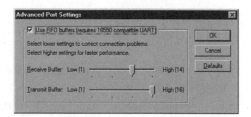

Part **V**
Ch **18**

4. Deselect the Use FIFO buffers option to disable it.

5. Click OK to close the dialog box, and click OK again to close the modem's Properties page.

TROUBLESHOOTING

My modem connects with the remote modem but locks up. Make sure that you are using the proper modem-to-computer flow control and error control for your modem (click the Advanced button on the Connection tab of the specific modem's Properties page). The preferred method to use is the Hardware option in the Use flow control area.

Advanced Connection Settings   The Advanced Connection settings govern the use of error, flow, and modulation control. *Error controls* ensure accurate data transmission; corrupted data sent across the line is automatically detected and retransmitted. If your modem supports error control, you can also choose to compress the transmitted data, which compacts the data before sending it across the lines. The receiving modem then decompresses the data before sending it to the computer. Compressed data travels faster and more efficiently over telephone lines.

Flow control designates the protocol used between your computer and the modem. The flow defines how fast the data can be transferred between your modem and computer. The protocol you choose must be compatible with your modem, the serial cable (if your modem is an external one), and your computer. You can use either hardware or software flow control. Most modems do not support the software-only option, whereas the hardware option is universally supported. Check your modem documentation for more information.

To change advanced connection settings, click the Advanced button on the Connection tab. The Advanced Connection Settings dialog box then appears (see Figure 18.8). In this dialog box, you can modify the following options:

FIG. 18.8
Set advanced settings such as flow control and modulation type.

■ *Use error control.* Activates or deactivates error control of the transmissions. If you deactivate this option, your data may not be reliably transferred.

■ *Use flow control.* Specifies the protocol used to control the flow of data between the modem and your computer.

- *Modulation type*. Specifies the modulation type compatible with both your modem and the modem you're connecting with. Standard works in most cases; however, if you're having trouble connecting, try the Nonstandard modulation type.

- *Extra settings*. Provides space in which you can enter additional initialization settings necessary for use with your modem.

- *Append to log*. Records your calls, errors, and so on in a file named MODEMLOG.TXT in the Windows folder. Use it to monitor calls and problems.

> **TIP** If you're unsure of any of the settings in the Advanced Connection Settings dialog box, refer to your modem's documentation.

Click OK to close the Advanced Connection Settings dialog box; click OK again to close the modem's Properties page. Then, to close the Modems Properties page, click OK.

Troubleshooting Modems

You can fix many common modem and connection problems yourself. Additionally, Windows includes a diagnostic tool that can help you identify your modem's connection, driver, speed, and so on.

> **TIP** One source of updated drivers is the modem manufacturer. You can try calling the manufacturer's technical support line or accessing its Web page if it has a presence on the Web.

The first things you should check when you have a modem problem may sound simple, but checking them can save you a lot of time and energy. The following list describes the initial checks you should make:

- Check to make sure that the modem is plugged in and connected to the phone line and that the phone line is connected in the wall jack. Do you hear a dial tone when you start your modem? If not, check the phone jack with a phone to see whether the jack is live. If not, call your phone company (using another line, of course).

- If the modem is external, make sure that it's turned on.

- Make sure that you're using a modem cable—a straight-through cable that connects the computer's pin 1 to the modem's pin 1.

- Check the phone number and area code you're dialing.

- Check the dialing properties, port, data bits, parity, stop bits, and so on to make sure that all settings are correct for your modem.

Using Diagnostics

Windows includes a Diagnostics tab in the Modems Properties dialog box; you can use it to help you identify your modem's connections and to find errors.

To use Windows' Diagnostics, follow these steps:

1. From the Modems Properties dialog box, choose the Diagnostics tab (see Figure 18.9).

FIG. 18.9
Use Windows Diagnostics to identify your modem's driver, port, interrupt, address, and so on.

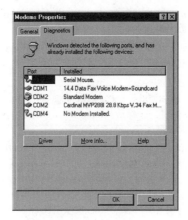

2. Select your modem in the Port list and choose the Driver button. Windows then displays a dialog box similar to the one in Figure 18.10.

FIG. 18.10
The Current Communications Driver dialog box describes the driver you're using for the modem.

3. Note the size, date, and time the driver was loaded. Installing a more recent or updated driver may solve your problem. Click OK to close the dialog box.

N O T E   If, when you install Windows 98, your modem is already installed and working, Windows Setup attempts to identify the modem and install drivers for it. If Windows can't identify the modem but can detect that it is there (two different things), Windows sets up a standard modem driver for it. This driver may not be the right driver to run your modem at its optimum. It might, for example, install a 28.8Kbps driver for a 33.3Kbps modem. This might be the case as well if you add a modem and Windows detects it when you start your system for the first time after installing the device. If this is the case, update the driver to one written specifically for your modem. See Chapter 5, "Installing and Configuring New Hardware and Software," for information on updating device drivers. ■

4. Click the More Info button. Windows displays a Please Wait message box while it checks your modem. Then it displays the More Info dialog box (see Figure 18.11).

5. The following text describes the options in the More Info dialog box. When you're finished, click OK to close the dialog box.

FIG. 18.11
Diagnostics checks
your modem and
communications port
and reports the results
in the More Info dialog
box.

More Info...

Port Information
Port: COM2
Interrupt: 3
Address: 2F8
UART: NS 16550AN
Highest Speed: No response

Cardinal MVP288I 28.8 Kbps V.34 Fax Modem
Identifier: ROCK_Cardinal8

Command	Response
ATI1	OK
ATI2	OK
ATI3	OK
ATI4	Cardinal V1.20h-V34_DS, 020 0458 501, ...
ATI5	022
ATI6	RC288DPi Rev 05BA
ATI7	000
AT+FCLA...	0,1,2

OK

Port Information Area

In the Port Information area of the More Info dialog box, the Port lists the port to which your modem is attached (almost always a serial port, such as COM1, COM2, and so on). Although PC architecture allows for as many as four COM ports, most systems have only two installed (COM1 and COM2).

When the serial port is installed to the system, it's configured to use specific interrupts and I/O (Input/Output) addresses. An *interrupt*, or *Interrupt Request* (*IRQ*), line enables access to the device; the I/O *address* is the port the modem uses to connect to the computer.

The standard IRQs and I/O addresses for the serial (COM) ports are as follows

Port	Interrupt	Address
COM1	IRQ4	03F8
COM2	IRQ3	02F8
COM3	IRQ4	03E8
COM4	IRQ3	02E8

Because no two devices can use the same COM port, a conflict may arise if, for example, your mouse and modem are assigned to the same port. Carefully read the documentation before installing any new hardware. You might even keep a list of addresses and IRQs you've already assigned to keep conflicts to a minimum.

If your modem is not working and you suspect an IRQ conflict, remove one of the devices, such as the mouse, and see whether the modem works. If the modem does work, the two devices were conflicting in interrupt or address. Open the Device Manager to help you diagnose and troubleshoot your modem problem.

 TIP You can use Microsoft Diagnostics (MSD), a program supplied with Windows, or purchase other diagnostic software programs that identify available IRQ lines and create a template detailing your communication channels.

Part
V

Ch
18

The *Universal Asynchronous Receiver/Transmitter,* or *UART, chip* controls breaking parallel data in the computer into serial format and then converting the data back again. A 16550A UART serial chip or higher is best suited for high-speed communications. If your UART is 8250, 8250A or B, or 16450, your problems could be coming from the slower chip. Lockups, slow communications, or inaccurate data could be caused by the UART chip. Additionally, the 16550 UART had a few bugs in the buffer area; the 16550A UART corrected these problems.

Highest Speed refers to the baud rate of the modem. *Baud rate* is the rate at which a signal between two devices changes in one second. Most modems transmit several bits per baud, so the actual baud rate is much slower than the bps rate. Use the highest speed listed in the More Info dialog box when your communication between modems is slow. If your modem speed is 14,400, for example, and the highest speed listed in the More Info dialog box is 56K, you know your port is fast enough to handle the modem speed, and the problem is more likely with the line connecting the two modems.

Modem Area

The Modem area of the More Info dialog box contains an area specific to your modem. Diagnostics runs *AT* (*ATtention*) *commands* to test the connection to your modem and then lists the response next to the command.

If you see an ERROR code listed in the Response window, something may be wrong with your modem. The command ATI2, for example, performs a checksum on firmware and as a response either returns OK or ERROR. Alternatively, an ERROR code can be returned for a command that is not applicable to your modem. For information about your modem's response to AT commands, see your modem's documentation.

TIP   Commands beginning with a plus sign (+) and an F designate a fax AT command.

TROUBLESHOOTING

I hear the call being answered at the other end, but there's no tone indicating a connection. The modem on the other end of the line is not working correctly, or no modem is there. To solve this problem, you must contact the person on the other end to turn on his or her modem. Or dial a different number that you know is connected to a modem that is turned on.

After connection, I see many data errors on the screen. Make sure that no one else is using the telephone line. Try calling the other modem again at another time or from a different phone line to get a better connection.

My modem cannot sign on to the remote modem. Check the communication parameters of the remote station and make sure that your software is configured for the same number of data bits, stop bits, and parity. (See the Connection tab of the specific modem's Properties page.)

CHAPTER 19

Configuring an Internet Connection

by Rod Tidrow

In this chapter

Why You Want an Internet Connection

The Internet is a global collection of independent networks and computers. These computers, which are sometimes called *hosts*, offer a wealth of information on thousands of subjects and allow millions of people to communicate with one another. Most users who connect to the Internet do so to access the World Wide Web. The Web, which is a part of the Internet, provides a graphical approach to accessing information and resources on the Internet. The range of resources for Internet hosts seems limitless, and more come online every day. With an Internet connection, you can make discoveries well beyond what radio, TV, newspapers, and magazines offer. Some of the reasons that you might consider connecting to the Internet include finding entertainment; accessing educational resources; staying in touch with news, sports, and weather; communicating with people from around the world; and accessing computer-related information and files.

The following basic services are available to you on the Internet:

- *Electronic mail (email)*. Electronic messages are created with email software and sent over Internet routers to their destinations, where recipients can read, print, send, save, or forward those messages to other users. Although the Web is one of the fastest growing segments of the Internet, email is still the most used and most popular service on the Internet.

- *Mailing lists*. Discussion topic areas employ the email system as the means of transmitting an endless stream of opinions and information on about 7,000 different topics.

- *Newsgroups*. You can post and read messages on these electronic versions of cork bulletin boards. Newsgroups store the ideas and opinions of millions of users on approximately 30,000 different subjects. You must use a program called a *news reader*, several of which exist. You can discuss virtually any topic from A to Z within the newsgroup system. Newsgroups are also called *Usenet News*, a reference to the store-and-forward system that carries the postings.

- *Telnet (remote login)*. From your own computer, you can log in to a network across the street or on another continent and use that remote computer as if you were there onsite.

- *FTP (file transfer protocol)*. Almost 1,300 host systems exist as computer file storage sites and allow you to log in to those sites and transfer copies of the files held there to the your own computer. These servers hold more than two million files and do not charge for the transfer.

- *Archie*. This database and search device locates files stored on FTP host computers.

- *Gopher*. This ingenious information retrieval program is menu based. When you log in to a Gopher session, a menu appears onscreen. As you select menu items, you see succeeding menus, layer after layer, until you locate what you want. Gopher incorporates other Internet tools such as file transfer and remote login. Gopher is fast, easy to use, and comprehensive.

- *Veronica and Jughead.* These two programs search Gopher menus. You enter a keyword, and either program searches all or a selection of Gopher machines for the text string you entered.

- *WAIS (Wide Area Information Server).* This database tool searches the contents of documents, not just the titles of those documents.

- *Internet Relay Chat (IRC).* You can participate in real-time "chatting" via the computer keyboard. IRC resembles CB radio, except that you "talk" by entering text from the keyboard while you are logged in to an IRC session.

- *World Wide Web.* The Web is an information-retrieval medium that has taken the online world by storm and appears to be doing nothing less than redefining how we get information. The Web employs the client/server model, in which a Web *client* program, such as Netscape or Internet Explorer, requests information from a Web *server*, a computer set up to dispense information to the client program. Upon receipt of the information, the client program processes the information and displays it. The retrieved information can take the form of text, photos, sound, and/or video. The Web uses *hypertext linking*, in which text, an icon, or photo on a Web screen page can link to another Web page or Web computer. The links can be endless. More than 10,000 Web servers provide a phenomenal amount of useful and fun information, and more servers go online every week. World Wide Web users also refer to it as *WWW, W3*, or simply the *Web*.

Understanding Windows TCP/IP and Other Internet Software

This section describes what Windows TCP/IP protocol is, what it does, and how it relates to Internet application programs that enable you to send email, browse the contents of other Internet host computers, and see the technicolor wonders of the World Wide Web. You will also see that the TCP/IP protocol is not all you need to make a connection to the Internet.

First, you need to understand two acronyms:

- *TCP,* which stands for Transmission Control Protocol
- *IP,* which stands for Internet Protocol

Basically, Transmission Control Protocol breaks your outgoing message or file into packets called *datagrams.* Internet Protocol routes the datagrams through the system in search of a target router. When the datagrams find the correct router, they navigate onward to the destination computer, where Transmission Control Protocol reassembles the packets into their original form.

Part

V

Ch

19

Understanding the Router

A *router* is just one of several pieces of special computer hardware that sends Internet messages through the Internet system. The following sequence of events and subsequent analogy may help you better understand the concept of routing:

1. Using Windows Internet tools, your computer and modem dial into an Internet service provider's (ISP's) computer system. Your message goes from your computer and modem to your ISP.

2. The provider's computer system is connected to special communications equipment, one item of which is a router. Your message passes through your ISP's system and out its router to a high-speed telephone line connected to another major Internet provider.

3. The systems belonging to the major ISPs also have routers, both incoming (to receive your message) and outgoing (to send your message to one of the many *backbones*, high-speed fiber-optic superhighways, that interlink the major providers). Your message now passes from the major ISP to the backbone system.

4. While riding the backbone, your message passes from router to router in search of the correct destination router and computer. Simply reverse the preceding steps to get your message to its destination.

5. Your message routes to a target major ISP, which hands the message off to the correct target mid-sized ISP, which then passes it to the correct target computer.

As you just learned, the TCP/IP program manages the datagrams from and to Internet hosts. But by itself, the TCP/IP stack is useless. (A *stack* is TCP/IP software.) It needs a connection to other routers. Windows provides that connection with a program that finds your modem, dials into a provider, and locates a PPP connection (which you learn about later) to the Internet. This program matches the Internet addressing information you gave Windows with the addressing information that the provider's system expects to see from Windows configuration.

After you have installed and configured the TCP/IP stack and the dialer, and Windows has made contact with your Internet service provider, you can finally connect to another Internet host and do something. You need separate application programs to send and receive email, contact Gopher servers, download files, log on to remote networks, view World Wide Web sites, and so on.

Understanding Internet Services

You can obtain an Internet connection in several ways. One method is to use standard communication software such as Procomm Plus for Windows. You can use this program to dial into a network or Internet service provider and use its computer system.

Procomm Plus does not work with the Windows TCP/IP program. Instead, it accesses Internet hosts indirectly by dialing into your Internet provider's network and turning your computer into a temporary terminal on your provider's network. This access, called *terminal emulation—*

usually accomplished through a *shell account*—is not as comprehensive as the kind of connection that Windows offers, but it does work. This chapter does not go into detail on shell accounts, but you can learn about them in Que's *Special Edition Using the Internet, Second Edition*.

A second method is to use an online service such as the Microsoft Network or America Online (AOL). You need special software provided by the online service to make a successful connection. Windows includes software for connecting to the following services:

- AOL
- AT&T WorldNet
- CompuServe
- Microsoft Network (MSN)
- Prodigy Internet

A third and more comprehensive way to obtain an Internet connection is to use the special Internet Connection Wizard software that is included in Windows.

Windows offers several ways to configure Internet connections. This chapter focuses on the steps needed to get a direct Internet session using a modem connected to a personal computer. If you access the Internet through a company or school network, some of the settings described may be different for you. Your organization's network manager or Information Services department should be able to give you the required configuration settings, if not install them for you.

Before you continue, make sure that you have installed and configured a modem for Windows.

PPP and SLIP Connections

Part
V
Ch
19

If you want to enjoy the full glory of the Internet, your computer must have direct access to the Internet system. Direct access to Internet routers and computers is achieved with expensive hardware and a special dedicated line wired right to your computer.

Most people cannot afford dedicated, leased-line access. But most *can* afford the functional equivalents, Point to Point Protocol (PPP) and Serial Line Internet Protocol (SLIP) connections. PPP and SLIP trick the Internet system into thinking that your computer has a dedicated line, even though PPP and SLIP are really dial-up communication protocols that need modems or networks as intermediaries between Internet routers and your computer.

PPP is newer than SLIP. A description of their differences is beyond the scope of this chapter, but most Internet service providers normally issue PPP, not SLIP, accounts. This chapter describes how to establish a PPP connection.

PPP and SLIP accounts are associated with the type of Internet addressing that routers understand. This addressing scheme is numeric and has four positions, separated by periods known as *dots*. An example of an IP (Internet Protocol) address is

198.6.245.121

This address identifies a specific host machine among millions of Internet hosts.

Because humans remember strings of letters better than strings of numbers, many numeric IP addresses have text equivalents. If a text equivalent, called a *Fully Qualified Domain Name (FQDN)*, exists, use it in lieu of the IP address.

FQDNs are constructed like this:

host_computer_name.location.domain_type

An example is **kiwi.wright.edu**. **Kiwi** is the name of the host machine you are addressing; **wright** is the location (Wright State University); **edu** is the domain type, or the type of facility that operates the host machine.

Table 19.1 lists the six major domain types.

Table 19.1   Domain Types

Domain	Description
com	Commercial organization
edu	Educational institution
gov	Government facility
mil	A military organization
net	Internet service provider
org	Miscellaneous, usually nonprofit, organization

Countries outside the United States use two-letter identifiers at the end of their fully qualified domain names. A few examples are **CA** (Canada), **UK** (United Kingdom), and **ES** (Spain).

Two Types of IP Addresses

If your computer has a *static* IP address, that IP address is permanently assigned to your computer. Whenever you go online with a PPP or SLIP connection, your computer uses and is identified with that address throughout the system. An advantage to a static IP address is that you can register a specific domain name to that static IP address; you or your business then can be identified all over the world with either the IP address or domain name.

Your computer may also have a *dynamic* IP address that your provider assigns from a pool of IP addresses available whenever you log in to a PPP or SLIP session. This approach is often a less expensive, but very viable, way of getting connected.

The difference between static and dynamic is important because Windows TCP/IP configuration asks you which IP address type you have.

Work closely with your Internet service provider as you configure your TCP/IP setup. When you set up your initial account with your ISP, be sure to gather all the information you need, including dial-up phone number, IP address, host name, your email address, and news server address. Also, ask your ISP about its technical support department, hours of operation, and telephone number.

How to Find an Internet Service Provider

You need an Internet service provider, or ISP, to establish a PPP or SLIP link. Most large- and medium-size cities in the U.S. now have providers who sell accounts at a reasonable rate, usually $20 to $40 per month depending on whether your PPP connection is static or dynamic. Also, several national providers now cover most of the country, including rural parts of the country. Dynamic IP accounts cost less than static IP accounts. Both function the same way while online. Again, static IP accounts afford you the advantage of establishing your own global identity.

Some ISPs give you a set number of hours for a set price, such as $20 for 15 hours. After you use up the set number of hours, the ISP charges an hourly rate, usually $1 to $3 per hour. This practice is called *metering*.

CAUTION

Do not subscribe to a set number of hours unless you know beyond any doubt that you will not use more hours than the set price permits. If you find that you will exceed those hours, contact your ISP for a revised arrangement. Many users find that they exceed a set number of hours.

Most ISPs offer quarterly, semiannual, and annual rates that permit you to stay online as long as you want and not worry about hourly charges.

As you'll see in the "Running the Internet Connection Wizard" section, the wizard downloads a list of ISPs in your area. You can use one of these ISPs or locate one on your own. If your phone book does not list a local ISP, ask someone at your local computer user group or computer store. If no local ISP exists, national ISPs such as UUNET/AlterNet sell accounts. National providers also may have toll-free 800 numbers or use the Tymnet or Sprintlink system to give you a local number. If you contact a national provider, it can explain the options that suit your needs and pocketbook. The last option, a toll call to the nearest dial-up number, is also available, but it is an expensive option.

Selecting an ISP takes some research because good ones and bad ones exist. If you live in a major metropolitan area such as Chicago or Washington, D.C., you have several ISPs from which to choose. If you live in a medium-sized city such as Dayton or Austin, you still have some flexibility. If you live in a small town away from a city or in a rural area, your choices are limited.

Part
V

Ch
19

Whatever choice you make, your ISP should charge a monthly, quarterly, or annual flat rate instead of charging by the hour. Technical support should be available during business hours and in the early evening. The ISP's connection from the backbone system to its system should be at least a T1 line, and enough incoming lines should exist so that you do not reach a continuous busy signal when you dial in. The ISP should offer all Internet services and should make most if not all Usenet newsgroups available without filtering out any of them.

On the other hand, you must be a good customer. Do your own research on Internet basics. Dozens of books are available on the subject, including Que's *Special Edition Using the Internet, Second Edition*, previously mentioned. Do not expect miracles. Providing Internet connectivity is a profoundly complex, expensive, and difficult task. If you are having trouble dialing in, make sure that your computer's hardware or software configuration is not the problem. If you have an older computer and a very slow modem (anything under 28,800 baud is too slow), you will probably be underpowered.

N O T E   The most important hardware components for a successful Internet session are those that bring data in and draw it to your screen. Ensure that your modem is fast and that you have a UART 16550 chip in your modem's COM port, at least 16MB of system RAM, and a fast graphics card. Currently, the fastest modems available for the mass consumer market are rated at 56Kbps with prices ranging from $59–199. If you have a 56K modem, ask the ISP whether it supports the V.90 modem standard. See Chapter 18, "Configuring Modems," for more information on this standard. ▧

TROUBLESHOOTING

My old ISP did not provide satisfactory service. What type of questions can I ask other ISPs to ensure that I can use Windows with their service? Ask the ISP the following questions:

- Does the access provider offer full Internet access?
- Does the access provider support PPP? SLIP?
- Does the access provider offer technical support?
- What kind of connection speeds does the access provider support?

What kind of information do I need from my ISP? You must obtain the following data from your access provider to use during configuration:

- Access phone number, preferably local
- Logon name and password
- Your host and domain name (be sure to repeat the numbers to the provider to ensure you have them written down correctly)
- The Domain Name System (DNS) server and IP address

Running the Internet Connection Wizard

Windows 98 makes setting up a connection to the Internet fairly easy. The easiest way is to use the Internet Connection Wizard (see Figure 19.1), which walks you through setting up a new connection or modifying an existing connection.

FIG. 19.1
Use the Internet Connection Wizard to set up or modify an Internet connection.

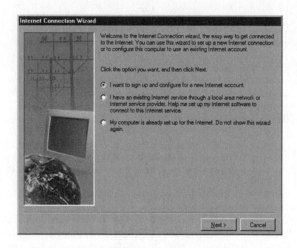

To run the Internet Connection Wizard, follow these steps:

N O T E   The following steps assume you have already set up a modem on your PC. If you have not, you will prompted to do so while using the Internet Connection Wizard. ■

1. Select Start, Programs, Internet Explorer, Connection Wizard. The Internet Connection Wizard then appears.
2. Click Next. Select one of the Setup Options. You can choose an Internet provider and set up a new account, set up a connection to an existing Internet account, or continue using an Internet connection you have already set up on this computer. The following steps show how to choose a provider and set up a new account.
3. Click Next. Enter the area code in which you reside.
4. Click Next. If you have File and Printer Sharing Microsoft (or NetWare) Networks, you are prompted to disable it. Click OK. Also, if Windows needs to install files to continue, a dialog box appears telling you that you may need to insert your Windows Setup disk. Click OK to install the files.
5. The Choose Modem dialog box appears (see Figure 19.2). Select the modem you want to use to connect to the Internet.

Part
V

Ch
19

FIG. 19.2

You must have a modem installed to set up an Internet account that uses a modem to connect to the Internet.

6. Click <u>N</u>ext. The Internet Connection Wizard now needs to connect to the Microsoft Referral Service to download a list of Internet service providers in your area.

7. Click <u>N</u>ext. The Internet Connection Wizard dials the Internet Referral Service to download a list of ISPs in your area. Make sure your modem is turned on and is connected to your phone line. The phone call is toll free.

After the list is downloaded, Windows display it (see Figure 19.3).

FIG. 19.3

The list you see may be different from the one shown in this figure.

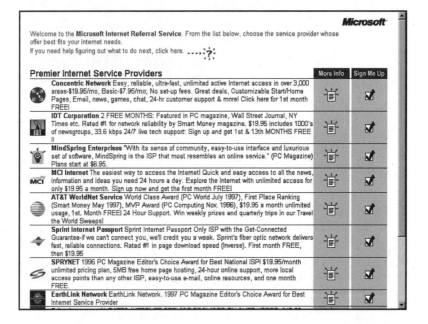

8. To specify a service provider you want to use, click the check mark in the Sign Me Up column. You can read more about an ISP by clicking the document icon in the More Info column. When you select an ISP, the Internet Connection Wizard dials the ISP of your choice so that you can set up an account with it. The actual sign-on process varies for each ISP, but most services request the following types of information from you:

- Name and address
- Credit card number or alternative payment method
- Your phone number

- Your modem speed
- Operating system

N O T E The list of ISPs may not represent the actual number of ISPs in your area. This list includes just the ones who are signed up for the Microsoft Internet Referral Service. Look in your local phone book for additional ISPs in your area. ▓

The steps here do not show the actual procedure for signing up with an ISP. You need to follow the instructions provided by the ISP of your choice.

9. After you've signed up with an ISP, you are given account information that you should write down. This information includes the following:

- Phone number to dial for your ISP
- User ID
- Email address
- Password

After you've set up your account, you are returned to the Windows desktop. You can now launch your Web browser or other Internet software, such as Internet Explorer 4. When you do so, you see the Dial-up Connection dialog box (see Figure 19.4). Click the Connect button to connect to your ISP and navigate the Internet.

FIG. 19.4
The Dial-up Connection dialog box automatically includes the username and password you just set up.

Configuring Dial-Up Connection Settings

You can modify the settings on the Dial-up Connection dialog box. One of the first changes you may want to make is to select the Connect automatically option so that Windows automatically connects to your ISP when you launch your Web browser, or when Windows is scheduled to download information from the Web (see Chapter 20, "Configuring Microsoft Internet Explorer 4.0").

To make changes to other Internet connection properties, click the Settings button. This action displays the Properties page (see Figure 19.5) for your ISP.

FIG. 19.5
If you need to change settings for your ISP, use this Properties page.

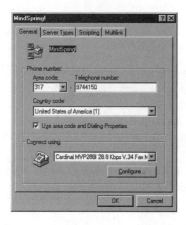

On the General tab, you can change the following settings:

- *Phone number.* Change the phone number that you dial to connect to your ISP.

- *Country code.* Select the country from which you are dialing.

- *Modem settings.* You can select a different modem from the drop-down list, or you can click the Configure button to display the Modem Properties page. From this page, you can set port, speed, and other modem properties. This Properties page is covered in more detail in Chapter 18, "Configuring Modems."

On the Server Types tab (see Figure 19.6), you can change the following settings:

FIG. 19.6
The Server Types tab enables you to set the type of Internet server you are connecting to as well which protocol Dial-Up Networking should use.

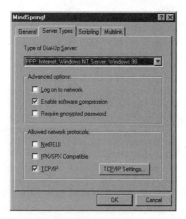

- *Type of Dial-Up Server.* If you have a PPP connection, select PPP: Internet, Windows NT Server, Windows 98. If you have a SLIP connection, select SLIP: Unix Connection.

- *Advanced options.* Select the Enable software compression check box. In most cases, you don't have to select the Log on to network check box unless your ISP requires it.

■ *Allowed network protocols.* Select TCP/IP. Deselect the NetBEUI and IPX/SPX compatible check boxes. Click the TCP/IP Settings button to change these settings on the TCP/IP Settings dialog box (see Figure 19.7).

FIG. 19.7
You can set IP and DNS information on the TCP/IP Settings dialog box.

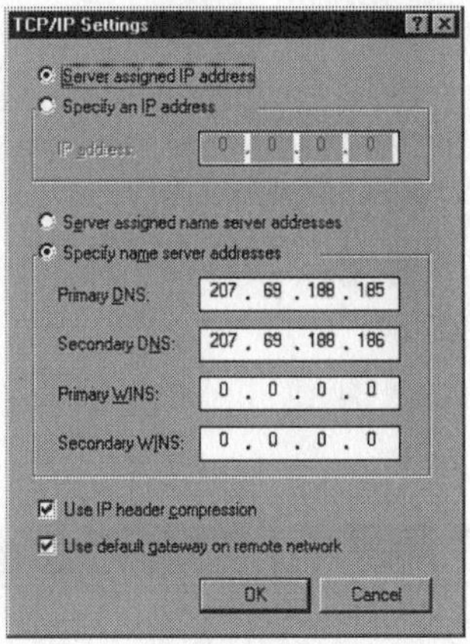

Use the TCP/IP Settings dialog box to set TCP/IP-specific information. If you use a dynamic PPP account, select the Server assigned IP address radio button. If you use a static PPP account, select the Specify an IP address radio button and enter your specific IP address. Check the specify name server addresses radio button, and enter your provider's Primary DNS number and Secondary DNS number—if it has a secondary number—in the fields provided under the radio buttons. Select the Use IP header compression and Use default gateway on remote network check boxes. Click OK to save your settings.

For some connections, you may need to create a script that processes the logon and user validation process when you connect to an ISP or Internet server. On the Scripting tab (see Figure 19.8), you can specify a path and filename for a dial-up script you must use to connect to your ISP. Click the Browse button to locate a dial-up script (.SCP files). In the \Program Files\ Accessories folder, you can find sample scripts provided by Windows. You can modify them by selecting one of them and clicking Open. Doing so returns you to the Scripting tab, where you can then click the Edit button to open the script in Notepad (see Figure 19.9) so that you can edit the script for your specific case.

Select the Step through script option if you want the script to run one command at a time while establishing a connection. This feature is handy when you need to troubleshoot scripting errors. After you get your script set, however, you should turn off this feature. Finally, select the Start terminal screen minimized if you don't want to view the terminal window as your script is running.

On the Multilink tab (see Figure 19.10), you can click the Use additional devices option so that you can set up additional devices to connect to your ISP. You can specify additional modems or ISDN lines. To do so, click the Add button and select the device from the Device Name drop-down list on the Add Extra Device dialog box.

Part
V
Ch
19

FIG. 19.8

Some ISPs require a
script to connect to the
Internet.

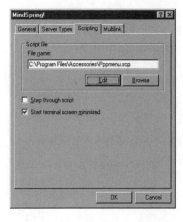

FIG. 19.9

You can edit a dial-up
script in Notepad.

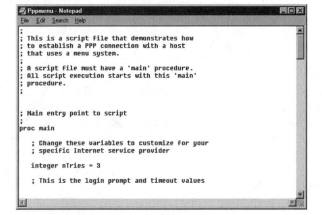

FIG. 19.10

You can modify the
Multilink tab when you
have multiple modem or
ISDN lines to use for
this connection.

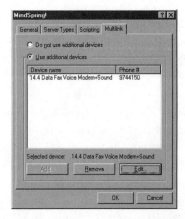

After you modify your ISP's connection settings, click OK to save them. You then return to the Dial-up Connection dialog box.

Dialing Your ISP

The big moment has arrived. Now you're ready to dial into your PPP session. To do so, follow these steps:

1. Click the Connect button on the Dial-up Connection dialog box. Windows 98 begins the dial-up process.

2. After you get connected, the Connected To dialog box is minimized on the taskbar tray. Unlike with the Connected To dialog box in Windows 95, you do not have to minimize this dialog box manually.

To disconnect from the Internet, double-click the Connected To icon and click Disconnect.

TROUBLESHOOTING

I have a 28,800-baud modem, but the fastest connection I get is 19,200. Sometimes the connection is choppy and laden with errors when I download files. Check for any of the following:

- Line noise

- Incorrect modem settings in your communication software

- Modem incompatibilities between your modem and your ISP's modem

- The presence of a 16450 or 8250 UART in your modem's COM port. High-speed communications require a 16550 UART.

If your phone company uses old switches in its central office, the only thing you can do is get faster, dedicated service or move.

My modem connects with my ISP's modem, and then it dumps the carrier (hangs up spontaneously). This problem is a potential nightmare with many sources. Check for these things:

- Did you set your parity to 8 bits, No stop bit, 1 parity bit?

- Is the initialization string in your communication software appropriate to your modem?

- Do the modem name and other settings in your communication software match your modem?

- Does an incompatibility exist between your modem and your ISP's modem?

Carrier dumping requires sleuthing. Be patient and work with your ISP until the problem is solved.

Using Other Windows 98 Internet Configuration Features

To take full advantage of the Internet's wealth of information, you should become familiar with a few standard tools. Telnet, FTP, and a TCP/IP configuration utility are all included in Windows 98. The following sections show you how to set up these utilities.

Starting the FTP Utility

File Transfer Protocol (FTP) is used to transfer files on the Internet from one site to another. Even if you have World Wide Web access, chances are you'll log in to an FTP site sooner or later. Windows 98 includes an FTP utility that you can use after you establish an Internet connection. To start an FTP session, click Start on the Windows 98 taskbar and choose Run. In the Open field, type **ftp** and click OK. The ftp window opens (see Figure 19.11).

FIG. 19.11

Windows includes its own FTP utility to access FTP sites on the Internet.

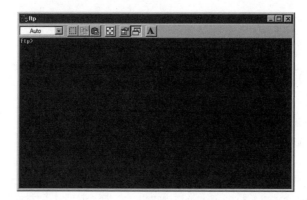

After you start FTP, you can log on to an FTP site by using the OPEN command, as in the following example:

      open ftp.microsoft.com

You can find other FTP commands by typing **?** at the ftp> prompt and pressing Enter.

Starting the Telnet Utility

Like files on FTP, much of the information on the Internet is available only if you use Telnet. This utility enables you to log in to another computer from your own and use the remote computer as if you were there. Windows provides a version of Telnet that you can run from the Start menu, as shown in the following steps:

1. Open the Start menu, choose Run, and type **telnet** in the Open field. Click OK. The Telnet window opens.

2. In Telnet, choose Connect, Remote Session.

3. In the Connect dialog box, type the host name of the Telnet site to which you want to connect in the Host Name field (see Figure 19.12).

FIG. 19.12
The Telnet utility enables you to log on to other computers remotely as if you were sitting in front of them.

4. In the Term Type field, select a terminal mode. The default is VT-100, which is a good place to start.

5. In the Port field, select a port. The default is Telnet.

6. To start the Telnet session, click the Connect button in the Connect dialog box.

Verifying Internet Connections with WINIPCFG

Windows includes an IP Configuration utility called WINIPCFG (see Figure 19.13), which you can use to display all the current TCP/IP network configuration values of your computer. Your computer must be running Microsoft TCP/IP to use WINIPCFG. To run WINIPCFG, click the Start button, choose Run, and type **WINIPCFG** in the Open field. Click OK.

FIG. 19.13
To see current IP settings, use the WINIPCFG utility available with Windows.

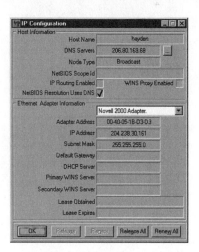

When you run WINIPCFG, you can see the current IP address allocated to your computer and other useful data about the TCP/IP allocation. The IP Configuration utility does not, however, dynamically update information. If you make any changes, such as disconnecting from your ISP, you must close the IP Configuration utility and restart it.

TROUBLESHOOTING

How do I know whether all my Internet connections are correct? You can use the PING command to get your answer quickly. To use the PING command, open a DOS session and type the following, which is the address for the Microsoft FTP server:

> **ping 198.105.232.1**

If this command works, then TCP/IP is set up correctly.

You also can start the WINIPCFG utility to see whether your IP addresses will appear. To run WINIPCFG, type **WINIPCFG** in the Open field after choosing Start, Run.

I'm connected to the Internet through my network at work. I have a DNS configuration error. Can you help? The best answer is to ask your network administrator to help you configure your Internet connection. He or she is the best qualified to designate these settings. However, you might check to make sure the DNS Configuration tab is set up correctly for your network. You can access this information by double-clicking the Networking icon in Control Panel, selecting TCP/IP, and clicking Properties. Click the DNS Configuration tab on the TCP/IP Properties page and ensure that these settings are properly configured.

CHAPTER 20

Configuring Microsoft Internet Explorer 4.0

by Rob Tidrow

In this chapter

Reviewing Features of Microsoft Internet Explorer 4.0

Internet Explorer 4.0 is the newest release of Microsoft's popular World Wide Web browser. Among other new features, the primary difference between Internet Explorer 4.0 and previous releases of Internet Explorer is its integration with Windows 98. Internet Explorer 4.0 is part of the Windows 98 shell, enabling it to act as a Web browser to display Internet and intranet content as well as browse and work with local PC files. This means users no longer need to switch between applications when locating documents or files on the Internet, local network, or their own workstations. Previous versions of Internet Explorer, on the other hand, were available as Web browsers and did not offer local PC accessibility.

Some of the new features of Internet Explorer 4.0 include the following:

- *Internet tools.* Internet Explorer 4.0 includes email, Usenet newsgroup, conferencing, broadcasting, and Web page development tools. With Internet Explorer 4.0, users have a complete suite of Internet tools built into their operating systems.

- *Webcasting.* With Webcasting, users can automatically receive updated live content from the Internet to their desktops. Also, Internet Explorer's Webcasting feature can inform users when their favorite Web sites have changed since they last visited them.

- *Java support.* Internet Explorer 4.0 includes enhanced Java support in which Java applets run faster, have enhanced security, and can access ActiveX controls.

- *Enhanced Web page support.* Internet Explorer handles a diverse number of document formats found on the Internet, including HTML 3.2, Dynamic HTML, style sheets, ActiveX, and Java.

- *Smart Toolbars.* Internet Explorer 4.0 uses Smart Toolbars, which dynamically change when you are viewing Web pages, folders, or files. Also, if you are not comfortable with the position and location of Internet Explorer's toolbars, you can move them, turn them off, or turn off their text labels.

- *Component architecture support.* With Internet Explorer 4.0, you can divide the screen to display sites you have saved in your Favorites, History, and Channels folders. Likewise, by clicking the Search button on the Standard toolbar, you can display the Search bar, which displays your search results in the main browser screen, while the search criteria displays on another part of the screen. This makes it easier to return to search engines after visiting a site. These separate "screens" are browser controls, not frames.

Configuring Internet Explorer 4.0

When you install Windows 98, Internet Explorer 4.0 is automatically installed. In most cases, you can begin using Internet Explorer as soon as you complete the Windows 98 installation.

You can, however, modify many Internet Explorer 4.0 options to meet your needs. To configure settings in Internet Explorer 4.0, launch it by double-clicking the Internet Explorer icon on the desktop or clicking the Launch Internet Explorer Browser toolbar button on the Quick Launch toolbar. You also can select Start, Programs, Internet Explorer, Internet Explorer. If you start Internet Explorer 4.0 without first connecting to the Internet, click the Stop button to stop it from attempting to connect to the default home page (http://home.microsoft.com). If you do not stop the connection process soon enough, the Connection Manager screen appears; you can click Work Offline to clear it from your screen.

Next, choose View, Internet Options from the Internet Explorer 4.0 menu bar. The Internet Options dialog box opens (see Figure 20.1). This dialog box includes six tabs: General, Security, Content, Connection, Programs, and Advanced.

FIG. 20.1
The Internet Options dialog box enables you to customize many of Internet Explorer 4.0's settings.

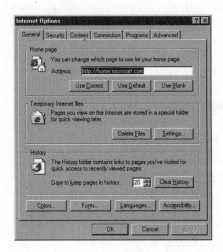

The following sections describe each of these tabs in more detail.

General Tab

The General tab is used to set multimedia, color, links, toolbar, and font settings. The following list explains each of these settings:

- *Address.* Enter the URL of a Web site or page you want to use as your default starting page. This page appears when you first start Internet Explorer 4.0. The default is http://home.microsoft.com. If you want to name an HTML file that resides on your hard drive, use the format file://C:*path_to_HTML_file*.htm. Fill in the actual filename for *path_to_HTML_file*.

 TIP To change the URL in the Address line without entering a URL, close the Internet Options dialog box and display the Web page you want to use as the default starting page in Internet Explorer's browser window. Next, choose View, Internet Options, select the General tab, and choose Use Current. This step saves the current page's URL as the Address URL. To change back to the default setting, click the Use Default button. You also can opt to display a blank starting page by clicking the Use Blank button.

■ *Temporary Internet Files.* The Temporary Internet Files folder holds cached copies of every file you download with Internet Explorer 4.0. These cached files are used when you return to a site for quick viewing later. They include every HTML document, image, icon, audio file, video file, cookie file, and other content. Needless to say, if you surf the Web for some time, you are bound to accumulate many files on your system that you may never use again. These files sit on your hard drive taking up valuable disk space. Click Delete Files to remove the cached files from your system. Choose Yes when prompted to delete all the files.

N O T E Before deleting files from the Temporary Internet Files folder, weigh the benefit of keeping the cached files in the Temporary Internet Files folder. These files make returning to a site extremely fast; you don't need to wait on the entire page to download. ■

To configure the Temporary Internet Files folder, click the Settings button to display the Settings dialog box (see Figure 20.2).

FIG. 20.2

You can change the amount of allotted space for your Temporary Internet Files folder by using the Settings dialog box.

In the Settings dialog box, you can designate how often you want Web pages checked against cached Web pages to see whether they have changed. You can specify that the page be checked every time you visit it, once each session of Internet Explorer 4.0, or never. You also can set the amount (in percentage) of disk space used by the Temporary Internet File folder. The default is 2 percent, which is a lot of disk space for large hard drives. You may want to limit the amount to 1 percent for most big drives.

Also in the Settings dialog box are options that enable you to move the Temporary Internet File folder, view all the files in the Temporary Internet File folder (if you have not deleted them), and view downloaded program files (click the View Objects button). Click OK to return to the General tab.

■ *Days to Keep Pages in History.* Set this option to the number of days you want to keep items in the Internet Explorer 4.0 History list. The default is 20, which may be too high for many users. You may want to set this value to 5 or 10 days to reduce the number of items stored on your hard drive.

TIP If you do a lot of Web surfing, your History list will grow out of control. History list files are stored on your hard drive, so your hard drive will soon contain numerous (sometimes thousands of) files associated with Web links. If you find that your hard drive space is limited, clear the History list or open the \WINDOWS\HISTORY folder, select all the files in the History folder, and press Delete.

- *Clear History.* Click this button to delete all items from your History list.
- *Colors.* Click the Colors button to display the Colors dialog box (see Figure 20.3). The Use Windows Colors option is used when you want Internet Explorer's text and background colors to be the default Windows colors. You must disable this option to be able to choose the Text and Background options, which then enable you to pick custom colors for the text and background. The Colors dialog box also includes options for setting hyperlink colors. By default, unvisited hyperlinks on a Web page are shown in blue; after you click a hyperlink, it turns to purple. Click the Visited and Unvisited options to change their color value. You also can set a hover color, which turns hyperlinks to a different color when you hover your mouse pointer over them. Click OK to return to the General tab.

FIG. 20.3
Use the Colors dialog box to set text, background, and link colors.

- *Fonts.* Click the Fonts button to display the Fonts dialog box (see Figure 20.4). This dialog box enables you to change the character sets, proportional fonts, fixed-width fonts, and font size for text that appears in Internet Explorer 4.0. These settings do not change the Web page you're viewing, only how Internet Explorer displays it. Click OK to save your settings and return to the General tab.

FIG. 20.4
The Fonts dialog box controls the way Internet Explorer 4.0 displays text.

Part
V

Ch
20

- *Languages*. Click the Languages button to display the Language Preferences dialog box. This dialog box enables you to specify languages Internet Explorer 4.0 will display if a Web page offers content in multiple languages. Click the Add button to specify additional languages from the Add Language dialog box. Click OK to return to the Language Preferences dialog box. Click the Move Up and Move Down buttons to prioritize your language preferences. Click Remove to remove a selected language. Click OK to return to the General tab.

- *Accessibility*. Click the Accessibility button to display the Accessibility dialog box (see Figure 20.5). This dialog box enables you to control formatting and style sheet options. You can choose the options described in Table 20.1. Click OK after setting these options.

FIG. 20.5

Use the Accessibility dialog box to set how Internet Explorer handles custom formatting and style sheets.

Table 20.1   Options in the Accessibility Dialog Box

Option	Description
Ignore Colors Specified on Web Pages	Instructs Internet Explorer 4.0 to use your text and background color settings (see Colors button discussion earlier) instead of any colors specified by the Web page.
Ignore Font Styles Specified on Web Pages	Instructs Internet Explorer 4.0 to use your font style settings (see Fonts button discussion earlier) instead of any fonts specified by the Web page.
Ignore Font Sizes Specified on Web Pages	Instructs Internet Explorer 4.0 to use your font size setting (see Fonts button discussion earlier) instead of any font sizes specified by the Web page.
Format Documents Using My Style Sheet	Instructs Internet Explorer 4.0 to use a local style sheet when displaying a Web page that supports style sheets. You must specify the file pathname to your local style sheet.

Click Apply to save your settings in the General tab.

Security Tab

The Security tab (see Figure 20.6) provides access to Internet Explorer security options, such as how Java applets run, how ActiveX controls are downloaded, how files are downloaded, and whether Active Scripting is enabled. The following describes each of the options on this page:

FIG. 20.6
Use the Security tab to set security zone settings.

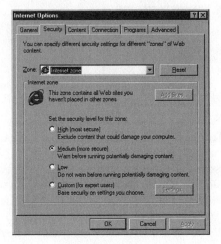

- *Zone.* Enables you to select security zones you want to configure. You can set up security zones to control how Internet Explorer displays Web content. You can, for example, specify the Internet Explorer security level of documents stored on your local intranet. When you select an option from the Zone drop-down list, the Internet Zone area changes to reflect options for each zone. The following are the four zones from which you can choose:

  - *Local Intranet Zone.* Displays security zone options for documents available on your company's intranet.
  - *Trusted Sites Zone.* Displays security zone options for Web sites you know are safe to display in Internet Explorer.
  - *Internet Zone.* Displays security zone options for Web sites that you have not added to the Trusted Sites or Restricted Sites zones. If you do not specify any Web sites in the Trusted Sites and Restricted Sites zones, all Web sites you encounter will use the security options you specify for the Internet Zone.
  - *Restricted Sites Zone.* Displays security zone options for Web sites that contain data or applications that may harm your computer.

- *Add Sites.* Displays a dialog box in which to specify specific sites or settings for each security zone. Figure 20.7 shows the Local Intranet Zone dialog box, which appears when you select the Local Intranet Zone option. In this dialog box, you can configure Internet Explorer to access all intranet sites that are not listed in other zones, all sites

Part
V

Ch
20

that do not use the proxy server, and all sites on a local area network path. Click the Advanced button to display the Local Intranet Zone dialog box, in which you can specify Web sites that use the security zone settings selected in the Local Intranet Zone dialog box.

FIG. 20.7

The Local Intranet Zone dialog box sets security zone options for intranet documents.

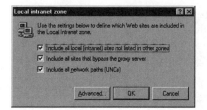

Figure 20.8 shows the Trusted Sites Zone dialog box, which appears when you select the Trusted Sites Zone option and click Add Sites on the Security tab. In this dialog box, you specify Web sites that use the Trusted Sites Zone settings. In the Add This Web Site to the Zone field, enter a URL you want to list as a trusted site. Click the Add button to add it the Web Sites box. To remove a Web site, select it in the Web Sites box and click the Remove button. If you want Internet Explorer to make sure your trusted Web sites are secure (that is, an HTTPS server is used) before connecting to them, click the Require Server Verification (https:) For All Sites in This Zone check box.

FIG. 20.8

You can enter specific URLs for Web sites that use the Trusted Sites Zone security settings.

Figure 20.9 shows the Restricted Sites Zone dialog box, which appears when you select the Restricted Sites Zone option and click the Add Sites button on the Security tab. In this dialog box, which is similar to the Trusted Sites Zone dialog box, you specify Web sites that use the Restricted Sites Zone settings.

NOTE The Add Sites button is not available when you select the Internet Zone option. ■

FIG. 20.9

You can enter specific URLs for Web sites that use the Restricted Sites Zone security settings.

- *Security Level Settings.* In the Restricted Sites Zone area, you set different security levels for each of the Zone options. Select the High setting when you want Internet Explorer to not display Web content that could damage your computer. For Internet Explorer to warn you of sites that may contain content that can damage your computer, select Medium. Select Low if you don't want any warning from Internet Explorer before entering a potentially harmful site.

  For more control over how Internet Explorer handles specific content, select the Custom option and click the Settings button. From the Security Settings dialog box (see Figure 20.10), set the way Internet Explorer handles files, programs, and fonts. To instruct Internet Explorer to handle an item automatically, click Enable. To instruct Internet Explorer to prompt you before proceeding with an item, click Prompt. Click Disable to instruct Internet Explorer to ignore the file or action. Table 20.2 describes each of the items you can set in this dialog box.

FIG. 20.10

The Security Settings dialog box provides control over potentially harmful actions, files, applications, and documents.

Part

V

Ch

20

Table 20.2   Security Settings

Item	Description
ActiveX Controls and Plugins	Enables you to specify how Internet Explorer handles ActiveX controls. The settings you can control include how Internet Explorer scripts ActiveX controls, if ActiveX controls can run on your computer, whether signed or unsigned ActiveX controls can be downloaded to your computer, and how ActiveX initializes and scripts ActiveX controls that are not marked as safe.
Java	Enables you to specify how Java Permissions are granted on your computer.
Scripting	Controls how Active scripting and scripting of Java applets are handled by your computer. If you cannot get Active scripting to work, be sure the Enable or Prompt option is selected.
Downloads	Controls how files and fonts are downloaded to your computer. By default, both of these settings are set to Disable, so you will be prompted when a Web site wants to upload a file or font to your system.
User Authentication	Enables you to control logon settings. If you want to have Internet Explorer log on to a Web site automatically, for example, click the Automatic Logon with Current Username and Password option.
Miscellaneous	Provides settings for controlling how nonencrypted form data is submitted, how applications and files in IFRAMEs are launched, and other options.

 To reset the Security Settings back to their default, click the Reset button. From the Reset To drop-down list, you can select the default security level that you want the default to return to, including High, Medium, and Low settings.

Click Apply to save your settings in the Security tab.

Content Tab

The Content tab (see Figure 20.11) includes settings that let you set content ratings (similar to the Motion Picture Association's ratings for movies), activate the certificates feature, and set personal information.

The following sections briefly explain each area on the Content tab.

FIG. 20.11
The Content tab
contains options to set
up content ratings,
certificates, and
personal information.

Content Advisor   Choose the Enable button to display the Create Supervisor Password dialog box (see Figure 20.12). Enter a password in the Password field, and enter it again in the Confirm Password field. You use this password when you want to change the Content Advisor settings. Keep this password secret, and do not let children know it. Click OK to save the password and display the Content Advisor dialog box (see Figure 20.13).

FIG. 20.12
Use the Create
Supervisor Password
dialog box to create a
password that you use
when you want to
change the Content
Advisor settings.

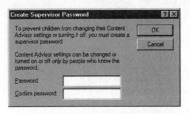

FIG. 20.13
You establish ratings for
the Content Advisor
settings in the Content
Advisor dialog box.

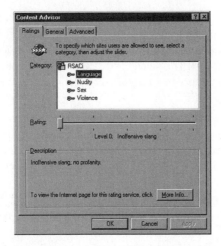

Part
V
Ch
20

N O T E For the Content Advisor settings to work on a Web site, that Web site must rate its page following the Recreational Software Advisory Council (RASC) rating service for the Internet. These ratings are based on the following categories: violence, language, sex, and nudity. If a site does not incorporate the RASC ratings in its pages, Internet Explorer 4.0 does not block users from these sites. You can learn more about RASC by clicking the More Info button on the Content Advisor dialog box, which sends you to the RASC s Web page at `http://www.rsac.org/ratingsv01.html`. ▮

In the Ratings page of the Content Advisor dialog box, click an item in the Category box (such as Language) and set the Rating slider bar for that rating. The slider bar appears below the Category box when you click a category. You can set the Rating slider bar from Level 0 (inoffensive slang) to Level 4 (explicit or crude language). Set each of the four categories to your tastes.

Click the General tab (see Figure 20.14) to set the following options:

FIG. 20.14

The General tab includes user and supervisor content settings.

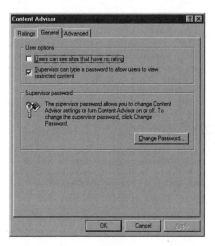

- *User Options.* In this area, you can set whether the user can see sites that have no ratings. If you leave this option blank, many sites will not be accessible to the user, including those that do not contain any offensive material (the majority of Web pages do not include RASC ratings yet). The default is to leave the option blank, but you may want to select it if you want to be sure that Internet Explorer displays only those sites on the Web that have ratings by RASC.

  In User Options, you also can enable the supervisor to enter a password that lets users (who happen to know the supervisor's password, such as the supervisor or a spouse) view pages with restricted content. This option is ideal if you want to block others from seeing specific content, but you (assuming you are the supervisor) want to access pages with this type of content.

- *Change Password.* Click this button to display the Change Supervisor Password dialog box and change the old password to a new one. In the Old Password field, enter the old password. Then enter the new one in the New Password and Confirm New Password fields. Click OK to save your changes.

Click the Advanced tab to set different rating systems and rating bureau information (see Figure 20.15).

FIG. 20.15

You can set up different rating systems in the Advanced tab.

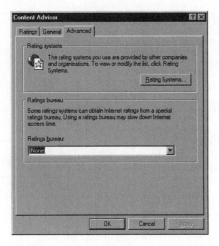

Options in the Advanced tab are described in the following list:

- *Rating Systems.* Click this button to select a new rating systems file to add to your rating systems list. By default, the RASCI.RAT file is provided with Internet Explorer 4.0 to set up the RASC rating system. You need to acquire new rating systems from other companies to add to your list. You also can delete systems from your list.

- *Rating Bureau.* Select a ratings bureau item from the Rating Bureau drop-down list. The options available in this list are determined by the rating systems files you add by using the Rating Systems button. The RASC rating system file, for example, does not contain any rating bureaus.

Click OK to save your settings and return to the Content tab. After you set the ratings, the Enable Ratings button changes to the Disable Ratings button. You can turn off ratings by clicking this button and entering the supervisor password. You also can change the content rating settings by clicking the Settings button. Again, you must enter the supervisor password, and then the Content Advisor dialog box appears.

Certificates   Use this area on the Content tab to designate certificate settings for identifying you, sites, and publishers of sites. Certificates are used to authenticate you (Personal button), the site on the other end (Authorities button), and the publisher of the information on the page you are viewing (Publishers button). You must obtain certificates (usually by purchasing them or receiving them from sites) before you can set them up in this section.

Personal Information   The Personal Information area of the Content tab includes settings for the Microsoft Profile Assistant. Here, you can set a Windows 98 Address Book entry for

Part

V

Ch

20

yourself, including your name, address, email address, and other personal information that is shared with Web sites you visit that request personal information from their visitors.

To set up your personal information, click the Edit Profile button to display your personal Properties page (see Figure 20.16).

FIG. 20.16

Your personal informa-
tion can be shared with
Web sites that prompt
for user information.

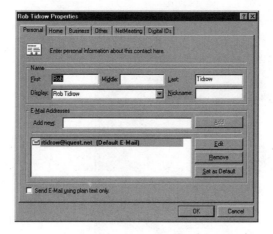

Fill out the information requested on the following pages and click OK:

- *Personal.* Enter your name and email address.
- *Home.* Enter your home address, phone number, fax number, cellular number, and Web page address (if applicable).
- *Business.* Enter your business information, such as company name, address, phone number, and Web page address.
- *Other.* Enter additional information about yourself.
- *NetMeeting.* Enter NetMeeting conferencing information about yourself, including your conferencing email address and the server used when conducting a NetMeeting conference.
- *Digital IDs.* Add, remove, or view digital IDs you may have. You need to click the Import button to select a digital ID file to import.

On the Content tab, click the Reset Sharing button to revoke all the permissions you granted to Web sites that use your personal information.

You also can set up Microsoft Wallet settings on the Content tab. Microsoft Wallet provides a secure way to conduct online shopping. Click the Addresses button to display the Address Options dialog box (see Figure 20.17) and to set up Microsoft Wallet addresses. Click Close to save your settings.

FIG. 20.17
Use the Address
Options dialog box to
specify an address that
should appear in the
Microsoft Wallet.

Click the Payments button to install the Microsoft - Credit Card extension. Click the Install
button when you are prompted to continue. The Payment Options dialog box then appears (see
Figure 20.18). Click the Add button to display the types of credit cards Microsoft Wallet supports, including Visa, MasterCard, American Express, and Discover. Select a credit card from
this list to launch the Credit Card Information Wizard, which walks you through setting up
information about the card you want to use with Microsoft Wallet. Click Close when you finish
adding new credit cards to the Payment Options dialog box.

FIG. 20.18
The Payment Options
dialog box includes
settings for the credit
cards Microsoft Wallet
uses to handle online
shopping.

 To remove a credit card from the Payment Options dialog box, click the Methods button, select the
credit card from the Select Payment Methods dialog box, and click OK.

Part
V

Ch
20

Click Apply to save your settings in the Content tab.

Connection Tab

The Connection tab contains information on how Internet Explorer 4.0 connects to the
Internet.

The Connection options are explained in the following sections.

Configuring Connection Settings   You can connect to the Internet using the Internet Connec-
tion Wizard. Click the Connect button to launch the wizard and to walk through setting up your
Internet connection settings. Chapter 19, "Configuring an Internet Connection," describes the
Connection Wizard in detail.

If you want to change the settings of your dial-up Internet connection, select the Connect to the Internet Using a Modem option and click the Settings button on the Connection tab. The Dial-Up Settings dialog box appears (see Figure 20.19).

FIG. 20.19

Use the Dial-Up Settings dialog box to change your dial-up Internet connection settings.

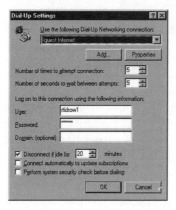

If, however, you connect to the Internet via a LAN, select the Access the Internet Via a Local Area Network option. You should then consult your LAN administrator before making any changes to your Internet configuration.

Configuring Corporate Proxy Server Settings   Click the Access the Internet Using a Proxy Server option on the Connection tab if you connect to the Internet via a proxy server. If you use Internet Explorer 4.0 from home, you don't generally use this setting. You need to worry about proxy settings only when you connect to the Internet from work and use a direct network connection (usually via a local area network) to the Internet. The proxy server is used to decrease the chances of users on the outside illegally breaking into your company's server using the Internet. In this case, ask your network administrator for the proper proxy settings to fill in.

Fill in the Address field with the URL of your proxy server. Fill in the Port field with the port number of the proxy server. Click the Advanced button to display the Proxy Settings dialog box (see Figure 20.20). In this dialog box, enter the URL and port numbers for the proxy servers that handle the following Internet protocols:

- HTTP
- Secure HTTP
- FTP
- Gopher
- Socks

If the same proxy server handles all the preceding Internet protocols, fill in the HTTP settings and click the Use the Same Proxy Server For All Protocols option.

For Web addresses that you do not want Internet Explorer to use the specified proxy server, enter those addresses in the Exceptions area. Separate each address with semicolons.

Click OK to close the Proxy Settings dialog box.

FIG. 20.20

The Proxy Settings dialog box includes addresses for different Internet proxy servers.

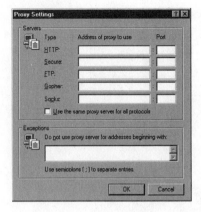

Using the Automatic Configuration Settings   If the system administrator has created a file that automatically configures your copy of Internet Explorer to run on your corporate network (to access the Internet or intranet), click the Configure button on the Connection tab. Doing so displays the Automatic Configuration dialog box (see Figure 20.21).

FIG. 20.21

The Automatic Configuration dialog box enables you to specify a URL to the file that automatically configures your copy of Internet Explorer.

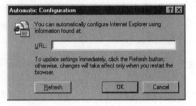

In the URL field, enter the URL to the file that automatically configures Internet Explorer. You should ask your system administrator for the address of this file.

Click Apply to save your Connection settings.

Programs Tab

The Programs tab, shown in Figure 20.22, includes settings for your Internet mail, news, conference, calendar, and contact list programs. You also specify in this tab whether you want Internet Explorer 4.0 to verify that it is always the default Web browser configured on your system.

Part

V

Ch

20

FIG. 20.22

The Programs tab enables you to set up programs to work with Internet Explorer 4.0.

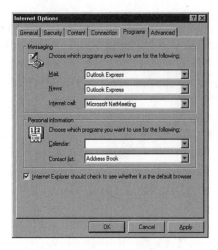

The following options are available on the Programs tab:

- *Mail*. Use this drop-down list to pick the email application you want to use when you click the Mail icon on the standard Internet Explorer 4.0 toolbar and select the Read Mail option. One example of an email program is Outlook Express. If nothing appears in this list, however, you must first install a supported email package and then return to this tab to specify it as your default email package.

- *News*. Use this drop-down list to pick the news reader application you want to use when you click the Mail icon on the standard Internet Explorer 4.0 toolbar and select the Read News option. If you have Outlook Express installed, Outlook Express appears in the News drop-down list as a news reader option.

- *Internet Call*. Use this drop-down list to select an Internet conference program to use with Internet Explorer. If Microsoft NetMeeting is installed, for example, you can choose the Microsoft NetMeeting option from the Internet Call drop-down list.

- *Calendar*. Use this drop-down list to specify the Internet calendar program to use with Internet Explorer.

- *Contact List*. Use this drop-down list to specify an address book to use with Internet Explorer, such as the Microsoft Address Book.

- *Internet Explorer Should Check to See Whether It Is the Default Browser*. Click this option if you want Internet Explorer 4.0 to check your system to see whether it is the default Web browser. If Explorer is not your default browser, a dialog box appears asking whether you want to make it the default browser.

Click Apply to save your Programs settings.

Advanced Tab

The Advanced tab (see Figure 20.23) includes several settings you can configure to change the behavior of Internet Explorer. These settings are covered in Table 20.3.

FIG. 20.23

Much of the way in which Internet Explorer looks and behaves is controlled by the Advanced tab settings.

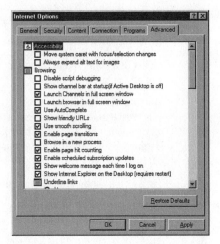

Table 20.3   Advanced Tab Options

Option	Description
Move System Caret with Focus/ Selection Changes	Moves the system caret (an accessibility feature) when you change the focus or a selection is made.
Always Expand Alt Text for Images	Specifies whether an image size is to expand to fit the alternate text area when you've turned off image display.
Notify When Downloads Complete	Indicates in the status bar when a page is completely downloaded.
Disable Script Debugging	Turns off script debugging so that errors in the script are not displayed when connecting to pages with script errors.
Show Channel Bar At Startup (if Active Desktop Is Off)	Displays the Channel Bar on your desktop when you start Windows.
Launch Channels in Full Screen Window	Displays channels in full-screen mode.
Launch Browser in Full Screen Windows	Starts IE 4.0 in full-screen mode.
Use AutoComplete	Automatically fills in the Internet address as you type a URL in the Address bar. The information filled in is based on URLs you've visited in the past.
Show Friendly URLs	Displays the full URL in the status bar.
Use Smooth Scrolling	Displays a page's content at a predefined speed when you use the scrolling bars to scroll through the page.

Part

V

Ch

20

continues

Table 20.3   Continued

Option	Description
Enable Page Transitions	Fades in a page you are connecting to, and fades out a page you are leaving.
Browse in a New Process	Starts a new IE 4.0 window each time you start IE 4.0, even if another occurrence of IE is running. This feature is useful if you double-click a Web page in Explorer and want that page to appear in its own IE 4.0 browser window.
Enable Page Hit Counting	Turns on a Web page's hit counter so that it tallies a page hit for every time you view the page. This feature works even when you are viewing the page offline.
Enable Scheduled Subscription Updates	Turns on the subscription feature so that it automatically updates as scheduled.
Show Welcome Message Each Time I Log On	Displays the IE 4.0 Welcome screen each time you start Windows.
Show Internet Explorer on the Desktop	Displays a shortcut to IE 4.0 on your desktop. Shut down and restart Windows if you change this option.
Underline Links	Shows hyperlinks with underline font. You can set this option to Always, Never, or Hover. Hover turns on underlining only when you hover the mouse pointer over the hyperlinked text.
Show Pictures	Turns on picture support in IE 4.0. Turn off this option if you want to load Web pages without images embedded, speeding up your download time.
Play Animations	Specifies that IE 4.0 plays animation files.
Play Videos	Specifies that IE 4.0 plays supported video files.
Play Sounds	Specifies that IE 4.0 plays supported sound files. This option does not turn off RealAudio sound support.
Smart Image Dithering	Smoothes images when displayed in IE 4.0.
Enable Profile Assistant	Turns on the Profile Assistant so that when you connect to a Web site that supports Profile Assistant information, you can enter information to share with the site.
PCT 1.0	Enables Private Communications Technology protocol to send and receive secure information. Some sites may not support PCT 1.0.

Option	Description
SSL 2.0	Enables Secure Sockets Layer Level 2 protocol to send and receive secure information. Some sites may not support SSL 2.0.
SSL 3.0	Enables Secure Sockets Layer Level 3 protocol to send and receive secure information. Some sites may not support SSL 3.0.
Delete Saved Pages When Browser Closed	Specifies the files stored in the Temporary Internet Files folder are deleted when you quit IE 4.0.
Do Not Save Encrypted Pages To Disk	Specifies that IE 4.0 does not save encrypted pages to your disk.
Warn If Forms Submit Is Being Redirected	Warns you that a form you submit is being sent to a Web site other than the one on which the form resides.
Warn If Changing Between Secure and Not Secure Mode	When connected to a secure page, IE 4.0 displays a message telling you that the page to which you're connecting is not a secure page.
Check for Certificate Revocation	IE 4.0 can check a certificate to see if it has been revoked before accepting the certificate and allowing you to connect to the site.
Warn About Invalid Site Certificates	IE 4.0 can warn you if a site you're visiting does not have a valid site certificate.
Always Accept Cookies	Specifies that IE 4.0 always accepts cookie files from sites. A *cookie* is a file on your computer that stores information about your identity and any properties you have set for a site. Not all sites use cookies, but many do to help track site activity, as well as store information about you so that the next time you return they will know your identity.
Prompt Before Accepting Cookies	Specifies that IE 4.0 asks whether you want to receive cookie files sent to you.
Disable All Cookie Use	Specifies that IE 4.0 does not download or upload cookie files when you connect to the Web.
Java Console Enabled	Turns on the Java console. Shut down and restart your computer if you change this setting.
Java JIT Compiler Enabled	Enables the built-in Java compiler in IE 4.0.
Java Logging Enabled	Creates a log file that tracks all Java activity when you run IE 4.0. You may want to enable this option to help diagnose and locate problems with Java applets.

Part

V

Ch

20

continues

Table 20.3 Continued

Option	Description
Print Background Colors and Images	Specifies that a Web page prints with its background colors and images included. This option may slow down the printing process and may reduce the quality of the printout.
Autoscan Common Root Domains	When IE 4.0 cannot locate a page you've indicated, this option specifies that IE 4.0 should search for a Web page using common root domains (such as .COM, .ORG, .EDU, and .GOV) to locate a page.
Search when URL Fails	Specifies whether IE 4.0 should automatically search for a Web page with a URL similar to the one you've entered in the Web address field or clicked in a page if the current page cannot be located. You can choose one of three settings: Never Search, Always Ask, or Always Search.
Show Font Button	Adds the Font button to the IE 4.0 toolbar. Select this option if you want to change font displays quickly in IE 4.0 when viewing a page.
Small Icons	Switches IE 4.0's toolbar buttons to small icons. Enable this option to increase the viewing area of IE 4.0.
Use HTTP 1.1	Enables IE 4.0 to use HTTP 1.1 when connecting to Web sites. HTTP 1.0 is the transport protocol for most sites on the Web, but HTTP 1.1 includes several enhancements, which is prompting many sites to upgrade. Clear this option if you have problems connecting with some sites.
Use HTTP 1.1 Through Proxy Connections	Enables IE 4.0 to connect to HTTP 1.1 Web site through a proxy server.

 T I P Click Restore Defaults to return all the options back to their default state when you installed Windows.

Click OK to save your Advanced settings and to return to the Internet Explorer main window.

Changing Toolbar Features

If you want to move toolbars on the Internet Explorer window, click and hold down the left mouse button on the toolbar to grab it. The mouse pointer changes to a four-sided arrow to indicate that you can move the toolbar in different directions. Next, drag the toolbar to its new location, such as above the menu bar or below another toolbar. You also can move it to the left or right of its current location. Release the mouse button when you have the toolbar in its new location.

You also can turn off toolbars by selecting View, Toolbars. Choosing this option displays a submenu of toolbar from which you can turn off, including Standard Buttons, Address Bar, Links, and Text Labels. These choices are also available on a context menu if you right-click a toolbar.

 TIP To turn off the display of toolbar button text labels, select View, Toolbars, Text Labels. Choosing this option shrinks the size of each toolbar to give you a little more browser window area. The Text Labels option does not affect the display of ToolTips, which appear above each toolbar button when you hover the mouse pointer over them. The ToolTips provide a brief explanation of a button's functionality.

Setting Thumbnail View

Internet Explorer provides a unique feature when viewing your favorite Web sites. Not only can you store a shortcut to a favorite Web site, but you also can store a thumbnail of a site. A *thumbnail* is a small image of a Web site.

To display thumbnail views in Internet Explorer, perform the following steps:

1. Select Favorite, Organize Favorites.
2. Right-click in the Organize Favorites window.
3. Select Properties from the context menu to display the Favorites Properties page (see Figure 20.24).

FIG. 20.24
The Favorites Properties page enables you to activate thumbnail view.

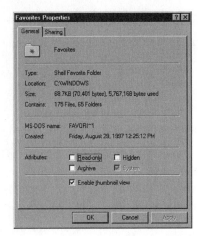

Part
V

Ch
20

4. Check Enable Thumbnail View and click OK.
5. Click Close to close the Organize Favorites window.

6. Reopen the Organize Favorites window (select F<u>a</u>vorites, <u>O</u>rganize Favorites).

7. In the Organize Favorites window, right-click and select <u>V</u>iew, <u>T</u>humbnails. Your view should now look like the one in Figure 20.25.

FIG. 20.25
You can see thumbnail views of your favorite Web sites.

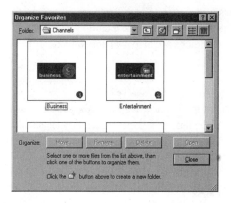

Setting Full-Screen Mode

For some Web sites, viewing a document in full-screen mode is a real advantage. Full-screen mode turns off all menu bars, desk icons, scrollbars, toolbars, and the status bar so that you can see more of a Web page. A floating toolbar of the Standard Buttons toolbar appears at the top of the full-screen mode.

Turn on full-screen mode by selecting <u>V</u>iew, <u>F</u>ull Screen (or click the Full Screen toolbar button). When you want to switch back to regular screen mode, click the Full Screen toolbar button (the third from the right).

Setting Subscriptions and Schedules

IE 4 can be set to check Web sites automatically to see whether new content is available on them. You do so by setting schedules for Web sites you subscribe to. IE 4 can then check on the Web sites daily, weekly, or monthly, depending on when you want a particular site checked. After a site is subscribed to and content is downloaded to your desktop, you can view the site while connected to the Internet or while offline.

To set up a subscription and schedule to a Web site, use the following steps:

1. Display the Web page to which you want to subscribe. You need to be connected to the Internet or an intranet to view your page.

2. Select F<u>a</u>vorites, <u>A</u>dd To Favorites.

3. From the Add Favorite dialog box (see Figure 20.26), select from the following options:

   - <u>Y</u>es, but only tell me when this page is updated
   - Yes, notify me of updates and <u>d</u>ownload the page for offline viewing

FIG. 20.26
Use the Add Favorite
dialog box to set up a
subscription to a Web
page.

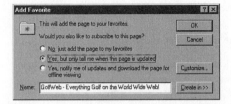

4. Click Customize to start the Subscription Wizard (see Figure 20.27).

FIG. 20.27
The Subscription Wizard
walks you through
setting up a Web page
subscription.

5. Select whether to receive an email message from the Web site to which you're subscribing when it changes.

6. Click Next. Fill in any username or password information required by the Web site.

7. Click Finish.

8. On the Add Favorite dialog box, click OK.

To configure subscription schedules, select Favorites, Manage Subscriptions. The Subscriptions window then appears (see Figure 20.28). Right-click a Web page you want to modify, and choose Properties from the context menu. The Properties page for that Web page then appears (see Figure 20.29).

Part
V

Ch
20

FIG. 20.28
You can view the
schedule of your
subscriptions in this
window.

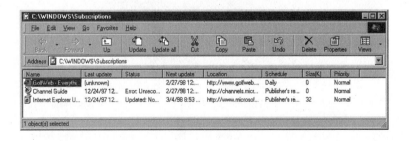

FIG. 20.29

The Subscription tab on the Properties page provides information about the subscribed-to Web page.

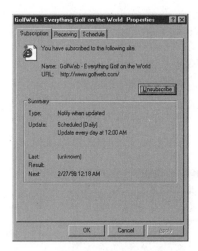

On the Subscription tab, you can click the Unsubscribe button if you want to remove the selected page from your subscription list.

If you want to change how IE 4 notifies you of a changed page, click the Receiving tab (see Figure 20.30) and set the Subscription Type and Notification options. They are similar to the options you selected in steps 3 through 5 in the preceding steps.

FIG. 20.30

The Receiving tab also includes the Login button, which enables you to modify username and password requirements for a page.

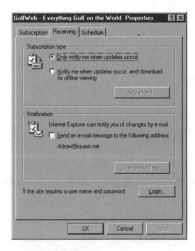

On the Schedule tab, set the schedule for how often the page should be updated. From the Scheduled drop-down list, select Daily, Monthly, or Weekly. Then click the Edit button to customize the schedule in the Custom Schedule dialog box. Make changes to when you want the update for the subscribed-to page to occur. Click OK to save your changes.

If you want to set up a new schedule for a subscription, click the New button on the Schedule tab and set up the new schedule.

TIP To have IE 4 automatically connect to the Internet via modem to update a subscription, be sure to click the Dial As Needed If Connected Through a Modem option. This feature is handy if you plan to update your subscriptions on off-hours, such as late at night or on weekends, when you usually are not connected to the Internet.

The Manually option is used if you don't want to schedule a time to update a subscription. Rather, you want to update the subscription manually by using the Update Now button on the Schedule page, or by right-clicking a subscription in the Subscriptions window and selecting Update.

Finally, select the Don't Update This Subscription When I'm Using My Computer option if you don't want IE 4 to update a subscription if you're doing something else with your computer. This way, IE 4 does not interfere with your work.

Click OK to save your settings. ●

Part
V

Ch
20

CHAPTER 21

Configuring Outlook Express

by Rob Tidrow

In this chapter

Viewing and Modifying the Outlook Express Window

New in Windows 98 is Outlook Express, software you can use for your messaging needs, including sending and receiving Internet email messages, participating in newsgroups, managing address books, and performing other communications needs. Outlook Express replaces the Windows Messaging and Microsoft Exchange clients available with Windows 95.

When you initially launch Outlook Express, the Internet Connection Wizard appears. If you've already set up an Internet connection, Windows 98 does not display the wizard; instead, Outlook Express appears. If you need to set up a connection, however, work through the Internet Connection Wizard, which also helps you fill out critical Outlook Express information, including your Internet email and newsgroup information.

After you run the Internet Connection Wizard, you can usually start using Outlook Express without any other setup required. If you bypass the Connection Wizard or want to reconfigure Outlook Express, you do so within Outlook Express itself.

One of the first configuration options you encounter with Outlook Express is setting your connection option. As Outlook Express launches, you see the dialog box shown in Figure 21.1. Here you can select the default connection you want Outlook Express to use upon startup. If you want to start Outlook Express so that it does not dial a connection, select Don't Dial A Connection from the Select the Connection You Would Like To Dial drop-down list. If you want to specify a connection method, such as a Dial-Up Networking connection, select the connection from the drop-down list.

FIG. 21.1

You can select a connection for Outlook Express to use during startup.

To make your selection the default connection, click the Set As the Default Startup Connection option.

For now, click Cancel to start Outlook Express to work offline.

The Outlook Express window then appears (see Figure 21.2). It is divided into three panes (you may need to click the Inbox folder to display all three panes). The folder list pane includes your mail folders, newsgroup server names, and newsgroups. You can use this pane to navigate quickly among these items and open them in the message list pane. In this pane, you can view email message headers and newsgroups to which you're subscribed. In the preview pane, you can read the body of email or newsgroup messages.

FIG. 21.2

The main window of
Outlook Express
contains three panes.

Folder list pane

Message list pane

Preview pane

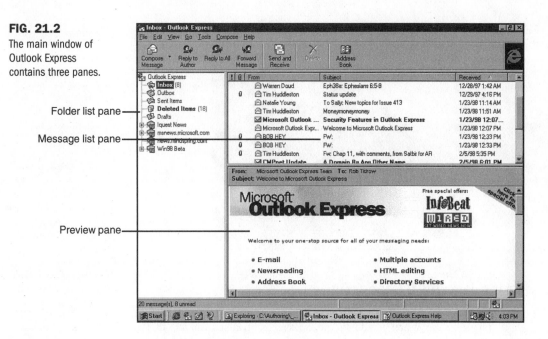

N O T E Showing you how to use Outlook Express is beyond the scope of this book. Consult *Special Edition Windows 98* for more information on using Outlook Express. ■

You can customize the Outlook Express window in a number of ways, as shown in the following sections.

Changing the Position of the Preview Pane

The preview pane enables you to view a message quickly without opening a separate window. This pane is located below the message list pane by default. You can, however, change it so that the preview pane appears next to the message list pane.

To change the preview pane position, follow these steps:

1. Select View, Layout. The Window Layout Properties dialog box appears (see Figure 21.3).

2. In the Preview Pane area, select Beside Message to have the pane appear to the right of the message list pane.

3. Click OK. The preview pane then changes its position.

To return the preview pane back to its original position, select the Below Messages option in step 2.

Part
V
Ch
21

TIP To resize an individual pane, grab the separator and move it left or right, or up and down.

FIG. 21.3

Use the Window Layout Properties dialog box to reposition the preview pane.

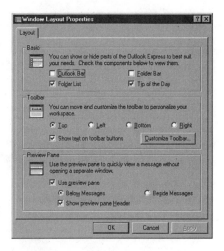

Turning Off the Preview Pane

If you want to view the body of your messages only in a separate window, you can turn off the preview pane. When you do so, the message list pane expands to fill the entire right side of the Outlook Express window.

To turn off the preview pane, do the following:

1. Select View, Layout.
2. In the Preview Pane area, deselect the Use Preview Pane option. The other preview pane options dim, making them unavailable until you turn the preview pane back on again.
3. Click OK. The preview pane is now gone, and any time you want to view a message, you need to double-click its subject in the message list pane.

Moving and Customizing the Toolbar

By default, the Outlook Express toolbar appears at the top of the window, just below the menu bar. If you want to move the toolbar, you can using the Window Layout Properties dialog box (select View, Layout).

From this dialog box, select Left, Bottom, or Right, to change the toolbar position (Top is the default).

If you don't have the Window Layout Properties dialog box open, right-click the toolbar and select Align and the alignment option (Left, Right, Top, or Bottom).

Another toolbar customization chore you can perform from the Window Layout Properties dialog box is to turn off text for each button by deselecting the Show Text On Toolbar Buttons option. You also can right-click the toolbar and select Text Labels.

You also can change the buttons that appear on your toolbar. Click the Customize Toolbar button to display the Customize Toolbar dialog box (see Figure 21.4). Select a button in the

Available Buttons list to add to your toolbar and then click Add. Doing so places this button on your toolbar. Use the Move Up and Move Down buttons to arrange the button where you want it. You also can select a button in the Toolbar Buttons list and click Remove to delete the button from the toolbar. To add a separate bar between buttons, select the Separator item in the Available Buttons list. Click Close when finished. Finally, if you want to return the toolbar to its original state, click Reset.

FIG. 21.4
The Customize Toolbar dialog box provides a set of buttons you can use on the Outlook Express toolbar.

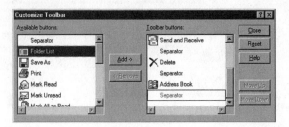

 To display the Customize Toolbar quickly, right-click the toolbar and select Buttons.

Making Outlook Express Look Like Outlook 97

If you use Outlook 97, which was distributed as part of the Microsoft Office 97 suite, you may have become accustomed to seeing and using the Outlook Bar that sits on the far left of the Outlook window. You can display the Outlook Bar on the Outlook Express window as well. Open the Window Layout Properties dialog box, and select the Outlook Bar option in the Basic area. If you turn on the Outlook Bar, the folder list pane is no longer needed. Turn it off by selecting Folder List.

Finally, to round out the transformation to Outlook 97, add the Folder Bar to the window so that it sits above the top of the message pane. Do so by selecting Folder Bar. Then click OK. The results of your changes are shown in Figure 21.5.

Configuring Outlook Express

Not only can you modify the appearance of Outlook Express, but you also can change its configuration settings. Next, select Tools, Options to display the Options dialog box (see Figure 21.6) for Outlook Express. This dialog box provides access to properties you can set for Outlook Express. The following sections discuss each of the tabs and their options.

Part
V

Ch
21

FIG. 21.5

The Outlook Bar and Folder Bar make Outlook Express look more like Outlook 97.

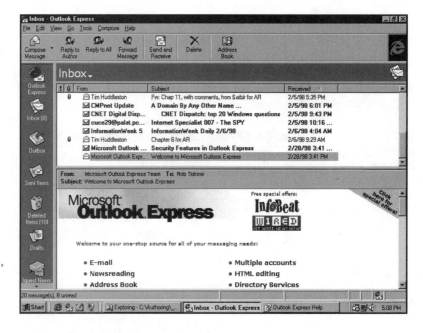

FIG. 21.6

Use the Options dialog box to configure Outlook Express features and preferences.

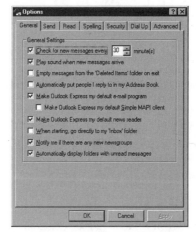

Modifying General Options

The following options are available on the General tab:

- *Check for New Messages Every x Minutes.* Set the number of minutes you want Outlook Express to check for new email automatically. The default setting is 30 minutes, but you may want to change this setting to a value that is more conducive to your mail patterns.

- *Play Sound When New Messages Arrive.* Use this option to set Outlook Express to play a sound when new messages arrive in your Inbox folder.

- *Empty Messages from the 'Deleted Items' Folder on Exit.* Select this option if you want to remove messages from the Deleted Items folder each time you exit Outlook Express. If you keep this option unselected, the Deleted Items folder retains every message you have deleted from another folder.

- *Automatically Put People I Reply To in My Address Book.* When you reply to a person via email, this option specifies that the recipient's name and email address be automatically added to your address book. This feature is handy if you have a habit of forgetting to include users' email addresses manually.

- *Make Outlook Express My Default E-Mail Program.* If you have more than one email program, such as separate ones for interoffice mail, Internet email, and online service email, you can establish Outlook Express as your primary one by using this option. By doing so, Outlook Express launches when you click an email message hyperlink in an HTML document or select an email program in your Web browser.

- *Make Outlook Express My Default Simple MAPI Client.* If you choose this option, Outlook Express is your default email program when you select the Send command from an application's File menu. An example of this is if you choose File, Send in Microsoft Word. When you set this option, you disable the Outlook 97 or Microsoft Exchange (also known as Windows Messaging) mail clients.

- *Make Outlook Express My Default News Reader.* You can make Outlook Express your main news reader by selecting this option. When you click an NNTP URL in an HTML document or select a news program in your Web browser, Outlook Express appears.

- *When Starting, Go Directly to My 'Inbox' Folder.* If you want Outlook Express to start by displaying the Inbox folder, use this option. You also can set this option on the first page that appears when you start Outlook Express if you click the When Starting, Go Directly To My 'Inbox' Folder option.

- *Notify Me If There Are Any New Newsgroups.* Use this option if you want Outlook Express to notify you when the news server you've attached to has new newsgroups in it.

- *Automatically Display Folders with Unread Messages.* If you have subfolders with unread messages, the folder list is automatically expanded to show those folders. You can direct new messages in a subfolder using the Inbox Assistant, as discussed in the "Configuring Your Inbox Assistant" section.

Modifying Send Options

The Send tab (see Figure 21.7) includes options that let you control how email and newsgroup messages are sent. On the Send page, you have the following options:

- *Mail Sending Format: HTML.* Select HTML if you want your email messages composed in HTML format. Before you choose this option, realize that not all email clients support HTML-formatted mail messages. If someone receives a message you send in HTML format and that person's mail client doesn't read HTML, the message will be difficult (if not impossible) to read. Click the Settings button to display the HTML Settings dialog box (see Figure 21.8). From here, you can set the bit and binary formats for encoding your message. Quoted Printable is the default, but you can select from None or Base 64 as well.

Part
V

Ch
21

FIG. 21.7
Among other Send tab options, you can set up your email and newsgroup messages to be composed in HTML or text file format.

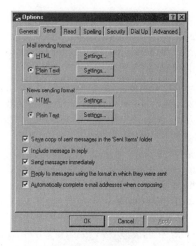

FIG. 21.8
Within the HTML Settings dialog box, you can set whether your HTML-formatted email messages will include embedded images.

To be able to send images used within an HTML-formatted message (such as a company logo), click the Send Pictures with Messages option. Otherwise, the message will contain a reference to that image, and the recipient will see it only if he or she has access to the image (or a copy of it). Select the Indent Message on Reply option if you want your original message indented when a reply is created.

■ *Mail Sending Format: Plain Text.* Select this option if you want your email messages created in plain text format. The advantage of plain text over HTML is that virtually all email clients that receive Internet email can handle plain text. Click Settings to change text format options (see Figure 21.9). For the most part, you should keep the MIME setting. You might want to use UUENCODE if your recipients' clients handle UUENCODED messages automatically. However, MIME is a better default.

FIG. 21.9
The Plain Text Settings dialog box provides options for modifying the way Outlook Express creates plain text-formatted messages.

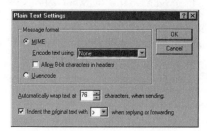

- *News Sending Format: HTML and Plain Text.* Select HTML or Plain Text to set how Outlook Express creates newsgroup messages. The options you can set by clicking the Settings buttons are identical to those discussed in the Mail Sending Format: HTML and Mail Sending Format: Plain Text options.

- *Save Copy of Sent Messages in the 'Sent Items' Folder.* Use this option if you want a copy of every message you send to be created in the Sent Items folder. This capability is handy if you want a record of all email messages you send for future reference or filing. This option is on by default.

- *Include Messages in Reply.* When you reply to a message, this option copies the original message and places > characters in front of the original text.

- *Send Messages Immediately.* Choose this option if you want your messages to be sent to the mail server as soon as you click the Send button after crafting your message. Clear this option if you want your messages queued before they are sent to the mail server. You then need to click the Send and Receive button on the Outlook Express toolbar to send your queued messages manually.

- *Reply To Messages Using the Format in Which They Were Sent.* Set this option when you want to use the same email or news message format as the format used in the original message.

- *Automatically Complete E-Mail Addresses When Composing.* When you're typing an email address in the To: line, Outlook Express can provide the rest of the address (or at least what it thinks is the rest) based on Address Book entries.

Modifying Read Options

On the Read tab (see Figure 21.10), you can set the way Outlook Express shows read and unread messages, how many newsgroup headers are downloaded at once, and other message viewing options. These options include the following:

FIG. 21.10
You may find the default Read options are fine for most situations.

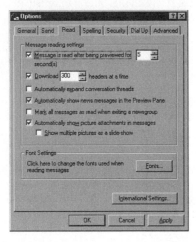

Part
V

Ch
21

■ *Message Is Read After Being Previewed for x Seconds.* You can set Outlook Express to change an unread email or newsgroup message header from bold to normal text after you've viewed the message for a specific number of seconds. The default is 5 seconds.

■ *Download x Headers at a Time.* Specifies the number of newsgroup headers that Outlook Express should download from a news server. The default is 300.

■ *Automatically Expand Conversation Threads.* You can have Outlook Express expand newsgroup threads in the message header pane. A thread is a response to a message. Some threads can be very long, so you may want to leave this option turned off so that more headers appear in the message header pane. On the other hand, if you're following or participating in a particular thread, you may want to select this option so that the thread is easier to follow.

■ *Automatically Show News Messages in the Preview Pane.* If you want a newsgroup message to appear in the preview pane when you click its header, use this option. Otherwise, you need to press Spacebar each time you select a message header and want to read it. The advantage of turning off this option is that Outlook Express will not download the body of a message if you simply select the message header.

■ *Mark All Messages as Read When Exiting a Newsgroup.* Use this option if you want newsgroup messages marked as read even if you have not read all of them.

■ *Automatically Show Picture Attachments in Messages.* This option enables Outlook Express to show JPG, BMP, or GIF images attached to a message. The image will appear at the end of message text in the body of the message.

■ *Show Multiple Pictures as a Slide-Show.* This option displays pictures one at time when a message includes two or more pictures. Backward and forward buttons are displayed with the slide show to enable you to navigate from picture to picture.

■ *Font Settings.* Click the Fonts button to change character set and font settings from the Fonts dialog box.

■ *International Settings.* Click the International button to remap character sets.

Setting Spelling Options

The Spelling tab provides options for setting the Outlook Express spell-check feature. The following are the options you can set:

■ *Always Suggest Replacements for Misspelled Words.* When a misspelled word is found in a message, you can have Outlook Express provide possible alternatives for the word.

■ *Always Check Spelling Before Sending.* You can have Outlook Express automatically spell-check your messages before they are sent. If you don't set this option, you must select Tools, Spelling from the message composition window each time you want to spell-check a message.

■ *Words in UPPERCASE.* Outlook Express can ignore words in all uppercase, such as if you use acronyms (DARPA) and initials (IBM) in your messages.

- *Words with Numbers.* Outlook Express can ignore words that have numbers within them, such as R2D2.

- *The Original Text in a Reply or Forward.* If you're replying to or forwarding a message, you can have Outlook Express not spell-check the original text. To do so, make sure this option is selected. Otherwise, you may spend a lot of time spell-checking text that is not part of your reply text.

- *Internet Addresses.* You can have Outlook Express ignore Internet addresses, including email addresses and URLs, when running a spell-check.

- *Language.* Set the language option Outlook Express should use for spell-checking your messages.

- *Edit Custom Dictionary.* Click this button to add new words to the spell-check dictionary.

Setting Security Properties

The Security tab (see Figure 21.11) includes the following settings:

FIG. 21.11
You should set security options to encrypt your messages.

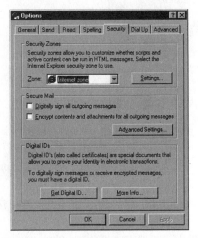

- *Security Zones.* This section sets security zone features for your Internet, intranet, and other connections. Because these settings also affect security zone settings in Internet Explorer 4.0, see Chapter 20, "Configuring Microsoft Internet Explorer 4.0," for details on these options.

- *Digitally Sign All Outgoing Messages.* Outlook Express can add a digital signature to each of your messages so that recipients know the message has not been tampered with.

- *Encrypt Contents and Attachments for All Outgoing Messages.* Outlook Express can encrypt your messages and their file attachments so that only those people with your digital ID can decrypt them. By default, all your messages also include your ID, so you may want to turn off this feature by clicking the Advanced Settings button. See "Setting Advanced Security Settings" later in this chapter for more information.

Part
V

Ch

21

■ *Get Digital ID.* You can obtain a digital ID by clicking the Get Digital ID button. This action launches your Web browser and connects you a Web site that enables you to obtain an ID.

■ *More Info.* Click this button to learn more about digital IDs.

Modifying Dial Up Options

On the Dial Up page (see Figure 21.12), you can configure how Outlook Express dials your online service, such as an Internet service provider, to download email and newsgroup data. You also can set some of the following options when you first launch Outlook Express:

FIG. 21.12

Dial Up settings are available when you have designated a dial-up connection to an online or Internet provider.

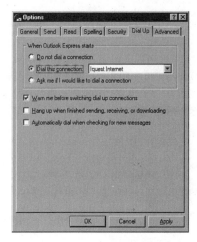

■ *Do Not Dial a Connection.* Use this option if you want Outlook Express to launch without dialing a service or displaying options to connect to a service.

■ *Dial This Connection.* This option specifies the dial-up connection you want Outlook Express to dial.

■ *Ask Me If I Would Like to Dial a Connection.* Use this option when you want Outlook Express to ask you to select a service to dial when you launch Outlook Express.

■ *Warn Me Before Switching Dial Up Connections.* If you have more than one dial-up connection set up, Outlook Express can prompt you if the first one isn't functioning, and you can switch to another connection.

■ *Hang Up When Finished Sending, Receiving, or Downloading.* If you just want to send and receive new messages, click this option so that Outlook Express disconnects after these tasks are performed. You then can read your messages or newsgroup posting while offline.

■ *Automatically Dial When Checking for New Messages.* Use this option when you want Outlook Express to dial the selected service automatically when you launch Outlook Express.

Setting Advanced Options

The options available on the Advanced tab (see Figure 21.13) relate to how messages are stored on your hard drive, as well as if log files are to be created. The following are the options for this tab:

FIG. 21.13

You may want to change some of the Advanced tab options after you have some experience with Outlook Express.

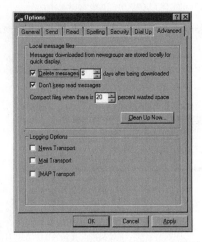

- *Delete Messages x Days After Being Downloaded.* This option sets the number of days in which downloaded newsgroup messages are retained on your hard drive. Five days is the default.

- *Don't Keep Read Messages.* After you read a message, Outlook Express can delete it when you exit Outlook Express. This option is selected by default.

- *Compact Files When There Is X Percent Wasted Space.* Newsgroup messages can be compacted (that is, eliminate wasted file space) when a percentage of wasted space on your hard drive is detected. The default is 20 percent.

- *Clean Up Now.* If you want to compact your newsgroup messages now, click the Clean Up Now button. Clicking this button displays the Local File Clean Up dialog box, from which you can select to compact, remove, or delete messages and message headers from your hard disk. You also can click the Reset button so that you can redownload messages from a newsgroup.

- *Logging.* You can specify whether all commands sent to your newsgroup, email, and IMAP servers are sent to a logging file. This capability is handy to troubleshoot problems with these servers.

Setting Advanced Security Settings

If you send confidential information in your email messages, you should consider acquiring a digital ID, or digital certificate. Digital IDs enable you to "sign" your messages electronically so that recipients are confident that the messages they receive from you have not been intercepted and tampered with.

Part
V

Ch
21

In Outlook Express, you use the Advanced Security Settings dialog box to set up your digital IDs. You must, however, obtain a digital ID from a certificate authority, which is a business that sells IDs to different users. One of these businesses is VeriSign and can be accessed via the Web at http://www.verisign.com. If you click the Advanced Settings button on the Advanced Security Settings page (select Tools, Options), you can attach to the Where To Get Your Digital ID page at http://www.microsoft.com/ie/ie40/oe/certpage.html.

After you set up an ID, you can associate it with other email accounts for which you want to use it. Use these steps to do so:

1. From Outlook Express, select Tools, Accounts. The Internet Accounts dialog box appears (see Figure 21.14).

FIG. 21.14
You must first associate your digital ID with a mail account.

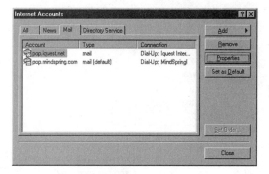

2. Select the account and click Properties. The Properties page for that account appears.
3. Click the Security tab (see Figure 21.15).

FIG. 21.15
The Properties page for the email account enables you to set with which account you want to associate an ID.

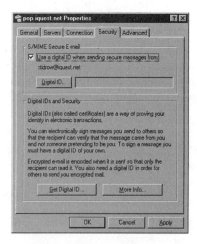

4. Click Use a Digital ID When Sending Secure Messages From option. The Digital ID button becomes available.

5. Click the Digital ID button. The Select Default Account Digital ID dialog box appears.

6. Select an ID and click OK.

7. Click OK to save your setting, and click Close to close the Internet Accounts dialog box.

Setting Internet Accounts

In Chapter 19, "Configuring an Internet Connection," you learned how to set up an Internet account. If you need to change this account or change it for your email or newsgroup settings, you can do so from Outlook Express. You also can set up or change properties for a directory service account. Directory services are Internet directories (LDAP) that your ISP or LAN uses to verify email addresses. These services are analogous to telephone yellow or white pages, but they contain email addresses. When you install Windows 98, a list of directory services is already set up for you.

To set or change Internet accounts, use the following steps:

1. From Outlook Express, select Tools, Accounts. The Internet Accounts dialog box appears. This dialog box includes tabs called All, News, Mail, and Directory Service.

2. Click the All tab (see Figure 21.16).

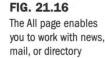

FIG. 21.16
The All page enables you to work with news, mail, or directory service accounts.

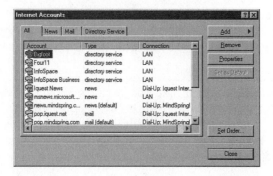

3. Select Add and choose the account you want to set up. If you choose Mail or News, the Internet Connection Wizard then appears. Work through this wizard as detailed in Chapter 19, "Configuring an Internet Connection."

   If you choose Directory Service, the Internet Directory Server Name screen of the Internet Connection Wizard appears. The following steps show how to work through this wizard.

4. Enter the Internet directory server address in the field provided. An example is `ldap.bigfoot.com`, for the Bigfoot directory. You may need to request this information from your ISP or from your system administrator.

5. Select the My LDAP Server Requires Me To Log On option if you must log on to the directory service.

Part
V

Ch
21

6. Click <u>N</u>ext. The Internet Directory Server Logon screen appears (see Figure 21.17). This screen appears only if you select the logon option in step 5. Otherwise, you see the Check E-mail Addresses screen, as described in step 7. Fill in the LDAP <u>A</u>ccount Name and <u>P</u>assword fields with your login information.

   Click the Log On Using <u>S</u>ecure Password Authentication option if your ISP uses SPA password authentication. You need to get this information from your ISP.

FIG. 21.17

Use this screen to enter logon and password information for your LDAP server.

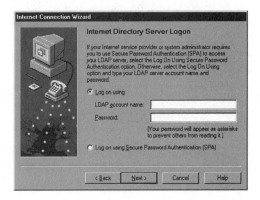

7. Click <u>N</u>ext. The Check E-mail Addresses screen appears. Here, you choose whether you want Outlook Express to check the new directory service to verify an email address. Click <u>Y</u>es if you want to; click <u>N</u>o if you choose not to. Note that you can change this setting later.

TIP If you choose to have Outlook Express check email addresses against a directory service, you will greatly increase the time it takes to send a message. This is due to the overhead required for Outlook Express to attach to the directory service, look for the email address, and then send the message. If an address cannot be found in the directory, you are informed of this situation. Your message, however, can still be sent. Your recipient just may not be registered in the same directory (or any directory) you are using.

8. Click <u>N</u>ext. Enter a name for the directory. By default, the address is used.

9. Click <u>N</u>ext. Then click Finish to save your settings. Your new directory service is added to the Internet Accounts dialog box.

To modify an account, select it and choose Properties. The Properties page for that account appears, such as the directory account page shown in Figure 21.18. The settings available here are the same ones you set up using the Internet Connection Wizard. You also have advanced options, which enable you to set port settings and search configurations.

If you select a news server account and choose Properties, the Advanced tab (see Figure 21.19) provides access to the following items:

FIG. 21.18
The Bigfoot Properties page provides access to settings for the Bigfoot directory service.

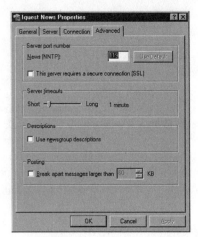

FIG. 21.19
You can set advanced settings for your news service account from this tab.

- *Port number.* Set the newsgroup port number, if different than the default.
- *Server Timeouts.* Adjust the timeout setting to a lower or higher setting as necessary. The longer the timeout period, the more time Outlook Express will attempt to connect to your news server before returning an error message that it cannot connect at this time.
- *Descriptions.* This option shows descriptions of each newsgroup.
- *Posting.* By selecting this option, you can have Outlook Express divide a posting into smaller files if the posting exceeds the file size you indicate. Some newsgroup readers cannot handle postings larger than 64KB.

Finally, if you select an email server account to modify, the Advanced tab (see Figure 21.20) includes settings you're already familiar with, such as configuring port and timeout settings, and instructing Outlook Express to break apart messages larger than a specific size. You also

Part

V

Ch

21

can specify to have Outlook Express retain a copy of email messages you've sent and received on the mail server. This capability is handy if you want to have a backup of your messages stored on the server. Some servers don't offer this feature. If this is the case with your email server, you receive a message telling you that messages can't be saved on the server after they've been received by the recipient.

FIG. 21.20

The Advanced tab on the email properties account is similar to the news server Advanced tab.

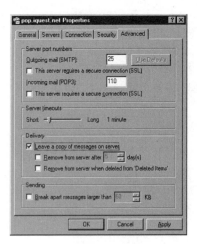

On the Internet Accounts dialog box, you also can set the order in which directory services are checked. Click the Set Order button to display the Directory Services Order dialog box. This capability is handy if you have several directory services and you want to have Outlook Express hit a specific one for the majority of your email messages. This service might be an LDAP server on your LAN that contains a list of employees in your company to whom you send mail often. Use the Move Up and Move Down buttons to set the checking order. Click OK to close the Directory Services Order dialog box.

Click Close on the Internet Accounts dialog box when you finish setting Internet account properties.

Configuring Your Inbox Assistant

Managing your email can be daunting at times. If you receive a great number of messages every day or every week, important messages can get buried underneath mail that is not so important, such as junk mail (*spam*). To help manage your incoming mail, you can set up rules that help you file messages that adhere to certain criteria you set up.

To do so, you use the Inbox Assistant. The Inbox Assistant is like having your own secretary organize your email into nice little stacks for you. You can, for example, specify that all mail coming from a certain user be stored in a specific folder. The key to using the Inbox Assistant is to pick up on trends in your email so that you can parse the messages as they are received.

Use the following steps to set up the Inbox Assistant:

1. Select Tools, Inbox Assistant. The Inbox Assistant window then appears. Until you add rules to the Assistant, the window is empty.

2. Click Add to display the Properties dialog box (see Figure 21.21). Here, you set up rules for your Inbox Assistant to follow.

FIG. 21.21

You must first set up properties for each rule in the Inbox Assistant.

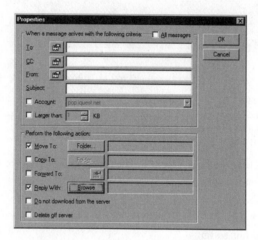

3. Specify the criteria for each of the properties listed on the Properties dialog box. If you want to parse all messages arriving from a user named Abby Lane, for example, place that name in the From text field. Click the contact icon next to the To:, CC:, and From: fields to access your Address Book, from which you can specify names stored there.

   You also can specify a subject that Inbox Assistant uses to parse messages. This capability is handy if you and others have standardized a subject line for specific documents. And, if you want to set up a rule for messages that are larger than a specific size, click the Larger Than option and set a size.

4. Select the action you want to be performed on the message that conforms to the preceding criteria. Actions include moving or copying to a specific folder, forwarding to another user(s), replying to a specific file, leaving the message on the server, or deleting it from the server without even downloading it.

TIP Click the Folder buttons to display the Move or Copy dialog boxes. From here, you can select a folder (such as the Inbox, Outbox, Sent Items, Deleted Items, and Drafts folders) or create a new one by clicking the New Folder button.

Part
V

Ch
21

5. Click OK to return to the Inbox Assistant window and to see the new rule you've just set up (see Figure 21.22).

FIG. 21.22

Periodically check to make sure the rules you apply are correct after you start receiving email.

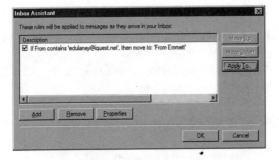

6. Continue creating as many rules as necessary by following steps 2 through 5.

7. Use the Move Up and Move Down buttons to determine priority of each rule.

TIP If messages conform to more than one rule, the rule closest to the top of the list in the Inbox Assistant window takes precedence.

To see the properties of a rule, select the rule and click Properties. Clicking this button opens the Properties dialog box, enabling you to modify rules if needed.

8. Use the Remove button to delete selected rules from the Inbox Assistant window.

9. Click OK to save your settings.

After you set a new rule, you should keep a close eye on your incoming messages to make sure that they adhere to the rules you have set up. If you notice action being done to messages other than what you originally intended, return to the Inbox Assistant and modify the properties of the rule to correct the action. ●

Configuring Windows 98 in a Networked Environment

CHAPTER 22

Configuring Windows 98 as a Network Client

by James Spann

In this chapter

Configuring Windows 98 as a Windows NT Client

Although Windows 98 has many powerful features for the desktop, some of its best features can be found in its networking capabilities. Whether you are connecting to a Windows NT network, a NetWare network, or just sharing files in a Windows 98 peer-to-peer network, Windows 98 has the capabilities you need built right in. This chapter shows you how to set up and configure your Windows 98 system as a secure network client that can participate in the network of your choice.

One of the first steps in configuring Windows 98 as a network client is to determine which type of network you will be connecting to so that you can add the appropriate client to the Network Properties. If you plan to connect to a Microsoft Windows NT network, you need to add the Client for Microsoft Networks to the Network Properties. For more information on that step, see "Configuring Network Properties" in Chapter 24, "Setting Up Windows 98 on a Peer-to-Peer Network." If you plan to connect to a Novell NetWare network, you need to add the Client for NetWare Networks to the Network Properties. For more information on that step, see "Configuring the Client for NetWare Networks" later in this chapter.

This chapter shows you how to configure the available options for the Microsoft Network client so that you can get the appropriate performance from your Windows 98 machine. If you configure your machine appropriately, you can provide some security for the information on your machine. You also can set up drive mappings to make the use of common programs easier and can share resources with other users on the network. This chapter also shows you how to define system policies for the user or users as well as how to set up roaming profiles using Windows NT.

Configuring the Client for Microsoft Networks

To configure the Client for Microsoft Networks, you need to edit the properties by going to the Network properties dialog box. You can access the Network properties dialog box from the Control Panel or by using one of the handy features of Windows 98.

N O T E If you have not already added the Client for Microsoft Networks to the Network Properties, turn to "Configuring Network Properties" in Chapter 24 and do that now. ■

To access the Network properties dialog box, follow these steps:

1. Click the Start Button, and select Settings, Control Panel.
2. When the Control Panel window opens, find and select the Network icon. If selecting the Network icon does not open a Network properties dialog box similar to the one shown in Figure 22.1, then you may need to double-click the Network icon.

N O T E   You can also access the Network properties dialog box more easily by right-clicking the
Network Neighborhood icon on the desktop and selecting Properties from the drop-down
menu. If the Network Neighborhood icon is not on your desktop, more than likely, you have not yet
configured any network clients. You have to follow the preceding method until you have added your
network client. ■

FIG. 22.1

Use the Network
properties dialog box to
change the Windows 98
network configuration.

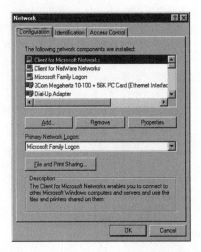

To configure the Client for Microsoft Networks, you can either double-click the icon or label
for Client for Microsoft Networks, or you can click once on that item to highlight it and then
click the Properties button. If you are successful, the next window that opens should look
similar to the one in Figure 22.2.

FIG. 22.2

The Client for Microsoft
Networks Properties
dialog box allows you
to choose the settings
for network drive
connections and
Windows NT domain
logons.

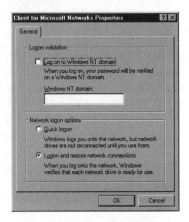

In Figure 22.2, you can see the two sections to the Client for Microsoft Networks Properties
dialog box: the Logon validation settings and the settings for Network logon options. Take a
look at the Logon validation settings first.

The first item in the Logon validation settings is the Log on to Windows NT domain check box. If you decide to set up this workstation to log on to a Windows NT domain, you can set additional security options for this workstation. A Windows NT domain provides a secure database of user accounts and security settings. If you have or will be creating a user account in a Windows NT domain, and you want to take advantage of these additional security options, you should click once inside this check box. Clicking places a check in the box to select the option; then you also need to fill in the Windows NT domain box with the name of the domain in which the user accounts are stored. After you have filled in these two items successfully, your Client for Microsoft Networks Properties dialog box should look like the one in Figure 22.3.

FIG. 22.3

Filling in the Client for Microsoft Networks Properties dialog box establishes logon validation from a Windows NT domain.

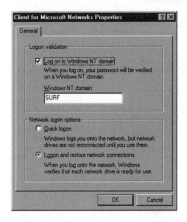

For your logon to be successful, you need to make sure that the Windows 98 workstation is connected to the network correctly and that one of the domain controllers for that domain is available to process logon requests. Additionally, you need to make sure that the username and password you enter at the logon screen are valid entries for the domain you will be logging on to. Now look at how the logon settings can be customized.

Configuring Logon Parameters

The next area on the Client for Microsoft Network properties dialog box is the Network logon options (refer to Figure 22.2). Only two settings are possible in this area, so selecting one of them automatically deselects the other. The choice you have to make depends on how quickly you want Windows 98 to start. For the fastest startup, you should select the top option, Quick logon. This option does not attempt to reconnect the network drive connections you have previously established. The drive letters for these network connections will still appear in your drive listings, but the connection to the actual resource will not be established until you attempt to use that drive.

On the other hand, if you want to make sure that all your network drive connections are reestablished as Windows 98 starts, you should select the lower option, Logon and restore network connections. To give you an idea of what this option can do for you, let me first explain what network drive connections are.

If you want to use network resources, you can browse the network to see what is available by using the Network Neighborhood. Each window that you proceed through using Network Neighborhood refines your search until you find the resource you want. However, if you use some network resources frequently, going through two windows to get to those resources would probably be easier than going through 5, 10, or more windows.

One way to make sure that commonly used resources are only a step or two away is to set up a drive mapping to that resource. A drive mapping assigns a drive letter to a network resource such as a folder on another computer on the network. For example, drive L: might be mapped to a folder (directory) called FILES that is located on another computer. Another way to view this situation is to look at the L: drive mapping as though it were a pointer to a network resource. Instead of having to search for that resource every time you need it, you can click on drive L: and it will "point to" the resource. That way, when you need the files, you can open drive L: and have access to them rather than having to search the Network Neighborhood for them again.

Now that you have an idea what drive connections are, look at the two possible settings for the Logon and restore Network connections box. If you select the first option, Quick Logon, when you start Windows 98, your network connection is not reconnected. You still have a drive letter L:, but the actual connection to the other machine is not established yet. When you select drive L:, the connection is established at that point, and setting up the connection may take a few seconds.

If you select the other option, Logon and restore network connections, Windows 98 tries to establish all your drive connections as the machine boots up. Depending on how many drive mappings you have set up, this process can slow down your startup time by anywhere from a few seconds to several seconds. The option you select depends on your preferences.

After you have finished making your selections, click the OK button to go back to the Network properties dialog box. If you do not have any other changes to make in the Network properties dialog box, you can click the OK button to close the dialog box. If you have made any configuration changes, Windows 98 will most likely want to copy some additional files, and you will probably be prompted to restart your computer.

Configuring Peer Resource Sharing

To make your Windows 98 resources available to other network users, you must first make sure that File and Printer Sharing for Microsoft Networks is one of the loaded services in your network configuration. To double-check this feature, right-click the Network Neighborhood icon and go to Properties. Scroll down through the list of the installed network components, and see whether File and Printer Sharing is one of the installed services. If it is not listed, follow these steps to add it:

1. Click the Add button in the Network Properties Configuration window.

2. From the Select Network Component Type window, select Service and then click Add.

3. From the Select Network Service window, select Microsoft from the list of manufacturers, and then select File and Printer Sharing for Microsoft Networks from the Network Service list.

4. Click OK. Setup then copies some files that are required for File and Printer Sharing. After the files have been copied, Setup prompts you to reboot your machine.

Now that you have installed File and Printer Sharing for Microsoft Networks, you can share directories and printers with other users. The most secure way to do so is to use user-level security by having the users authenticated by a secure server such as a Windows NT machine or a NetWare server. User-level security cannot be set up using only Windows 98 machines. Because this section deals with Windows NT, these steps demonstrate how to set up user authentication using a Windows NT machine as the authentication device:

1. To set up user-level security rather than share-level security, you must use the Network applet in the Control Panel. To get there, right-click Network Neighborhood and select Properties.

2. Select the Access Control tab to bring up the choices shown in Figure 22.4.

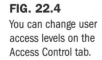

FIG. 22.4

You can change user access levels on the Access Control tab.

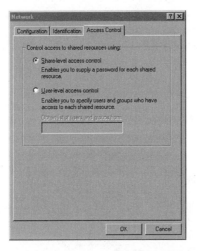

To enable User-level access control, select the appropriate button and fill in the blank titled Obtain list of users and groups from with the name of the Windows NT machine that will house the user accounts. This machine is then used to verify the correct login and passwords of all the users. After you make these settings, you can start sharing files and printers with specific users and groups with various levels of security.

To understand how much control you now have, look at the following example of how to set up user-level security for a shared folder.

To set up a shared folder and enable user-level access to it, find the folder you want to share and right-click it. From the drop-down menu, select Sharing and you then can make changes to the sharing properties for that folder. The first thing you need to do is check the Shared As radio button. Then you need to fill in a share name and a comment if necessary. Now you can add users to the list by clicking the Add button and selecting the users to whom you would like to give Read Only, Full Access, and Custom Access. Figure 22.5 shows an example of pulling up the user list on the server to assign users and privileges.

FIG. 22.5

You can assign access on the Add Users window.

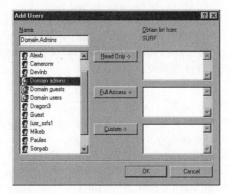

If you give some users Custom Access, when you click OK, the Change Access Rights window pops up, as shown in Figure 22.6, to let you configure the custom access for those users.

FIG. 22.6

You can change the access rights for custom access to Windows 98 in the Change Access Rights window.

After you have set up the custom rights, clicking OK takes you back to the sharing properties window. From this window, you can now select individual users or groups and modify their access privileges on a one-by-one basis if you like. The levels of access you can assign for these users and groups include the following:

- *Read Files.* Includes the ability to run most executables and batch files.
- *Write to Files.* Gives users the ability to add to or modify existing files.
- *Create Files and Folders.* Gives users the ability to add new files and folders.

- *Delete Files.* Gives the users the ability to remove files and folders.
- *Change File Attributes.* Gives the users the ability to modify the DOS file attributes.
- *List Files.* Gives users the ability to see the files as if they had used the DIR command to list the files.
- *Change Access Control.* Allows users to determine who has access and who does not.

With this capability, you can assign very detailed levels of access to individual users or groups of users based on the user information that is contained on the NT machine. You can also customize each user's environment by setting up profiles for each user. The next section details how to set up and use user profiles in Windows 98.

Configuring User Profiles

Another feature of Windows 98 is the ability to create and modify user profiles. A user profile is a complete set of parameters that identify a user's preferences for things like desktop colors, shortcuts, and documents. To start using user profiles, you must first create a user. To do so, go to the Control Panel and select the Users icon. Depending on your current desktop configuration, you might need to double-click the icon to run the Users applet. When you run the Users applet for the first time, it starts the wizard that walks you through setting up a user account. Figure 22.7 shows the first dialog box the wizard presents you with.

FIG. 22.7
Running the Users
applet for the first time
brings up the Enable
Multi-user Settings
dialog box.

Click Next to move to the next dialog box.

Follow these steps to complete the setup of user profiles:

1. The next dialog box prompts you for a username. After you have entered the username you want to add, click Next.
2. The wizard now prompts you to enter and reenter the password for this new user, as shown in Figure 22.8.

FIG. 22.8
You can enter
passwords in the Enter
New Password dialog
box to add a new user.

3. After you complete the password entry successfully, click Next, and the wizard prompts
   you for the personalized item settings for this new user. This dialog box allows you to
   configure the items that this new user can personalize and for which he or she can keep
   his or her own configuration.

As you can see from Figure 22.9, the possible options each new user can personalize are as
follow:

- The Desktop Folder and the Documents Menu
- The Start Menu
- The Favorites Folder
- Downloaded Web Pages
- The My Documents Folder

FIG. 22.9
In this wizard dialog
box, you can change the
personalized items
settings for multiuser
setup.

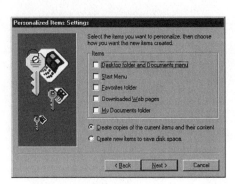

For each one of the items that you select, Windows 98 makes a new instance of that item and
stores it in a new folder named whatever the new username is. For example, if the new
username is User1, then a new folder named User1 is created. This new folder is stored in the
Profiles folder that is normally located just below the Windows folder (directory).

> **N O T E** After adding your first new user, take a moment to browse the Windows\Profiles folder
> to see its contents and the contents of the new folder it contains. Browsing this folder will
> give you a little more insight as to how Windows 98 is keeping up with which user has which settings.
> Look for folders such as Desktop, Favorites, and Start Menu within the new user's folder. The folders
> present depend on the options you selected for this new user. ▪

After you have decided which items this user will have customized settings for, you need to make one additional choice at the bottom of the Personalized Items Settings dialog box. As you can see from Figure 22.9, you now have to decide whether to copy the current items and their settings or to create totally new items for the user to modify. In Figure 22.9, note that the second option of creating totally new items can conserve some disk space, so you might want to choose this option if you are concerned about the available disk space. Otherwise, choosing the first option provides some benefits. The best benefit to this option is that by setting up your current items before you create this new user, you will, in effect, be creating the new user's desktop. For example, an administrator might want to configure the default desktop, My Documents folder, and other items to the settings that most users will need and then create the user accounts by copying the current items and their settings. Using this method prevents the administrator from having to go back and log in as each different user and modify the items and settings individually.

After you have selected your choices, click Next to move on. In the next window the wizard presents, you can click Finish to complete the setup process. When you click Finish, the wizard copies some files and folders and prompts you to restart the computer to complete the setup process. When the computer restarts, you are presented with a logon screen similar to the one in Figure 22.10.

FIG. 22.10

Here, you can log on using the Windows 98 Multi-user Logon screen. (Microsoft Family Logon is selected as the primary network logon.)

On the new logon screen, select the new username and enter the appropriate password. Then click OK to log on to Windows. Now that you have configured Windows 98 for multiple users, take a look at some of the additional options you now have available to you.

First of all, if you return to the Users applet in the Control Panel, starting it brings up the User Settings window that enables you to configure additional users (see Figure 22.11). Clicking the New User button starts the wizard to add an additional user (as mentioned previously). Highlighting a username in the list and clicking the Delete button generates a message that warns

Part
VI

Ch
22

you that this option will delete a user and his or her associated settings and folders. Clicking the Yes button shown in Figure 22.12 removes the user and his or her preferences.

N O T E Be very careful when deciding to delete a user. If the user has put customized documents in desktop folders, they will be deleted when the user is deleted. ■

FIG. 22.11

Here, you can see the User Settings dialog box of the Add New User Wizard.

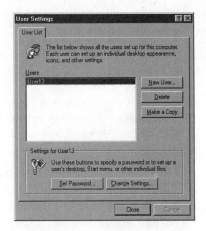

FIG. 22.12

In the delete user dialog box, be absolutely sure you want to delete the user before continuing.

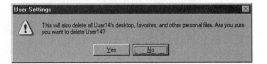

In the User Settings dialog box, you can use the Make a Copy button to duplicate a user's settings quickly by making a new user from the old one. The Set Password button can be used to change the password for this Windows user. The Change Settings button allows you to go back and modify which items this user has control over changing.

After you have decided to set up user profiles for individual users, you might want to consider the option of being able to have users get the same profile no matter which Windows 98 machine they log on to. To do so, you must configure a roaming profile setup using a Windows NT server. The next section covers this process in detail.

Configuring Roaming Users on a Windows NT Server

Through the combination of the power of the Windows NT platform and the configuration of the Windows 98 setup, you can set up a profile for a user so that the user gets it every time he or she logs on to Windows 98. The user will still have that profile even if he or she logs on to a different machine every time.

To set up roaming profiles, you must make sure that a couple of conditions are met. First, each of the Windows 98 workstations must be set up to log in to a Windows NT domain. Second, the Windows NT domain must have been created and exist on the network so that the Windows 98 machines can see it. Additionally, the user accounts for each user must exist in the NT domain. You do not need to set up each user on each Windows 98 machine. As a matter of fact, it would be best in this scenario if each Windows 98 machine were not configured for multiple users. Otherwise, the users and possibly the administrator may become confused when they are changing user preferences such as user passwords.

For example, when you're changing a password, you would have to stop and think, "Am I changing the password for the Windows 98 user account or for the Windows NT user account?" Then you would have to make sure that you were changing it in the right place. To avoid this confusion, it would be easier to set up only multiple users with roaming profiles using user accounts on a Windows NT domain. If you follow this technique, you would have no reason to set up the Windows 98 machines for multiple users, and you would be able to avoid this possible confusion.

When you're setting up users on a Windows NT domain, a utility called the User Manager for Domains enables you to set up and configure user accounts. One of the settings for the user accounts is the user profile settings. Figure 22.13 shows an example of configuring the user profile settings for a Windows NT domain user. For the Windows 98 users to have roaming profiles, the options on this screen must specify a location in the domain where the user's profile will exist. This profile would normally be located on an NT server in the domain. That way, when a user logs on from a Windows 98 machine, no matter which one he or she chooses, the profile that user gets will be the one that exists on the domain.

FIG. 22.13

The User Environment Profile dialog box is from the Windows NT User Manager for Domains User Profile Settings for a new user.

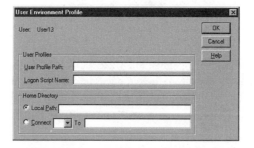

For roaming profiles to work on all the Windows 98 machines, you must configure each Windows 98 machine to log on to a domain. If you look back at Figure 22.2 earlier in this chapter, you will see the option for configuring the Client for Microsoft Networks to log on to a Windows NT domain. This option must be set up on all the Windows 98 machines for roaming profiles to work.

When you configure the NT domain and the Windows 98 machines, you create a file called USER.DAT for each user who logs on to the domain. The USER.DAT file is stored in the place specified by the settings for that user's domain profile configuration. If you want to make sure that the user cannot change any of his or her profile settings (desktop colors and other prefer-ences), all you have to do is change the name of the USER.DAT file to USER.MAN after it is cre-ated.

The best way to carry out this procedure is as follows:

1. Log on as the user whose profile you want to create, and then configure the desktop and the rest of the user environment in the manner you would like for it to be set for that user.

2. When you log off as that user, the settings you just defined are stored in a new USER.DAT file that is created for that user.

3. Locate the USER.DAT file and rename it USER.MAN.

Renaming the file to USER.MAN creates what is called a *mandatory profile*. Mandatory profiles ensure that users always get the same environment every time they log on. That way, if a user makes a mistake and changes colors to some color scheme in which he or she cannot read the screen anymore, all the user has to do is log out and log back in to the domain. Then the user's desktop appears just like it always did. Note that users can make changes to their environ-ments even if they have mandatory profiles. The difference is that the changes are not saved if the USER.DAT file has been renamed with the .MAN extension.

If you want to restrict the users even further and make sure they do not have access to items such as the desktop settings, you need to consider setting up system policies for the Windows 98 machines. The next section discusses the utility for setting up policies and how to configure them for your machine.

Setting Up System Policies

Before I discuss the System Policy Editor, I must warn you that it is an incredibly powerful tool. It is so powerful that you can end up making changes to the Windows 98 system that are very difficult, if not impossible, to fix without reinstalling Windows 98. You should be very careful when using the System Policy Editor.

Because the System Policy Editor is such a powerful tool, it is not installed during the normal installation of Windows 98. You must go back and specifically add the System Policy Editor by using the Add/Remove Programs applet in the Control Panel. After you have installed the System Policy Editor, it is available as a System Tool from the Start menu. Just select Start, Programs, Accessories, System Tools, System Policy Editor.

You can work with the System Policy Editor in two ways. The first way is to modify the Registry of the machine on which it is running. To do so, you select File, Open Registry to see options for configuring the Local User and the Local Computer.

The other option available with the System Policy Editor is to create a policy for the Default User and Default Computer. If you decide to choose this option, you can add individual users and computers to the policy as you configure it.

Opening the Default Computer allows you to customize the user environment in great detail, but once again caution is advised. Look at Figure 22.14, which shows an example of just some of the settings that can be configured for the Default Computer.

FIG. 22.14

You can configure the Default Computer Properties with the System Policy Editor.

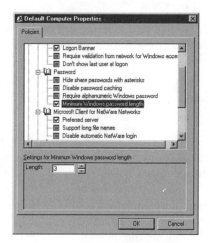

After you have created your policy, you should save the file with a .POL extension. You can name the file whatever you want, and you can even create multiple policy files. However, you normally do not need to create more than one policy file per machine, and you usually need to create only one policy file that applies to all the computers and users.

If you would like to make the policy apply to all your Windows 98 machines and users, you should copy the policy file to the NETLOGON folder on the Windows NT Primary Domain Controller and make sure that all users are logging on to the domain. That way, when users log on to the domain, the policy file is used to define their environment. You can set this up in a larger environment with multiple NT authentication machines in other ways. They are explained in the Resource Kit under the load-balancing feature.

Configuring Windows 98 as a Novell NetWare Client

So far, this chapter has shown you how to configure the available options for the Microsoft Network client so that you can get the appropriate performance from your Windows 98 machine. Looking at how to configure your machine in a Novell NetWare environment is also important. The following sections do just that. If you configure your machine appropriately, you can provide some security for the information on your machine. You also can set up drive mappings to make the use of common programs easier and can share resources with other users on the network.

Installing and Configuring Network Adapters

To participate on a network, you need a Network Interface Card (NIC). Although this section describes how to install and configure NICs, this chapter covers only the software installation necessary to get the NIC to perform with Windows 98. If you need assistance with the physical installation of the hardware, consult the documentation provided with the card.

If the NIC you are adding to the machine is a Plug and Play adapter, and the machine you are using is Plug and Play compliant, Windows 98 automatically finds and configures the NIC for you while only stopping to ask you for a driver disk if one is necessary. If you are configuring a legacy device or do not have a Plug and Play system, you may need to consult the documentation provided with the NIC for accurate installation and setup of the device.

If you just need to add the software for the new NIC, right-click the Network Neighborhood icon and select Properties. If you do not yet have a Network Neighborhood icon on your desktop, you can also get to the Network Properties by selecting Start, Settings, Control Panel and then selecting the Network applet. When you are ready to modify the Network Properties, your screen should look similar to the one in Figure 22.15.

FIG. 22.15
You can modify the Network Properties in this dialog box.

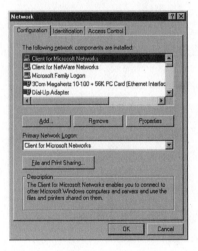

To add a NIC, click the Add button and select Adapter from the list of choices. Then click the Add button. In Figure 22.16, you can see that you may have choices for both Plug and Play (PnP) adapters and non-PnP adapters.

The other box shown in Figure 22.16 gives you a list of manufacturers to choose from. For each manufacturer, corresponding adapter types are listed in the right-hand pane of the window. Select the appropriate manufacturer and network adapter type. If a disk came with your NIC, click the Have Disk button and follow the onscreen instructions. Click OK to proceed; Windows 98 then installs the software for the adapter.

FIG. 22.16

You can select a network adapter in this dialog box.

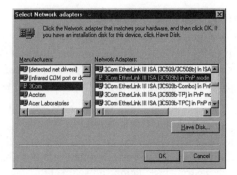

Each adapter has different options that can be configured. Because I cannot cover all the possibilities, this section just gives you an idea of how to make changes to your adapter. When the adapter has been added to the list of network components, you can select it from the list and click the Properties button. In Figure 22.17, you can see the 3Com adapter, which is highlighted before the Properties button is clicked.

FIG. 22.17

Notice that the 3Com adapter is highlighted before clicking Properties.

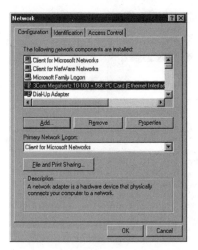

Although Figure 22.18 shows an example of the network adapter properties for a 3Com PC Card NIC, it is just an example of what the network adapter properties might look like. Each adapter type has its own options, tabs, and configuration parameters. They should all have a Bindings tab similar to the one displayed in Figure 22.18. This tab is important because it lets you configure which protocols are used with this NIC. In this figure, you can see that the Fast Infrared Protocol is not being used with this NIC. If you want to bind this protocol to this NIC, you simply check the check box to select it. In this case, selecting the check box causes an error because the 3Com device is not Infrared enabled, as some of the other devices on this machine are.

FIG. 22.18
On the Bindings tab for this network adapter, notice that the only installed protocol that is not bound to this device is the Fast Infrared Protocol.

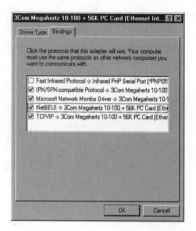

After you have finished making changes to the configuration for the NIC, click OK and then click OK again on the Network properties dialog box. This way, you force Windows 98 to update itself with any changes; it may require you to reboot your system. After you have your adapter installed and configured, you can move on to configuring the client software for the network of your choice. The Client for NetWare Networks is covered next. See the beginning of this chapter for information on configuring the Client for Microsoft Networks.

Configuring the Client for NetWare Networks

To configure the Client for NetWare Networks, you need to edit the properties by going to the Network properties dialog box. You can access the Network properties dialog box from the Control Panel or by using one of the handy features of Windows 98.

N O T E If you have not already added the Client for Microsoft Networks to the Network Properties, turn to "Configuring Network Properties" in Chapter 24 and do that now. ■

To access the Network Properties dialog box, follow these steps:

1. Click the Start Button and select Settings, Control Panel.
2. When the Control Panel window opens, find and select the Network icon. If selecting the Network icon does not open a Network properties dialog box similar to the one shown in Figure 22.1, you may need to double-click the Network icon.

N O T E You can also access the Network Properties dialog box more easily by right-clicking the Network Neighborhood icon on the desktop and selecting Properties from the drop-down menu. If the Network Neighborhood icon is not on your desktop, more than likely, you have not yet configured any network clients. You have to use the preceding method until you have added your network client. ■

To configure the Client for NetWare Networks, you can either double-click the icon or label for Client for NetWare Networks, or you can click once on that item to highlight it and then click the Properties button. If you are successful, the next window that opens should look similar to the one in Figure 22.19.

FIG. 22.19

You can set the properties in the Client for NetWare Networks Properties dialog box.

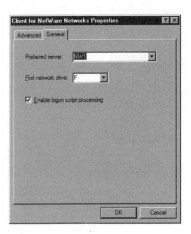

As you can see from Figure 22.19, this dialog box normally has at least two tabs of properties to configure. The General tab has three configurable options that let you define the NetWare environment for this machine. The first option, Preferred server, lets you decide with which NetWare server you want to authenticate the logon name and password. The second option, First network drive, allows you to determine the drive letter to start with when setting up network drive connections. This setting normally defaults to drive F: for NetWare networks. The last option is a check box that you can select to enable NetWare login scripts to be processed as part of the login procedure. If you do not want the login scripts to be executed when you log in, deselect the check box.

To be able to log in to the NetWare server of your choice and Windows 98 at the same time, you must also check to make sure that the Primary Network Login has been configured to reflect Client for NetWare Networks. To check this setting, look at the Network properties dialog box in the section titled Primary Network Logon.

Now that you have successfully logged in to the NetWare network, you're ready to explore your ability to share resources with other users in a secure fashion. The next section describes how to establish shared resources in a NetWare environment and set them up with security.

N O T E You may also want to consider using the intraNetWare Client for Windows 95 from Novell. The Novell client, which has been designed for access to Novell networks and servers, has some capabilities that the Microsoft client does not have. One of the biggest advantages is the ability to log in to multiple NDS trees with one login. The Novell client also supports the 32-bit NetWare Administrator and the NetWare Application Launcher. If you are primarily using Novell NetWare or intraNetWare as your network operating system, you should check out the Novell client. ■

Configuring Windows 98 as a Novell NetWare Client

Configuring Peer Resource Sharing

To make your Windows 98 resources available to other network users, you must first make sure that File and Printer Sharing for NetWare Networks is one of the loaded services in your network configuration. To double-check this setting, right-click the Network Neighborhood icon and go to Properties. Scroll down through the list of the installed network components and see whether File and Printer Sharing for NetWare Networks is one of the installed services. If it is not listed, follow these steps to add it:

1. Click the Add button in the Network Properties Configuration window.

2. From the Select Network Component Type window, select Service and then click Add.

3. From the Select Network Service window, select Microsoft from the list of manufacturers and then select File and Printer Sharing for NetWare Networks from the Network Service window.

4. Click OK. Setup then copies some files and may even need to reboot your machine.

After you have File and Printer Sharing for NetWare networks installed, your Network properties dialog box should look something like Figure 22.20.

FIG. 22.20

This Network properties dialog box shows File and Printer Sharing for NetWare Networks installed.

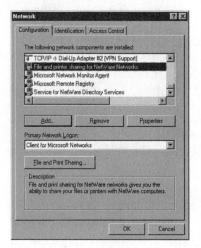

If you need to make any changes to the properties for the File and Printer Sharing for NetWare Networks, simply select and then click the Properties button. It is unlikely that you will need to change these settings because they are used only in more advanced scenarios.

Now that you have File and Printer Sharing for NetWare Networks installed, you can share directories and printers with other users. The most secure way to do so is to use user-level security by having the users authenticated by a secure server. Because this section deals with NetWare, these steps demonstrate how to set up user authentication using a NetWare server as the authentication device:

1. To set up user-level security rather than share-level security, you must use the Network applet in the Control Panel. To get there, right-click Network Neighborhood and select Properties.

2. Select the Access Control tab to bring up the choices shown in Figure 22.4.

To enable User-Level access control, select the appropriate button and fill in the blank titled Obtain list of users and groups from with the name of the NetWare server that will house the user accounts. This machine is used to verify the correct login and passwords of all the users. After these settings have been made, you can start sharing files and printers with specific users and groups with various levels of security.

To understand how much control you now have, look at the following example of how to set up user-level security for a shared folder.

To set up a shared folder and enable user-level access to it, find the folder you want to share and right-click it. From the drop-down menu, select Sharing. In the resulting window, the first thing you need to do is check the Shared As radio button. Then you need to fill in a share name and a comment if necessary. Now you can add users to the list by clicking the Add button and selecting the users you want to give Read Only, Full Access, and Custom Access. Figure 22.21 shows an example of pulling up the user list on the server to assign users and privileges.

FIG. 22.21

In this dialog box, you can add users to a shared resource.

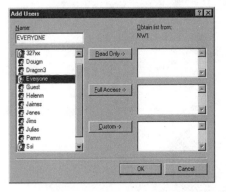

If you select to give some users Custom Access, when you click OK, the Change Access Rights window pops up to let you configure the custom access for that user or users.

After you have set up the custom rights, clicking OK takes you back to the sharing properties window. From this window, you can now select individual users or groups and modify their access privileges on a one-by-one basis if you like. The levels of access you can assign for these users and groups is discussed earlier in this chapter in the Windows NT section titled "Configuring Peer Resource Sharing."

With this capability, you can assign very detailed levels of access to individual users or groups of users based on the user information that is contained on the NetWare server. You can also customize each user's environment by setting up profiles for each user. The next section details how to set up and configure roaming users with Novell NetWare in Windows 98.

Configuring Roaming Users on a NetWare Server

Through the combination of a Novell NetWare server and the configuration of the Windows 98 setup, you can set up a profile for a user in such a way that the user gets the same profile every time he or she logs on to Windows 98. The user will get this same profile even if he or she logs on to a different machine every time. To set up these roaming profiles, you must set up user profiles for the users. If you are unfamiliar with user profiles, look at the section titled "Configuring User Profiles" earlier in this chapter.

To set up roaming profiles on a NetWare server, you must make sure that a couple of conditions are met:

- First, each of the Windows 98 workstations must be set up to log in to a Novell NetWare server.
- Second, the Novell NetWare server must exist on the network so that the Windows 98 machines can see it.
- Additionally, the user accounts for each user must exist on the NetWare server.

You do not need to set up each user on each Windows 98 machine. As a matter of fact, it would be best in this scenario if each Windows 98 machine were not configured for multiple users. When you're setting up users on a NetWare server, each user automatically gets a MAIL folder (directory). The user profile for a user must be stored in the user's MAIL folder for the NetWare server to provide roaming profiles for the users. When a user logs on to the NetWare server from a Windows 98 machine, Windows 98 examines the MAIL folder for that user and looks for a user profile. If one is found, it is used to define the initial user environment. That way, when a user logs on from a Windows 98 machine, no matter which machine he or she chooses, the profile that user gets will be the one that exists on the NetWare server.

For roaming profiles to work on all the Windows 98 machines, you must configure each Windows 98 machine to log on to the NetWare server. If you look back at Figure 22.19 earlier in this chapter, you will see the option for configuring the Client for NetWare Networks to log on to a preferred NetWare server. This option must be set up on all the Windows 98 machines for roaming profiles to work.

When you configure the NetWare server and the Windows 98 machines, you create a file called USER.DAT for each user who logs on to the domain. The USER.DAT file must be stored in the MAIL folder for that user on the NetWare server. If you want to make sure that the user cannot change any profile settings (desktop colors and other preferences), all you have to do is change the name of the USER.DAT file to USER.MAN after it is created.

The best way to carry out this procedure is to log on as the user and configure the desktop and the rest of the user environment in the way you would like for it to be set. When you log off as that user, the settings you have defined are stored in that user's USER.DAT file. Locate the USER.DAT file, move it to the appropriate NetWare MAIL directories, and rename it USER.MAN.

Renaming the file to USER.MAN creates what is called a *mandatory profile*. Mandatory profiles ensure users always get the same environment every time they log on. That way, if a user makes a mistake and changes colors to some color scheme in which he or she cannot read the screen anymore, all the user has to do is log out and log back in to the server. When the user logs back in, the desktop appears just like it always did. Note that users can make changes to their environments even if they have mandatory profiles. The difference is that the changes are not saved if the USER.DAT file has been renamed with the .MAN extension.

If you want to restrict the users even further and make sure they do not have access to items like the desktop settings, you need to consider setting up system policies for the Windows 98 machines. I covered setting up system policies and configuring them earlier in this chapter in the Windows NT section titled "Setting Up System Policies." ●

CHAPTER 23

Configuring Network Hardware

by Christopher Gagnon

In this chapter

Installing Network Interface Cards

Hundreds of network cards are available today. If your card manufacturer has done its homework, installation can be as simple as installing the card and booting the PC. Unfortunately, with the recent boom in multiplayer gaming, everybody and his brother has decided to jump into the marketplace. You will undoubtedly find lots of great deals on network cards, but these prices are usually subsidized by unstable drivers and a lack of support. Remember that you get what you pay for. If the choice is between an unknown company and a big company with a $20 difference in price, spend the extra buck for the well-known company. Fortunately, Microsoft has eased the installation process of nearly every network adapter by including every network card driver it could get its hands on with Windows 98. In the following sections, you'll learn about the installation and configuration of network adapters in your system.

Checking Network Hardware on Your System

Before you install any new network cards in your machine, checking for any existing or previously installed equipment is a good idea. Network cards eat up system resources such as IRQs and static memory ranges. If you have multiple cards in your machine, you should note these settings before you install. This way, you can avoid conflicts during the installation process itself.

The easiest way to check the status of network equipment is through the Device Manager (see Figure 23.1). You can access the Device Manager by selecting the System from the Control Panel. The Device Manager lists all the hardware installed on your system. You can view the network cards installed in your system by clicking the plus (+) sign next to network adapters.

FIG. 23.1
The Device Manager allows you change resource settings for every device in the PC.

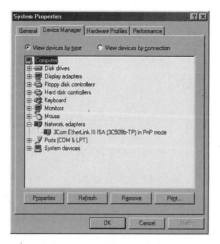

N O T E Network adapters do not appear in the Device Manager if you do not have a network adapter installed. ■

The three areas in the Network Adapters section of the Device Manager are as follow:

■ *General.* The General tab gives you basic information about the card such as device type, manufacturer, and hardware version (see Figure 23.2). It contains an area called Device Status, which tells you if the card is working properly. Finally, it contains a Device Usage area, which allows you to disable the device or add it to all hardware profiles.

FIG. 23.2
The General tab gives you basic information about your network card.

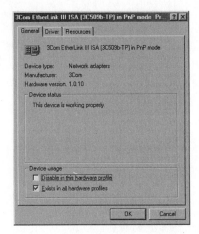

■ *Driver.* The Driver tab has two functions (see Figure 23.3). First, it allows you to view the actual driver files for the card. This capability is useful when you suspect a missing or corrupted file is causing problems. Second, it allows you to use the Upgrade Device Driver Wizard to apply updated drivers to your network card.

FIG. 23.3
The Driver tab allows you to perform driver-specific functions.

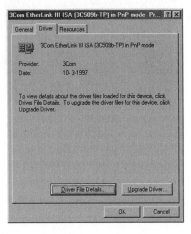

■ *Resources.* The Resources tab shows you the current resources used by the card (see Figure 23.4). It also contains a section that tells you which resources, if any, are conflicting with another device. If you want to change the resource settings for this card,

Windows 98 allows you to select between several preset configurations that were included with the driver. You can also change each setting manually. To change the resource settings, you must first uncheck the Use Automatic Settings check box. Then you can just double-click the setting you want to change. The Resources tab also has a handy section called the Conflicting Device List. This list shows you which resources, if any, are in conflict. You will learn about changing resource settings later in this chapter.

FIG. 23.4

The Resources tab shows you which system resources are in use by your adapter.

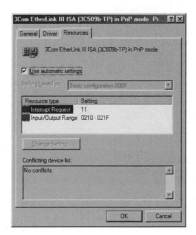

N O T E Some network cards do not allow you to change certain settings. If you have a resource conflict but cannot change the settings on your network card, you have to change the resource on the conflicting device. ▧

Installing a Network Interface Card

The network interface card is your PC's passport to the network. Most network adapters contain a port for whichever type of network you are installing and a link light to verify the connection status. The installation process is pretty straightforward and happens in one of two ways. In the following sections, you will examine both the Plug and Play and manual installation methods.

Plug and Play Plug and Play technology, which was introduced in Windows 95, is one of the most useful features to carry over into Windows 98. This technology allows you to install a piece of supported hardware without much user input. To install a Plug and Play card, use the following process:

1. Install the card in a free expansion slot following the manufacturer's instructions.
2. Boot the PC.
3. Windows 98 then detects the card and informs you that it has detected new hardware.
4. The installation process then completes, and the machine finishes booting.

N O T E By default, Windows 98 assigns protocols and services to your network card. You need to verify that the protocols and services you need are configured correctly. ▓

Depending on your network card, you may be asked to verify certain settings for the card. If you are unsure of the settings, just accept the defaults. In most cases, they work just fine. As you can see, the Plug and Play process is quick and easy. Sometimes, however, the card may not be detected properly, or you may just need to install manually. You'll examine that process next.

Manually Adding Network Cards   Although most network cards now support Plug and Play, some on the market still do not. If this is the case or if you just want to install the card yourself, you can add it manually.

Be sure you have the following information if you are installing your network card manually:

- The IRQ you want to use
- The I/O Address you want to use
- The Memory Range you want to use

This information will help you prevent resource conflicts before they happen.

The manual installation process can start from either the Add New Hardware interface or from the Network Properties dialog box (see Figure 23.5). Both are accessible from the Control Panel. Because the Network Properties dialog box allows you to alter all network settings from a unified interface, I cover that method here. The Add New Hardware Wizard is covered elsewhere in this book. If you choose to use it to manually add your network card, you should review that section of the book before proceeding. To install a card manually, follow this procedure:

FIG. 23.5

The Network Properties dialog box allows you to add components manually.

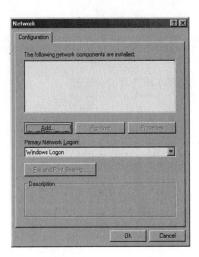

Part

VI

Ch

23

1. In the Network Properties dialog box, click the <u>A</u>dd button. This action opens a selection window asking you what you want to add (see Figure 23.6).

FIG. 23.6

Select Adapter from the dialog box.

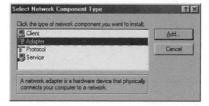

2. Choose Adapter and click Add. The next screen presents you with a list of all the manufacturers that provided drivers to Microsoft that are included on the CD.

3. Choose the manufacturer of your network card on the left side of the screen. A list appears on the right showing every model of network card that is included with Windows 98 for this manufacturer (see Figure 23.7).

FIG. 23.7

This dialog box lists almost every network card manufacturer on the market.

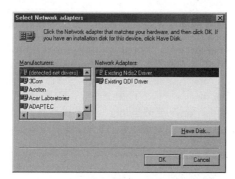

4. Scroll through the list, select your card (as shown in Figure 23.8), and click OK.

FIG. 23.8

Select your card from the list of models on the right side of the window.

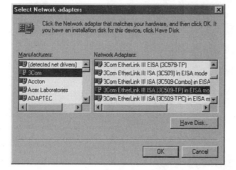

TIP

You can get to Network Properties more quickly. Just right-click the Network Neighborhood icon and choose Properties from the list.

After you click OK, you are prompted to insert your Windows 98 distribution CD. After the files are copied, you are returned to the Network Properties dialog box. You then need to reboot for the changes to take effect.

Part
VI

Ch
23

> **CAUTION**
>
> Because you are installing the adapter manually, Windows 98 assigns only Client for Microsoft Windows and TCP/IP to your card (see Figure 23.9). This may not be the logical configuration you need. Be sure you understand the concepts of network services and protocols before you attempt a manual installation. This process is covered in the next chapter.

FIG. 23.9

After you add a network card manually, the default network bindings are TCP/IP and Client for Microsoft Networks.

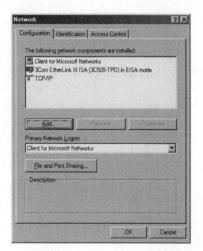

Configuring Your Network Interface Card

Sometimes network cards require additional configuration because they require several resources that may be in use by other hardware. The three most important network card settings are Memory Range, IO Address, and Interrupt Request. These settings must be unique to the network card and cannot be in use by any other equipment on the PC (see Figure 23.10). Depending on the equipment in your PC, you may have to make some changes to these settings. These changes can be made from the Device Manager.

You can access the Device Manager by selecting the System icon from the Control Panel. As described earlier, the Device Manager allows you to change resource settings for every piece of hardware in the PC. It also allows you to track down resource conflicts between devices.

FIG. 23.10

This figure shows a resource conflict between the network card and other devices.

TIP You also can use a shortcut to get to the Device Manager. From the desktop, simply right-click My Computer and choose Properties from the list.

To change the resource settings for your adapter, go into the Device Manager, select your network card from the Network Adapters list, and select the Resources tab. Deselect the Use Automatic Settings check box. Now you can change any of the settings that are relevant to the card. For example, to change the IRQ, you double-click the IRQ listing and choose a new setting from the list (see Figure 23.11). On the Resources tab, the Conflicting Device List lets you know if the new resource is in use by another device. Keep changing the resource value until you find a setting that has no conflicts.

FIG. 23.11

To change the conflicting IRQ, just scroll through the list until you find a setting with no conflicts.

If you try to change a setting and receive a message stating that the desired resource cannot be changed, your network card is forced to use that setting. If you have a conflict, you need to change the resource setting on the conflicting device (see Figure 23.12).

NOTE Some network cards install a new icon in the Control Panel to allow you to configure the card's resources. Although handy, these interfaces do not include the Conflicting Device List, which lets you know in real time if your new settings conflict with other devices. ■

FIG. 23.12
The Conflicting Device List shows no conflicts after the IRQ setting is changed.

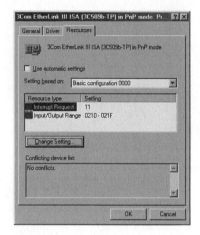

Configuring the Identification Tab

The Identification tab in the Network Properties dialog box allows you to identify your computer to the network (see Figure 23.13). The three settings on this tab are as follow:

- ■ *Computer Name.* The computer name must be unique on the network. This is the friendly name that will show up in the Network Neighborhood. The computer name cannot exceed 15 characters and cannot contain spaces.

- ■ *Workgroup.* Workgroups are logical collections of computers on the network. When you look at Network Neighborhood, you see the different computers divided into workgroups. Workgroup names are also restricted to 15 characters and cannot contain spaces.

- ■ *Computer Description.* The computer description can be anything you want from *Bob's PC* to *Payroll Computer on the Third Floor*. This field is not required but is useful for identifying other machines on the network.

Configuring the Access Control Tab

The Access Control tab allows you to choose the type of security you want on your shares. The two types of security available in Windows 98 are both described here.

NOTE The Access Control tab may not be available if you do not have File and Print Sharing installed. This topic is covered in the next chapter. ■

FIG. 23.13

The Identification tab controls how your PC is identified on the network.

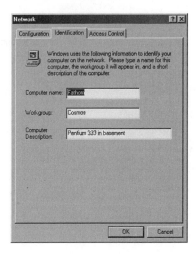

Share-Level Security Share-level security allows you to assign permissions on a per-share basis (see Figure 23.14). This means that each share you create on your machine has its own set of permissions. The disadvantage to this strategy is that you have to manage passwords for each share you create. If you create a large number of shares, keeping up with all the passwords can be difficult.

FIG. 23.14

Share-level security allows you to assign permissions to the share itself.

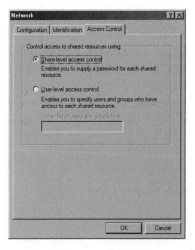

When share-level security is enabled, you have three security options for each share (see Figure 23.15), as listed here:

■ *Read-Only.* The read-only option allows people to open and copy files from your shares. However, read-only access does not allow them to change, save, or delete files that exist on your machine. You have the option of assigning a password to your read-only shares. This way, you allow access only to those who know the password.

- *Full.* Full access permissions allow other users to create, delete, copy, and modify files in the shared folder on your machine. If you decide to assign full access permissions to your shares, you need to be sure you can trust everyone on the network. You also have the option of assigning a password to this type of share. Because full access can present a considerable security risk, it is recommended that you always assign passwords to these types of shares.

- *Depends on Password.* This option allows you to set permissions based on the password used. This way, you can create one share with two passwords. You can give the full access password to those people you trust while still allowing others to connect with the read-only password.

FIG. 23.15

Share-level security gives you two security levels: Full and Read Only.

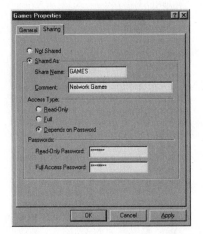

User-Level Security   User-level security is much more robust than share-level security because you assign permissions to users instead of particular shares. This way, you don't have to keep up with passwords for each share. When you are setting up user-level security on a share, you choose the users who you want to access the share along with the access level. The disadvantage to this type of security is that you must have a Windows NT or a Netware Server on the network (see Figure 23.16) because Windows 98 does not contain a system for managing and tracking individual users across the network.

To implement user-level security, Windows 98 uses a method called *passthrough security.* Windows NT and Netware servers are capable of managing thousands of users across the network. When a Windows 98 machine needs to validate a particular user, it queries the Windows NT or Netware server for the user's list of access permissions (see Figure 23.17). If the user has been granted the appropriate permissions, the Windows NT or Netware server sends the okay to the Windows 98 computer, and the user is given access to the share. Because Windows NT and Netware are expensive and are not required for small workgroup networks, this option is less popular than share-level security.

FIG. 23.16
When selecting user-
level security, you are
required to provide the
name of the Windows NT
server that validates
users.

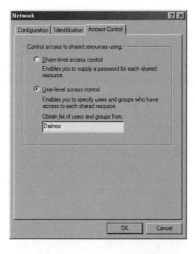

FIG. 23.17
User-level security
allows you to assign
share access by adding
valid users to a list.

Installing Network Cables

Computer networks have seen a burst of evolution in just a few decades. This rapid growth has led to several types of networking strategies, equipment, and cables. In the following sections, I'll briefly review the most common cable types while pointing out the benefits and shortcomings of each type. I'll also explain the correct installation procedures for each type.

Unshielded Twisted Pair

Unshielded twisted pair (UTP) is the most common type of network cable in use today. It is fast, reliable, and relatively inexpensive. Category 5 UTP, which is used for networking, consists of four pairs of thin copper wire. Each pair is twisted together—hence, the name twisted pair. Twisting the pairs together helps to prevent a phenomenon known as *crosstalk*. Crosstalk occurs when the signal from one wire is picked up by a nearby wire. This creates a false signal that can cause problems on the network. The four pairs are encased in a plastic jacket. Because the wires are not shielded, they are more susceptible to electromagnetic noise; thus any application of this cable would need to contain some type of error checking. Category 5 UTP is used primarily in Ethernet networks. The connector used in this configuration is called an RJ-45 connector. It looks like a big phone plug, but it has eight leads (to connect the four twisted pairs) instead of the six leads present in the RJ-11 connectors used for telephones. To install the cable, all you need to do is plug one end of the connector into the port on the network card and the other end into the hub.

Shielded Twisted Pair

Shielded twisted pair (STP) is similar to UTP, but it consists of only two wires that are twisted together in a single pair. The pair is then wrapped in a shielding material before the outes jacket is applied. The shield is usually made of either a wire mesh screen or a metallic foil. This shield protects the twisted pair from electromagnetic interference, providing a cleaner, more reliable connection. The connector used with STP is called a D-shell connector. It is a large plastic connector that is shaped like the letter *D*. The most common use for STP is in token-ring networks. Because token ring is not generally used in workgroup situations, I will not cover it in much detail.

Coaxial Cable

Coaxial cable is constructed from a single conductive strand surrounded by insulation and a second conductive sheath. A plastic jacket is then wrapped around the cable. Coaxial cable can be used in a variety of applications, including cable television and Ethernet networks. Because Ethernet over coaxial cable is installed in a bus topology, a central connection point like a hub or a switch is not needed. The connector used with coaxial cable is called a BNC connector. Unlike cable television connectors that either push or screw into place, the BNC connector has a quarter-turn locking system, which holds it to the device it is connected to. When coax is connected to a PC, a component called a T-adapter is plugged into the PC. The coax is then plugged into one side of the T-adapter. The next PC in the chain is connected to the other side of the T-adapter. This process is used to chain the PCs together to form the network. The PC at each end of the chain is then affixed with a terminator that reflects the signal back onto the network when it reaches the end of the bus. The disadvantage of this type of network is, if a machine is unplugged from the network, the network is effectively cut in two. Because the two network halves are both unterminated at one end, network reliability drops to nil.

Installing a Workgroup Hub

Hubs are centralized connection points for networks with a star topology. The main purpose of a hub is to redirect all network traffic to each machine on the network. In this section, I'll discuss the purpose of hubs and walk you though the installation process.

Hub Description

A hub is a small box with RJ-45 ports in it. Hubs can contain anywhere from 5 to 24 ports with a link light for each port. All hubs are designed differently, but usually the link light is either green if a connection is made or off if a problem occurs with the connection. Check your documentation for your hub's link light configuration. When you plug your PC into the network, you physically plug it into a hub. Because hubs are passive and are not directly attached to the PC, you don't need to install a driver. In fact, Windows 98 is not even aware of the hub. The network card handles all communication with the hub.

To truly understand the purpose of a hub, you need to be aware of the network topology behind it. The network in this case is laid out in a star topology. Every machine on the network is plugged into a central point, or hub. The benefit of this strategy is that you can unplug a machine from the network without interrupting service to any of the other machines. Another benefit is that you can monitor the network load because all traffic flows through a central location.

Installing the Hub

Hub installation is quick and easy. Usually, the hub is a small plastic box with a power supply and several RJ-45 ports. When placing the hub, you should find a location that allows you to plug in each PC without creating a big mess of cables. After you select a location, all you need to do is plug it into a power source and attach the network cables from the PCs. Because hubs are passive devices, they need no further configuration.

Troubleshooting Network Hardware

Setting up a network requires so many steps that you are bound to forget something along the way. Here's a list of simple things to check that will solve 50 percent of your network problems:

- *Check your cables.* You would be surprised how easy it is to forget to plug in a cable. The easiest way to verify this problem is to check for a link light on the hub and on the back of the network card for each machine.
- *Be sure your hub is plugged into a power source.* Hubs are passive devices from a networking standpoint, but they do require a separate power source because the signal's strength is boosted before it is reflected to the other machines. If your hub does not receive power, the network does not function.
- *Check your network adapter settings for resource conflicts.* As I stated earlier, network adapters use up a lot of system resources. Use the Device Manager to check for resource conflicts.

You might not get a successful link for several reasons. They could range from malfunctioning equipment to using the wrong cables. Use the following steps to troubleshoot your connection.

1. The first step is to check your cables. Cables are much more susceptible to malfunctions than network cards and hubs. The easiest way to test a cable is to try to establish a link

with a known good cable. Also, you can try the suspect cable on another machine that has an established connection. Make sure that you are using the correct kind of cable for your network configuration. Several types of devices that use RJ-45 connectors may look like network cables. One way to check your cable type is to look at the pin-outs. UTP has four pairs of wires, for a total of eight wires. Standard Ethernet cable uses a straight-through pin-out. This means that if you look at the RJ-45 connectors side by side, the wire colors match from left to right. For example, if one end of the cable has a pin-out of red-orange-yellow-green-blue-white-brown-black from left to right, the other end of the cable should have the same configuration. Also, make sure that you are using network-grade cable. Standard Ethernet cable uses Category 5 cabling. Sometimes you can find Category 3 cabling with RJ-45 connectors in the correct pin-out configuration. This cable is rated only for telephone applications and is not reliable enough for data transmission.

Part

VI

Ch

23

2. If the cable is working, you need to check your network card. If Windows 98 reports that the card is working with no conflicts, you should try to install the card in another machine. If you have an identical card handy, replace the suspect card with it. Most network cards come with diagnostic disks. The easiest way to check a network card is to run the manufacturer's diagnostics. If the diagnostic program reports that the card is not installed in the system, you probably have a bad card.

3. You need to check the hub. One of the ports in the hub may be malfunctioning. This malfunction causes the problem to appear to come from the card because the other machines in the network work fine. The easiest way to check for a bad port in a hub is to plug a working machine into it. Also, be sure that the port is not set up as a crossover port. Some hubs have a port with the cable pin-outs reversed so that you can attach a second hub. If you plug a computer into a crossover port, it does not work. If the port is not a crossover port, and you still cannot get a link, the port is probably bad.

4. Be sure that your network cards are all set to the same speed. Many cards are now supporting 100Mbps as well as 10Mbps.

CHAPTER 24

Setting Up Windows 98 on a Peer-to-Peer Network

by Rob Tidrow

In this chapter

Reviewing Windows 98's Peer-to-Peer Capabilities

Windows 98 can be configured as a node on several different network configurations, including Windows NT, Novell NetWare, and Banyan VINES. One problem with these types of networks is the cost of implementing and supporting them. If you cannot afford or do not require a network setup based on one of these larger network operating systems, you can set up two or more Windows 98 machines in a peer-to-peer network. You also can set up Windows 98 in a peer-to-peer network even if you're running another network operating system.

With a Windows 98 peer-to-peer network, users can share resources without the overhead of a dedicated server managing access to resources. This way, you can use all your PCs for sharing resources and for performing workstation duties, such as running applications for a user. The only extra hardware required is a network interface card (NIC) and cable, such as coaxial, twisted-pair, or fiber-optic cables, or wireless devices. If you plan to connect more than two PCs, you might also want to invest in a workgroup hub, which is used in a star topology network.

N O T E In a *star topology network*, workstations are connected to a hub, much like the points of a star connect to its center. A *topology* is the way a network's nodes are connected to each other.

Another popular topology is the *bus topology*, in which nodes are connected in linear segments. Each node is connected to a main (backbone) cable. One disadvantage of bus topology networks is that if there is cable failure anyplace in the segment, the entire network is affected. On the other hand, cable failures on a star topology affect only those nodes using that particular cable connection. ■

Some features of a Windows 98 peer-to-peer network include the following:

- *Sharing files*. Files can remain on the workstation on which they were created and then be shared across the network. This way, the person responsible for creating a specific type of document, for instance, can maintain the document on his or her PC. The folder or drive in which the document resides can be shared so that all users can access it, or just specific users can access it via password-protection.

- *Sharing printers*. A printer connected to a PC on the network can be shared by other users. This enables you to distribute the cost of the printer across the entire department or team without requiring a separate printer server to be installed. Any user who is part of the network can access a shared printer. Or, password-protection can be enabled to limit who has rights to a printer.

- *Sharing drives*. Similar to sharing printers, drives, including CD-ROM drives, can be shared by users on a Windows 98 peer-to-peer network. For instance, if your PC does not include a 5 1/4-inch floppy disk drive (not standard on PCs anymore), but you have a 5 1/4-inch floppy you need to read, use a PC on the network that includes this drive type. Similarly, PCs not equipped with CD-ROM drives can use the drive from another machine to access files or programs stored on CDs.

■ *Distributed administration.* On a server-based network (such as Windows NT), there usually is a person (or entire department) dedicated (full or part time) to administrating the server. Because there is not a dedicated server, a dedicated (full-time or part-time) network administrator is not often needed for a peer-to-peer network. Users at each workstation can perform administration duties such as assigning shared access privileges to resources, backing up data, and so forth.

N O T E You can use Microsoft Backup to back up files on your hard disk to another computer on the network. ■

■ *Sharing fax modems.* With Windows 98, you can share fax modems and thereby decrease the amount of money invested in fax modems, if you also have the Microsoft Fax service from Windows 95 installed. You can set up a shared fax modem on one workstation and let other users on the network use that modem to send and receive fax messages.

Part
VI

Ch
24

Sharing Privileges

You've read a little about how you can limit access to shared resources using passwords. On a pure Windows 98 peer-to-peer network, you have only one type of security level: *share-level security*. With share-level security, you can share printers and folders with other users on the network. These users can access resources with or without a password, depending on how you've set up the shared rights to them.

Unlike *user-level security*, which is supported on Windows NT and NetWare networks, share-level security does not enable you to grant permissions on a per-user, per-group, or per-resource level. This means that you need to be aware of who is part of your peer-to-peer network and set up shares only to those resources you want shared. If, for instance, you have a folder in which you store confidential documents, do not share your entire drive. Instead, share only those folders that do not contain confidential documents. This might mean going through the process of sharing 49 of 50 folders (if you have 50 folders on your drive, for instance), but the time is well spent if your documents are protected. You're shown how to share folders in the "Sharing Drives and Folders" section later in this chapter.

N O T E On a Windows 98 peer-to-peer network, you also cannot restrict and permit access on a per-file level because the Windows 98 file system does not allow file-specific access rights. ■

Configuring Network Properties

To set up a Windows 98 peer-to-peer network, install network interface cards in the PCs you want to connect. You also need to connect the PCs with a cable of some sort.

▶ **See** Chapter 23, "Configuring Network Hardware," for information on installing and configuring network hardware.

After your PCs are connected, install the Client for Microsoft Network client on each computer. Then configure the clients so that they can communicate with one another across the LAN. Finally, configure shared resources. The following sections show how to perform these tasks.

Add Client for Microsoft Networks

To begin configuring workstations for a Windows 98 peer-to-peer network, you need to install the Client for Microsoft Networks component. This installs the 32-bit networking client that enables your computer to speak to other Windows 98, Windows 95, Windows for Workgroups, and Windows NT computers running the Client for Microsoft Networks client.

To add the Client for Microsoft Networks, do the following:

1. Select Start, Settings, Control Panel, Network. The Network properties sheet displays.
2. Click Add. The Select Network Component Type dialog box appears (see Figure 24.1).

FIG. 24.1
Use the Select Network Component Type dialog box to select the networking components to install, including Client for Microsoft Networks.

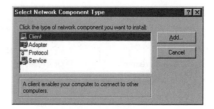

3. Select Client and click Add. The Select Network Client dialog box appears (see Figure 24.2).

FIG. 24.2
The Select Network Client dialog box includes type of clients you can install for your networks.

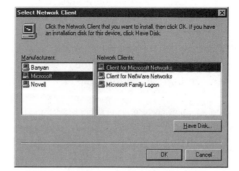

4. Select Microsoft in the Manufacturers list and then select Client for Microsoft Networks from the Network Clients list.
5. Click OK. You're prompted to insert the Windows 98 CD-ROM or floppy disk. Click OK.

The Client for Microsoft Networks appears in the network components list on the Network properties sheet. You next have to install the protocols you want to use over your new network.

Add Protocols: IPX/SPX, NetBEUI, and TCP/IP

For your Windows 98 computers to communicate with each other over the LAN, they must all use the same protocol. *Protocols* are a set of "rules" for communicating among computers, governing format, error control, timing, and sequencing. If the other computers on the network are running IPX/SPX, for example, you must install that protocol on your Windows 98 computer.

The TCP/IP, NetBEUI, and IPX/SPX-compatible protocols are installed by default when a network adapter driver is installed. You might want to keep these protocols for your network, or use another one, such as the Novell IPX ODI protocol. Unless you are required to use a third-party protocol to communicate with other computers, such as if your company has adopted another protocol, you should use one of the Microsoft protocols provided with Windows 98 to take full advantage of the Windows 98 networking features. Not only is it easier in most cases to use the Windows 98-provided protocols, but the third-party protocols often require extra components, licenses, and configuration.

The three most popular protocols to use over a Windows 98 peer-to-peer network include the following:

Part
VI

Ch
24

- *NetBEUI.* The NetBIOS Extended User Interface (NetBEUI) protocol is one of the easiest protocols to implement. Besides supplying the computer name and workgroup name, NetBEUI does not require the configuration of additional network addresses. NetBEUI also includes fast communication and dynamically self-tuning performance. One disadvantage of NetBEUI is that it is not routable.

- *IPX/SPX.* Commonly used with NetWare networks, the IPX/SPX protocol is a routable protocol. The Microsoft implementation of IPX/SPX includes support for automatic detection frame type, network address, and other settings. It's also a great protocol for mixed networks, such as if you're running a Windows 98 peer-to-peer network on top of a Microsoft NT or Novell NetWare network.

- *TCP/IP.* Transmission Control Protocol/Internet Protocol (TCP/IP) is probably the most implemented protocol because of its use on the Internet. You also can install TCP/IP on your LAN to take advantage of its speed and error-checking capabilities. Because you must set up IP addresses for each computer, many smaller installations don't want to take the time to set up TCP/IP protocols on their workstations. Instead, they use IPX/SPX or NetBEUI.

To install a protocol on a Windows 98 computer, follow these steps:

1. On the Network properties sheet, click <u>A</u>dd. The Select Network Component Type dialog box appears.

2. Select Protocol and click <u>A</u>dd. The Select Network Protocol dialog box appears (see Figure 24.3).

FIG. 24.3

Select the protocol you want to use on your network from this dialog box.

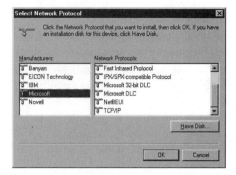

3. Select Microsoft from the Manufacturers list. Select the protocol you want to run from the Network Protocols list.

4. Click OK.

The new protocol is added to the list of installed components. It is also automatically bound to an installed adapter, which you might not want. For instance, if you have the Dial-Up Adapter installed for an Internet connection, you do not need it bound to any other protocol except TCP/IP. If this is the case, select the protocol bound to that adapter and click Remove.

After you install the protocol for your LAN, you can configure properties for it. The following sections show properties for three of the most common protocols.

IPX/SPX Protocol Configuration Settings   The IPX/SPX protocol can be configured in the following way:

1. Select the IPX/SPX-compatible Protocol component from the Network properties sheet.

2. Click Properties. The IPX/SPX-compatible Protocol Properties sheet appears (see Figure 24.4).

FIG. 24.4

You can configure IPX/ SPX settings from this properties sheet.

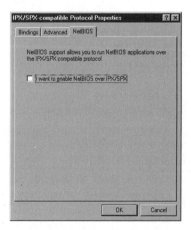

3. On the NetBIOS tab, select the I Want to Enable NetBIOS Over IPX/SPX if you want to be able to execute NetBIOS applications over your network. NetBIOS (network basic input/output system) provides a link between the operating system and the network protocol stacks. It provides a layer where network requests are sent, which are then translated and sent to the appropriate transport stack. It's analogous to the BIOS (basic input/output system) in your computer. Not all networks need this enabled, but if an application you're trying to run over the network requires NetBIOS support, choose this setting.

4. On the Advanced tab (see Figure 24.5), you can set values for the following properties:

FIG. 24.5

The Advanced tab for the IPX/SPX-compatible protocol.

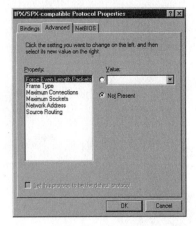

Part
VI

Ch

24

- *Force Even Length Packets.* This should be set to Not Present unless running Ethernet 802.3 implementations that cannot use odd-length packets.
- *Frame Type.* Specifies the type of frame used by your network adapter. The recommended setting is Auto, but you can choose values for specific settings such as Ethernet 802.2, Ethernet 802.3, Ethernet II, Token Ring, and Token Ring SNAP. Select the same frame type for all computers on the network to improve performance. Also, some IPX applications, such as Btrieve, require that you select a specific frame type.
- *Maximum Connections.* Shows the maximum number of connections that IPX can handle.
- *Maximum Sockets.* Shows the maximum number of IPX sockets that IPX assigns.
- *Network Address.* Indicates the network address as a 4-byte value.
- *Source Routing.* Used only on Token Ring networks, this value shows the cache size used with source routing. The recommended value for Token Ring networks is 16 entry cache. Other networks should be set to Off.

5. On the Bindings tab (see Figure 24.6), set the component that will use IPX/SPX to communicate over the LAN. In this case, we've only set up the Client for Microsoft Networks, so make sure that it is selected.

FIG. 24.6

Select the component that will use the protocol over the LAN.

6. Click OK to save your settings.

NetBEUI Protocol Configuration Settings If you decide to run NetBEUI as your LAN protocol, you can configure it using the following steps:

1. Select the NetBEUI component from the Network properties sheet.

2. Click Properties. The NetBEUI Properties sheet appears (see Figure 24.7).

FIG. 24.7

The NetBEUI Properties sheet includes the Bindings and Advanced tabs.

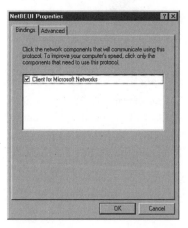

3. On the Bindings tab, set the component that will use NetBEUI to communicate over the LAN. In this case, we've only set up the Client for Microsoft Networks, so make sure that it is selected.

4. On the Advanced tab (see Figure 24.8), you can set the following properties and values:

FIG. 24.8
On the Advanced tab, you can set Maximum Sessions and NCBS settings.

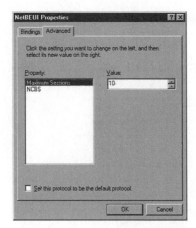

- *Maximum Sessions.* Specifies the maximum number of connections to remote computers that can be supported. You can change this setting here or in the `sessions=` line of the `PROTOCOL.INI` file.

- *NCBS.* Specifies the network control blocks (NCBS) to identify the maximum number of NetBIOS commands that can be used.

5. Click OK to save your settings.

TCP/IP Protocol Configuration Settings   To configure the TCP/IP protocol on a Windows 98 computer, follow these steps:

1. Select TCP/IP from the Network properties sheet and choose Properties. The TCP/IP Properties sheet appears.

2. Select the IP Address tab (see Figure 24.9). Select Obtain An IP Address Automatically if there is a Dynamic Host Configuration Protocol (DHCP) server on the network configured to supply this machine with an IP address. DHCP is run on several types of systems, including Windows NT Server. However, because we're showing how to set up a Windows 98 peer-to-peer only network, you need to select the Specify An IP Address option and type the IP address and subnet mask in the spaces provided. Each machine on your LAN must have a unique IP address.

CAUTION

An incorrect IP address or subnet mask can cause communication problems with other TCP/IP nodes on the network. If an IP address is the same as another already on the network, the machine that attaches to the network second will disable its TCP/IP support. Make sure that you assign unique TCP/IP addresses to each client.

Part
VI

Ch
24

FIG. 24.9

The IP Address tab of
the TCP/IP Properties
sheet.

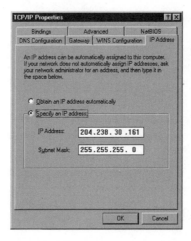

3. On the WINS Configuration tab (see Figure 24.10), make sure that Disable WINS
   Resolution is selected. This setting is for networks running WINS on a Windows NT
   Server network.

FIG. 24.10

On Windows 98
peer-to-peer networks,
you cannot set up a
WINS configuration.

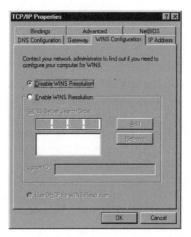

4. On the Gateway tab (see Figure 24.11), enter the IP address of the default IP router on
   the LAN. Click Add to add the gateway to the list of Installed Gateways. Most small peer-
   to-peer networks will not require a gateway.

FIG. 24.11

You can specify IP router addresses on the Gateway tab.

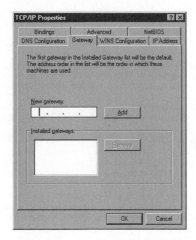

5. On the DNS Configuration tab (see Figure 24.12), enter the DNS information for your computer and LAN. If you do not use DNS to resolve names to IP addresses, click the Disable DNS option. Otherwise, fill out the Host, Domain, DNS Server Search Order, and Domain Suffix Search Order fields. When you install TCP/IP on a Windows 98 computer, a HOSTS file is created, which provides mappings of IP addresses to host names. You must enable DNS to be able to use the HOSTS file. For additional information on the HOSTS file, open the file from the Windows folder and read the sample file information.

FIG. 24.12

You probably won't have a DNS server on your Windows 98 peer-to-peer network, so this tab can be left unchanged.

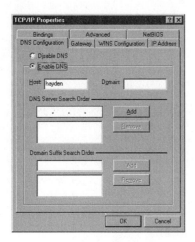

6. On the NetBIOS tab (see Figure 24.13), indicate whether you want to run NetBIOS over TCP/IP. This option is available if you're running over a WINS-enabled network.

Part

VI

Ch

24

FIG. 24.13
The NetBIOS tab allows you to configure whether you want NetBIOS applications to run over TCP/IP.

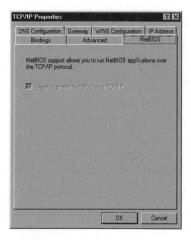

7. On the Bindings tab, set the component that will use TCP/IP to communicate over the LAN. In this case, we've only set up the Client for Microsoft Networks, so make sure that it is selected. By the way, the Advanced tab is blank, so no configurations are necessary.

8. Click OK to save your settings.

Add File and Printer Sharing for Microsoft Networks

Your network is not complete until you've set up the service that enables you to share file and printer resources. To do this, take the following steps:

1. Click Add on the Configuration tab of the Network properties sheet. The Select Network Component Type dialog box appears.

2. Select Service and click Add. The Select Network Service dialog box appears (see Figure 24.14).

FIG. 24.14
Use the Select Network Service dialog box to choose the file and printer sharing for Microsoft Networks service.

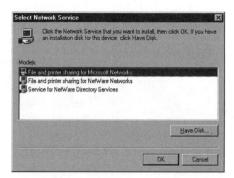

3. Select file and printer sharing for Microsoft Networks.

4. Click OK.

The File and Printer Sharing for Microsoft Networks services appears on the Configuration tab. You now need to enable the service for your computer:

1. Click the File and Print Sharing button. The File and Print Sharing dialog box appears (see Figure 24.15).

FIG. 24.15

You must enable file and print sharing so that others can access resources on your computer.

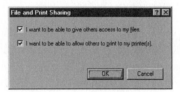

2. Select both options to enable others to share files from your system and to use your printers. Or, select the option you want to enable for your PC.

3. Click OK.

Bind Adapter to Protocol

You read earlier in the "Add Protocols: IPX/SPX, NetBEUI, and TCP/IP" section that when you add a new protocol it automatically binds to all available adapters. If, however, you want to change the bindings for an adapter, take the following steps:

1. Select the adapter name on the Configuration tab of the Network properties sheet.

2. Click Properties. The properties sheet for that adapter appears.

3. Click the Bindings tab (see Figure 24.16).

FIG. 24.16

The Bindings tab shows all the protocols installed and which ones are bound to the selected adapter.

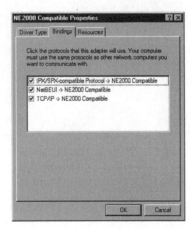

4. Click the bindings(s) you want to disable. Check marks appear next to those that are bound.

The more bindings an adapter uses will greatly affect its performance. If you notice your network is slow, see whether you can disable one or more bindings. Remember that every computer on the network must use the same protocol, so make sure that you don't disable the protocol(s) shared by other PCs.

   5. Click OK to save your settings.

Set Computer Identification Properties

To identify your PC on the network and to specify the workgroup to which your PC belongs, you use the Identification tab (see Figure 24.17) of the Network properties sheet.

FIG. 24.17
The Identification tab provides fields for identifying this computer on the network.

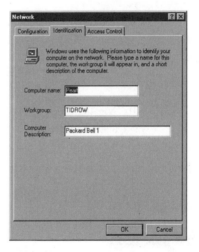

In the Computer Name field, enter a name for the computer. Each computer on the network must have a unique name given to it to distinguish it from other computers. You might use proper names, usernames, or numbers to identify the computers. Each name can be up to 15 characters and cannot include spaces.

In the Workgroup field, enter a workgroup to which this computer belongs. A *workgroup* is a logical grouping of computers, such as in teams, divisions, or other setups. You might, for instance, create a workgroup for all users in the accounting department. Another workgroup could be set up for users in the engineering department. Or, you can opt to have one workgroup, to which all users belong.

Finally, fill in a description of this computer in the Computer Description field. Other users on the network will be able to see this description by viewing the properties sheet of the computer (see Figure 24.18).

FIG. 24.18
An example of viewing a computer's properties sheet from Network Neighborhood.

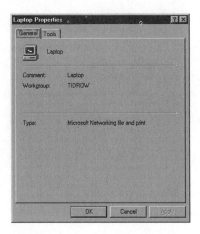

Set Access Control

Another task you must perform is to enable share-level access for this computer. Do this by clicking the Access Control tab and selecting Share-Level Access Control (see Figure 24.19). This will enable users to share resources on your PC.

FIG. 24.19
If users can't access resources on your computer, make sure that the Share-Level Access Control option is selected.

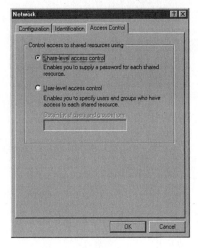

Click OK to save your new network settings. Click Yes to restart your computer. When Windows restarts, notice the Network Neighborhood icon on your desktop (if you didn't have any network support installed prior to these steps).

Installing and Configuring Shared Devices

Your network is only as good as what it can enable users to share or communicate with one another efficiently. A network without some sort of shared resource or email configuration is not that helpful. Out of the box, Windows 98 enables you to share folders (and files within them), printers, and drives. The following sections show how to set up these resources.

Sharing Drives and Folders

If you have File and Printer Sharing for Microsoft Networks installed, you can share your drives, folders, and files with other users on the network.

To set up shares for these resources, follow these steps:

1. Start Explorer and select a folder on your hard drive.

2. Right-click the selected folder and choose Sharing from the context-sensitive menu. The Properties sheet for that folder appears.

3. Select the Sharing tab and click Shared As (see Figure 24.20).

FIG. 24.20

The Sharing tab includes controls for setting up shared folders.

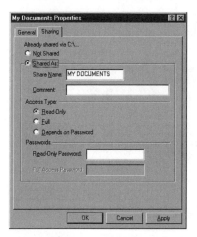

4. Enter a name in the Share Name field. This is the name other users on the network will see for the shared folder.

5. Enter a description of the share in the Comment field.

6. Select one of the following access types:

   - *Read-Only.* Select this type if you want others to be able to read but not edit, delete, or move files in the selected folder. You can set up a password for this access type in the Read-Only Password field.

   - *Full.* Select this type if you want others to be able to read, edit, move, and delete files in the selected folder. You can set up a password for this access type in the Full Access Password field.

- *Depends on Password.* Select this type if you want to assign one password for read-only rights and another for full rights. You can then distribute passwords for each access type to the people who need them.

7. Click OK to save your settings.

Shared folders appear with a small hand holding the contents of the folder. You can use these same steps to set up shares to drives.

Sharing a Printer

To share a printer, you use the Sharing tab of the printer's properties sheet. To do this, use the following steps:

1. Open the Printers folder (select Start, Settings, Printers, or open My Computer and double-click the Printers folder).

2. Right-click the printer you want to share and select Sharing. The Sharing tab of the printer's properties sheet displays.

3. Click Shared As (see Figure 24.21).

FIG. 24.21

You can share a printer using the Sharing tab.

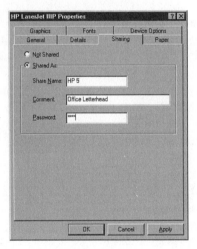

4. Enter a name for the printer, a description, and password (if necessary) for the share. Assigning a password to a printer is handy if your printer should be used only by certain users (be sure to tell them the password). Also, if your printer will be filled with special paper most of the time, such as forms, letterhead, and the like, you might want to limit those who can access this printer by using a password.

5. Click OK to save your settings.

A hand holding a printer icon appears to indicate that the printer is now shared.

Part

VI

Ch

24

Installing a Network Printer

If you're connected to a peer-to-peer Microsoft Network, you can use another user's printer across the network. If someone else on your network has designated his or her printer, for example, as a shared resource and designated you as having access to that resource, you can print to that printer from any of your Windows applications.

Installing a network printer is similar to installing a printer connected to your own computer. To install a network printer, follow these steps:

1. Select Start, Settings, Printers.

2. In the Printers window, double-click the Add Printer icon. The Add Printer Wizard dialog box appears.

3. Choose Next, and the second wizard screen appears.

4. Click the Network Printer option and click Next. The third wizard screen appears.

5. Enter the path to the printer in the Network Path text box. Choose whether to use MS-DOS-based programs with the printer. Click Next.

6. The next wizard dialog box appears. Enter a name to represent the printer on your computer and click Next.

7. The last wizard dialog box appears, asking whether you want to print a test page. Choose Yes to print a test page or No to skip this step. If you choose Yes, a dialog box appears confirming the test page printed correctly. If you choose No, Windows tries to diagnose the problem.

8. Choose the Finish button. The installed printer icon appears in the Printers window as a network printer. You can print to this printer as you would a printer attached directly to your computer.

▶ **See** the section "Sharing a Printer" earlier in this chapter to learn how to set up network share permissions for each network printer.

Setting Up Deferred Printing

Windows 98 supports *deferred* printing (also known as *offline printing*), which enables you to create print jobs when your computer is not physically connected to a printer. When you do connect to a printer, the print jobs are then sent from your PC to the printer.

To use deferred printing, the printer to which you want to print is usually set up as a network printer. Deferred printing is set up automatically for your portable computers when you are not connected to the network printer and you send a print job to it.

You also can turn on deferred printing manually from the Printers folder. Open this folder by choosing Start, Settings, Printers. Select the network printer and choose File, Work Offline. A check mark indicates that the Work Offline command is turned on. The printer icon in the Printers folder also becomes dimmed when the Work Offline command is turned on.

TIP Even if your printer is not on a network, you can defer print jobs until later. To defer a print job on a standalone computer (that is, a computer that never is connected to a network), navigate to the Printers folder and select the printer on which to defer print jobs. Choose File, Pause Printing. Jobs you send to this printer will now be held until you're ready to print them. At that time, choose File, Pause Printing again to turn off the Pause Printing command. Your print jobs will begin printing.

After you have deferred printing set up, you send print jobs to the deferred printer as you do any other printer. When you get back to the office and reattach to the network, open the Printers folder and deselect Work Offline. Windows sends your print jobs to the printer.

Installing Shared Fax Modems

Adding a shared fax modem from your network is similar to adding a regular modem (one that is connected to your computer system) to the Microsoft Fax server. The Microsoft Fax configuration program is started from the Control Panel Mail and Fax sheet. Select the Microsoft Fax profile and click the Properties button to begin configuring this service.

> **CAUTION**
>
> You must have the Microsoft Exchange or Windows Messaging service installed in Windows 95 and then upgrade to Windows 98 to have the shared fax modem service available. See Appendix B, "Configuring Windows Messaging and Microsoft Fax," for more information.

On the Microsoft Fax properties sheet, select the Modems page to configure the network modem. Click the Add button to add a new modem to the fax service. This brings up the Add a Fax Modem dialog box, which asks you to specify the type of modem you are adding. You should select Network Fax Server.

You now need to enter the shared fax folder in the usual \\COMPUTER\FOLDER form. If you are not sure of the computer or folder name, ask your network administrator.

After you have specified the network fax folder, you should be able to use the Microsoft Fax service.

NOTE If you use Microsoft Exchange or Microsoft Messaging as your primary fax software, faxes you receive on a shared fax modem are not automatically routed to the proper recipient. Instead, the fax messages are saved on the machine that receives them, and the administrator or other user must manually distribute the faxes to each recipient, such as by electronic mail. ∎

Installing Shared CD-ROM Drives

CD-ROM drives that are shared on the network are mounted just like any other directory shared on your network. You can mount a shared CD-ROM drive by choosing Tools, Map

Part **VI**

Ch **24**

Network Drive in the Explorer. The system prompts you for the machine name and share name; if you don't know these, open the Network Neighborhood and look for the machine that has the CD-ROM shared on it.

After you have found the machine and the share name, you can mount the CD-ROM on your system. It appears as a new drive letter and can be accessed from the Explorer or My Computer icon. You can specify the drive letter on the Map Network Drive sheet. ●

CHAPTER 25

Configuring the Personal Web Server

by Serdar Yegulap

In this chapter

Basic Features of Personal Web Server

Microsoft Personal Web Server (PWS) is a modest but useful Web server program that runs under Windows 98. It uses some of the same core technologies as Microsoft's professional-level Web server, Internet Information Server (IIS). PWS includes many of the capabilities of its bigger brother, including the capability to connect to databases and use Active Server Pages to create dynamic content.

PWS is scaled down from IIS for less demanding Web-server tasks, such as an in-office intranet. You can still use PWS to serve pages to the Internet at large, if your page demands and hardware allowances are modest, and this chapter will go into some detail about that. You can also use PWS to test Web sites before they are deployed for real.

PWS was originally created and deployed for Windows 98 as a downloadable add-on and could be found on Microsoft's Web site, in Microsoft's developer's kits, and in many shareware repositories around the world. When Windows 98 began to take shape, it was added as a standard component that could be installed from the Windows 98 CD-ROM.

Personal Web Server allows you, quite simply, to turn your computer into a Web server more than powerful enough to meet most modest Web server needs. If you have an Internet connection, or have your computer installed on a local area network (LAN), you can publish HTML documents without having to invest in a separate server. When used in conjunction with a Microsoft-compatible Web publishing tool, such as FrontPage, PWS can also be used to publish databases.

PWS can be used independently of the type of Internet or network connection it uses, provided that the connection supports the TCP/IP protocol. Anything from a LAN or a T1 connection to a 28.8 dial-up will work, albeit at different speeds.

PWS is *not* designed to function as a commercial-level Web server that handles, for instance, financial or secured transactions. That sort of capability is better handled by Microsoft's Internet Information Server, which runs on Windows NT and provides a far more robust platform for deploying merchant-style Web-based services.

N O T E　There has been a great deal of confusion regarding Windows NT's server capacities, especially as opposed to Windows 98. Windows NT Workstation has a built-in limit of ten inbound NetBIOS connections. (The number of TCP/IP connections is not limited, which allows NT Workstation to be used as a quick-and-dirty Web server without trouble.) Windows NT Server has no practical connection limit, but you must buy licenses for each connection on a per-server or per-seat basis. Windows 98 does not have any hard-wired limitations, in licensing or otherwise, to the number of connections that it can satisfy. The only real limit is the power of the host computer, the bandwidth of the connection, and the robustness of Windows 98 itself. Windows 98 can be used satisfactorily for a modest Web server. ■

Personal Web Server was originally designed as a downloadable add-on for Windows 95 Service Release 2. It appears, with some modification and updates, in Windows 98 as a feature that can be installed directly from the Windows 98 CD-ROM.

Hardware Requirements

Because PWS is small and designed to run light, running PWS doesn't require a lot of hardware power. Any computer that can run Windows 98 will do for a start and should fit this bare bones description:

- 486/50 or better Intel or Intel-compatible processor; Pentium or higher preferred.
- 16MB of RAM.
- 200MB hard disk space.
- A network connection.

The network connection is the most indispensable part of PWS because it's impossible to get access to the server without a network link of some kind. PWS doesn't care whether the pages are being accessed through a dial-up connection, a LAN or a WAN, as long as a network link that uses TCP/IP is available to it.

In general, the better the configuration, the better everything will run, including PWS.

TIP On the whole, PWS is more disk- and memory-intensive than processor-intensive. If you have a choice between using a machine that has a faster processor and a machine with more memory or a faster drive, use the one with more memory or the faster drive. The performance payoff is more visible and immediate.

As a guideline, try to dedicate a machine for your PWS installation. If someone else is working with the machine, the performance hit on the server software will be noticeable, especially if the user is running memory- or CPU-intensive applications. The less the system is doing besides running PWS, the better.

Part
VI

Ch
25

Installing PWS

To install the Personal Web Server, insert the Windows 98 disk into the CD-ROM drive and click Start, Run. Type the following command:

```
[driveletter]:\add-ons\pws\setup.exe
```

Replace [driveletter] with the letter of your CD-ROM drive. The Personal Web Server Setup program appears (see Figure 25.1). To start the installation, click Next, and read through the licensing agreement.

N O T E Don't be confused by the "Microsoft Windows NT 4.0 Option Pack" statement at the top of the licensing agreement. Many core components of PWS were taken directly from IIS, and the licensing arrangement is similar. ■

> **CAUTION**
>
> The licensing agreement is more than boring legal folderol. If you're planning on using PWS in any kind of
> public or professional application, read the agreement front to back and make sure that you're not using
> PWS in a fashion that violates the agreement. You might need a full-blown, properly licensed Web server for
> what you're doing, so save yourself the risk of being embarrassed later and read the document.

Click Next to move on to the installation options menu.

Installation Options

There are three basic types of installation that you can do with PWS. You choose between the
types of installations by clicking the appropriate button in the installation options menu.

- *Minimal.* Click this to install only the bare minimum of components needed to run
  Personal Web Server. If you're tight on space or just want to get a basic idea of what PWS
  is like, this is a good choice. This contains the binaries needed to run the program but no
  documentation or transactional components.

- *Typical.* The Typical installation option installs everything from the Minimal installation,
  plus basic documentation and the minimum of tools needed to create Web applications
  (that is, Web-enabled databases).

- *Custom.* This option lets you pick and choose among the bevy of system components
  available for PWS. Some components are required for PWS and are checked by default;
  most are optional.

If you choose Custom, a list of components appears that you can select or deselect (see Figure
25.1). Here is a quick rundown of the components available in PWS through the Custom menu
option:

- *Common Program Files.* These components make up the core of PWS, so this option
  shouldn't be deselected.

- *FrontPage 98 Server Extensions.* This installs components that allow the server to operate
  with Microsoft's FrontPage 98 Web authoring program. If you plan on using FrontPage
  98 to do Web authoring with PWS, check this component; otherwise, you can safely leave
  it off.

- *Microsoft Data Access Components 1.5.* The Data Access Components allow PWS to
  interact with databases. If you are planning on serving only static pages through PWS,
  you can uncheck this option.

- *Microsoft Message Queue.* This component is a critical part of PWS's Web-application
  technology. Message Queue allows PWS to communicate with other networked applications and should be loaded if you're planning to use PWS to publish dynamic content like
  databases.

- *Personal Web Server.* This is the other critical set of core components for PWS and shouldn't be unchecked.

- *Transaction Server.* This enables PWS to run Web-based applications that consist of ActiveX objects. Again, if you're not planning to publish live content or create a Web database, you can safely uncheck this option.

- *Visual InterDev RAD Remote Deployment Support.* This is a toolkit that allows you to create remotely deployable applications through PWS. If you don't plan on doing any Web application development through PWS, you can safely uncheck this option.

FIG. 25.1

The Microsoft Personal Web Server Setup dialog box.

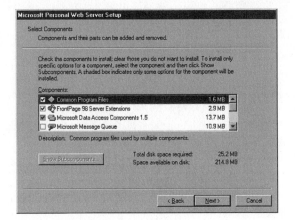

If you check every box on the list, you'll install *everything* included in the PWS package— development tools, documentation, FrontPage 98 server extensions, and so on. Be warned that a full install of PWS will use 52.6 megabytes of disk space, so this should only be done on a system that you're sure has the space for it, and if you really need all the pieces.

The component list does not appear if you do not select Custom.

After you've finished selecting which components you want to load, click Next. The PWS installation program asks you for the name of the directory you are going to keep your Web page files in (see Figure 25.2). This defaults to [rootdrive]:\Inetpub\wwwroot but can be changed to anything you want. The other two directories (FTP Service and Application Installation Point) are not available in PWS and are therefore grayed out by default.

Click Next to begin copying the PWS installation files from the CD-ROM. A progress meter will indicate how far along the copying process is. When the files have finished copying, you will be asked to reboot your machine. PWS will start up automatically after the next reboot.

FIG. 25.2

The PWS default directory text boxes.

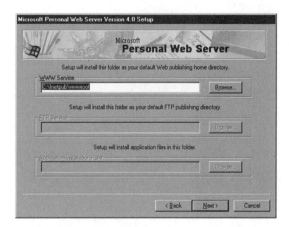

Running and Configuring PWS

While running, PWS normally appears as an icon in the system tray. The icon changes depending on the state of the server (running, paused, or stopped). Right-clicking the icon brings up a list of quick options for PWS.

- *Start Service.* This is normally grayed out because the PWS service is set to run by default, but when deactivated or paused, it is enabled. Select this to start up PWS when it's not already activated.

- *Stop Service.* This shuts down PWS completely. When Stop Service is selected, the icon changes, and a "stop sign" icon appears over the main PWS icon.

- *Pause Service.* This stops PWS from communicating but doesn't unload it from memory. When Pause Service is selected, the icon changes to have a "yield" sign appear over it.

- *Continue Service.* This is only enabled if the service is paused. Selecting it will cause Web services to resume as before and will change the tray icon for PWS back to its original appearance.

- *Properties.* Selecting this option is the same as double-clicking the icon itself and will bring up the Properties sheet for PWS.

PWS Properties Sheet/Personal Web Manager

The PWS properties sheet, also known as the Personal Web Manager, comes up when the user double-clicks the tray icon, or selects Properties from the icon's right-click menu. It can also be accessed from the Start button, by selecting Programs, Microsoft Personal Web Server, Personal Web Manager. See Figure 25.3 for an example of the Personal Web Manager.

The Manager is divided into two panes, with the left-hand pane containing the five main program options: the Main screen, Publish, Web Site, Tour, and Advanced. Clicking each of these will bring up the appropriate information in the right-hand pane. The default is Main.

Main Pane   The Main pane is subdivided into two sections: Publishing and Monitoring.

FIG. 25.3
The Main pane of the
Personal Web Manager.

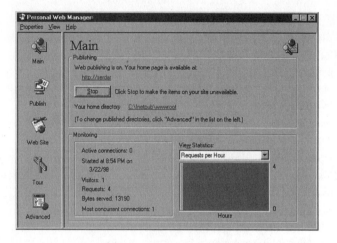

Part
VI

Ch

25

Publishing   The Publishing subsection of the Main pane describes the basic attributes of PWS's functioning: whether it's on or not, what the proper URL is to view the site from your local machine, and what the server's home directory is currently registered as. The two URLs shown in the Publishing subsection are live: they can be clicked and will bring up a copy of Internet Explorer to display the contents of the URL. This is a good, quick way to preview what's on the Web site.

The Stop button has the same functionality as the Stop command on the tray icon's right-click menu. Once clicked, it changes to a Start button (again, same functionality), and the hotlinks to the PWS site vanish. The statistics in the Monitoring section also vanish. To reactivate the Web site, simply click the Start button.

Using Pause instead of Stop is a good way to make quick tweaks without actually turning off the Web server. If you shut down the server completely, the server won't respond to outside requests at all. If the server is paused, it will at least fire back a message stating that the site is temporarily unavailable.

CAUTION

You will need to shut down the server completely if you need to add or remove components, or change the directory structure of the server. You cannot make changes of that nature when the service is running or paused.

Monitoring The Monitoring subsection of the Main pane provides live statistics about the PWS site. These statistics are continually updated; you do not need to click a button to bring them up to date. The statistics listed are as follows:

- *Active Connections.* This is how many connections there currently are to the Web site. This is not the same thing as the number of users currently accessing the site because a user might have more than one connection open at a time. For that statistic, see Visitors.

- *Started at....* This is the time and date at which the Web server was last activated.

- *Visitors.* This is the total number of individual IP addresses there have been to the site since the last reactivation of the Web site. The server stores only 50 addresses for comparison, so a repeat visit is not counted as another visitor unless more than 50 new addresses have contacted the server since the last visit.

- *Requests.* This is the number of separate requests for objects that the server has received since its last inception. A Web page is a discrete object, but each graphic on that page, for instance, also counts as a discrete object.

- *Bytes Served.* This is the total number of bytes that have been sent out by the Web server since it was last turned on.

- *Most Concurrent Connections.* This is the maximum number of connections that the Web server has had to satisfy at any given time since its last activation. This statistic can be useful in gauging at a glance how much of a load the Web server is taking on. If the number is unusually high, you might want to consider a faster machine or subdividing the Web site across several different servers.

- *View Statistics.* This is a drop-down list that lets you select four different types of Web site statistics to be displayed graphically: visitors per hour, visitors per day, requests per day, and requests per hour. Again, they provide a good sense of the frequency and concentration of the hits to the site and can be used to get an idea of when the highest numbers of users hit the site.

Publishing Wizard The Publishing Wizard is a quick way to create and publish simple documents on PWS. It is not a substitute for a full-fledged HTML publishing program such as Microsoft FrontPage, but it is a good way to get a page up onto the server quickly and without programming.

Windows 98 comes with a copy of FrontPage Express, a stripped-down version of FrontPage's HTML editor. It does not do full-fledged site management, but it's good for editing individual pages.

The Publishing Wizard is activated by clicking the Publish icon in the left-hand pane of the Personal Web Manager. When you do this, the Publishing Wizard (see Figure 25.4) opens in the right-hand pane.

FIG. 25.4
The first screen of the Publishing Wizard, running in the Personal Web Manager.

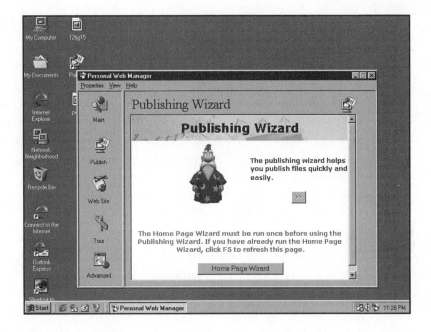

N O T E If you've never created a document with the Publishing Wizard before, the program will prompt you to run the Home Page Wizard first. ▦

The Publishing Wizard contains several controls (depicted in Figure 25.5) used to publish a desired page.

FIG. 25.5
The Publishing Wizard screen.

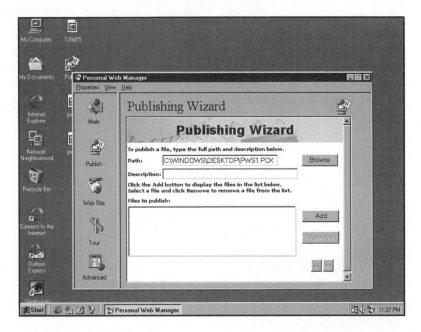

■ *Path.* Fill in the pathname of the document in question, or click Browse to look through your hard drives and select a file. If you've opened the wizard by dragging and dropping a file to the Publish icon, this field will already be filled in, and you do not need to complete it.

■ *Description.* Provide a description of the file in question, which can be any text. If you have directory browsing enabled, this description will appear next to the published file in the browsed directory. This field is optional.

■ *Files to Publish.* This contains a list of the files that will be published.

■ *Add.* Click the Add button to add the page described in the Path and Description text boxes to the Files to Publish list.

■ *Remove.* Click Remove to delete a selected file from the Files to Publish list. (Click a filename in the list to select it first.)

Home Page Wizard   The Home Page Wizard creates a quick and attractive home page on the server by prompting the user to answer several basic questions.

1. The Home Page Wizard has several *themes* from which you can choose a design for your home page. They are:

   • *Looseleaf.* The page design resembles a page from a loose-leaf notebook.

   • *Journal.* This design is intended to resemble a diary or blank tablet.

   • *Gunmetal.* A gray, high-tech look.

   Click the design you want to use and then click the right arrow (the ">>" symbol) to advance.

2. You can install a *guest book* on your home page. This is a section of your home page where visitors can sign in and leave comments. Click Yes or No to allow or disallow a guest book; then click the right arrow to go on.

N O T E   At any time during the Home Page Wizard, you can click the list at the left-hand side of the frame to go back and change a previously defined option. For instance, during the guest book page, the only other option is "theme"; clicking that will bring you back to the themes choice page and let you redo your choices there. ■

3. You can have a *drop box* placed on your page. This is a section for private messages from your visitors to you. Click Yes or No depending on whether you want a drop box; then click the right arrow to go on.

4. The next page is opened in Internet Explorer, or whatever the currently installed browser is, and is both a recap of the previous options, plus the capability to add personal information to your home page (name, address, email, interests, hobbies, links to outside pages, and so on).

After the Home Page Wizard is run, the Publishing Wizard will allow you to edit and make changes to pages already available.

The Publish Desktop Icon   The Publish desktop icon is placed on the desktop when you first install PWS. If you drag any file to this icon, including HTML files, the Publishing Wizard appears and will allow you to publish the selected document in your Web site. After the drag-and-drop, the Publishing Wizard appears, which is detailed in the section devoted to the Publishing Wizard.

The Personal Web Manager Tour   The Product Tour of Personal Web Manager, which appears in the right-hand pane when you click the Tour icon in the left-hand pane, is a noninteractive summary of PWS's major features.

Advanced Options   The Advanced Options pane (see Figure 25.6) lets you control some of the less commonly used but also important settings of PWS. Someone using PWS in a fairly passive context—that is, setting it up and leaving it alone—will probably not need to use any of the advanced options. However, someone looking to get the most use out of the Web server will want to make themselves familiar with the Advanced Options screen.

FIG. 25.6

The Advanced Options screen.

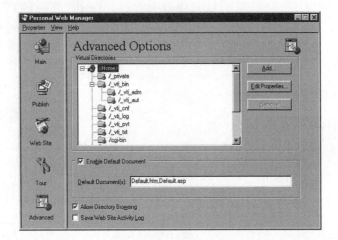

Part

VI

Ch

25

Virtual Directories   Virtual directories are a way of more freely structuring the content on a Web site. Generally, the entire directory structure of a Web site is virtual—that is, there's no direct correspondence between the directory structure on the Web site and the organization of the files on the server. For instance, if you have a Web site that has a virtual directory named /main, the virtual directory system in your Web server will allow you to place the files for /main anywhere on your hard drive. The same goes for any other directory in the entire hierarchy.

The Virtual Directories subsection of the Advanced Options pane lists all the virtual directories currently on the web server.

> **CAUTION**
>
> Do not edit the virtual directory structure unless you're absolutely sure that you know what you're doing. The directories that appear by default in the virtual directory window are created by PWS during the installation process and provide a good deal of the Web site's basic functionality, especially the /SCRIPTS and / IISADMIN directories. Delete them at your own risk.

Next to the Virtual Directories window is a list of buttons that provide control over the Virtual Directories list: Add, Edit Properties, and Remove.

Add   The Add button lets you insert a new virtual directory into the hierarchy below the directory currently highlighted. For instance, if the highlighted directory is /New, the Add button creates a directory underneath /New. To create a virtual directory off the root directory, highlight the <Home> directory by clicking it and then click Add.

Clicking Add brings up the Add Directory window. Consider each entry in the Add Directory window before clicking OK to confirm the new directory.

- *Directory.* This is the physical directory on your hard drive that will be shared. Click the Browse button to open an Explorer-style directory tree and choose the directory you want graphically. Alternatively, if you know the pathname, you can simply type it in the Directory text box.

> **CAUTION**
>
> You can only publish files from your local drive. The Personal Web Manager Publishing Wizard will not publish a file that resides on a network drive. This is for security reasons.

- *Alias.* This is the name that you want to give the virtual directory, as it will be seen on the Web site. Alias names have to be made according to the naming conventions used to construct all URLs: they can only contain upper- or lowercase alphanumeric characters, underscores, or dashes—no spaces or backslashes.

Edit Properties   The Edit Properties button lets you bring up the properties of a virtual directory, which are the same as in the Add Directory window, and change them. To make changes to a virtual directory's properties, click on the virtual directory to highlight it and then click the Edit Properties button.

Remove   The Remove button deletes the selected virtual directory. As with Add and Edit, a directory is deleted by clicking the directory first to highlight it and then clicking the Remove button.

Access   The Access subsection of the Add Directory window controls how you want to re-strict or allow access to a given virtual directory.

- *Read.* Allows users to fetch documents from that directory and read them.
- *Execute.* Allows users or the Web server to run executables in that directory.

■ *Scripts*. Allows a script engine—such as a CGI program—to run in this directory without having Execute permission set. Use Script permission for directories that contain ASP scripts, Internet Database Connector (IDC) scripts, or other scripts. Script permission is safer than Execute permission because you can limit the applications that can be run in the directory.

CAUTION

Don't set Execute or even Scripts on a directory unless you're absolutely sure that the executables you're providing are set up properly and cannot be used to harm your computer. For safety's sake, never set both Read and Execute permissions on any directory.

Click OK to finalize the settings and set up the new virtual directory, or Cancel to bail out.

CAUTION

Never delete any directories created by the PWS setup process. These include any directories that start with the letters IIS or MS, and the /SCRIPTS and /WEBPUB directories. PWS needs all these directories for internal management.

Enable Default Document   The Enable Default Document check box lets you allow PWS to automatically display a document (you provide the name) whenever the user browses a directory without providing a specific document name. By default, this is set to Default.htm and Default.asp (for Active Server Pages). Therefore, if you provided a file named Default.htm into a virtual directory named /Sub, a user who asked for just the /Sub directory without specifying a file would get whatever was in Default.htm. Default documents are enabled by default.

Default documents are a powerful way to control how content is delivered in your Web site. The root virtual directory, which is described as <Home> in the Virtual Directories list, contains a Default.htm file that can be edited freely by the user. This will change the information automatically delivered to a user when she asks for your Web site without specifying a directory or document name.

If you deselect the Enable Default Document check box, then PWS will not deliver the default document in any directory. This change is global and cannot be performed on a directory-by-directory basis. This should generally only be done in rare circumstances.

N O T E   Some Web site software programs use Index.htm rather than Default.htm as the default document. O'Reilly's WebSite is one such program. If you are transporting a Web site from a server that used such software, you will either have to rename all Index.htm files to Default.htm (and rename all corresponding links within pages), or change the default document to Index.htm. Keep in mind that changing the default document name will cause some preinstalled PWS functions, such as the Publishing Wizard, to malfunction. ■

Allow Directory Browsing   The Allow Directory Browsing check box, when enabled, allows users to look at the contents of a directory in the Web site by simply providing the pathname. If no default document is in that directory, or if default documents have been turned off, then the entire contents of the directory are listed, with each filename hyperlinked (see Figure 25.7). This is useful if you want to publish entire directories of files quickly. Directory browsing is disabled by default.

FIG. 25.7

A browsed directory, with files.

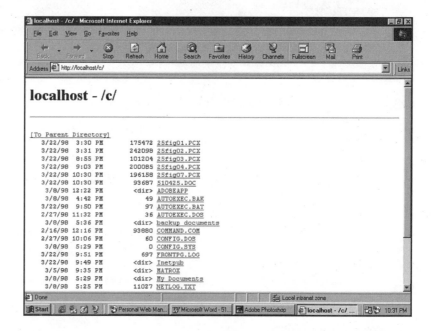

> **CAUTION**
>
> Allowing directory browsing can be dangerous. If you allow unrestricted access to the contents of a directory that might contain sensitive information, you are inviting trouble. Don't enable directory browsing unless you've confirmed that everything being published through the Web site is intended for unrestricted use.

Save Web Site Activity Log   Enabling the Save Web Site Activity Log check box causes all Web site activity—requests from the outside, files sent, the IP addresses of Web site users—to be logged to a file. This is a powerful alternative way of evaluating usage, aside from the built-in usage charting. Logs are saved to the \System\LogFile\W3spc1 directory. After each month of activity, a new log is started. Logs are written in the NCSA log file format and can be viewed in any text editor. Logging is disabled by default.

Getting the Most out of Personal Web Server

Here are several suggestions for intelligent usage, optimizing performance, and getting the most out of PWS in general.

Defragment the Server System Frequently

Any computer used as a Web server is going to experience a lot of disk activity. Use the Task Scheduler to set the system to be defragmented at least once a week. Also, if the machine you're running PWS on is being used primarily as a Web server and not much else, use the Application Launch Accelerator in the Disk Defragmenter to place PWS and its associated files near the front of the disk for faster access.

Use the Activity Logs to Determine Better Usage Policy

Use the quick-glance usage charts and the activity logs to get a better idea of when the peak times for traffic to the Web site appear. If the machine is being used for more than just Web services, you can make a standing policy to keep local users off the Web server during peak hours.

Use PWS as a "Proving Ground" for a Web Site

One of the best uses for PWS is to provide a localized way of testing a Web site before deploying it for real. If you use PWS in conjunction with a Web publishing tool such as Microsoft FrontPage, you can leverage a good deal of PWS's power in testing everything from static pages to dynamic content, including databases and Active Server Pages.

Part
VI

Ch
25

> **CAUTION**
>
> Web sites tested with PWS should be double-checked for correctness if they are to be deployed on a server that does not use a Microsoft-variety Web server. Static pages will generally not be a problem, but anything that uses even simple executables, such as CGI scripts, should be written in as close to a platform-neutral manner as possible. Also make sure that the way you have the directories that hold your CGI executables locally mirrors the way that CGI is executed on the server. Contact your Web hosting company for details on how to best accomplish this.

Using Personal Web Server on the Net Full Time

One of the best things about Personal Web Server is its cost-effectiveness. It enables an ordinary desktop computer to serve Web pages to the Internet on any network backbone. This makes it possible for someone to use his desktop computer to create a World Wide Web site from nothing more sophisticated than his existing Internet dial-up account.

Until recently, this wasn't practical for one reason. Most Internet service providers, or ISPs, use "dynamic IP" for their dial-up clients. This means that every time someone dials in and connects to the Internet, he is assigned one of a pool of IP numbers specifically reserved by the ISP for dial-up clients. Unfortunately, this means that users rarely get the same IP address twice when they dial in. This makes it impossible to do reliable full-time hosting of a Web site through a dial-up connection because a domain name can't be given to a dynamic IP address.

There have been some intermediate solutions to this problem. For instance, there are many shareware programs that, upon connection, determine your current IP number and post it to a Web page, FTP site, or even an IRC channel. But this still requires that someone know where to look to get the IP address and can be more trouble than it's worth.

Now there is a more reliable solution to this problem. There are companies that, for a fee, will allow you to assign your dynamic IP address to a subdomain machine in their domain, such as "mycomputer.dynamic.net". This isn't as impressive as a top-level domain name like "www.mycomputer.com", but it makes it many times easier for you to create and maintain a presence on the Web and attract continuing visitors to your site. To make this feasible, the user downloads and installs a program that notifies the dynamic IP host every time the computer gets a new IP address (that is, every time it dials in). The clients themselves are generally small and unobtrusive.

There are disadvantages to doing this. One is low bandwidth because the fastest "pipe" that a dial-up connection can currently offer is 56KB inbound (and 33.6KB outbound). The other disadvantage is that it requires a phone line to be dedicated to the computer continually and should be used in an area where there is either no charge for call time (only per-call charges), or where local calls are not charged. Still, if you're not planning to serve out anything more demanding than text pages and the occasional graphic, this is a good option to investigate. For instance, nonprofit organizations and information clearinghouses might want to investigate this option because it provides some of the best results for the least expense.

As of this writing, there are two major providers of dynamic IP hosting—Monolith Internet and DynIP.com.

Monolith Internet

One of the most popular dynamic IP hosts, Monolith Internet (`http://members.ml.org/`) provides a dynamic IP hosting project, named DynDNS, at no charge. Monolith is subsidized by funds from other projects, which allows it to provide DynDNS for free.

Monolith hosts all dynamic IP clients from a subdomain called `dyn.ml.org`. Therefore, if your machine is named `myserver`, your URL would be `myserver.dyn.ml.org`.

Many people like Monolith for its openness and user-friendliness. Monolith provides the technical details of its service online, which makes it easy to write a client program to update the DynDNS IP address database. Many people have written clients for Monolith, not just for Windows but for many other OSes as well.

Because Monolith is a volunteer and not-for-profit project, its services are occasionally less dependable than a commercial service like DynIP.com. However, the fact that it's free and quite dependable the vast majority of the time more than makes up for it.

The best Monolith client for Windows 95, 98, and NT is generally considered to be DynamoDNS, a shareware program by Rage Creations, and is available through Monolith's own Web site as well. It features a wealth of options, is extremely flexible, and can be set to work with one or more modems at a time, if you use line pooling or ISDN.

DynIP.com

DynIP.com, a division of CanWeb Internet Services, Ltd., is another service that provides dynamic IP hosting, but for a price. DynIP.com will host a dynamic IP address for $19.95 a year, with a 30-day free trial period. DynIP.com also allows you to look up other users online through its Web site.

DynIP.com also has one other drawback as compared to Monolith: you are required to use its client software. Fortunately, it has very good clients for Windows, Macintosh, and even Linux and FreeBSD. ●

Running Your Software on Windows 98

CHAPTER 26

Using Windows 98 Software

by Rob Tidrow

In this chapter

Exploring the Windows 98 Architecture

Before you delve into the nitty-gritty of how applications work with Windows 98, it is important that you understand a few foundation concepts regarding the Windows 98 architecture. As you know, Windows 98 is an operating system. *Operating systems* provide the link between hardware and software. When a software application needs to write a file to the hard disk, print a document, or display something onscreen, the operating system provides these services.

Windows 98 executes software differently, depending on the type of software you are running. Software is divided into three basic categories:

- Applications written for DOS
- Applications written for Windows 3.1 (generally referred to as *16-bit applications*)
- Applications written for Windows 95, Windows 98, and Windows NT (generally referred to as *32-bit applications*)

The Windows 98 application execution environment changes depending on the type of software. The key architectural areas that differ include the Virtual Machine (VM), multitasking, and internal messaging.

Simulating Computer Resources with Virtual Machines

To meet the various needs of each type of software application, Windows 98 creates a fictional computer called a virtual machine. A *virtual machine* is an environment created by the operating system and processor that simulates a full computer's resources. To the software application, the virtual machine appears to be a real computer.

The operating system keeps track of the application needs and hardware resources. Windows 98 determines which resources each application will have access to and when it can have access. All software applications in Windows 98 run in virtual machines (VM).

Each DOS application runs in a separate MS-DOS VM. For example, if you ran a DOS-based version of WordPerfect and a DOS-based version of Lotus 1-2-3, Windows 98 would create two separate MS-DOS VMs, one for each DOS-based program. Providing each DOS application with its own VM is beneficial because most DOS-based programs were created in a single application environment. That is, DOS-based programs usually assume that they are the *only* program executing at any particular point in time. This single-mindedness of DOS applications has been known to cause grief (system hang-ups, sudden reboots, and general protection faults) when running DOS applications under Windows 3.x.

Another benefit of the single DOS VM is that each DOS application is shielded from other DOS applications as well as Windows 3.x and Windows 98-type applications. Thus, a misbehaving DOS, Win16, or Win32 application cannot bring down another DOS application (that is, suspend its execution). The MS-DOS VM insulates the DOS application from other misbehaving programs.

In addition to the MS-DOS VM, Windows 98 creates another virtual machine environment called the System VM. The System VM executes the following:

- System services
- 16-bit applications
- 32-bit applications

The system services, such as the *kernel* (which is the core program of the operating system), graphics, and Windows management execute in a separate area (memory address). Each Windows 98 32-bit application executes in its own separate memory address. This design prevents 32-bit applications from interfering with other currently executing 32-bit, 16-bit, or DOS applications.

However, the 16-bit Windows applications all run in the same memory address within the System VM. This design aspect of the Windows 98 architecture was done to maintain downward compatibility with the old Windows 3.x 16-bit applications. So although Windows 98 is compatible with the older Windows 3.x applications, Windows 98 doesn't offer any better protection against misbehaving 16-bit applications than did Windows 3.x. That is, a misbehaving 16-bit application can still bring down all currently executing 16-bit applications (and can crash Windows 98 at times).

Multitasking Your Applications

Running multiple programs at the same time is called *multitasking*. Windows 98 provides a multitasking feature that enables multiple applications to run concurrently by sharing processor cycles. A *processor cycle* is a time slice that the operating system gives a program so that the program can use the CPU, or central processing unit. In Windows 98, this enables you to print a document while sending email and editing a spreadsheet at the same time. Under the PC cover, all three applications are sharing CPU time, one slice at a time.

First, you need to familiarize yourself with some terms:

- A *process* is an executing application.
- A *thread* is a unit of execution within a process, such as one task within a process.

N O T E Windows 98 supports multitasking on one microprocessor. Windows 98 doesn't support *Symmetric Multiprocessing* (SMP), which enables the use of multiple microprocessors within one PC. Windows NT and OS/2 Warp do support SMP. ■

In Windows 98, each executing DOS and Windows application is a single process. For example, if you have Word for Windows 97, Paradox for DOS, and Lotus 1-2-3 for Windows 3.x running, the CPU is handling three processes (in addition to the operating system work). Within a process, Windows 98 allows 32-bit applications to schedule individual threads of execution. This is called *multithreaded processing*.

How an application multitasks depends on the type of application (DOS, 16-bit, or 32-bit). For DOS and 32-bit applications, Windows 98 uses *preemptive multitasking*. In preemptive multitasking, each thread is executed for a preset time period, or until another thread with a higher priority is ready to execute. The Windows 98 Task Scheduler manages multitasking and ensures that no one application monopolizes the processor. At any time, the operating system can *preempt* (take control away from) an application and hand the system resources to another application with a higher priority task.

For Windows 3.x (16-bit) applications, Windows 98 uses a *cooperative multitasking* system. In cooperative multitasking, the program (rather than the operating system) is in control of CPU scheduling. Although programs should yield to the operating system after a reasonable amount of time, we have all encountered the Windows 3.x program that fails to return control of the system resources back to the operating system and eventually locks up the entire system. Windows 98 uses the less reliable cooperative multitasking model to provide compatibility with existing 16-bit Windows 3.x programs.

For Windows 98 (32-bit) applications that choose to schedule their own threads of execution (multithreaded processing), Windows 98 again uses the cooperative multitasking method. Up to 32 levels of priority can be assigned.

How Applications Communicate

Applications communicate with the operating system via the Windows 98 messaging system. The *messaging system* passes information between the hardware, the applications, and the operating system. For example, when a user moves the mouse, Windows 98 converts the hardware interrupt into a message that is sent to the appropriate message queue.

> **CAUTION**
>
> Although each DOS and 32-bit application has its own message queue, all the 16-bit applications share one common message queue. Thus, if a 16-bit application hangs, all running 16-bit applications must wait until the hung application is cleared. If the hung application is not cleared, all 16-bit applications might lose their messages.

Understanding Windows 98 Software Features

Since the release of Windows 95 in the fall of 1995, many applications have been released that are written for Windows 95, including business applications, games, multimedia applications, and graphics and design packages. In many cases, applications released for previous versions of Windows, the Macintosh, MS-DOS, or IBM's OS/2 have been upgraded for Windows 95. These same applications can run on Windows 98 just as they did on Windows 95. This means that if you've standardized on an application or suite of applications to run under Windows 95, you can often find an upgrade product that runs well under Windows 98.

The following sections describe features and benefits of Windows 98 applications.

Reviewing the Designed for Windows Logo Program

If you are upgrading to Windows 98 from Windows 95, you probably have purchased applications that adhere to the Designed for Windows 95 *Logo* program. This logo is used to let consumers know that an application is designed to take full advantage of the Windows 98 environment. Likewise, each Windows 98 application must adhere to specific guidelines issued by Microsoft to receive the authorization to place the Designed for Microsoft Windows logo on its packaging.

In March 1997, Microsoft released the Designed for Windows NT and Windows 95 Logo program, which includes specifications for applications to run on both Windows 95 and Windows NT. Applications designed to run on Windows 98, must adhere to these same guidelines, plus additional ones designed to take advantage of new features in Windows 98. The following list describes some of the Windows 98 logo requirements:

- *Support long filenames and Universal Naming Convention (UNC).* Windows 98 applications must support UNC, which enables users to set up logical connections to network resources. Support of UNC makes applications work better in network environments. In addition, Windows 98 applications must support filenames that have up to 255 characters. Previous versions of Windows (prior to Windows 95) and MS-DOS were restricted to filenames of eight characters, with a three-character extension (this is referred to as the *8.3 naming convention*). Along with the long filename, Windows 98 also saves a truncated filename that uses the 8.3 convention for compatibility with 16-bit applications. A Microsoft Excel for Windows 98 file called YEARLY_TOTALS.XLS, for instance, might be truncated as YEARLY~1.XLS. Files also are truncated if you start an MS-DOS session under Windows 98 and open a file created with a long filename.

- *Adhere to the Windows user interface style guidelines.* To make applications easier to learn and use, Microsoft published the *User Interface Style Guidelines 4* for application developers to follow in creating their user interfaces. These guidelines describe how each Windows 98 application should look so that a common look and feel is consistent between all Windows 98 applications.

- *Use the Win32 API.* Windows 98 applications must use the Win32 API, which is the architecture layer between applications and the Windows 98 subsystem. The Win32 API enables Windows 98 applications to take advantage of Windows 98's preemptive multitasking, memory address allocations, and multithreaded processing features.

- *Include install and uninstall wizards.* Windows 98 applications must provide an installation wizard that guides users through the process of installing the application. In many cases, the install wizard provides options to install all or parts of the application. Windows 98 applications must also provide an uninstall feature that helps users remove all components of the application, as well as removing listings in the Windows 98 Registry. This helps users maintain their systems and keep them clean of unwanted files and Registry settings.

Part VII
Ch 26

■ *Include Object Linking and Embedding (OLE) support.* Windows 98 applications must be OLE-compliant, to help applications communicate and share information. OLE enables you to create a file in one application (say a table in a database application) and then reuse that information in another file in another application (such as including the database table in a document created by a word processor). This provides an environment in which users can quickly and easily recycle information without re-creating it each time a new document is created. Applications must also support drag-and-drop functionality.

■ *Support for the Internet.* Windows 98 applications that have ActiveX controls must have digital signatures for the controls. This means that users of the application will know who has developed the ActiveX control. Microsoft recommends developers obtain Authenticode digital signatures from the Web site at `http://www.microsoft.com/workshop/prog/security/authcode/codesign-f.htm`.

N O T E   To find out more about the Windows logo requirements, visit the Designed for Microsoft Windows Logo Programs Web site at `http://www.microsoft.com/windows/thirdparty/winlogo`. When an application developer submits an application to be tested for compliance to the Windows 98 logo requirements, Microsoft does not do the testing. Rather, a third-party, independent testing laboratory at Veritest, Incorporated (`http://www.veritest.com/microsoft.htm`) conducts the testing.

You also can learn about the PC 98 System Design Guide, a related program headed by Microsoft and Intel, that presents guidelines for Windows 98 and Windows NT Workstation 5 computers. Visit `http://www.microsoft.com/hwdev/pc98.htm` to see the guidelines for designing hardware devices for these operating systems. ■

Reviewing the Zero Administration Windows (ZAW) Initiative

In a move to make network computing easier, Microsoft released the Zero Administration Windows (ZAW) Initiative in late 1996. ZAW attempts to reduce the cost of ownership by lessening the burden of administrating desktop operating systems and applications by automating many tasks, such as automatic updates of operating systems and automated application installation. The Windows Update feature in Windows 98 is an example of ZAW (see Chapter 2, "Installing Windows 98 on a Desktop and Laptop"). Administrators will have the capability to "lock-down" users' configuration settings, eliminating inadvertent system changes on the part of the user. In addition, ZAW provides users the flexibility of roaming between PCs without requiring applications and files to be transferred from one computer to another. Instead, applications, operating system properties, and files reside on a centralized network server.

N O T E   You can read more about ZAW on the Web at `http://www.microsoft.com/windows/platform/info/zawmb.htm`. Developers and administrators interested in implementing ZAW should get the Zero Administration Kit from Microsoft. You can find information on how to download the kit from the Get the Zero Administration Kit Today Web page at `http://www.microsoft.com/windows/zak/getzak.htm`. ■

Examining Benefits of Windows 98 Software

For many users and organizations, upgrading to Windows 98 applications means investing a large amount of time and economic resources. Before investing in new versions, you might want to consider some of the advantages of using Windows 98 applications on Windows 98. The following are some key advantages of Windows 98 software:

■ 32-bit processing

■ Preemptive multitasking

■ Multithreaded processing

■ Easy maintenance

In the following sections, you learn how each feature can save you both time and money.

Fast Processing

The easiest way to understand the difference between 16-bit processing and 32-bit processing is to imagine each as a highway with 16 or 32 lanes. Imagine your data as buses and cars commuting at rush hour. When the traffic is heavy and the heat is on, 32 lanes provide for more throughput, fewer accidents, and less stress on system resources. In your computer, the Windows 98 operating system is already running at 32-bit speed. The more 32-bit applications you use, the more work gets done, fewer GPFs occur, and less stress is on the computer resources.

As covered in the beginning of this chapter, DOS applications execute in separate virtual machines (VMs). Windows 3.x (16-bit) applications execute in the System VM in a single address space. Windows 98 (32-bit) applications also run in the System VM but in separate address spaces. This means that if DOS applications crash, they cannot bring down the system, other DOS applications, or other Windows (16- or 32-bit) applications. On the other hand, Windows 3.x (16-bit) applications can bring down other 16-bit applications if they crash running under Windows 98. The fastest, best protection exists for the 32-bit applications, which execute within the 32-bit Windows 98 operating system. Windows 98 (32-bit) applications, however, cannot bring down other 32-bit, 16-bit, or DOS applications if they crash.

Part
VII

Ch
26

Preemptive Multitasking

The 32-bit applications use *preemptive multitasking*, where each thread is executed for a preset time period, or until another thread with a higher priority is ready to execute. The Windows 98 Task Scheduler manages multitasking and ensures that no one application monopolizes the processor. At any time, the operating system can *preempt* (take control away from) an application and hand the CPU to another application with a higher priority task.

This is better than the quirky Windows 3.x (16-bit) applications, which use a cooperative multitasking system in which the program (rather than the operating system) is in control of CPU scheduling. Although programs should yield to the operating system after a reasonable amount of time, we have all encountered the Windows 3.x program that fails to return control and eventually locks up the entire system.

Multithreaded Processing

Windows 98 32-bit applications can take advantage of *multithreaded processing* (schedule their own threads of execution). Multithreaded processing is not available for DOS or Win16 applications. The advantage of multithreading is that each thread can use the same address space as its parent process and provides an environment in which you get to do your work faster. For example, printing a document in Word for Windows 98 is much faster than in Windows 3.1, and you get control of your document back quicker because Word for Windows 98 takes advantage of multithreaded processing for print jobs.

Easier Maintenance

Consolidation of the system initialization and setup files into a single database—which is maintained by the operating system—makes the Win32 platform easier to use. Once consumers move to Win32 and no longer need DOS or Win16 applications, the AUTOEXEC.BAT, CONFIG.SYS, WIN.INI, SYSTEM.INI, and other INI files will no longer be needed. This information is kept in the Registry database and automatically modified as software and hardware is installed, removed, and updated. This feature coupled with the Plug and Play standard makes Windows 98 a self-configuring system.

How Windows Uses the Registry

DOS depended on the AUTOEXEC.BAT and CONFIG.SYS configuration files to initialize and set system parameters on what resources were available and how they should be used. Windows 3.x relied on initialization files (which had a file extension of INI) to tell Windows and Windows applications what resources were available and how to work with those resources.

When Microsoft began designing Windows 95, they identified many problems with these resource setting files. These files were difficult to maintain, often contained remnants of old program setups no longer needed, and usually required user intervention to improve performance. To solve these problems, Windows 95 borrowed a good idea from Windows NT: the Registry. Windows 98 uses the same Registry introduced in Windows 95.

The Registry is a single database that contains system and application execution information. Ultimately, the Registry replaces all INI files as well as AUTOEXEC.BAT and CONFIG.SYS. (Most systems, because of their need to support legacy hardware and device drivers, still use the AUTOEXEC.BAT and CONFIG.SYS files.) The Windows 98 Registry replaces REG.DAT, which was used by Windows 3.1 to store file extension application associations and register OLE applications.

Exploring the Registry

The Windows 98 Registry consists of three data files:

- ▪ *USER.DAT*. Stores user preferences such as the Desktop,
- ▪ *SYSTEM.DAT*. Stores the computer's hardware configurations such as drives, printers, and sound card settings.

■ *POLICY.POL*. Stores administrative policies set up on a network server. (POLICY.POL is not part of the Registry if System Policies are not invoked.)

Precautions are taken to protect these data files. First, the Registry data is kept in binary format, so that the files cannot be read or edited by a regular text editor. Second, the file attributes are set to read-only, hidden, system files. This prevents accidental deletion.

When you first install Windows 98, the setup program creates the SYSTEM.DAT file and enters the data regarding installed hardware. If you installed to the Windows 3.x directory, setup copies the data from REG.DAT into the new SYSTEM.DAT file. From then on, whenever you install new hardware or change a configuration, Windows 98 automatically updates the SYSTEM.DAT data file.

You can view the hardware data stored in SYSTEM.DAT by opening the Control Panel folder and selecting System. Figure 26.1 shows the installed devices, as reported by SYSTEM.DAT.

FIG. 26.1

The Device Manager page displays installed devices by type.

Using the Registry Editor

The Registry Editor (REGEDIT) is located in the Windows 98 folder. To run the Registry Editor, choose Run from the Start menu, type **REGEDIT**, and press Enter. Figure 26.2 shows the Registry Editor and data for My Computer.

Part
VII

Ch
26

FIG. 26.2
The Registry Editor stores information about your computer.

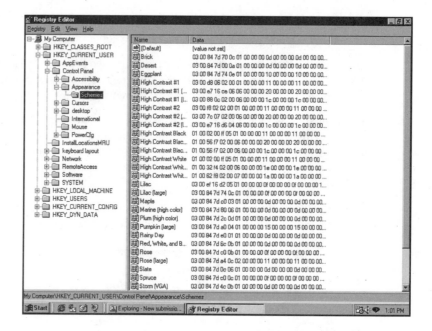

CAUTION

Before you open the Registry Editor and start modifying the settings, be sure that you understand what you are changing and why. If the modification you want can be effected by using Control Panel or by setting some other property, make the change there. Avoid using the Registry Editor unless it is absolutely necessary.

Microsoft advises that you don't use the REGEDIT utility unless you are on the phone with one of their technicians. That's why they didn't include a shortcut or program item for it by default—you have to manually create one.

Incorrect edits to the Registry could prevent Windows from working properly and result in a loss of critical data.

Any time you edit the Registry, you should make a backup copy of the SYSTEM.DAT, SYSTEM.DA0, USER.DAT, and USER.DA0 files in case you experience problems with Windows 98 or an application after modifying the Registry. Depending on the size of these files, you might be able to back them up to floppy disks. In some cases, these files can become too large to store on one floppy disk, requiring that you back up the files on to a tape backup or other device (such as an Iomega Zip drive).

The Registry is organized into matched keys and values. The keys are listed on the left pane as a hierarchical tree. As you double-click items and drill-down within branches, the values appear in the right pane. To change a key's value, right-click the value in the right pane. The Registry Editor then displays an object menu: Modify, Delete, and Rename. Figure 26.3 shows the Edit Binary Value dialog box for a Registry value.

FIG. 26.3
Enter or edit the Value Data in the Edit Binary Value dialog box.

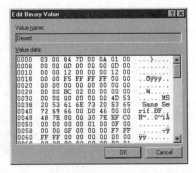

As you change entries, the Registry Editor automatically changes the applicable database file (DAT). However, many changes don't take effect until you restart Windows 98.

N O T E Windows 98 maintains backup copies of the Registry data in the Windows 98 folder. Windows uses this data during the startup process if the previous shutdown process was interrupted or Windows was shut down improperly. The backup files SYSTEM.DA0 and USER.DA0 are used by Windows 98 in the event that the actual DAT files become corrupt. ▪

Using the Remote Registry Service

To edit Registry files on a remote computer, run REGEDIT.EXE and choose Registry, Connect. You also must have the Microsoft Remote Registry Service installed on all remote computers. To install this, use the following steps:

1. Open Control Panel and double-click the Network application.
2. Click the Add button to display the Select Network Component Type dialog box.
3. Double-click the Service component to display the Select Network Service dialog box.
4. Click the Have Disk button to display the Install from Disk dialog box.
5. Click the Browse button and locate the \ADMIN\NETTOOLS\REMOTREG folder on the Windows 98 CD-ROM. Click OK to display the Select Network Service dialog box.
6. Select the Microsoft Remote Registry option in the Models listbox and click OK. This installs the Remote Registry Service on the system. Do this on each computer you want to connect to via a remote connection.

Handling Application Crashes

Sometimes you might experience system crashes or *GPFs* (*General Protection Faults*) running applications under Windows 98. Although Windows 98 is designed to handle GPFs much more efficiently than Windows 3.x, you might have situations in which your entire system locks up, causing you to reboot the computer. Under normal situations, Windows 98 applications that experience GPFs only require that you close the offending application, enabling you to continue running Windows 98 and other applications you may be running.

Part
VII

Ch
26

One reason for applications to behave in a nonstandard way (that is, applications that lock up the entire system) is because of missing, outdated, or corrupted Dynamic Link Libraries (DLLs). You can fix this problem by reinstalling the application or querying the manufacturer for any known bugs about the application.

Another reason why a Windows 98 application fails to perform as designed is because of a known bug in Windows 98. To search for known bugs published by Microsoft, use the Microsoft Knowledge Base. This is available from several sources, including on the World Wide Web at http://www.microsoft.com/kb/default.asp. You can get the Knowledge Base on CD-ROM as well by subscribing to the Microsoft Developer Network (1-800-759-5475).

To handle a GPF, press Ctrl+Alt+Del. This displays the Close Program dialog box, which shows the status of all running applications including the application that crashed. Select the offending application and click End Task. The application closes. If, when you display the Close Program dialog box, an application is still executing or if Windows still thinks an application is still executing, another dialog box displays telling you that the application is still executing and that you need to wait until it's finished or end it prematurely. Click End Task.

Understanding File Systems and Modifying Their Properties

Before you start fine-tuning the file system for running your applications, you might want to explore the design of the Windows 98 file system. Operating systems use a file system to organize files, store files, and control how files are named. Windows 98 continues to use the DOS *file allocation table* (FAT) file system as its default file system. However, Windows 98 uses the *installable file system* (*IFS*) introduced in Windows 95. IFS is a program that provides an interface between the application file requests and various supported file systems.

Windows 98 ships with the following installable file systems:

- *Virtual file allocation table* (VFAT)
- *CD-ROM file system* (CDFS)
- Network Redirector

In addition to these supported file systems, vendors may create and add their own installable file systems. A vendor might create an installable file system to enable users to access and work with UNIX or Apple files, for example.

The IFS Manager can work with *Application Programming Interface* (API) calls from Win32 applications and interrupt 21 (INT 21H) calls generated by Win16 or DOS applications. The file-system design in Windows 98 supports up to 32 layers from the *input/output subsystem* (IOS) down to the hardware level. Each layer has defined interfaces with the layers above and below. This enables each component to cooperate with its neighbors.

VFAT

The FAT file system was developed to work with DOS. A clear advantage of FAT is that a drive formatted for FAT can be read by DOS, Windows NT, Windows 98, and OS/2. However, the DOS FAT file system has the following limitations:

- Filenames are limited to eight characters plus a three-character extension.
- Every file access from a Windows-based application requires the system to switch to 8086 mode to execute DOS code, which slows down performance.
- The use of the INT 21H interrupt as the sole interface to every file-system function causes conflicts between TSRs, disk caching, disk compression, and network systems.

VFAT is a 32-bit virtualized FAT file system. The VFAT.VXD *file system driver* (FSD) controls this file system and uses 32-bit code for all file access. VFAT is a protected-mode implementation of the FAT file system. The VFAT system supports long filenames (up to 255 characters), eliminates the over-reliance on INT 21H, uses 32-bit processing, and allows multiple, concurrent threads to execute file system code.

CDFS

The CDFS replaces MSCDEX TRS, which is used to support most CD-ROM devices. CDFS is a 32-bit protected mode ISO 9660–compliant CD-ROM file system. With Windows 98, CD-ROMs larger than 4GB are supported using the CDFS.VXD and CDVSD.VXD drivers. Applications send file requests to the CDFS, which handles the request and passes it to the IOS. The IOS routes the request to the *type-specific driver* (TSD), which converts the logical request to a physical request. From there, a special SCSI translator sends the request to the SCSI port driver and then to the Miniport driver.

Network Redirector

The Network Redirector installable file system is a 32-bit protected mode VXD responsible for implementing the structure of a remote file system. When an application sends or receives data from a remote device, it sends a call to the Redirector. The Redirector communicates with the network via the protocol driver. Windows 98 supports two kinds of redirectors:

- Windows Networking (SMB over NetBEUI protocol)
- Microsoft Client for NetWare (NCP protocol)

Using FAT32

Windows 98 includes a new 32-bit file system called FAT32. FAT32 first was released in an *original equipment manufacturer* (OEM) release of Windows 95 called the Windows 95 *OEM Service Release 2* (OSR-2). The FAT32 file system can support disk partitions in excess of 2GB. The new FAT32 file system also uses 4KB clusters for partitions of up to 8GB. This improves on the old MS-DOS FAT system that uses 32KB clusters, which results in a large amount of wasted hard drive space for small files (in essence, if you have a file that is only 1KB, it consumes 32KB of your hard drive).

Part

VII

Ch

26

One downside to the 4KB cluster size is if you work with mostly very large files, the system works longer to read all these smaller clusters compared to the time it takes to read larger clusters. Overall, however, your system should see a performance gain when converting to the FAT32 system.

You can set up your file system as a FAT32 file system by running the Drive Converter (FAT32) utility. The conversion process can take several hours to complete, during which time you cannot use your system. When you are ready to convert your file system to FAT32, use the following steps:

1. Choose Start, Programs, Accessories, System Tools, Drive Converter (FAT32). The Drive Converter (FAT32) Wizard appears.

2. Click Next.

3. Select the drive you want to convert, as shown in Figure 26.4.

FIG. 26.4
Use the Drives field to select the drive you want to convert to FAT32.

4. Click Next. A dialog box appears, telling you that some operating systems will not be able to access a FAT32 drive.

5. Click OK. Drive Converter looks for applications that may conflict with a FAT32 file system.

6. Click Next. You can create a backup of your files before setting up FAT32 on your system. This ensures that you can revert to these backed up files in case FAT32 conversion inadvertently corrupts your drive.

7. Click Create Backup to start Microsoft Backup. Otherwise, click Next. Windows needs to restart your computer in MS-DOS mode to begin the conversion process.

8. Click Next to continue.

Working with Long Filenames

Whereas DOS limited users to filenames that were up to eight characters plus a three-character extension (8.3), Windows 98 supports the use of *long filenames* (LFNs). The long filenames follow these filenaming rules:

- Filenames can contain up to 255 characters, including extensions.
- Uppercase and lowercase are preserved but are not case-sensitive.
- Filename characters can be any characters (including spaces), except for the following:
  ? / \ " : < > | *

N O T E   An *exabyte* is a billion gigabytes. A stack of 3 1/2-inch disks equal to the capacity of 16EB would be 2,300 times the distance from the earth to the moon. ■

Preserving Long Filenames

Windows 98 maintains FAT 8.3 filenames for each long filename. A file named `East Coast Sales.EXCEL`, for example, would have a FAT name of `EASTCOAS.EXC`. By doing so, Windows 98 ensures that a program designed for FAT filenames can access and work with files created under Windows 98. Long filenames also provide additional information about a file, such as the date of the last file modification.

The following rules are used by the Windows 98 file system to convert long filenames into the DOS 8.3 format:

- Remove special characters (such as spaces).
- If unique, use the first eight characters of the LFN.
- If not unique, use the first six characters, a tilde (~), and a number (for example, `EASTCO~2.EXC`).
- For the extension, use the first three characters following the last period.

If you have three files in Windows 98 called `East coast budget.xls`, `East coast expenses.xls`, and `East coast sales.xls`, for example, their 8.3 DOS filenames become `EASTCO~1.XLS`, `EASTCO~2.XLS`, and `EASTCO~3.XLS`, respectively.

Note that 8.3 filenames do not preserve the case of characters (all uppercase).

Several problems arise when using a file in a Windows 98 application and in a non-LFN–aware application:

- Changing the LFN filename or copying the LFN to a new name while in a non-LFN application deletes the long filename.
- LFNs are lost if you modify a Windows 98 document in a 16-bit application.
- Files created according to the 8.3 filenaming rules have an LFN that is the same as the 8.3 filename.
- Files created according to the LFN filenaming rules have a different 8.3 filename (as outlined in the prior rules).
- LFNs use a previously reserved area of the FAT. DOS utilities that also use this area of FAT may damage this section of FAT.

Part
VII

Ch
26

■ LFNs are not supported on Novell NetWare servers unless you have IBM OS/2 Namespaces running on the server.

N O T E The Windows NT 4.0, Windows 95, and Windows 98 long filename schemes are compatible. However, Windows NT 3.5 and earlier versions do not support LFNs in the FAT file system. Windows 98 supports LFNs in FAT and FAT32.

Also, the OS/2 LFN naming scheme is not compatible with Windows 98 LFNs. ■

CAUTION

Do not use disk or backup utilities that are not aware of long filenames. If you need to use a backup/restore utility that does not support LFNs, Microsoft supplies a utility called *Long File Name Backup* (LFNBK) that preserves the LFNs. (This comes on the Windows 98 CD-ROM, or you can contact Microsoft for this utility.) You also can download a copy of this file from the Microsoft Web site at

http://www.microsoft.com/windows95

Modifying File-System Properties

Windows 98 automatically sets file-system properties to optimize the performance based on the current configuration. However, at times, you might need to set a certain property or become aware of a unique need to boost performance. The System Properties dialog box, which is accessed through the Control Panel, enables you to view and set disk and CD-ROM file-system properties.

To set file-system properties, follow these steps:

1. Choose Start, Settings, Control Panel.

2. Double-click the System icon.

3. Select the Performance page in the System Properties dialog box that appears.

4. Click File System. The File System Properties dialog box appears, as shown in Figure 26.5.

FIG. 26.5

Increase the read-ahead optimization to speed up performance.

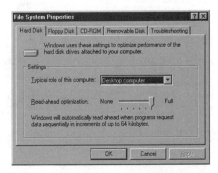

5. Set the desired options.

6. Select the CD-ROM page and set CD-ROM properties as desired, as shown in Figure 26.6. You learn more about these options in Chapter 12, "Installing and Configuring CD-ROM and DVD Drives."

FIG. 26.6

To optimize the CD-ROM performance, select the correct access pattern.

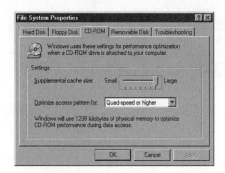

7. Choose OK twice to implement the changes the next time Windows 98 loads.

Troubleshooting the File System

If an application does not respond properly to the Windows 98 file system, you can use the File System Troubleshooter to detect the cause of the problem. Using the Troubleshooter, you can disable the following Windows 98 file-system features:

- File sharing and locking
- Preservation of long filenames in non-LFN programs
- Protect-mode, hard drive interrupt handler
- 32-bit, protect-mode disk drivers
- Write-behind caching for all drives

To start the File System Troubleshooter, follow these steps:

1. Choose Start, Settings, Control Panel.
2. Double-click the System icon.
3. In the System Properties dialog box that appears, select the Performance page.
4. Choose File System.
5. Select the Troubleshooting page, as shown in Figure 26.7.
6. Select the setting to be tested.
7. Click OK twice to test the setting.

Part
VII

Ch
26

FIG. 26.7

Use the Troubleshooting page to disable file-system properties when trying to locate a problem.

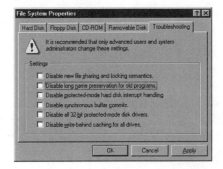

CHAPTER 27

Using DOS Software

by Rob Tidrow

In this chapter

Running DOS Applications in Windows 98

Before Windows became the standard operating system on the majority of personal computers, MS-DOS was the standard. Because of this, thousands of applications were created to run specifically under MS-DOS. Many users want to make sure their old DOS programs still will run under Windows 98. In many cases, Windows 98 will run older DOS programs, and in some cases, Windows 98 will run them more efficiently than in a standalone DOS environment.

On a Windows 98 computer, DOS is available in two flavors:

- DOS session (multitasking)
- MS-DOS mode (single task, real mode)

The DOS session starts from within Windows 98. You can switch the DOS session between a windowed view and a full-screen view. From a DOS session, you can switch back to Windows 98 and to any other currently running application. Windows 98 is a multitasking environment, and each DOS session runs in a separate MS-DOS *virtual machine* (VM). In a windowed DOS session, Windows 98 even provides a toolbar for quick access to cut, copy, and paste operations; property pages; and fonts. The property pages are similar to the old Windows 3.*x* PIF files. The property pages for DOS sessions enable you to control the MS-DOS VM and what the DOS program sees. (You can even hide Windows 98 from the DOS program!)

▶ **See** "Using Windows 98 Software" **p. 471**

You can start MS-DOS mode from within Windows 98, or you can access MS-DOS during bootup. *MS-DOS mode* (also known as *real mode*) is a single-task environment. No other programs are in memory, so you cannot switch over to another program. Windows 98 leaves a small footprint of itself in memory so that when you close your DOS application (or type **exit** at the DOS prompt), Windows 98 can load automatically. In MS-DOS mode, you cannot cut, copy, or paste to the Clipboard. The DOS application has complete control of the CPU and all resources.

For DOS programs that you start from MS-DOS mode, you can specify certain properties. Properties that require Windows 98, such as fonts, memory management, and screen display, are not available. However, you can specify a custom AUTOEXEC.BAT and CONFIG.SYS to be run for each DOS program running in MS-DOS mode (no more creating separate boot disks for finicky DOS programs that require special treatment).

Displaying the DOS Command Prompt

Although most of the time Windows 98 provides tools for your computing needs via a user-friendly graphical interface, there might be times when you need to or (for us old-timers) want to access DOS. You don't need to exit Windows 98 to access the DOS command prompt or to issue a DOS command.

 To start a Windows 98 program from the command prompt, type the new DOS command **START** followed by the program name.

TIP A handy utility available with Microsoft Power Toys is DOS Prompt Here 1.1. This utility enables you to start an MS-DOS prompt from any folder by clicking a button from the folder of your choice. Download this utility by visiting

> http://www.microsoft.com/windows95

and clicking the Free Software button on the left side of the Web page. Then select Shareware and Utilities from the fly-out menu. Next, click the Power Toys hyperlink. You can download Command Prompt Here 1.1 by itself (about 7KB) or with the Power Toys Set (about 204KB).

To display the DOS command prompt from within Windows 98, follow these steps:

1. Choose Start, Programs, MS-DOS Prompt. By default, Windows 98 opens a windowed DOS session (see Figure 27.1).

FIG. 27.1
The windowed DOS session provides you with more control over the DOS environment.

2. If you prefer working in a DOS full-screen session, press Alt+Enter (see Figure 27.2).
3. If you need to switch between the DOS session and Windows 98, press Alt+Tab.
4. When you finish, type **exit** at the DOS prompt to close the DOS session. If you are working in a DOS Window, click the close (x) button in the upper-right corner.

CAUTION

Be careful when using the x button to close a windowed DOS session. You could lose data in any open DOS applications or data files that contain unsaved data, or your files could be corrupted as a result. Always close data files and end DOS applications before using the x button.

N O T E To display help for a DOS command, type the name of the command you want, followed by a space and **/?**. For example, type **MD /?** to display help text on the Make Directory (MD) command.

Adding the pipe character (|) and the word **MORE** to the end of the statement displays help text one screen at a time, as in this example:

MD /? | MORE

FIG. 27.2

A full-screen DOS session lets you see more onscreen.

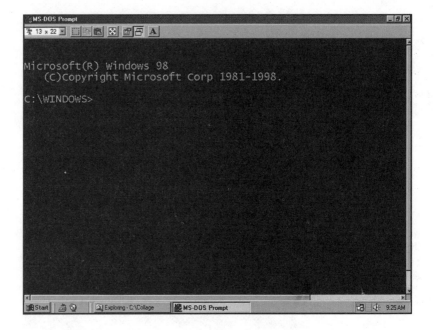

To start the computer at the DOS prompt in MS-DOS mode, follow these steps:

1. Choose Start, Shut Down.

2. Choose Restart the Computer in MS-DOS Mode? A full-screen, single-application DOS prompt appears.

3. When you finish, type **EXIT** to start Windows 98.

N O T E   You also can enter MS-DOS mode when your machine boots up. When the message
Starting Windows 98 appears, press F8 and select Command Prompt Only to boot up
the computer in the real-mode version of DOS. When you finish, type **EXIT** to start Windows 98. ■

Working with DOS Commands

The Windows 98 set of DOS commands is functionally the same as in prior versions of DOS. You can view a list of these commands by opening the \WINDOWS\COMMANDS folder. File-manipulation commands such as COPY, DIR, and RENAME have been enhanced to support long filenames. You can use a long filename that contains spaces, for example, by enclosing the long filename in quotation marks:

```
RENAME eastsale.wk1 "Eastcoast Sales.wk1"
```

> **CAUTION**
>
> Be careful when using long filenames. Although the Windows 98 DOS commands support long filenames, existing DOS and Windows 3.x programs do not. Furthermore, be careful when using a file in Windows 98 with a long filename and then accessing the file in a DOS or Windows 3.x program. Doing so deletes the long filename!
>
> Finally, you can store only 512 files in the root directory when using the FAT file system. Long filenames consume two directory entries, so keep this in mind as you create and add new files to your system.

The DIR command has been enhanced to display a seventh column that shows the long filename. DIR also sports a new command-line switch called verbose: /v. The verbose switch displays additional information, such as file attributes and the last-access-date stamp.

Windows 98 DOS also supports the *Universal Naming Convention* (UNC). UNC makes it easier to refer to and use networked resources such as printers and network folders. (You no longer need to map folders and remember those cryptic addresses.) To copy a file to a shared network folder named Accounting Sales Data, for example, you would issue the following command line:

```
COPY "Eastcoast Sales.wk1" "\\Accounting Sales Data"
```

Many of the DOS commands included in prior versions of DOS are not included in Windows 98 because they no longer are needed. In these cases, Windows 98 provides the features elsewhere. Furthermore, if your computer did not have DOS installed prior to installing Windows 98, you will not have some of the older DOS commands that Windows 98 does not need but leaves in the old DOS folder.

A powerful command included in Windows 98 is the START command. You can use START to launch DOS and Windows programs from the DOS command prompt. (START is not available in MS-DOS mode.) You can use two syntax forms. The first supplies the program name. The second syntax supplies the document name. For the document name to launch the program and display the document, the filename extension must be registered properly:

```
START [options] program [arg...]
START [options] document.ext
```

The options available follow:

/m	Runs the new program minimized (in the background)
/max	Runs the new program maximized (in the foreground)
/r	Runs the new program restored (in the foreground); this is the default
/w	Does not return until the other program exits

Suppose that files with the extension DOC are registered as Word for Windows files. Then issuing the following command loads Word for Windows and the document sales.doc:

```
START sales.doc
```

Part
VII

Ch
27

Using START at the command prompt to load a DOS program actually opens a new MS-DOS VM for that program. If, instead, you type the name of the DOS program without the command START, the DOS program loads in the current MS-DOS VM.

N O T E If you type the DOS command **VER** at the command prompt, the version information that appears is Windows 98. However, DOS programs that ask internally for the DOS version get the number 7. This could cause conflicts with DOS programs that work only for a specific DOS version number. ■

Some DOS commands should *not* be used in Windows 98:

CHKDSK /F	You can run this command at the DOS prompt but not in Windows 98.
FDISK	Avoid running this command at the DOS prompt; it can't be used when Windows 98 is running.
RECOVER	This command exists from an older version of DOS, and it doesn't work well with Windows 98 or at the command prompt.

 T I P To configure the DOS command-line sessions, set file properties for COMMAND.COM, which is located in Window's Command folder.

Starting a DOS Program

Starting a DOS program takes a few more steps than you might be used to, but it does have the advantage of being less cryptic than navigating the DOS prompt and cryptic command lines.

To start a DOS program, follow these steps:

1. Open the My Computer folder.
2. Locate the program file.
3. Double-click the program file.

You also can start a DOS program by using any of the following options:

■ Choose Run from the Start menu.

■ Type the **START** command at a DOS command prompt.

■ Create a shortcut on the desktop or menu.

Working in a DOS Window

When you work in a DOS window, Windows 98 provides you with a very helpful toolbar for easy access to the following features:

■ Copying, cutting, and pasting to and from DOS windows

■ Changing fonts and font sizes

- Switching between exclusive and foreground processing
- Changing property pages without leaving the DOS window

N O T E You cannot paste text into a DOS program when it is running in full-screen mode. ■

 T I P To select text by dragging the cursor over the selection, open the Properties dialog box for the DOS program, select the Misc tab, and click QuickEdit.

To view the toolbar, click the MS-DOS icon in the title bar and click Toolbar.

Configuring DOS Applications

In Windows 3.x, DOS applications were configured by editing a *program information file* (PIF). The PIF file had to be manually created and maintained by the user via the PIF Editor. This was cumbersome at best. Windows 98 automates PIF creation and moves the configuration maintenance into a series of Properties dialog boxes.

When you first start a DOS application, Windows searches for a PIF file with the same name as the executable file. If Windows finds an existing PIF file, Windows uses the program info file file settings. If no PIF file exists yet, Windows uses default settings to control the DOS application. Windows 98 uses a database of known DOS application settings to create the PIF. The PIF files are viewed and maintained via the property pages.

N O T E Windows 98 stores all PIFs in a hidden PIF folder in the Windows 98 directory. This keeps novice users from inadvertently altering the actual PIF files. ■

Displaying DOS Property Pages

You set properties for a DOS program the same way you set properties for any object in Windows 98—by right-clicking the object and choosing Properties. Windows 98 then displays the property pages for the DOS application (see Figure 27.3). DOS program properties are organized into six property pages. You'll learn more about each of the property pages in the following sections.

To display the property pages, follow these steps:

1. Open the My Computer folder, or open Explorer.
2. Locate the DOS file and right-click it.
3. Choose Properties. Windows 98 displays the property pages for that DOS file.

T I P To display property pages while running the DOS program session, press Alt+Spacebar and choose Properties.

Part
VII

Ch
27

FIG. 27.3
You control how DOS programs execute in Windows 98 by setting program properties.

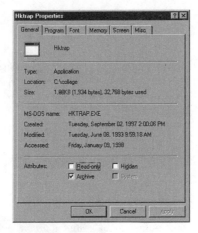

Setting General Properties

The General property page displays the filename, size, location, file type, and other general information (refer to Figure 27.3). The only configuration settings you can change are the file attributes. Changing file attributes here is identical to using the DOS ATTRIB command at a DOS prompt. Table 27.1 describes each file-attribute setting.

Table 27.1   File Attribute Settings

Attribute	Description
Read-Only	Specifies that the file can be read, moved, and copied, but that it cannot be changed or erased.
Archive	Marks a file as having been changed since it was backed up last.
Hidden	Specifies that the file is not displayed in directory listings. Most DOS commands, such as COPY and DEL, won't work on hidden files.
System	Marks a file as belonging to the operating system (Windows 98 or DOS). System files are not shown in directory listings. Currently, Windows 98 does not enable you to set the System attribute here. However, if a file has the System attribute set, it will appear checked, although dimmed.

Setting Program Properties

The Program properties page enables you to control many application settings, such as the command line, working directory, shortcut key, and icon (see Figure 27.4). From the Program properties page, you can click Advanced to configure how Windows 98 emulates the DOS environment for this program. Clicking Change Icon enables you to browse through icon files and select a new icon for the program.

FIG. 27.4
On the Program
properties page, you
can specify the working
folder.

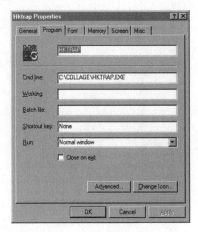

To set Program properties, follow these steps:

1. Open the Property folder for the desired DOS program.

2. Edit the Name text box as needed.

3. Edit the Cmd Line field as needed.

4. Edit the Working field as needed.

5. If you would like to run a batch file each time this program executes, enter the name of the batch file in the Batch File field. This is handy if the application uses a *terminate-and-stay-resident* (TSR) file when it runs.

6. If you would like to assign a shortcut key, move to the Shortcut Key field and press Ctrl and/or Alt and the other key.

7. From the Run drop-down listbox, select the window size: Normal Window, Maximized (full-screen window), or Minimized (a button on the taskbar).

8. If you want the MS-DOS window to stay open after you exit the program, deselect the Close On Exit check box. Otherwise, Windows 98 will close the MS-DOS window on exit.

9. Click OK to save your changes or Apply to save the changes without closing the Properties dialog box.

Setting Advanced Program Properties   The Advanced Program Settings dialog box enables you to configure the DOS environment where the DOS program will run (see Figure 27.5). You can hide Windows 98 from the DOS program, allow Windows 98 to switch to MS-DOS mode as needed, or require that the DOS program always be run in MS-DOS mode. Table 27.2 describes the Advanced property settings available.

Part
VII

Ch
27

FIG. 27.5

Use the Advanced Program Settings dialog box to control the DOS program execution environment.

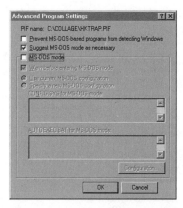

Table 27.2   Advanced Program Settings

Setting	Description
Prevent MS-DOS-Based Programs from Detecting Windows	Hides Windows 98 from the DOS program. This option is not enabled if MS-DOS mode is selected.
Suggest MS-DOS Mode as Necessary	Tells Windows 98 to detect whether the DOS program runs better in MS-DOS mode. If so, Windows 98 executes a wizard to set up a custom icon to run the program. This option is not enabled if MS-DOS mode is selected.
MS-DOS Mode	Runs the program in MS-DOS mode.
Warn Before Entering MS-DOS Mode	Tells Windows 98 to display a warning message that it will close all programs before running MS-DOS mode.
Use Current MS-DOS Configuration	Tells Windows 98 to use the existing (default) AUTOEXEC.BAT and CONFIG.SYS files when it enters MS-DOS mode.
Specify a New MS-DOS Configuration	Creates alternative CONFIG.SYS and AUTOEXEC.BAT files. Enables the CONFIG.SYS and AUTOEXEC.BAT text boxes and the Configuration button.
CONFIG.SYS for MS-DOS Mode	Enables you to edit as needed to create a custom CONFIG.SYS file for MS-DOS mode.
AUTOEXEC.BAT for MS-DOS Mode	Enables you to edit as needed to create a custom AUTOEXEC.BAT file for MS-DOS mode.
Configuration	Tells Windows 98 to create custom configuration files for you. (This helps you avoid typing in commands.)

By default, DOS programs run from Windows 98 in a DOS window. Alternatively, DOS programs can be executed in MS-DOS mode (also called *single-application mode* or *real mode*). In MS-DOS mode, the DOS program controls all system resources. Before running a program in MS-DOS mode, Windows 98 closes all active Windows and DOS programs. Only a small portion of Windows 98 remains in memory so that Windows 98 can reload itself into memory when you exit the program. Setting up a program to use MS-DOS mode is the same as shutting down Windows 98, restarting in MS-DOS mode, and then rebooting your machine to Windows 98. MS-DOS mode generally is used for DOS programs that will not run under Windows, such as DOS games.

N O T E Windows 98 property pages exist for all DOS programs, whether started in MS-DOS mode, from the command prompt, or as a Windows 98 DOS session. For those applications set up to run in MS-DOS mode, many properties do not apply and therefore are not available. When MS-DOS mode is selected, only the following properties are enabled:

General	File attributes
Program	Icon Text, Command Line, Close on Exit, Change Icon, and the advanced MS-DOS mode options

Font, Memory, Screen, and Misc pages are blank. ■

T I P If a DOS program detects Windows 98 and won't run properly, select Prevent MS-DOS-based Programs from Detecting Windows in the Advanced Program Settings dialog box.

To allocate all system resources to a DOS program (run in real-mode or single-application mode), follow these steps:

1. Open the Properties folder for the DOS program.
2. Select the Program tab.
3. Click Advanced.
4. Choose MS-DOS Mode.
5. If you do not want the warning message, deselect Warn Before Entering MS-DOS Mode.
6. If you do not want to use the current MS-DOS configuration, choose Specify a New MS-DOS Configuration.
7. For manual configuration, type or edit configuration commands in the CONFIG.SYS and AUTOEXEC.BAT text boxes.
8. To have Windows 98 generate the configuration commands for you, click Configuration. The Select MS-DOS Configuration Options dialog box appears, as shown in Figure 27.6. Select the desired options and click OK to return to the Advanced Program Settings dialog box.
9. Click OK to return to the Properties dialog box.

Part
VII

Ch
27

10. Click OK to save your changes, or click Apply to save your changes without closing the Properties dialog box.

FIG. 27.6
For programs starting in MS-DOS mode, you can create custom AUTOEXEC.BAT and CONFIG.SYS files by selecting options.

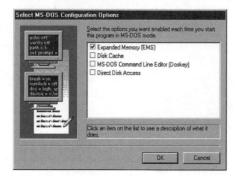

Changing Program Icons

Changing Program Icons   As with every object in Windows 98, DOS-based programs have a graphical picture called an *icon* associated with the program file. By default, the icon can appear in the following places:

- In file lists
- When you press Alt+Tab to switch between running applications
- On the Start menu
- On the taskbar

If the program file doesn't specify an icon, Windows 98 uses the MS-DOS icon. You can change the icon by opening the DOS Properties dialog box and clicking Change Icon. Windows 98 displays the Change Icon dialog box, as shown in Figure 27.7. To view the contents of another icon file, type the filename or click Browse to find the file. After selecting the icon, click OK twice to save your changes.

FIG. 27.7
The PIFMGR.DLL file contains many icons that you can assign to program files.

NOTE You can find more icons in the following folders:

`\SYSTEM\SHELL32.DLL`   `\MORICONS.DLL`

`\SYSTEM\ICONLIB.DLL`   `\PROGMAN.EXE`

Setting a Shortcut to a DOS Program

Assigning a shortcut key to a DOS program gives you quick access to your favorite DOS programs. You can use the shortcut key to start the program or to switch back to it once it is running.

Windows 98 contains many shortcut keys (called *access keys*), so you need to be careful when assigning your own shortcut keys. Here is a list of the rules:

■ Use Ctrl and/or Alt and another key (for example, Alt+W).

■ The other key cannot be Esc, Enter, Tab, SpaceBar, Print Screen, or Backspace.

■ No other program can use this key combination.

■ If the shortcut key is the same as an access key used by a Windows program, the access key won't work. (The shortcut key does work.)

Setting Font Properties

A feature in Windows 98 that is not supported in Windows 3.*x* is the capability to control font size and appearance. Windows 98 enables you to use any bitmapped or TrueType font installed on your computer. The font settings work in full-screen and windowed DOS sessions. Figure 27.8 shows the Font property page you can use to improve the display of your DOS sessions.

FIG. 27.8

You can reduce eye strain by changing the font type and size.

Part

VII

Ch

27

In addition to giving you control over the font type and size, Windows 98 provides an Auto font-size feature (located in the Font Size scroll box) that automatically adjusts the font size to fit the size of the DOS window. This feature enables you to see all 80 characters, even when you reduce the size of the DOS window.

 TIP Use the Auto font-size setting to automatically scale DOS session windows.

To set font properties for a DOS program, follow these steps:

1. Open the Properties folder for the DOS program.

2. Select the Font tab.

3. Select the available types to list in the Font Size scroll box: Bitmap Only, TrueType Only, or Both Font Types.

4. Select a font size in the Font Size scroll box. Windows 98 shows you what your selection will look like in the Window Preview and Font Preview boxes.

5. Click OK to save your changes, or click Apply to save the changes without closing the Properties dialog box.

Setting Memory Properties

The settings on the Memory page control the way the DOS application uses the PC's memory (see Figure 27.9). Settings are provided to control conventional, expanded (*Expanded Memory Specification* or EMS), and extended (*Extended Memory Specification* or XMS) memory. Note that since each DOS application executes in its own MS-DOS VM, the memory settings apply only to that DOS application. Other executing DOS, Windows 3.*x*, and Windows 98 applications are not affected by these memory settings. Table 27.3 describes the Memory property settings.

FIG. 27.9
You can customize the memory configuration for each DOS application.

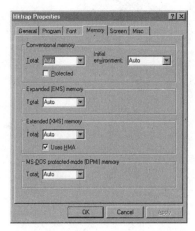

Table 27.3   Memory Settings

Setting	Description
Conventional Memory	
Total	Specifies the amount of conventional (lower 640KB) memory the program requires. If you are unsure about this setting, choose Auto.
Initial Environment	Specifies the number of bytes to reserve for COMMAND.COM. If set to Auto, the size is determined by the SHELL= line in CONFIG.SYS.
Protected	Protects the system from any problems caused by the program. The program might run slower when this check box is enabled.
Expanded Memory (EMS)	
Total	Specifies the maximum amount of expanded memory allotted to the program. The Auto choice sets no limit. If you experience problems, try a setting of 8192.
Extended Memory (XMS)	
Total	Specifies the maximum amount of extended memory allotted to the program. The Auto choice sets no limit. If you experience problems, try a setting of 8192.
Uses HMA	Indicates whether the program can use the *High Memory Area* (HMA).
MS-DOS Protected Mode Memory (DPMI)	
Total:	Specifies the maximum amount of DOS protected mode memory (DPMI) to allocate to the program. The Auto setting lets Windows 95 configure this based on your setup.

Setting Screen Properties

The settings on the Screen property page control the way the DOS application appears (see Figure 27.10). You can set up the DOS program to load in a window or full-screen—with or without a toolbar—and determine how many lines of text should appear. In addition, you can set display performance features such as dynamic memory allocation and fast ROM emulation. Table 27.4 describes the Screen properties.

Table 27.4   Screen Settings

Setting	Description
Usage	
Full-Screen	Starts the program in full-screen mode.

continues

Part
VII

Ch
27

Table 27.4 Continued

Setting	Description
Usage	
Window	Starts the program in a window.
Initial Size	Sets the number of screen lines displayed (25, 43, or 50 lines). A setting of Default uses the program's number of lines.
Window	
Display Toolbar	Displays the toolbar if the program is running in a window.
Restore Settings on Startup	Restores the font and screen settings when you close the program (if you are running the program in a window).
Performance	
Fast ROM Emulation	Controls the read-only video-memory usage. Select this to speed up the screen display and refresh feature. If the program has problems writing text to the screen, disable this check box.
Dynamic Memory Allocation	Controls the amount of memory available to switch between text and graphics mode in a DOS program. If you want to maximize the amount of memory available to other programs while this program runs, check this box. If you want to maximize the memory available to this program, disable this check box.

FIG. 27.10

By turning on dynamic memory allocation, you can speed up the display performance of a DOS program.

Dynamic memory allocation

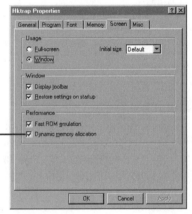

Setting Miscellaneous Properties

The remaining DOS program properties are grouped on the Misc page (see Figure 27.11). On the Misc property page, you can control foreground and background settings, the mouse, shortcut keys, and other items. Table 27.5 describes the miscellaneous settings.

FIG. 27.11

The Misc property page enables you to resolve conflicts between Windows shortcut keys and DOS programs.

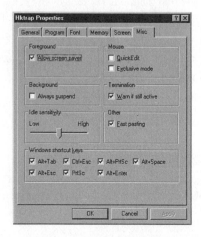

Table 27.5   Miscellaneous Settings

Setting	Description
Foreground	
Allow Screen Saver	Enables the screen saver to work even when the program is active.
Background	
Always Suspend	Prevents the program from using system resources when not active.
Idle Sensitivity	
Low to High	Specifies how long Windows allows the program to remain idle before redirecting CPU resources to other programs. Slide toward Low to give the DOS program a longer idle time (more resources). Slide toward High to take resources away from the DOS program sooner.
Mouse	
QuickEdit	Enables the Quick Edit feature, which enables you to select text for cutting and copying functions with the mouse (otherwise, you must mark text first).

continues

Part

VII

Ch

27

Table 27.5   Continued

Setting	Description
Mouse	
Exclusive Mode	Specifies that the mouse is controlled exclusively by the DOS program. The mouse no longer is available in Windows.
Termination	
Warn If Still Active	Specifies that a warning message is displayed if you try to close a running DOS application.
Other	
Fast Pasting	Enables the fast-paste feature. Could cause problems with older DOS programs.
Windows Shortcut Keys	
Alt+Tab Alt+Esc Ctrl+Esc PrtSc Alt+PrtSc Alt+Enter Alt+Space	Enables you to deselect certain Windows shortcut keys to disable those keys when the program is running.

Configuring Common Peripherals

CHAPTER 28

Configuring Input Devices

by Rob Tidrow

In this chapter

Configuring Pointing Devices

Windows 98 provides support to a wide range of pointing devices, including mouse devices, trackballs, joysticks, touch screens, touch pads, pen and tablet, and integrated keyboard devices (such as the TrackPoint "J" key). You can have multiple input devices running on the same computer, such as a mouse and touch pad. This enables you to switch from one input device to another without reconfiguring Windows or restarting your system.

When Windows installs, it looks for a pointing device and will attempt to set up yours. You can have the device set up on COM1 through COM4. Some of the manufacturers and models supporting "out of the box" include the following:

- Anchor USB mouse
- BTC USB keyboard mouse
- Compaq's Internal Trackball (PS/2 and Serial) and PS/2 Port Mouse
- ELO TouchSystems USB touch screen
- Kensington Serial Expert mouse
- Logitech's Bus Adapter, PS/2 Port, Serial, USB, and USB Wheel mouse devices
- Microsoft's Bus Adapter, InPort Adapter, and PS/2 mouse devices, Serial BallPoint, Serial EasyBall, Serial IntelliMouse, Serial IntelliMouse TrackBall, and USB IntelliMouse.
- Texas Instruments QuickPort BallPoint
- Toshiba AccuPoint

Other input devices are also supported by Windows, for some of which you need to provide drivers. Once you have your input device installed, you can set different properties for it. The most common input device is the mouse. The following sections show how to set mouse properties.

Setting Pointing Device Properties

Your pointing device doesn't need to be a boring little arrow that moves around on-screen. You can decide what it looks like. If you're left-handed, you don't need to suffer in a right-handed world—you can reconfigure the buttons for the left hand. If you don't like to move your pointing device around a lot, or you think you're required to double-click too fast, you can adjust the sensitivity of the device. Also, manufacturers sometimes provide additional features specific to their device.

You use the Mouse Properties sheet to adjust your pointing device. You can access this sheet by selecting Start, Settings, Control Panel and double-clicking the Mouse icon. From this sheet, you can set buttons, pointer styles, mouse motions, and general properties, as described in the following sections.

Setting Buttons Properties   The Buttons page is the default page displayed when you open the Mouse Properties dialog box (see Figure 28.1). You can specify the button configuration for a right- or left-handed user. You also can adjust how fast or slow you double-click the mouse button.

FIG. 28.1

In the Buttons page, you can set button configuration and adjust the double-click speed of your pointing device.

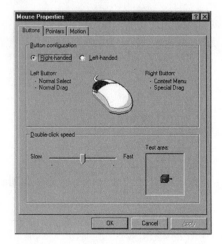

To set the pointing device as a left-handed device, click the Left-Handed button in the Button Configuration area. Conversely, to specify a right-handed device, click the Right-Handed button.

To adjust the double-click speed, follow these steps:

1. In the Double-Click Speed area, drag the slider left or right to adjust the speed. If you drag the slider to the right, Windows requires you to shorten the amount of time between the first and second click. If you drag the slider to the left, Windows allows more time between the first and second click.

2. To test the amount of time between clicks of a double-click, try your settings by double-clicking the jack-in-the-box in the lower-right Test Area. If Windows understands the speed of your double-click, the jack-in-the-box jumps out of or back into its box.

Modifying the Look of the Pointer   The Windows pointer takes various shapes, such as when a program is busy working on something or your pointer is positioned over the edge of a window. Now, with Windows 98, you can choose your own pointers—even animated, color pointers.

You can change your pointers individually or as a scheme (such as a set of 3D-styled pointers). To quickly change the set of pointers from the current scheme to another scheme, select the Pointers page in the Mouse Properties sheet. Open the Scheme drop-down list (see Figure 28.2) and pick a new scheme. If no schemes are listed, you haven't created any yet. You'll learn how to create a scheme in the following steps.

Part
VIII

Ch
28

FIG. 28.2

Use the Scheme drop-down list on the Pointers page to change the pointers Windows displays.

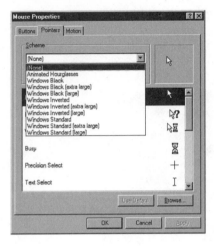

You also can change a single pointer instead of all the pointers at the same time. To do this, follow these steps:

1. From the pointers list, highlight the pointer you want to change and choose the Browse button. The Browse dialog box displays (see Figure 28.3).

 TIP You can double-click the pointer for faster access to the Browse window.

FIG. 28.3

Select a new look for your pointer by selecting a pointer name in the Browse window.

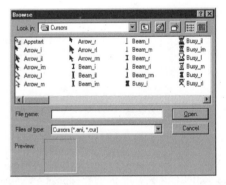

2. From the Browse window, select a new pointer from the \Windows\Cursors folder. Only pointers with an .ANI or .CUR extension are listed. When you highlight a pointer name, the Preview area shows what the pointer looks like.

3. After you find the pointer you want, click the Open button to select the cursor file and associate your choice with the pointer in the Pointer properties list. You can customize as many pointers as you like. If no pointer names appear in the Browse window, the extra mouse pointers were not installed when Windows 98 was installed. To add them, use the Windows Setup page of the Add/Remove Software Wizard.

CAUTION

Even though it's fun to use color-animated cursors in a pointer scheme, consider using those that have some relationship to the pointer's original appearance. For example, if you change all your pointers to a set of animals, you may have a hard time remembering which animal stands for which type of pointer.

4. If you don't like a change you've made to a particular pointer, you can set it back to the default Windows 98 pointer. Select the pointer in the list and choose the Use Default button.

TIP If you want to reset all your pointers to their defaults, choose the Scheme drop-down list and set the scheme name to (None).

5. After making changes to the pointers, you may want to save the set of pointers as a scheme. Do this by clicking the Save As button at the top of the Pointers page. The Save Scheme dialog box displays (see Figure 28.4).

FIG. 28.4

Give your pointer scheme a name in the Save Scheme dialog box.

6. In the Save Scheme dialog box, give your scheme a name and click OK to save it.

CAUTION

Windows does not warn you if you are about to save your new scheme with the same name as an existing scheme. You will replace the existing scheme if the new scheme has the same name.

7. If you want to delete a pointer scheme, select the name from the Scheme drop-down list. Then choose the Delete button. When you delete the pointer scheme, you don't delete the actual pointers. You just break the association of the pointers from the \Windows\Cursors folder to the Pointers list.

8. To apply all the changes you've made to your pointer settings, choose the Apply button. This saves your changes and leaves the sheet open for you to make other adjustments to your mouse. If you are finished making changes, click OK to save all your changes and close the Mouse Properties dialog box.

Part
VIII

Ch
28

CAUTION

If you've added or deleted schemes, choosing Cancel does not undo those actions. Adding or deleting a scheme is permanent.

Modifying Pointer Speed and Trail Settings

Perhaps you notice that you're moving the pointer too much or too little compared to the actual pointer movement on-screen. If you use a portable computer, you may have difficulty following the pointer around on the small screen. In either case, you want to select the Motion page on the Mouse Properties sheet (see Figure 28.5).

FIG. 28.5

You change your pointer's movement in the Motion tab of the Mouse Properties dialog box.

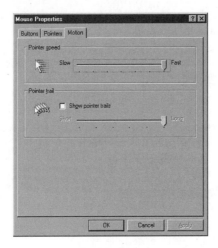

To adjust the sensitivity of the pointing device, follow these steps:

1. Drag the Pointer Speed slider left and right to adjust the sensitivity. Dragging the slider toward Slow requires you to move the pointing device more to make the pointer on-screen move. Dragging the slider toward Fast means you need to move the pointing device less to make the pointer on-screen move.

2. Choose the Apply button to save your changes and to leave the sheet open to other adjustments to your pointing device.

3. If you are finished making changes, click OK to save all your changes and close the Mouse Properties dialog box.

TROUBLESHOOTING

My pointer seems to skip around the screen. What's wrong? Your computer is probably busy performing a task. If you share a folder on your hard drive, other users may be heavily reading and writing information in it. This can also happen when several programs are running at the same time and you have less than 16MB of RAM installed in the computer.

If you have trouble following the pointer on your portable computer screen, try turning on *pointer trails*, which help you locate your pointer onscreen. To turn on pointer trails and adjust their length, follow these steps:

1. Click the Motion page of the Mouse Properties sheet.

2. In the Pointer Trail area, select the Show Pointer Trails check box. Then drag the slider left and right to adjust the trail length. Dragging the slider toward Short displays less of a trail. Dragging the slider toward Long displays a longer trail.

3. Choose the Apply button to save your changes and to leave the sheet open to other adjustments to your pointing device.

4. If you are finished making changes, click OK to save all your changes and close the Mouse Properties sheet.

TROUBLESHOOTING

My pointer moves in one direction but not another. Try cleaning your mouse ball, track ball, or any internal motion contacts (usually small plastic wheels). If you're using a mouse, clean the glide pads on the bottom (if you have them). If you use a mouse pad, be sure to clean it regularly to prevent a build-up of dirt. Be sure to follow the cleaning and care instructions provided by your manufacturer.

TROUBLESHOOTING

My pointer moves erratically. If shaking the cable makes the situation better or worse, verify that the connection to your computer is secure. Sometimes the connector has come loose from the port on your computer. If this solution doesn't work, inspect the cable for breaks or cuts. If your cable is broken or pierced, repair or replacement is necessary. If you see no visible breaks, a wire inside the cable may have broken. Breaks can be caused by severe twisting of the cable, placing a heavy object on the cable for long periods of time, or dropping a heavy object on it.

Configuring Keyboards

Another input device you rely on is the keyboard. Windows provides support for many types of keyboards. Most keyboards you purchase now are compatible with the PC/AT Enhanced Keyboard 101/102 key standard.

As Windows installs, it will detect the type of keyboard you have connected to your PC and install drivers for it. If Windows can determine the make and model of the keyboard, it may set up specific drivers for it based on the list of keyboard manufacturers and models Windows maintains. If Windows cannot determine your specific keyboard, it will set up the generic driver, Standard 101/102 or Microsoft Natural Keyboard. Although this driver should work fine with your keyboard, you may want to change it to one written specifically for your keyboard to activate any special features of the keyboard.

Examining the Types of Keyboards Windows 98 Supports

Windows 98 supports a wide variety of keyboards, including the Microsoft Natural keyboard, Universal Serial Bus keyboards, and a number of keyboards that come as standard devices

Part
VIII

Ch
28

with news PCs. Unless your PC's keyboard is damaged, you probably won't have any problem getting it to work properly with Windows 98. Some of the manufacturers and models supported by Windows 98 are included in the following:

- Olivetti keyboards (including 102, 83, 86, and A101/103 key models)
- PC/AT keyboard (84-key)
- Microsoft USB keyboard
- Compaq Enhanced Keyboard
- BTC USB Keyboard
- Maxi Switch (including #1101, #1102, #2101, and #2102)
- Acer API Ergo USB and API Generic USB keyboards
- Keytronic USB Keyboard
- Samsung USB Keyboard versions 1 and 2

N O T E   Most hardware manufacturers have designed keyboards that enable users to customize key settings or have pre-built customized keys that perform specific Windows actions. A Packard Bell keyboard, for instance, includes two Windows keys that, when pressed, display the Start menu and its options. A third Windows key displays the context menu of the selected object when pressed. Read the documentation that comes with your keyboard to determine if your keyboard has special features. ■

If you need to upgrade or purchase a new keyboard, if it is defective (keys have been lost or you've spilled liquids on it), look for one that has a nice feel to it. Many users have opted for ergonomically designed keyboards to decrease the stress placed on their hands and wrists. The Microsoft Natural Keyboard, for instance, includes a specially designed case to let your wrists rest on the keyboard, as well as let your hands remain in comfortable and less stressful position during keystroking. The Microsoft Natural Keyboard also includes special keyboard shortcuts that perform specific tasks in Windows, including the following:

- *Windows key.* Displays the Windows 98 Start menu
- *Windows+R.* Displays the Run dialog box in Windows 98
- *Windows+F1.* Displays Windows 98 Help
- *Applications key.* Displays context menu of the current application window

N O T E   You can learn more about the Microsoft Natural Keyboard at http:// www.microsoft.com/products/prodref/310_ov.htm. ■

Another type of keyboard available is compliant with the USB I/F Human Interface Devices (HID) Firmware specification. Universal Serial Bus (USB) is a technology created coopera-tively between Compaq, Digital Equipment Corp (DEC), IBM, Intel, Microsoft, NEC, and Norhern Telecom that describes devices that use a universal driver for multiple devices, such as modems, keyboards, and mouse devices. With Windows 98, you can, for instance, have two

USB-compliant keyboards set up on the same PC and used at the same time. The input from each of these keyboards is merged and used in the active application. You can learn more about USB by visiting their Web site at http://www.usb.com.

Changing Your Keyboard Properties

Your keyboard has a variety of properties that dictate how it enables you to interact with the computer. In many cases, they are configurable according to your individual preferences. These include the language used by the keyboard, its layout, and the speed at which keys repeat when pressed. Keyboard resource settings can also be viewed and changed, such as I/O and interrupt request settings (IRQs).

You can change the properties associated with a keyboard using the Keyboard icon from the Control Panel. To display the Keyboard property sheet, use these steps:

1. Select Start, Settings, Control Panel.

2. Double-click the Keyboard icon. The Keyboard Properties sheet appears (see Figure 28.6), containing two tabbed pages: Speed and Language.

FIG. 28.6
The Keyboard Properties sheet.

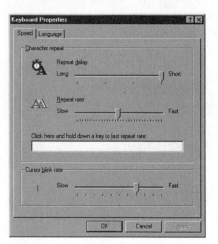

Changing How Keys Repeat   One keyboard property you can change is the way keys are repeated when you press and hold down a key. Depending on your typing style, you may want to speed up or slow down the repeat rate. You can change the way your keyboard keys repeat by using the Speed page, as shown in the following:

1. To change the time that elapses before a pressed-down key begins to repeat, drag the Repeat Delay slider to the right for a shorter time, to the left for longer.

2. To change the speed at which characters repeat when you hold down a specific key, adjust the Repeat Rate slider.

3. When you have settled on a suitable repeat setting, click Apply.

Part
VIII

Ch
28

Changing Your Cursor Blink Rate You can also change the speed at which your cursor blinks. After accessing the Keyboard Properties control panel, do the following:

1. On the Speed page, adjust the cursor blinking speed by dragging the Cursor Blink Rate slider to the right to make it faster, or to the left to slow it down.

2. When you have it blinking at the speed you want, click Apply.

Changing a Keyboard Layout When you press a character on the keyboard, Windows has to know which character you want displayed. For users in the United States, the standard keyboard is the QWERTY 101-key keyboard. This means the top row of letters on the keyboard are QWERTYUIOP. If you use a different keyboard, or want to change the layout of your keyboard (such as to the Dvorak layout), you do so from the Language page of the Keyboard Properties sheet.

1. Select the Language page (see Figure 28.7). The top section of the Language page displays the Installed Keyboard Languages and Layout list.

FIG. 28.7

The Language page in Keyboard Properties is where you can change your keyboard layout.

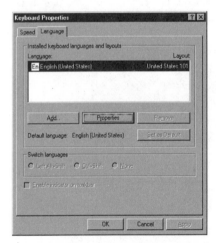

2. From the Language list, select the language and keyboard layout that you want to change.

3. Click the Properties button. The Language Properties dialog box appears (see Figure 28.8).

FIG. 28.8

The Language Properties dialog box enables you to change the layout of your keyboard.

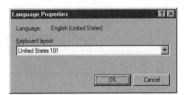

4. Select the new keyboard layout from the Keyboard Layout drop-down list box.

5. Click OK twice save your settings.

Adding Another Language or Layout   If the keyboard layout or language you want to select does not appear in the Language list on the Language page, just add it. From the Language page, do the following:

1. Click the Add button. The Add Language dialog box appears.

2. Select the language you want from the Language drop-down listbox.

3. Click OK. The Add Language dialog box disappears, and the language you just selected now appears on the Installed Keyboard Languages and Layouts area on the Language page.

4. Select the language you want to use as your primary language from the list.

5. Click the Set as Default button.

6. Click OK.

Your new language is now defined as the default language.

T I P   At the bottom of the Language page on the Keyboard Properties sheet is an option box called Enable Indicator on Taskbar. If this is checked, an indicator, called En, appears on the Windows 98 taskbar. To quickly change between languages, click this indicator and a list of available languages appears. You can instantly switch between available languages by clicking the language you want from that En list.

Deleting a Language or Layout   You can also delete a language or layout from the Keyboard Properties control panel. Having opened the Language page, do the following:

1. Select the language and layout you want to delete from the Installed Keyboard Languages and Layouts list.

2. Click the Remove button.

3. Click OK.

The Keyboard Remap Utility

The Windows 95 Keyboard Remap utility available with the Microsoft KernelToys enables you to change the placement of your keyboard keys. For example, to change the placement of the Caps Lock, Ctrl, and Alt keys to suit your needs and user habits, do the following:

1. Download the Remap utility from `http://www.microsoft.com/windows95/info/ kerneltoys.htm`. Click the `Windows 95 Keyboard Remap` hyperlink to start the download.

2. After you download Remap, double-click the `KEYREMAP.EXE` file to uncompress it on your hard drive.

3. Next, right-click the `KEYREMAP.INF` file and select Install to install the Keyboard Remap utility on your system. When prompted to provide the `KEYREMAP.DLL` file, point Windows to the folder in which you uncompressed the `KEYREMAP.EXE` file.

Part
VIII

Ch
28

4. To use Keyboard Remap, double-click the Keyboard icon in the control panel and click the Remap page. This page appears only after you install the Keyboard Remap utility (see Figure 28.9).

FIG. 28.9
The Keyboard Remap utility enables you to quickly remap different key settings.

5. On the Remap page, choose options in the When This Key Is Pressed area and map them with options shown in the Act as if This Key Is Pressed. You can remap keys on both the left and right sides of the keyboard.

6. Click OK after you make all your changes.

 You can remove Keyboard Remap by opening the Add/Remove Programs Properties sheet and selecting Key Remap from the list of applications to remove. Click Add/Remove to uninstall the utility.

Changing or Viewing Keyboard Resource Settings

You can change resource settings for your keyboard via the Device Manager accessed through the System Properties sheet.

You might need to change the settings if another component you're adding needs to use those same resources, or if you are adding another similar device, such as another keyboard, that wants the same settings.

To make changes to the keyboard resource settings, do the following:

1. Select Start, Settings, Control Panel.

2. Double-click the System icon. The System Properties sheet appears.

3. Click the Device Manager page.

4. Click the plus sign next to the Keyboard device type.

5. Double-click the keyboard for which you are interested in changing the resource settings.

6. Select the Resources page (see Figure 28.10).

FIG. 28.10

You can identify the specific resources using the Resources page.

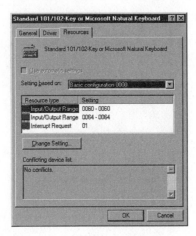

7. Make the changes to the keyboard resource by double-clicking the resource you want to change.

CAUTION

For a component to work properly, it must have the correct resource settings assigned to it. Do not change resource settings unless you know exactly what you are changing. A new component might need certain resources assigned to it, in which case either the product will specify them or Windows 98 will tell you what to use when you run the Add New Hardware Wizard.

8. Click OK to save your settings.

TIP

If the Use Automatic Settings option in the Resources page is checked, you will not be able to change the resource settings, and the Change Setting button will be grayed out.

TROUBLESHOOTING

I have a Microsoft Natural Keyboard, but it does not work with my IBM PS/2 computer. What can I do to make it work? You need to make sure the DASDDRVR.SYS device driver for your IBM computer loads before the Natural Keyboard driver loads. You can set this setting in CONFIG.SYS. Make sure the DASDDRVR.SYS driver, which is an IBM ROM BIOS patch driver, is written for your specific computer. This driver is usually found on the SETUP disk that came with your PC. You cannot use a DASDDRVR.SYS driver that is created for another PS/2 model.

CHAPTER 29

Configuring Printers

By Rob Tidrow

In this chapter

Installing a Printer to a Single PC

Windows makes installing any printer quick and easy with the help of the Add Printer Wizard. The wizard guides you, step-by-step, to configuring the printer and loading the driver. You can use any of Windows' supplied drivers, or you can use your printer manufacturer's disk when installing your printer.

N O T E   When you install a printer in Windows 98, you really are installing your printer's device driver to work with Windows 98. ■

If you have trouble installing your printer, there are a few things you can try to solve the problems. Additionally, you use Windows' Device Manager to view printer port settings and see if the problem you're having is with the hardware.

N O T E   Windows autodetects your printer when you install the Windows program; use the Add Printer Wizard when you add a printer after Windows is installed. ■

Using the Add Printer Wizard

By using the Add Printer Wizard, you can quickly and easily add any printer to your system. Before installing the configuration and driver files to your computer, make sure that you attach the printer to your computer and turn on the printer.

To install a printer to your PC, do the following:

1. Select Start, Settings, Printers. The Printers window appears (see Figure 29.1). Alternatively, you can open My Computer and double-click the Printers folder.

FIG. 29.1
The Printers window lists the current printers and enables you to add new printers.

2. Double-click the Add Printer icon. The Add Printer Wizard screen appears.
3. Click the Next button to display the second Add Printer Wizard dialog box. You can choose to install a local printer or a network printer. A local printer, which is featured in

these steps, is a printer attached to your computer. For steps on setting up a network printer, see "Installing a Network Printer," later in the chapter.

4. Click the <u>L</u>ocal Printer option and click the Next button. The third wizard screen appears (see Figure 29.2).

 TIP If you need to review or modify your choices in an Add Printer Wizard screen, click the <u>B</u>ack button to go to the previous wizard screen.

FIG. 29.2
You install the driver and configuration files by choosing the manufacturer and model in this wizard screen.

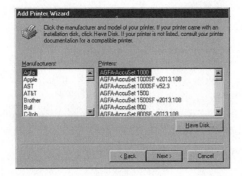

5. In the <u>M</u>anufacturer list, choose the maker of your printer. The list of <u>P</u>rinters changes to reflect those printers made by the selected manufacturer.

6. Select the exact model of your printer in the <u>P</u>rinters list.

   If your printer is not listed, you can insert the manufacturer's disk that came with your printer and click the <u>H</u>ave Disk button. Windows installs the configuration files and driver from the disk and then returns to this wizard box. Not all printer vendors provide a disk that works with Windows 98; call the printer manufacturer to inquire if an updated printer driver for Windows 95 or Windows 98 exists.

CAUTION

In general, you should avoid using printer drivers that are written for Windows 3.1 in Windows 98. Many times these drivers are not compatible with Windows 98 and will cause your prints job to fail or cause Windows 98 to crash. On the other hand, you should have few or no problems using printer drivers created for Windows 95 under Windows 98.

For updated printer drivers, contact the manufacturer of your printer, visit manufacturer's Web sites (if available), or visit the Windows 95 Device Driver Library page on the Microsoft Web site at `http://premium.microsoft.com/support/kb/articles/q135/3/14.asp`.

7. Click the Next button. The fourth Add Printer Wizard screen appears. This wizard screen displays the port to which your printer is attached, such as LPT1, LPT2, File, and Fax. The file port should be used if you want to set up your printer to print to a file.

8. Select the port to which the printer is attached.

   If you select to print to a parallel port, such as LPT1, you can change the following LPT port settings (see Figure 29.3) by clicking the Configure Port button:

FIG. 29.3

The Configure LPT Port dialog box.

- *Spool MS-DOS Print Jobs.* If checked (default setting), spools the documents you print from MS-DOS-based applications. Spooling controls the number of pages sent to the printer at one time so that printing is more efficient.

- *Check Port State Before Printing.* Runs a check on the connection before sending jobs to the printer.

   If you select to print to a serial port, such as COM1, click the Configure Port button to display the COM Properties dialog box. Configure the COM port settings as needed.

   Choose OK to close the Configure LPT Port or COM Properties dialog box.

9. Choose Next. The fifth Add Printer Wizard screen appears.

10. In the Printer Name field, accept the suggested name or enter a new name for the printer. The printer appears in the Printers folder to help you distinguish it from other printers you may have set up on your computer.

T I P You can easily change a printer name after the printer is installed. To do this, open the Printers folder, click twice on the printer icon (don't double-click the icon), and change its name.

11. If you want this printer to act as the default printer for your Windows applications, choose Yes. If you've already assigned another printer as the default printer, choose No.

12. Click Next. The sixth Add Printer Wizard screen appears asking if you want to print a test page. Choose Yes to print a test page or No to skip this step. If you choose Yes, Windows displays a dialog box asking if the test page printed OK; if you choose No in this dialog box, Windows tries to diagnose the problem for you.

13. Click the Finish button. Windows may prompt you for the necessary files to set up the printer; insert the Windows CD-ROM or disks. The installed printer icon appears in the Printers window.

Troubleshooting Printer Installation

Following are a few common installation problems you might encounter with your printer. If you need further help with your printer configuration, see the section "Configuring Your Printer" later in this chapter and consult your printer's documentation for more information.

If your printer is not listed in the Add Printer Wizard dialog box, you must use your printer's manufacturer's disk to install the configuration files and driver. If you did not receive a disk with your printer, call the dealer who sold you the printer and ask for the disk.

TIP Some printers are designed to emulate other printers. In some cases, for instance, laser printers may be able to emulate the Hewlett Packard LaserJet line of printers. If you cannot find your specific printer when you set up a new printer under Windows 98, consult the printer's documentation to see if it can emulate a printer listed in the wizard screen. If so, choose that printer.

If your selected port is not working with your printer, confirm that you're designating the correct port on your computer. Printer ports are usually the parallel ports LPT1 or LPT2. Next, make sure that your printer cable is appropriate for the port and that the cable is firmly attached to both the computer and the printer.

Confirm that the printer's power cord is plugged into a power outlet and into the printer. Check that the printer is turned on and that the printer's control panel lights are on.

If you're still having trouble with the printer port, follow these steps:

1. Select Start, Settings, Control Panel.
2. Double-click the System icon in the Control Panel. The System Properties sheet appears.
3. Choose the Device Manager page.
4. Find the Ports (COM & LPT) icon in the list and double-click it. The available ports appear below the icon.
5. Select the Printer Port and then click the Properties button. The Printer Port Properties sheet appears (see Figure 29.4).

FIG. 29.4
Use the Printer Port Properties sheet to spot problems with the port.

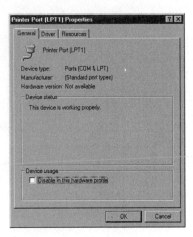

6. On the General page, look in the Device Status area. If the port has a problem, it's listed here with a suggested solution. If there is no problem listed, go on to step 7.

T I P Note any problem code or number in the Device Status area in case you need to call the printer manufacturer's support line. The number helps them identify the problem.

7. In the Device Usage area of the General page, make sure the Disable In This Hardware Profile option is unchecked. If checked, this disables the printer for your current hardware profile.

8. To find out about the printer port driver file, choose the Driver tab of the Printer Port Properties sheet (see Figure 29.5).

FIG. 29.5

Windows supplies the printer port driver, but you can change to your own driver or an updated driver.

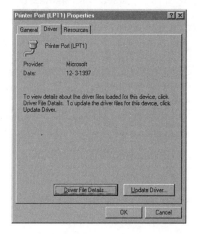

9. Click the Driver File Details button, to display the Driver File Details dialog box (see Figure 29.6). The Windows-supplied drivers for your printer port are listed in the Driver Files area. The default drivers include the C:\WINDOWS\SYSTEM\LPT.VXD and C:\WINDOWS\SYSTEM\VMM32.VXD. The VXD extension denotes a 32-bit driver. If your driver has an DRV driver, you are not using a 32-bit driver. Click OK and return to the Driver page of the Printer Port Properties sheet and click the Upgrade Driver button. This launches the Upgrade Device Driver Wizard, which walks you through the process of upgrading your port driver. Follow the onscreen instructions to finish the wizard.

10. To review the resources assigned to your printer, click the Resources page on the Printer Port Properties sheet (see Figure 29.7).

11. In the Conflicting Device List box, check to see if there is a conflict.

    To change a conflicting resource setting, clear the Use Automatic Settings option and click the setting Based On drop-down list box to display other configuration settings you can use. Check the Conflicting Device List to ensure the configuration setting you choose does not cause conflicts with other devices. If so, select a different configuration. If there are no configuration options available, you cannot change your port settings.

FIG. 29.6
The Driver File Details
dialog box lists the
driver files for your
printer port.

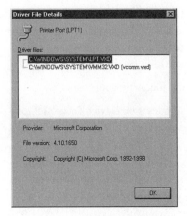

FIG. 29.7
Your safest bet is to
use Windows'
automatic settings
unless there's a device
conflict.

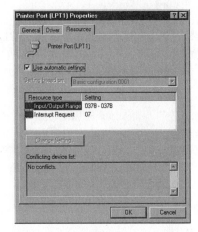

CAUTION

It's best to not change the resources manually because then the resources assigned to the printer become permanent. This limits the resources Windows can configure to other devices during system start up.

Also, if you change a configuration from the default, your port may not work correctly. It could slow considerably and may also lose some functionality.

12. When you're finished, choose OK to close the Printer Port Properties sheet and then choose OK again to close the System Properties sheet.

Another common problem with printers not working is outdated or incorrect printer drivers. When you purchase a printer, make sure it is designed to work with Windows 95 or Windows 98. This does not necessarily mean that the printer is a Plug and Play printer, but does imply that the printer driver is updated to work with Windows 95 or Windows 98. If you encounter problems with the printer and suspect the driver is at fault, contact the printer manufacturer to find out if a new driver is available. Sometimes the manufacturer will have a download service or Web site from which you can acquire the new driver.

You also can find updated drivers at the following sources:

- *World Wide Web*. Windows 95 Windows 95 Device Driver Library page on the Microsoft Web site at `http://premium.microsoft.com/support/kb/articles/q135/3/14.asp`.

- *Anonymous FTP site*. `ftp.microsoft.com/softlib`. Download the `index.txt` file to see a list of files available in the `MSLFILES` directory. When you find the file you want, change to the `MSLFILES` directory and download the file(s) you want.

- *Microsoft Download Service*. Dial 206-936-6735 from your modem. Note that this is a toll call and you are billed for your time online.

- *Update Driver feature*. A new feature in Windows 98 is the capability to automatically search for updated drivers from the Drivers tab (open a printer's properties sheet and click Driver). Click the Update Driver button and you can choose locations to search, including floppy, CD-ROM, Windows 98 Setup disks, or the Internet. See Chapter 5, "Installing and Configuring New Hardware and Software," for more information on this feature.

N O T E If you still have problems printing from Windows, try the Windows Troubleshooter. Choose Start, Help. In the Help Topics dialog box, choose the Index tab. Type **Printers Trouble-shooting,** click the Print Troubleshooter topic from the Topics Found dialog box, and click Display. The Print Troubleshooter appears in the right pane of the Help window. Click the Click Here hyperlink to start the Print Troubleshooter. Follow the directions onscreen. ■

Configuring Your Printer

After you install a printer to Windows, you can change its configuration to better suit your working practices. Windows makes it easy for you to change the port, paper size and orientation, graphics mode, font options, and more.

N O T E Some printer manufacturers include their own configuration utilities to change printer settings. Consult your printer's documentation for specific directions for your printer. ■

When you configure the printer through the printer's Properties sheet, the changes you make apply to all applications in which you use the printer. If, for example, you set the orientation to landscape, landscape becomes the default orientation when you print a page in your applications. You can, of course, change the printer setup in most applications to override the defaults in that application.

To open the printer's Properties sheet, follow these steps:

1. Select Start, Settings, Printers. The Printers folder appears.

2. Right-click printer icon you want to configure and choose Properties. The specific printer's Properties sheet appears (see Figure 29.8).

FIG. 29.8
Each installed printer has a properties page you use to set specific printer configurations.

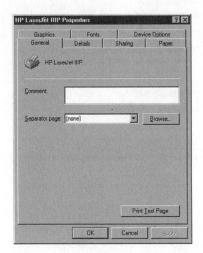

N O T E The pages and options available on the printer Properties sheet vary depending on the printer you are configuring. Some printers, for instance, include the Paper page, whereas other printers do not. The pages and options shown in the following sections are representative of the HP IIIP LaserJet printer, which may not match the printer you have installed. ■

The following sections discuss each printer property tab. If you want to set options on more than one tab, click the Apply button before changing tabs to make sure that the changes are activated.

 You can use the Microsoft System Information tool to help you gather information about your printers. You can launch this tool by selecting Start, Programs, Accessories, System Tools, System Information. In the left hand pane of the Microsoft System Information window, click the Components category and then click the Printing item to display the item and value information for your installed printers in the right hand pane.

Using the General Page

The General page of the printer's Properties sheet contains options that are handy if you're sharing your printer on a network. Additionally, you can print a test page from this page to make sure your printer is working correctly.

The options you can choose from include the following:

- *Comment*. The Comment area of the General page enables you to enter a description or comment about your printer, such as what its best use is. When sharing a printer, others on the network who install your printer see the comment.

- *Separator Page*. Select whether to insert a page between each document that's printed from your printer. You may want to use a separator page if several people are printing documents at once; the separator page makes it easy to divide the jobs. You can choose either a Full or Simple page to use as a separator. The full contains a graphic, and the simple contains only text.

N O T E You can also click the Browse button beside the Separator Page option to specify a custom separator page, such as a Windows Metafile. ■

- *Print Test Page*. Click the Print Test Page button to send a page to the printer. The page contains various fonts and graphics, depending on your printer. If the test page prints, your printer is attached and working.

Using the Details Page

The Details tab of the printer's Properties sheet enables you to set options such as printer port, capture printer port, spool settings, and so on. Figure 29.9 shows the Details tab.

FIG. 29.9

Configure ports and drivers in the Details tab of the Properties dialog box.

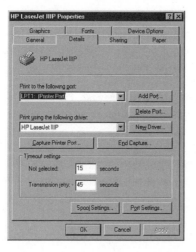

The following options can be found on the Details tab of the Properties dialog box:

- *Print to the Following Port*. This box displays the port to which your printer is connected. If you're using a network printer, the box displays the path to that printer. If you change the connection to your printer, you also need to change the port. Click the down arrow beside this option to display available ports and select one. Alternatively, you can add a port by clicking the Add Port button and typing a path in the Specify Path text box.

When you add a port, the Add Port dialog box appears. Specify whether the port is Network or Other (such as faxmodem or local) and enter the path or select the type of port you want to add. Choose OK to close the Add Port dialog box and return to the Properties dialog box.

Select a port and choose Delete Port if you want to delete a port.

■ *Print Using the Following Driver.* The driver you're currently using appears in this box, but you can change the driver if your printer supports or emulates the new driver. Click the down arrow for a list of installed drivers or click the New Driver button to change the driver.

If you click the New Driver button, you are prompted that the new driver will change your printer settings. Click Yes to continue. The Select Device dialog box displays (see Figure 29.10). This is the same dialog box you are presented in steps 5 and 6 in the "Using the Add Printer Wizard" section earlier in the chapter. Select your printer's manufacturer and model from this dialog box. Or, click the Have Disk button if your new driver is contained on a disk. Click OK. Windows 98 copies the new driver file you request. You may be prompted to insert the Windows 98 Setup disks or CD-ROM, or insert your printer manufacturer's driver disk. After the driver is installed, you see it in the Print Using the Following Driver list of the Details page.

FIG. 29.10

The Select Device dialog box enables you to change your printer driver.

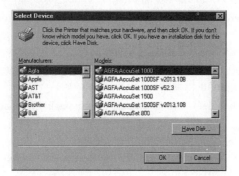

■ *Capture Printer Port.* Capturing a printer port is the same as mapping to a network printer. Choose the Capture Printer Port button to display the Capture Printer Port dialog box. If the path is not displayed, enter the path to the network printer in the Path text box, choose the Reconnect at Logon option, and choose OK. The next time you start Windows on the network, the network printer is automatically mapped to your drive and ready for you to use. Note that you must have rights to the network queue you are capturing to.

■ *End Capture.* Click the End Capture button to cancel the mapping to the network printer. If you want to use the network printer after canceling the capture, you must either recapture the printer or work your way through numerous folders to get to the printer.

■ *Timeout Settings.* The Not Selected option refers to how many seconds Windows waits for the printer to be online before it reports an error. Enter the amount of time you want Windows to delay.

Transmission Retry specifies the number of seconds Windows waits for the printer to be ready to print before reporting an error.

■ *Spool Settings.* Spool settings govern how your document is sent to the printer. Click this button to display the Spool Settings dialog box (see Figure 29.11).

FIG. 29.11

The Spool Setting dialog box provides options for controlling how your document is sent to the printer.

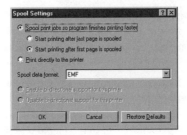

The first options specify whether to spool a job or print it directly to the printer. If you spool the job, you can choose to start printing after the first page was sent or after the last page was sent. You spool a print job so that your program can get back to work more quickly while the print queue does all the work. If you choose to print directly to the printer, your computer remains tied up until the entire job is sent to the printer.

The Spool Data Format option refers to the way your computer stores the data to be printed. Use EMF (metafile) format to free up your program faster; use RAW format if you have problems with the EMF. RAW format does take longer to print, though.

Choose the Enable or Disable Bi-directional Support for this Printer to specify whether your printer should communicate with your computer.

Select the Restore Defaults button to change all options in the Spool Settings dialog box back to the default.

■ *Port Settings.* Click the Port Settings button to display the Configure LPT Port dialog box (refer to Figure 29.5), in which you can choose to spool DOS application print jobs and/or to check the port before printing.

Using the Sharing Page

The Sharing page refers to how your printer works with a network, such as the peer-to-peer Microsoft Network. If you choose Not Shared, others on the network cannot access your printer. If you choose Shared As, you can specify a password to limit others' access to your printer. Figure 29.12 illustrates the Sharing page with the Shared As option selected.

N O T E You must have File and Printer Sharing for Microsoft Networks or File and Printer Sharing for NetWare Networks service installed for the Shared As option to be active. You learn how to install these services in Chapter 22, "Configuring Windows 98 as a Network Client." ■

FIG. 29.12
Share your printer with others on the network, but limit access with a password.

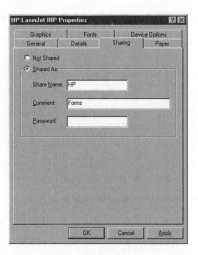

In the Shared As area, enter a name to identify your computer on the network in the Share Name text box and enter a Comment if you want. You can also enter a Password to limit those with access to your computer. After you enter the password, Windows displays a confirmation dialog box in which you enter the password again to confirm it.

To stop sharing your printer with the network, click the Not Shared option on the Sharing page.

Using the Paper Page

Use the Paper page of the printer's Properties sheet to set defaults for paper size, orientation, paper source, copies, and so on. The defaults you set on this page are applied to any application using the printer, unless you change printer setup in the specific application. Figure 29.13 illustrates the Paper page.

FIG. 29.13
Set defaults for the printer that apply to all applications that use it.

The following are the options available on the Paper tab:

■ *Paper Size*. Select the paper size you want to print from as a default. You might, for example, set up one printer on your network to print only number 10 (commercial-sized) envelopes. Choose the envelope size on this page. To choose a size of paper or envelope, click the icon in the scroll box; its size description appears above the scroll box.

■ *Orientation*. Choose either Portrait (vertical orientation) or Landscape (horizontal orientation) as the default paper orientation for this printer. If you select Landscape, you can select the Rotated option to rotate the data printed on the page 180 degrees.

■ *Paper Source*. Specify the paper source for your printer. You can choose, for example, to use the upper tray or lower tray, or manual feed as with an envelope feeder.

■ *Copies*. Enter the default number of copies to print.

■ *Unprintable Area*. Click this button to display the Unprintable Area dialog box. The unprintable area is the margin around the outside of the page that a laser printer, for example, cannot print to. You can change the area not printed to suit your printer or for special print jobs. Enter the amount of unprintable area for the Left, Right, Top, and Bottom of the page. Choose OK to return to the Paper page of the Properties sheet.

■ *About*. Click to display the About dialog box, which displays the printer name and driver version. Choose OK to close the dialog box.

■ *Restore Details*. Click the Restore Details button to change all options in the Page page back to their defaults.

Using the Graphics Page

Use the Graphics page to specify graphics resolution, dithering, intensity, and so on. The settings on this page affect only graphics, not text. Figure 29.14 shows the Graphics page of the Properties sheet.

FIG. 29.14
You can speed up your print jobs by choosing options in the Graphics page.

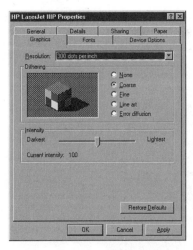

The following are the options available on the Graphics page:

■ *Resolution*. Listed in the Resolution box are the available choices for printing graphics. Higher resolutions (600 dots per inch, for example) produce high-quality graphics but take longer to print. Lower resolutions (75 dpi) produce coarse and grainy graphics but print quickly.

■ *Dithering*. Dithering blends grays in black and white printing or colors in color printing to produce smoother transitions. Choose None if you do not want dithering. Choose Coarse for a grainy effect or Fine for a higher quality, smooth effect. If your resolution is low—150 dpi or less—choose Fine Dithering to improve the look of the graphics. Choose Line Art if there are no shades of gray in the graphics; the contrast between blacks and whites will be sharper. Choose Error Diffusion for sharpening the edges of photographs.

■ *Intensity*. Click and drag the lever to Darkest for darker graphics or to Lightest for lighter graphics. The default intensity is 100. The lowest intensity is 0, which would produce black or nearly black graphics; and the highest intensity is 200, which would produce white or nearly white graphics.

Using the Fonts Page

Use the Fonts page to specify how TrueType fonts are printed and to indicate any font cartridges you use with your printer. Figure 29.15 illustrates the Fonts page of the Properties sheet for an HP IIIP laser printer.

FIG. 29.15
Identify your font cartridges, install printer fonts, and specify TrueType fonts in the Fonts page.

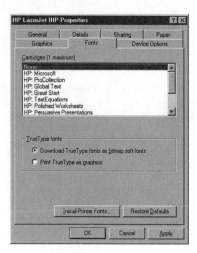

The following are the options available on the Fonts page:

■ *Cartridges*. Some printers, mostly Hewlett-Packard printers, enable you to use a font cartridge to add to your list of available fonts. Font cartridges can contain two or 20 fonts and various styles of fonts, such as bold, italic, and so on. If your printer uses a font cartridge, select the cartridge in this list to enable the use of those fonts in your Windows applications.

■ *TrueType Fonts*. Use the Download TrueType Fonts as Bitmap Soft Fonts option for lower quality output and the Print TrueType as Graphics for artistic effects, such as printing graphics over text so that only part of the character is printed.

■ *Install Printer Fonts*. If your font cartridge is not listed in the Cartridges list, choose to install the fonts using the Install Printer Fonts button. From the Font Installer dialog box (see Figure 29.16), click the Add Fonts button. Windows prompts you to insert a disk containing the font files or to enter a directory where the fonts can be found. Choose OK, and the Installer copies the fonts.

FIG. 29.16

The Font Installer dialog box is used to install printer fonts.

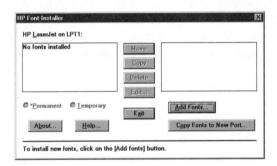

■ *Restore Defaults*. Click this button to erase any changes you made and to restore the defaults to the Fonts page.

TROUBLESHOOTING

The print quality of my graphics is poor. Is there anything I can do? If the print quality is poor for graphics, make adjustments to the Graphics page of the printer's Properties sheet. If text quality is poor, adjust the print quality settings in the Device Options page of the printer's Properties sheet.

Using Device Options

Use device options to set the print quality of the text and to control printer memory tracking. Figure 29.17 illustrates the Device Options page of the Properties sheet for the HP IIIP printer.

FIG 29.17

The amount of printer memory, RAM, is listed in the Device Options page of the Properties sheet.

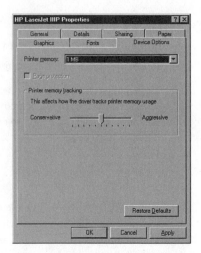

The following are the options available on the Device Options page:

- *Printer Memory*. This area lists the amount of RAM in your printer. With some printers, the amount is fixed; with other printers, you can change the amount of memory if you add memory to your printer.

- *Page Protection*. If available with your printer, this option applies some of the printer's memory to complex pages when printing. Although this option produces better printing result, it also uses more printer memory resulting in slower printing times.

- *Printer Memory Tracking*. This feature controls printer memory tracking. When printing complex documents, adjust the tracking by dragging the lever to Conservative or Aggressive. The more aggressive the tracking, the more likely the printer driver will attempt to print a complex document; however, the printer's memory may be exceeded, and the print job fails. The more conservative the tracking, the more likely the printer's memory will be available, but the less likely the printer driver will print the complex document.

- *Restore Defaults*. Choose this button to erase any changes you made and to restore the defaults to the Device Options page.

TROUBLESHOOTING

I can't get complex pages or graphics to all print on the page; the printer divides it into two pages. What can I do? Try changing the Printer Memory Tracking in the Device Options page of the printer's Properties sheet. If you still have trouble, consider adding more memory to your printer.

Creating a Printer Shortcut

To quickly access a printer, place a shortcut to it on the desktop. This is handy if you want to print documents to a printer by dragging and dropping files on the printer shortcut icon.

To create a printer shortcut, open the Printers folder and drag and drop the printer's icon on the desktop. Windows asks if you want to create a shortcut to the printer (it also lets you know you can't move or copy the printer to the desktop). Click Yes. Windows creates a shortcut to the printer.

Deleting a Printer

Not only can you install a printer under Windows 98, you also can delete one. Before deleting one, however, make sure you really want to. Once you delete it, it's deleted for good. You'll need to reinstall the printer following the instructions shown in "Installing a Printer On a Single PC."

To delete a printer, follow these steps:

1. Open the Printers folder and click the folder you want to delete.
2. Press the Delete key. The Printers dialog box displays asking if you want to delete the printer.
3. Click Yes. You are asked if you want to delete files that are used only for the printer you're deleting. Click Yes to delete these files, or click No if you want to retain them on your system. Regardless of your response, the printer is removed from your system.

CHAPTER 30

Configuring Scanners

by Rod Tidrow

In this chapter

Finding the Right Scanner

While joysticks, mouse devices, tape backup drives, and modems are relatively commonplace among computers running Windows, scanners and digital cameras are not likely to be found attached to an average Windows workstation. There are many reasons for this trend, including the high price tags that were attached to such peripherals in the past. But now that prices for this hardware are dropping, and demand for faxing and document storage is rising, you may be considering the purchase of a scanner.

Finding the right scanner for you and your work is not a difficult task, but can be frustrating at times. Scanners come in several different types: flatbed, sheet-fed, hand-held, and card scanner. The latter, card scanner, has been adapted for single photo scanning as well.

If you're in the market for a scanner, you should consider some of the following buying tips:

- *Quality of scan.* When you purchase a scanner, you want to get the best quality for the price you can pay. The way to judge quality is to see how closely the scanned image on your screen compares to the actual photo or page you've scanned.

- *Interoperability with other devices.* If you plan to connect your scanner to a parallel port, you may also have to connect a printer or other device (such as backup device) to that same port. Make sure the scanner and these other devices work flawlessly with each other. If this means trying out a scanner before buying it or returning it within the specified return date, do so. You don't want to get stuck switching cables every time you want to scan, print, or perform another task.

- *Color depth.* For most users, 24-bit color (also called high-color) is all they need. Those planning to output to graphics shops should, however, look for scanners that support 30- to 36-bit color depths.

- *Company support.* Read the manufacturer's warranty and support license. Warranties of over one year are probably the best, but you may have difficulty finding free technical support. Because the most difficulty with scanning usually is a result of the scanning software you use (of course, once you get the device configured), inquire about the technical support offered by the software manufacturer, which is usually different than the hardware manufacturer.

- *DPI (dots per inch).* DPI relates to the number of individual dots (pixels) that are squeezed into a square inch. The higher the number (such as 2400) means more dots make up the image, resulting in a higher quality image. For most business scanning, such as document imaging and OCR, a 300×600 dpi rating is fine. For higher-quality images, look for DPI ratings over 600×600.

- *Single-pass versus three-pass devices.* Flatbed scanners that scan on a single pass—that is, the image is scanned the first time the scanner passes over the image—scan faster than those that require three passes. If your shop will be scanning a large number of images or documents, consider a single-pass model.

■ *Price.* Generally, the higher the price of scanners, the better quality and higher number of colors that can be reproduced. Flatbed scanners can be purchased for under $100 today. These may not be the best scanners if you plan to create high-quality presentations and advertisements. However, for document imaging, OCR (optical character recognition) tasks, and general business scanning, these low-priced scanners should suffice. Likewise, hand-held scanners can be found in the $69 range, but you should opt for a hand-held only if you can't afford a flatbed scanner.

■ *Software bundle.* Ask the vendor what type of scanning software is available with the scanner. Without software, you can't scan. So look for a scanner that includes scanning and OCR software. Some software bundles are actually "lite" or demo versions. Watch out for this and try to get a bundle that includes full-featured versions.

Installing Scanner Hardware

Most scanner hardware is connected to your computer through a separate interface board (usually a SCSI card); however, some hand-held scanners and flatbed scanners can connect to your computer's parallel port. If you have to install a scanner adapter into your computer, turn your computer off and perform the following steps.

 If your adapter has dip switches or jumpers that are used to configure the adapter, write down the current settings before you install the adapter.

1. Install the scanner adapter board into your computer. Follow the manufacturer's installations guidelines closely.

2. Restart your computer.

3. Run the Add New Hardware Wizard as detailed in Chapter 5, "Installing and Configuring New Hardware and Software." If your scanner is not detected automatically by Windows, you need to specify the Imaging Device type or Other Devices type to manually install your scanner. If your scanner connects to a SCSI port, you'll need to make sure that port is installed and configured first. Then connect your scanner to the port and install the drivers necessary for your scanner. See how to install hardware in Chapter 5.

If the Add New Hardware Wizard cannot automatically detect your scanner board, you have two options:

■ You can run the Add New Hardware Wizard again and select No when the wizard asks to automatically detect your new hardware. You can then manually install the Windows 98 drivers by selecting from a list of manufacturers and their adapter boards. If you cannot find your exact adapter board listed, load the driver disk that was shipped with your scanner adapter. Select Have Disk, which will search the manufacturer's disk for a Windows 98 device driver. If the Add New Hardware Wizard can find a Windows 98 driver for your scanner adapter, the wizard will display the adapter driver in a list, and the installation procedures may continue from step 6 in the preceding installation steps.

■ The Add New Hardware Wizard may not detect your adapter and the manufacturer disk may not contain a Windows 98 device driver. When the driver disk for your adapter only contains DOS and Windows 3.x device drivers, you need to follow the manufacturer's installation instructions for installing the device drivers on your system. Some manufacturers may offer a Windows 98 or Windows 95 installation section within their manuals if their native Windows 98 drivers are not ready yet. Check to see if the scanner you have or want to purchase will work with Windows 98 or if there are specific installation instructions for Windows 98; otherwise, follow the standard installation procedures outlined in the manuals.

N O T E   If you are installing a hand-held scanner or a flatbed scanner that connects to your computer's parallel port, you may not need to run any hardware installation procedures. Check your installation manuals regarding this matter. You may only need to install software that works with your scanner. ■

TROUBLESHOOTING

After I installed my scanner, I can't seem to scan anything into my word processor. What's wrong?
If you are not using the scanning software, you won't be able to scan anything into your word processor. If you are trying to scan text from a document into the word processor, you will need to use special software that uses Optical Character Recognition (OCR) to actually convert the image into text data. This software may have been shipped with your scanner; you should review the operation of the OCR software and its usage for scanning into word processing documents.

Installing and Configuring Scanner Software

Scanner software communicates with the hardware through a Windows device driver. The device driver controls the way the scanner works when capturing an image. The scanner software is usually written by the manufacturer of the scanning hardware, because each scanner has various capabilities and resolutions.

Some common controls that the scanner software manages include

■ Color resolution (if your scanner supports color)

■ Image resolution, usually expressed in dots-per-inch (dpi)

■ Image enhancement

■ Image cropping, enlargement, and reduction

■ File format for the captured image

Proprietary Solutions

Since the scanning software is so closely linked to the scanner hardware, you may not have any choice but to use the software that was provided by the manufacturer to perform your scanning. If you have purchased a brand-name scanner with a good reputation, the software that is delivered will probably be mature and reliable and may even be a 32-bit Windows 98 program. The features included in this software will probably be what you are looking for, plus some additional features that may be new to you.

To install your scanning software, follow the instructions provided in your scanner's installation manual. This procedure is typically very quick because there are few options to most scanning software. Once your software is installed, you will be able to start scanning images into your computer.

Scanning Software Example

To give you an idea of some of the functions that are available through scanning software, let's take a look at the iPhotoPlus scanning software.

Figure 30.1 shows the iPhotoPlus software's main screen. On the left side of the screen are the main controls for configuring the operation of the scanner, while the right side of the screen shows a preview image of the scanner.

FIG. 30.1
iPhotoPlus' software lets you preview the images you are scanning.

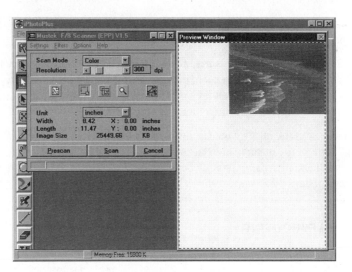

When scanning an image, it is common for the scanning software to offer a preview mode for cropping an image. The preview mode will perform a fast scan of the entire scanning bed to allow you to see where your image is positioned in the scanner. Once you can see where the entire image is, you can choose the portion you want to scan at a higher quality. Looking back to Figure 30.1, notice that the entire scanning area is represented by the box on the right side of the screen.

Once you have completed the preview scan, you can crop the image to the desired size. This will prevent the scanner from scanning in blank space which not only makes your image look poor, but also requires more hard drive space to store and much longer time to scan.

Take the example of a business card. If you walked up to a photocopy machine and placed the card on the machine, you would end up with an 8 1/2 by 11-inch piece of paper with a business card located somewhere on the page. What you really wanted was a copy of the business card, not a copy of the photocopy machine's cover.

If you placed that same business card on a scanner, you could view the preview scan and crop only the business card by drawing a box around that part of the scanning area. When the scanner digitizes that image, it will only include the part of the scanning area you cropped. Again, this saves time and disk space while giving you the image you want.

In addition to the cropping features, another important feature includes the scanning mode in which your image is captured. Since images may be used for many different purposes, you may have to change the scanning mode from time to time. Some images you will only view on the computer screen, so these images should match the number of colors your video mode can support. Other images will be included in word processing or spreadsheet documents, which will be printed in black and white. Still others may be advertising images that are being sent to a high-quality color printer for proofing. Each of these images has different quality needs that your software should handle.

The iPhotoPlus software provides an image quality selection that allows you to use one of several preset image settings or create your own.

There are many other features that the iPhotoPlus software provides, including automatic contrast and brightness correction, multiple file format support, multiple size settings, and image scaling. But this is not a review of the iPhotoPlus software, it is simply a benchmark against which you can measure other scanning software.

Once you scan the image, you can view and manipulate it in the iPhotoPlus window (see Figure 30.2). Some of the manipulation tasks you can perform include resizing, retouching, enhancing, and changing color depths. Depending on the software you get with your scanner, you may or may not have these same features.

TROUBLESHOOTING

I bought a scanner to do OCR, but I never thought I'd have to do so much re-typing. Why can't the computer do a better job at reading the documents into my word processor? It sounds like your expectations were a little too high for this technology. While some OCR software can read text with 99.7 percent accuracy, that still means you could have between 5 to 10 errors on a "good" page and many more on a page with illegible writing or poor text quality. OCR is wonderful technology, but don't expect it to replace your secretaries anytime soon.

FIG. 30.2
With iPhotoPlus, you can scan an image and then manipulate it into a final digital image.

Scanning Tips

Once you have your scanner working, take some time to get comfortable with it. Although the quality of the scanner and the features of your scanning software determine much of how your finished scanned image looks, you can follow these guidelines to improve your scans:

- Always use the best quality original as possible. This way you don't have to touch up the image after it's scanned.

- When using a hand-held scanner, scan as slowly as possible. If the device has a slow scanning command, turn it on to see if your scans improve. Also, place the scanner against a straight-edge place on your image.

- Make single sheets and pages of books and magazines as flat as possible.

- When scanning a news clipping, place a sheet of white paper underneath it. This places a sharp edge on the scanned image, as well as eliminates bleed-through from the other side of the news clipping.

- Keep the scanner surface clean, including the runners on hand-held scanners and the scanning window on a flat bed device.

CHAPTER 31

Configuring Game Cards and Joysticks for Windows 98

by Rob Tidrow

In this chapter

Installing Your New Game Card into Your PC

The first task in getting a game card to work with Windows 98 is installing the new piece of equipment into your PC. A *game card* is an adapter you install in your computer that enables game software to work with a joystick plugged into the game card. Many sound cards, in fact, have a *Musical Instrument Digital Interface* (MIDI)/joystick port included. If your sound card does have this port (see the sound card documentation or look on the card itself), you won't have to bother installing a separate game card. In fact, after you install the sound card, you might have very little (or no) work to do to configure Windows 98. If you have a Plug and Play system and the card is Plug and Play compatible, for example, Windows 98 does all the work necessary to configure your new game card. In this section, you learn how to install your game card into your PC and how to recognize whether your PC and card are both Plug and Play compatible.

 Before you start to configure a new game card or joystick, be sure that you have any relevant documentation handy. You might need to supply information included in the user manual. Also, be sure that you have any floppy disks or CD-ROMs supplied with the device; Windows 98 might need software that is supplied on these.

The steps necessary to install a new game card into your PC follow. Be sure to check the documentation provided with your game card for specific installation instructions:

1. Shut down Windows 98, turn off the power on your PC, and follow the instructions enclosed with the card to install the card into your PC. You should leave the PC plugged in to keep it grounded. You also might want to wear an antistatic wrist strap to eliminate static electricity, which can damage your card. You'll need to remove the PC case to install the card inside the computer.

2. Turn on your PC and boot Windows 98.

3. If the game card is a Plug and Play model, Windows 98 notifies you that it has detected and identified the new card. Windows may prompt you for the location of the driver of the game card. This driver probably is located on the floppy disk. If so, enter the path to the driver's location in the dialog box.

4. If the game card is not a Plug and Play model, Windows 98 does not prompt you for any information. You should start the Add New Hardware Wizard to configure your new game card (see the following section).

Starting the Add New Hardware Wizard

Game cards are identified and configured for use in Windows 98 through the Add New Hardware Wizard. The Add New Hardware Wizard in Windows 98 automates most of the work you had to complete in Windows 3.x and MS-DOS to set up a new game card. This wizard is located in the Control Panel folder.

When you run the Add New Hardware Wizard, select the Sound, Video and Game Controllers option from the Hardware Types listbox, as shown in Figure 31.1. Refer to Chapter 5, "Installing and Configuring New Hardware and Software," for specific instructions on using the Add New Hardware Wizard.

FIG. 31.1

Be sure to select the Sound, Video and Game Controllers hardware type when installing your game card.

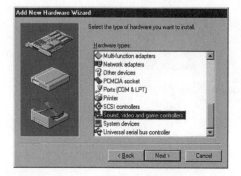

Troubleshooting Your Game Card

If your game card does not work properly after installing it under Windows 98, you can perform some basic troubleshooting procedures to get it working. In many cases, the conflict is a result of Windows not enabling the device, a hardware resource being allocated improperly or not at all to your new game card, or a device driver conflict. The following sections discuss these issues in more detail.

Enabling Your Game Card

The following steps show how to use the game card Properties dialog box to enable your game card:

1. Choose Start, Settings, Control Panel and double-click the System icon. The System Properties dialog box appears.

2. Select the Device Manager page.

3. Click the plus sign next to the Sound, Video and Game Controllers item.

4. Double-click the specific game card device you want to change. The Properties dialog box for your game card appears (see Figure 31.2).

5. In the Device Status area on the General page, read the status of the game card. If the Enable Device button is available, click it to enable the game card. The System Settings Change prompt appears, informing you that your hardware settings have changed and asking whether you want to restart Windows now.

   If the Device Status area indicates that the game card is working properly, see the following section, "Running the Hardware Troubleshooter."

Part
VIII

Ch
31

FIG. 31.2

Use the game card Properties dialog box to modify the card's configuration.

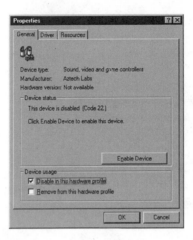

> **CAUTION**
>
> When you enable your new game card, it may disable another hardware device—namely, any with which it is currently conflicting. Be sure to check to see whether the device you're disabling no longer is needed.

  6. Click Yes to restart Windows.

Running the Hardware Troubleshooter

After Windows 98 restarts, if your game card is still not working correctly, you can run the Hardware Troubleshooter to help diagnose and fix the problem. Follow these steps to use the Hardware Troubleshooter from your new game card Properties dialog box:

  1. Perform steps 1 through 4 in the preceding procedure to open the game card Properties dialog box.

  2. Click the Hardware Troubleshooter button on the General page to start the Hardware Troubleshooting Wizard. (This button does not appear if your hardware does not conflict with your system or if the Hardware Troubleshooter cannot be used to fix your device's problem.)

  3. Read the Hardware Troubleshooting Wizard screen to find out what the Hardware Troubleshooter has diagnosed as the problem with your device and how it plans to fix it. If you want to continue with the Hardware Troubleshooting Wizard, click Next. However, if the Troubleshooter plans to change a setting you do not agree to (such as freeing resources when you are not sure you want this to happen), click Cancel.

  4. On the next Hardware Troubleshooting Wizard screen, you are given further information about what is wrong with your hardware device. Click Next.

  5. In the example shown in Figure 31.3, the Hardware Troubleshooting Wizard displays devices you can disable to free resources for your new game card. Click More Choices

to examine more devices you can disable. Click Cancel if you don't want to disable any of the choices, or select a device to remove and click Next. Be sure the device you remove is one you do not want to use again.

FIG. 31.3
Any device you remove must be reinstalled before you can use it again under Windows 98.

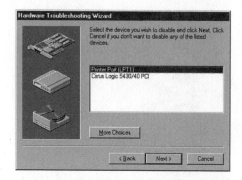

6. (If you clicked Next in step 5 to disable a device.) Click Next to disable the selected device. If Windows cannot free the resource or disable the selected device, you are prompted to select a different device. Otherwise, Windows removes the device and prompts you to restart Windows. Click Yes to restart Windows.

N O T E   After Windows restarts, if your new game card still does not work, check the game card Properties dialog box; make sure that the Disable in This Hardware Profile check box is *not* enabled (refer to Figure 31.2). ■

Updating Your Game Card Device Driver

Another change you can make to get your game card working is update its device driver. Use the following steps to update your game card driver:

1. Display the game card Properties dialog box.
2. Select the Driver tab (see Figure 31.4).
3. Click Upgrade Driver. The Upgrade Device Driver Wizard starts.
4. Click Next. The next wizard screen appears, presenting you with two options (see Figure 31.5). Selecting Search for a Better Driver Than the One Your Device Is Using Now (Recommended) instructs Windows to look for a driver newer than the one currently installed. Click Next to see a list of locations where Windows will look for new drivers; choices include Floppy Disk Drives, CD-ROM Drive, Microsoft Windows Update, and Specify a Location (see Figure 31.6). Clear the check box for location(s) you don't want Windows to search. If you keep the Microsoft Windows Update check box enabled, you need a dial-up or direct link to the Internet. Click Next to begin your search, and follow the specific instructions when Windows locates a new driver.

Part
VIII

Ch
31

FIG. 31.4

The Driver page for your new game card.

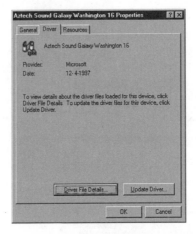

FIG. 31.5

You can have Windows search for a new game card driver or instruct Windows to create a list of drivers residing in a specific location.

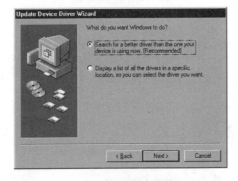

FIG. 31.6

Windows 98 will look for a new driver in various locations, including the Internet.

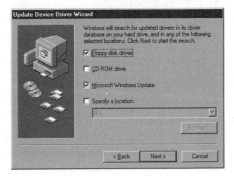

N O T E If Windows locates a driver that matches the one already installed for your device, you'll see a wizard screen recommending that you keep the current location. You can click Next to finish the Upgrade Device Driver Wizard or Back to install a specific driver, as discussed in the following steps. ■

If you want to manually select a new game card driver, select the Display a List of All the Drivers in a Specific Location, So You Can Select the Driver You Want option. This option instructs Windows to create a list of drivers from which you can select the new keyboard driver. The following steps assume that you have selected this option.

5. Click Next. The Update Device Driver Wizard screen shown in Figure 31.7 appears. In the Mo<u>d</u>els listbox, select the model that matches your keyboard. If your model is not listed and you have a new driver on a disk, click <u>H</u>ave Disk and specify where this new driver is located.

FIG. 31.7
Windows 98 shows a list of manufacturers and models that might match your installed game card.

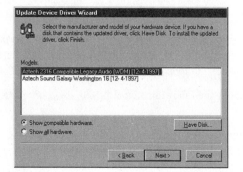

Part
VIII

Ch
31

 TIP The Mode<u>l</u>s listbox displays the keyboard models compatible with your hardware. Make sure that the Show <u>C</u>ompatible Hardware option is selected. If the keyboard you want to set up is not on the list, you should select the Show <u>A</u>ll Hardware option. The list changes to show all such keyboards.

6. Click the Next button. You are prompted to insert the disk that contains the new driver. Click OK after you insert the disk, or click OK if the disk already is inserted (such as a CD-ROM or your hard drive).

7. After the driver is installed, you are returned to the Update Device Driver Wizard. Click Finish.

8. You are prompted to restart Windows 98 to finish the driver update. Click <u>Y</u>es to restart your computer.

Calibrating Joysticks with the Game Controllers Applet

After you configure your new game card, attach a joystick (or other gaming device, such as a game pad) to the connections available on the game card. *Joysticks* are hardware devices used primarily for games. Your game card (or your sound card, if your game adapter is part of a sound card) has a 15-pin D-shell–type socket into which you can connect the male end of the joystick cable.

After you attach a joystick to the game card, you're ready to calibrate it to work with Windows. In Windows 98, the Joystick applet (which was introduced in Windows 95) in the Control Panel has been replaced with the Game Controllers applet. This applet enables you to configure and test game controllers (including joysticks and game pads).

N O T E PC game pads are similar in function to joysticks, but they resemble game pads used with game systems, such as SEGA Genesis and Nintendo 64. You can use the information presented in this section to set up and calibrate many game-pad devices. You should consult your game-pad manual or online documentation for additional instructions for your specific game pad, however. ■

Connect your game port (which is a 15-pin port on the back of your computer), and attach your joystick's game-port connector to it. Next, install the joystick software based on the instructions accompanying the joystick. Reboot Windows 98 to finish the installation process.

After Windows 98 reboots, use the following steps to calibrate your joystick using the Game Controllers applet:

1. Choose Start, Settings, Control Panel and double-click the Game Controllers icon. The Game Controllers dialog box appears (see Figure 31.8). Your new joystick should appear in the Game Controllers listbox.

FIG. 31.8

Use the Game Controllers applet to calibrate your new joystick.

2. On the General page, select the joystick you want to calibrate in the Controller column.

 T I P If your joystick does not appear in the Game Controllers listbox, click Add to display the Add Game Controller dialog box (see Figure 31.9). Find the type of joystick you want to set up in the Game Controllers listbox and click OK.

FIG. 31.9

The Add Game Controller dialog box enables you to add a new joystick.

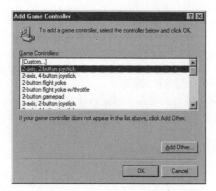

3. Click Properties to display the Game Controller Properties dialog box.

4. Select the Test page (see Figure 31.10). Test the functionality of your joystick by moving the joystick and watching the Axes section. The plus-sign (+) indicator in the Axes section should mimic the movement and rotation of your joystick. Also, move the hat-switch button (if available) on your joystick and watch the Point of View Hat section. The movement of the arrow indicator (which only appears when you start moving the hat switch) should mimic the movement of the hat-switch button. Finally, click each joystick button to make sure that the corresponding light in the Buttons section lights up.

Part
VIII

Ch
31

FIG. 31.10

Use the Test page to test your game controller's functionality.

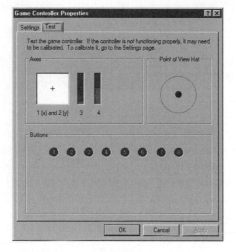

If your joystick functions properly, click OK twice. If it does not function properly, continue these steps.

5. Select the Settings page.

6. Click <u>C</u>alibrate to calibrate your joystick. The Calibration dialog box for your joystick appears. Figure 31.11 shows the SideWinder 3D Pro Calibration dialog box, which appears if you use the Microsoft SideWinder 3D Pro joystick. Follow the instructions on the Calibration dialog boxes to calibrate your joystick. Click <u>N</u>ext after you perform each action. In the last Calibration dialog box, click <u>F</u>inish to complete the calibration procedure. (The actual number of Calibration dialog boxes you see depends on the model of the game controller you have installed.)

FIG. 31.11
The Calibration dialog box enables you to set your joystick's center position, range of motion, and point-of-view hat.

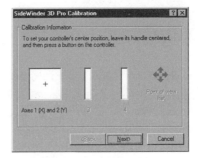

7. Enable the <u>R</u>udder/Pedals check box on the Settings page if your joystick includes an attached rudder or pedal device.

8. Click OK to return to the General page of the Game Controllers dialog box.

9. Click OK to save your settings.

 T I P To remove a game controller, select the controller name and click <u>R</u>emove. The Remove Controller confirmation box appears, asking whether you are sure you want to remove the selected controller. Click <u>Y</u>es to remove it.

N O T E Microsoft manufactures a line of gaming devices called SideWinder; it offers the SideWinder Standard and SideWinder 3D Pro joysticks and the SideWinder game pad. These devices are designed to work well with Microsoft games developed for Windows 98. Many users find that these products do not work perfectly with games produced by other manufacturers, however. Some of the problems range from users having to recalibrate the joystick each time they reboot the system to Windows 98 not recognizing the game card when playing certain games.

One of the best ways to get information about a specific problem you are experiencing with these products is to join the Microsoft Hardware Products newsgroup at

    microsoft.public.microsofthardware.products

You also can read the Frequently Asked Questions page for SideWinder 3D Pro at

    http://www.microsoft.com/HardwareSupport/SideWinder/content/faq/

Changing the Game Controller Port Driver and ID Settings

Windows 98 enables you to set a specific port driver for a game controller. This capability is handy if your joystick or game pad requires a specific port driver that Windows does not set up automatically. Also, you can assign a game controller an ID, which certain games use to identify your game controller.

To set the ID and port driver settings, follow these steps:

1. Choose Start, Settings, Control Panel and double-click the Game Controllers icon. The Game Controllers dialog box appears.

2. Select the Advanced page (see Figure 31.12).

Part

VIII

Ch

31

FIG. 31.12

You use the Advanced page of the Game Controllers dialog box to set controller IDs and port drivers.

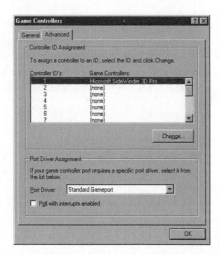

3. In the Controller ID's column, select an ID you want to assign to a controller. If the ID for your controller is correct, you do not need to change it.

4. Click Change to display the Change Controller Assignment dialog box (see Figure 31.13).

5. In the Game Controllers listbox, select the game controller you want to assign to the ID that appears in the Selected ID field.

6. Click OK to return to the Advanced page.

7. In the Port Driver drop-down listbox, select the port driver your game controller port requires. If the port driver is correct, you do not have to change it.

8. If you are experiencing modem problems while playing online games, disable the Poll with Interrupts Enabled check box.

FIG. 31.13

You use the Change Controller Assignment dialog box to assign new controller IDs.

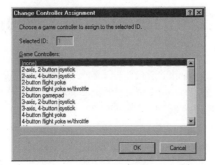

TROUBLESHOOTING

I use the Microsoft SideWinder Game pad device under Windows 98, but I cannot get it to work with MS-DOS. Why not? The Microsoft Gamepad is designed to work with Windows 98 and sends digital-signal values to the joystick port. These digital signals are interpreted by a device driver in Windows 98. These drivers do not exist for MS-DOS. There is no word from Microsoft as to whether it will release updated drivers or *terminate-and-stay resident* (TSR) programs to work with MS-DOS.

Configuring Digital Cameras

by Keith Underdahl

In this chapter

Choosing the Right Digital Camera

Digital cameras occupy one of the fastest growing segments of consumer electronics, and as they grow in popularity, prices are dropping rapidly. But although price is important, it is not the only thing you should consider. Before you buy, evaluate image quality, the methods used to store images in the camera, accessories, and compatibility with your computer.

This section discusses what you should look for as far as the type of PC interface the camera should have. This is important because PC compatibility is probably one of the main reasons you bought digital in the first place. Beyond that, you should also consider image quality. Higher quality cameras almost always cost more, so you will have to decide what suits both your needs and budget. If you plan to use the images in a Web site, or if you want to print them using a color printer, 640×480 pixels should be your bare minimum, with higher numbers equating to higher quality.

Also consider what extra items come with the camera and what accessories are available. For instance, does the camera include any free image editing software, such as Adobe PhotoDeluxe or PhotoShop? Is there an LCD preview screen built into the camera? Can you buy accessories, such as a printer or spare storage cards?

Another important thing to consider is how the images are stored. The least desirable method is for images to be stored in internal memory; images stored in memory are susceptible to loss if the camera battery dies. Also, you can only take as many pictures as the memory has room for. Ideally, the camera should use some type of removable storage medium such as a card or disk. This helps to ensure image integrity, and with spare storage media, the number of pictures you can take is unlimited.

Some digital cameras use 3.5-inch floppy disks to store images. This greatly simplifies the configuration process because you can simply put the "film" (in this case, a floppy disk) right into the floppy disk drive of your computer. However, this also makes the camera bulkier, and a single disk might store fewer than ten high-quality images.

Whatever you decide, some careful research and shopping beforehand will help you get the camera that is right for you. Reading through this chapter *before* you buy will help you be a more informed and knowledgeable consumer.

Hardware Setup

Your first step in configuring a digital camera should be to make sure that both your PC and the camera itself are ready to be connected to each other. A physical connection must exist if you hope to download all those great new photos you just took, so this first step is critical. Begin by carefully reading all the documentation that comes with your camera. Every device is different, so this material will no doubt contain invaluable instructions and tips to guide you through the process.

TIP Your new camera probably contains instructions for installing the device on a PC running Windows 3.1 or Windows 95, or on a Macintosh but says nothing about Windows 98. Worry not! In general, you should be able to follow the instructions given for Windows 95, along with the steps in this chapter, without any problem. We have tested this with several cameras and met with success every time.

Deciding Which Port to Use

Begin by determining what kind of port will be needed to connect the camera to your computer. Most digital cameras currently on the market have provisions for connecting to an RS-232 (D-SUB 9) serial port, an RCA-style video jack, or a Macintosh serial port. Some cameras connect to a parallel port rather than a serial port, and a few of the latest cameras use a USB (Universal Serial Bus) port.

Most digital cameras use either the serial, parallel, or USB port. If your camera has an RCA jack for video output, it is probably meant primarily for use with a VCR or TV. However, you might be able to connect the RCA jack to a video capture board, so be sure to check all the documentation to see just what you can and cannot do. Considering the fact that you bought this book, you probably won't have much use for the Macintosh serial adapter. Be careful not to confuse the Macintosh serial adapter with a PS/2 port.

Which port you use depends largely on what type of interface cable comes with the camera. Again, the documentation should provide some help with this. Also, this all assumes that your computer has an available port of the same type supported by the camera. Your best bet is to check the back of your computer before buying a camera to ensure that you get one with the right interface.

Part
VIII

Ch
32

Connecting the Camera

After you've located an available port on the back of your computer, it's time to plug things in. Perform the following:

1. Gather together the camera, cables, and any documentation you might need.

2. Shut down the computer and make sure that the power is turned off.

CAUTION

Most digital cameras do not support "hot connections," meaning that you must turn off the power on both the camera and the PC before connecting or disconnecting any wires. Plugging in the cords while the power is on could damage the camera and could also void your warranty.

3. Connect the cable to the appropriate ports on the computer and camera.

4. If the camera uses a pass-through style connector for the PC's parallel port, connect the cable to the computer, and plug in any devices (such as a printer or external modem) that were previously connected there to the port.

5. Turn on the camera's power.

6. Turn on the computer and wait for Windows 98 to start.

What If You Don't Have an Available Port?

It is entirely possible that when you look at the back of your computer for an open port you won't find one. Fortunately, you have some options:

■ Purchase a video capture board. This will allow you to quickly and easily connect the camera's video output jack to the video-in connection on the board. Most video capture boards plug into a PCI slot on your motherboard, so make sure that you have one free.

■ If you don't have an open PCI slot, you can also get a video capture device, such as ZipShot, that connects via a parallel port pass-through connector.

■ Some cameras actually come with their own expansion board (ISA or PCI). Although these cameras tend to be more expensive, they can also solve your port availability problems.

■ Do you have a serial mouse? If so, it's connected to a working RS-232 port right now. If your computer has an open PS/2 port, buy a PS/2 mouse and use the serial port for your camera. Alternatively, you could just live without the mouse for a short time while you download images from the camera. This might be the most inexpensive alternative.

■ Another inexpensive alternative is to buy a serial expansion board, available at many computer stores for less than $40. This will give you another serial port (as well as an extra parallel port) to plug your camera into.

Installing the Camera Software

After the hardware has been installed, you must install the software that accompanies the camera. Your camera should come with a CD-ROM or floppy disk with some utility and driver software. Depending on your camera, you will need to install one or more of the following:

■ *Device driver.* This will probably be a TWAIN-compliant driver. TWAIN drivers provide a standard method for imaging devices such as digital cameras and scanners to communicate with Windows applications. A device driver must be installed before the camera will work.

■ *Utility software.* Utilities usually allow you to control certain functions of the camera directly from your PC. The utility software (see Figure 32.1) might also allow you to make adjustments that the controls on the camera itself might not be able to do, such as adjust the internal clock. The camera utility is usually mandatory, although image editors can serve many of the same functions.

■ *Image editor.* Some cameras come with free image editing software, such as Adobe PhotoDeluxe. This software allows you to modify and edit digital images after they have been downloaded from the camera. You might also be able to use the image editor to acquire images directly from the camera, without opening the camera utility.

FIG. 32.1

This utility software accompanies Olympus digital cameras, and allows you to control the camera from your PC.

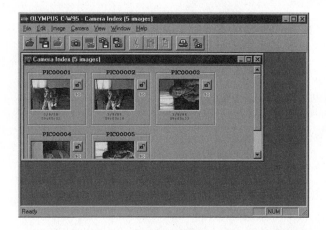

Your first step should be to install the camera's device driver. If the software comes on a CD-ROM, a setup wizard might start automatically when you insert the disk into the CD-ROM drive. Follow the onscreen instructions to complete the setup. Otherwise, follow the installation instructions that come with the CD-ROM or perform the following:

1. Insert the disk into the appropriate drive.

2. Open My Computer and then open the drive that the disk is in.

3. If the disk has folders for different operating systems, such as the disk shown in Figure 32.2, open the one for Windows 98.

Part

VIII

Ch

32

FIG. 32.2

Open the folder for your operating system. In this case, the Win95nt4 folder is the best choice.

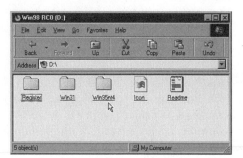

4. Look for an icon called Setup. Click it to open the file and begin installation. Follow the wizard screens that appear to install the driver.

5. Restart the computer if prompted to do so.

After the driver has been installed, you may continue installing any other software in a similar manner. Again, keep in mind that your camera might not contain instructions specifically for Windows 98. If this is the case, instructions for Windows 95 should suffice.

Configuring the Camera

One drawback of digital cameras is that most of them are not Plug and Play compatible. Plug and Play is a standard used by many hardware devices to simplify the installation process. Installation of Plug and Play devices is almost effortless because Windows and the device's software automate configuration, ensuring that resource conflicts do not exist. But as we said, most digital cameras are not Plug and Play, so you will probably have to do some manual configuration.

How you configure the camera depends in large part on how it is connected to your computer. See the "Hardware Setup" section earlier in this chapter.

 One of the most common reasons for a nonresponding camera is simply that the power isn't on. Most digital cameras have a feature that automatically turns them off after two or three minutes of inactivity to preserve battery power. Checking this often saves time and frustration as you hunt down a problem.

Universal Serial Bus (USB) Cameras

Digital cameras using the USB interface are still rare, but they should grow in popularity in the near future. USB cameras present the fewest potential configuration problems, due to the nature of the bus. Also, USB devices allow "hot" plugging, which means you won't have to turn off the computer to connect or disconnect the camera.

Unlike cameras using other styles of interfaces, all USB cameras *are* Plug and Play compatible, so you should not encounter any configuration problems. Windows 98 fully supports USB technology, so if it's also supported by your computer and camera, installation should go smoothly. Simply install the camera's device driver, and you're ready to go!

Serial Port Cameras

Many current digital cameras utilize an RS-232 (D-SUB-9) serial port. Virtually all PCs have a serial port, so using one for the camera makes sense. Most PCs have two serial ports, and one of them is usually used by the mouse. You should be able to connect your camera to the open serial port and test it using the camera utility software. However, if the camera does not respond, there are several things you should check.

First, you'll need to check several things in the system CMOS/BIOS setup utility, which you must access by restarting the computer. As soon as the computer begins to turn on again, you should see it running through a memory test, and a message will appear on the screen that says something like, "Press DEL to run SETUP." Press the Delete key on your keyboard to run CMOS setup. You might need to browse through several submenus to check the following items:

- Look for settings for Onboard Serials Ports one and two. Make sure that both are enabled and write down the COM and address information. It will probably look something like Listing 32.1.

Listing 32.1   Serial Port Settings

```
ONBOARD SERIAL PORT 1          COM1/3F8
ONBOARD SERIAL PORT 2          COM2/2F8
```

- Check the Interrupt Request (IRQ) settings for your COM ports and write down that information. Make sure that the appropriate IRQs are enabled, as shown in Listing 32.2.

Listing 32.2.   IRQ Settings

```
IRQ3 (COM2):    ENABLE
IRQ4 (COM1):    ENABLE
```

If you made any changes (such as enabling a disabled IRQ), make sure that you save them to the system BIOS before exiting the setup utility. Test the camera to see whether that fixed the problem. If not, it's time to check system resources for other possible conflicts. Most PCs have four COM ports. Either COM 3 or COM 4 is usually used by a modem, and COM 1 and COM 2 should be assigned to the serial ports.

If your camera is connected to a serial port but won't work, you might want to make sure that another device is not conflicting with it. First, refer to the notes you took from the CMOS setup utility. In a perfect world, the COM settings assigned to the serial ports should not be assigned to anything else, but sometimes they are accidentally assigned to a modem. To check this, perform the following:

1. Click the Start button and choose Settings, Control Panel.
2. Click the Modems icon. On the General tab, highlight the modem and click Properties.
3. The Modem Properties dialog box will show you which COM port is assigned to the modem, as shown in Figure 32.3.
4. If the COM port conflicts with one of the serial ports (that is, if it is set as COM1 or COM2), click the drop-down arrow for the Port list and select a different port. It is best to use COM3 or COM4 for the modem.
5. Click OK and Finish when you are done. If you have more than one modem, make sure that you check this information for each one.

A final possibility for hardware conflicts involves IRQ settings. You can check the current settings from the Control Panel by opening the System icon and selecting the Device Manager tab. Highlight Computer at the top of the list and choose Properties. With the Interrupt Request (IRQ) radio button selected on the View Resources tab, the Computer Properties dialog box will display current IRQ settings (see Figure 32.4).

Part
VIII

Ch
32

FIG. 32.3

This modem correctly uses COM3.

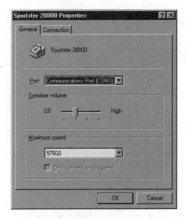

FIG. 32.4

Computer Properties displays the current IRQ settings.

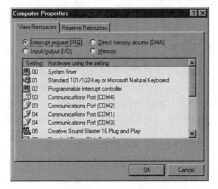

Based on the information shown in Figures 32.3 and 32.4, we can begin to investigate the conflict. Here is what we know so far:

■ The computer has a serial mouse using either COM1 or COM2.

■ According to Figure 32.3, the modem uses COM3.

■ The modem and mouse both function properly, but the camera does not.

Given these facts, we can surmise that the serial port used by the mouse must be COM2. If the mouse used COM1, the modem would not function because it would also operate on the same interrupt. The mouse should not share an IRQ with any other device. However, COM2 must use IRQ3, and COM1 must use IRQ4. The logical solution would be to change the IRQ setting for COM3 or COM4, and if your system BIOS allows you to do that, you're in luck. Unfortunately, many motherboards are poorly designed, and you might not be able to make this change.

If you're stuck in this situation, you have several possible solutions. One, if your motherboard will support a PS/2 mouse, you could start using one of those to free up the serial port. Check the documentation that came with your PC to find out whether you can do this. Another solution might be to purchase a serial expansion board, available from many computer and consumer electronics stores for less than $40. These boards fit in a PCI or ISA expansion slot and usually contain extra serial and parallel ports.

> **CAUTION**
>
> Make sure that any serial expansion board you buy allows you to assign an IRQ other than three or four to the COM ports.

A third solution might be to create a second hardware profile specifically for the camera. You can call the second profile "Camera" or something similar, and in that profile you would disable to modem so that it does not conflict with the second serial port. Of course, this would require you to reboot every time you wanted to download images from the camera and then reboot again when you're done, but it is one possibility. See Chapter 5, "Installing and Configuring New Hardware and Software," for more on creating hardware profiles.

A variation on the theme mentioned earlier involves using an external modem. The modem and camera could share a serial port via a switch box, or you could manually switch the cables. To do this, you would still need to create multiple hardware profiles.

These steps should solve your problem. As a last resort, you could shut down the computer and connect the serial cable for your camera where the mouse usually plugs in, and simply use keyboard commands to download the images. If you do this, create a second hardware profile in which the mouse driver is disabled. Obviously, this is not exactly a desirable choice, so try the other solutions first.

Parallel Port Cameras

The parallel port is a popular place to plug in peripherals, and "daisy-chaining," or connecting several devices inline, is becoming increasingly common. The device most often connected to the parallel port is a printer, but it can also be used for external modems, scanners, and external storage devices. Now add to that list digital cameras.

Using the parallel port makes sense. For one thing, you probably won't have the resource conflict problems that accompany serial ports, although some parallel devices such as modems and disk drives might prevent other devices from sharing the port. Parallel port cameras usually come with a pass-through cord, as demonstrated earlier in this chapter.

The most important thing to remember about using the parallel port is that of all the devices connected to the port, only one can be used at a time. For instance, if you are printing a large document and you want to download images from the camera, you'll have to wait until the printer is done using the port.

Part
VIII

Ch
32

Adjusting the Camera Settings with the Camera Utility

You might need to make some adjustments to the camera itself using the camera's utility program. To do so, open the utility using the path specified in the documentation. The utility program will probably be installed in the Programs menu, and it should have a name indicative of the device's name or manufacturer.

After the program is open, look through the options in the menu bar and find a selection called Options or Preferences. Here you will see a variety of configuration settings for the camera, including port settings (see Figure 32.5). If the camera uses a serial port, make sure that the correct COM port setting is shown.

FIG. 32.5
Check the camera's
configuration settings.

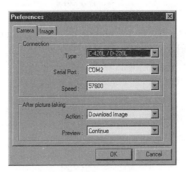

Another setting you might see is the port speed. Consult your camera's documentation for an appropriate speed. If no recommendation is given, choose 57600 bps. Click OK when you are done making adjustments.

Using Windows Imaging to Download Images

Many digital cameras include image editing software, such as Adobe PhotoDeluxe or PhotoShop. These programs allow you to manipulate or retouch digital images in a variety of ways. However, if your camera did not include such software, Windows 98 includes a light-featured but handy applet that gives you some basic editing capabilities called Windows Imaging. You can launch Imaging by clicking the Start button and choosing Programs, Accessories, Imaging.

Downloading images

Your first step will be to set Imaging to read from the digital camera. On the Imaging menu bar choose File, Select Scanner to open the Select Scanner dialog box (see Figure 32.6). All digital imaging devices installed on your PC will be listed here. If the camera is not shown, then it has not been installed properly. Refer to the installation and configuration sections of this chapter.

 If you just installed the camera and it is not shown in the Select Scanner list, restart the computer and try again.

FIG. 32.6
Select the device you
want Imaging to read
from.

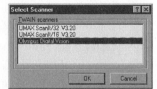

Highlight the listing for the camera and click OK. Now you're ready to begin downloading
information from the camera. On the Imaging menu bar choose File, Scan New. Imaging will
automatically download thumbnails of images currently stored in the camera (see Figure 32.7).
From here, you can select all images—or only a few—for download.

FIG. 32.7
Imaging is ready to
control the camera.

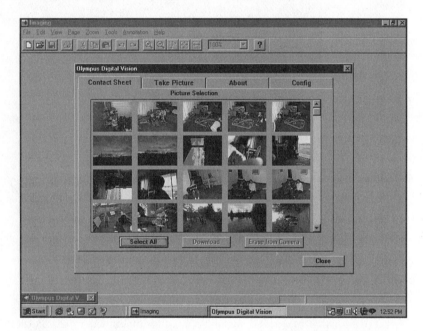

To select a single image, click it to highlight its border. To select multiple images, hold down
Ctrl as you click each image. Click Download when you have selected the ones you want. As
you can see, many other options for controlling the camera are available here. You can erase
images from the camera's memory, take pictures, or change configuration settings.

Editing Images

Windows Imaging is not without its drawbacks. The most important shortcoming is that it can
only save files in bitmap (.BMP), TIFF (.TIF), or fax document (.AWD) format. These formats
are not compatible with the Internet, so you won't be able to use them on a Web page. Fortunately, many cameras automatically save images in JPEG (.JPG) format, so you might still be
able to use them in a Web page. However, you will not be able to edit them using Windows

Imaging. On the other hand, if you only plan to make direct prints of the images with your color printer, or if you will use them in non-Web related documents, Imaging is sufficient.

You can begin editing a bitmap or TIFF image by clicking the Open icon on the Imaging toolbar and navigating to the desired file. If the picture is a different format—such as JPEG—you will need to save it as a bitmap or TIFF before you can begin editing. After the image is open, choose File, Save As from the menu bar. Type in a new name, select a format, and click Save. Now you're ready to edit the image (see Figure 32.8).

FIG. 32.8

Imaging is ready to edit the picture.

Truth be told, the editing capabilities are limited. There are three things you might find useful:

- *Rotate the image.* Sometimes you rotate the camera when you take a picture. If you were taking a full length picture of a standing person, for instance, you would probably turn the camera on its side to take the picture. Use the Rotate Left and Rotate Right icons on the Imaging toolbar to put your subject right side up.

- *Add text.* On occasion, you might want to add text directly to a picture. Use the controls on the Annotation toolbar to add and edit text.

- *Crop the image.* Sometimes you might want to trim off excess parts of a picture. For instance, suppose that you want to trim the image shown in Figure 32.8 so that Cole takes up more of the picture. Click the Selection tool icon on the Imaging toolbar, and then click and drag a selected area on the image. Now click the Cut icon on the Standard toolbar, so that a white space is left where you cut the selected area (see Figure 32.9).

FIG. 32.9
Cole has been cut from the picture.

Using the Selection tool again, select the entire image and press Delete. Now right-click in the image area and choose <u>P</u>aste. The final product should look something like Figure 32.10.

FIG. 32.10
The picture has been cropped to a smaller area.

Again, Imaging is not the most advanced image editor available, but it will give you some basic options if you have nothing else. ●

Part
VIII

Ch
32

Appendixes

What's New with Windows 98

by Keith Underdahl

In this appendix

Accessibility Wizard

Windows 98 offers support for persons with disabilities and significantly reduces the need for costly hardware add-ons. The Accessibility Wizard improves the setup process, ensuring that the PC is more accessible than ever. Improvements include visual enhancements for people with vision disabilities, as well as StickyKeys, MouseKeys, and ShowSounds to help those with other specific handicaps. See Chapter 3, "Selecting Windows 98 Components," for more on accessibility options.

Backup

The improved Backup utility provides enhanced support for various backup devices, including newer items such as ZIP drives. Backup helps you preserve important data in the event of a system malfunction or other loss. Backup is discussed in Chapter 13, "Setting Up Backup Systems."

Desktop Enhancements

Among the most obvious changes to come with Windows 98 are the many visual enhancements made to the desktop. The biggest news involves the new *Web style navigation*. With *Web style navigation*, you can now open icons and folders with only a single mouse click rather than the double-click you probably used with the *Classic Style navigation* of Windows 95 and earlier. And where before you might have single-clicked an item to select it, you now only have to point to an item to select it. These techniques also apply to other common windows, including My Computer and Windows Explorer. These features are discussed in greater detail in Chapter 6, "Configuring Windows 98 Classic and Web View Desktops." If you have already been using Internet Explorer 4.0 with Windows 95, you might be familiar with these and other features.

Improved Start Menu

In addition to the new navigation methods used on the desktop, the Start menu has also been substantially revised. You can use drag and drop to add or remove items in the Start menus, and several of the menus have been reorganized. The reorganized menus arrange items into more logical subgroupings (see Figure A.1).

New Desktop Themes

Four themes from the Microsoft Kids! accessory program are included with Windows 98. In addition, all the themes that were previously part of the Microsoft Plus! add-in for Windows 95 are now included with Windows 98. Most of the other visual enhancements that used to come with Plus! are also incorporated, including smooth edges for screen fonts and the capability to show window contents when dragging. You can adjust these features by opening the Display Properties dialog box and choosing the Effects tab.

The Accessories menu has been simplified
by the creation of new submenus

FIG. A.1
The improved
Windows 98
Start menu.

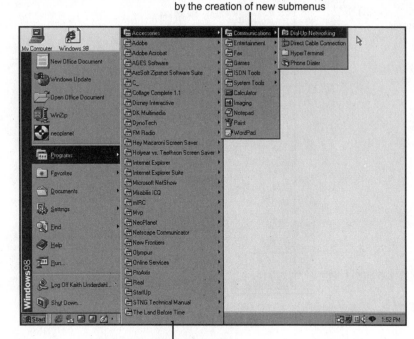

Click here to scroll down and view
more of the Programs menu

Quick Launch Toolbar

The Quick Launch toolbar (see Figure A.2) provides a convenient way to open the programs you use most. It is located on the taskbar next to the Start button, and by default includes buttons for Internet Explorer, Outlook Express, TV Viewer, WebTV, Show Desktop, and Channels. The Show Desktop button works just like the Minimize All Windows command in the taskbar shortcut menu. You can also drag and drop shortcuts for other programs to the Quick Launch toolbar, or drag items off that you don't use often.

Dial-Up Networking Server Support

Support for making your computer a Dial-Up Networking server is now built in to Windows 98. This eliminates the need for specialized software previously required.

FIG. A.2
The Quick Launch
toolbar.

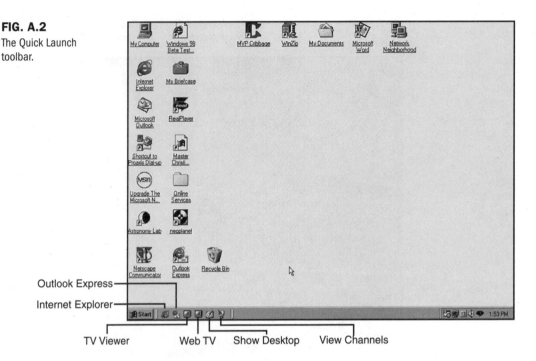

Outlook Express
Internet Explorer

TV Viewer   Web TV   Show Desktop   View Channels

Drive Converter (FAT32)

The Drive Converter is easily one of the most important features of Windows 98. It converts
your 512MB or larger hard drive to a 32-bit File Allocation Table (FAT32), without the need to
reformat your drive and lose existing data. FAT32 makes much more efficient use of the available space on your hard drive, eliminating the need for disk compression. It also allows hard
drives larger than 2GB to be partitioned as a single drive. Learn more about the Drive Converter and partitioning in Chapter 10, "Installing and Configuring Hard Disk Drives."

> **N O T E**   If you are upgrading from the OSR-2 version of Windows 95, your hard drive might already
> be partitioned with FAT32. To check your version of Windows 95, right-click the My
> Computer icon, choose Properties, and check the listing under System on the General tab. If the
> version number is 4.00.950A, you do *not* have OSR-2. ▪

Internet Connection Wizard

The Windows 98 Internet Connection Wizard greatly simplifies the process of starting an
Internet account on your PC and getting connected. What before was a confusing and often
maddening process involving DNS numbers and scripting tools is now much easier to deal
with.

Maintenance Wizard

The Maintenance Wizard automates many of the system maintenance functions that should be run periodically. You can choose from a list of utilities, including Scan Disk, Disk Cleanup, Disk Defragmenter, and others, as well as select when and how often they should be run. These utilities help your PC run more efficiently, and they can provide more free space on your hard drive. Chapter 14, "Configuring Memory, Disks, and Devices," covers proper housekeeping for your hard drive.

Multimedia Support

In keeping with technology trends in the world of PCs, Windows 98 offers vastly improved multimedia support through such programs as DirectX, NetShow, and more. See Part IV of this book for more on Windows 98 multimedia capabilities.

Multiple Display Support

Windows 98 supports the use of multiple displays on your computer. Assuming that you have the right hardware, you can in theory use as many monitors as you want, each one functioning as part of your Windows desktop. The most common use of this feature would be to enable two monitors, arranged side by side. If the monitors are set to 600×800 resolution, this setup would actually give you a 600×1600 desktop. Likewise, four monitors arranged in a grid would provide a 1200×1600 grid. See Chapter 7, "Configuring Monitors and Video Cards," for more on multiple display support.

New Hardware Support

Support for new hardware and technologies is an important feature of Windows 98. On the multimedia front, Windows 98 provides software support for DVD drives, allowing you to view DVD movies right on your PC. Also, WebTV for Windows supports TV-PC cards and integrates Web-based content with regular television viewing capabilities. Windows 98 also supports new bus technologies such as IEEE-1394 (Firewire), Universal Serial Bus (USB), and Accelerated Graphics Port (AGP).

Power Management

Advanced Configuration and Power Interface (ACPI) is a new power management standard for emerging computer and peripheral technologies. Windows 98 provides support for this specification, ensuring efficient power usage for all of your devices. Learn more about configuring power-saving devices in Chapter 2, "Installing Windows 98 on a Desktop and Laptop."

Registry Checker

It doesn't take too much fiddling in the system Registry to completely corrupt your PC. Fortunately, Windows 98 automatically makes a backup copy of your Registry every time you boot up, just in case a problem occurs. The Registry is checked during each boot sequence, and if a problem is found you will be able to restore your system by using the backup Registry copy. Windows 98 also provides a System File Checker that looks at critical system files to see whether they have been corrupted.

Scan Disk

Scan Disk is nothing new; it is a useful utility that has been around since the days of DOS. What's new is that Windows 98 automatically runs Scan Disk during startup whenever the system was not shut down properly.

Web Integration

Another new key feature of Windows 98 is the integration of Web content into the user interface. The World Wide Web figures prominently in almost every aspect of the Windows 98 operating environment, and you can quickly and easily access Web pages from almost anywhere in Windows. Most windows contain an Address bar (see Figure A.-3) where you can type in paths to files and folders on your hard drive, or URLs for Web sites.

FIG. A.3
My Computer can be used to view contents of your hard drive, or a Web page.

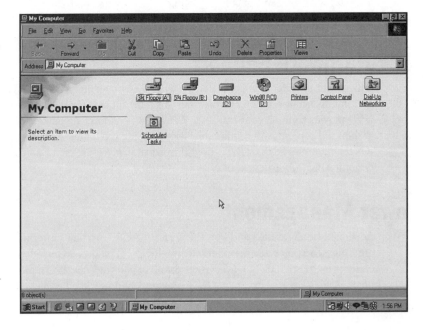

Internet Explorer 4.0

The Internet Explorer 4.0 suite is an integral part of Windows 98. It includes the Internet Explorer Web browser, the Outlook Express email and newsgroup client, NetMeeting for Internet conferencing, and the FrontPage Express HTML editor. Components of Internet Explorer are covered in Part V of this book.

Channels

The Channels that are a part of Windows 98 use what is known as *push technology*. Channels are hosted by a variety of media and culture sources on the Internet, and when you subscribe to one, its content is automatically updated on your computer on a regular basis. In theory, this saves time because the information is already downloaded when you are ready to view it.

Active Desktop

Windows 98 offers a unique method of Web integration with the Active Desktop. It fully integrates the Internet into your Windows desktop, making it possible even to use a Web page on your desktop in place of wallpaper (see Figure A.4).

FIG. A.4

The Active Desktop enables you to set a Web site as your desktop wallpaper.

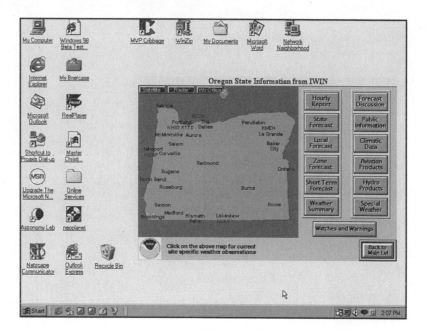

Windows Support from Microsoft

Microsoft has improved its support of Windows 98 in several ways. First, the Windows Help applet has been improved and is now easier and quicker to use. But more interesting is Windows Update, a method for obtaining new hardware drivers and other software updates quickly and efficiently via the World Wide Web. You can begin the updating process by clicking Start, Windows Update. ●

Configuring Windows Messaging and Microsoft Fax

by Rob Tidrow

In this appendix

Read This First

One of the most popular communications components of Windows 95 is Microsoft Fax. With Windows 98, however, Fax is not an option to install. To use Fax under Windows 98, you must have previously installed Fax under Windows 95. During the Windows 98 Setup process, Fax is left intact. You can then use Fax to send and receive fax messages.

This appendix assumes you want to be able to run Microsoft Fax under Windows 98, but you have not installed Windows 98 yet. You need to work through this appendix before running Windows 98 Setup. This appendix also assumes you have Windows 95 running and that Windows Messaging (formerly called Microsoft Exchange in early releases of Windows 95) is installed. If you don't have Windows Messaging installed, refer to your Windows 95 documentation.

> **CAUTION**
>
> If you uninstall Microsoft Fax under Windows 98, you cannot re-install it under Windows 98. You must re-install Windows 95, install Fax, and then upgrade to Windows 98 again.

Identifying the Features of Microsoft Fax

Microsoft Fax enables you to send and receive faxes through your fax modem on your computer. You can use Microsoft Fax on a separate computer to service one user, or connect it to a network to use it as a fax server in a workgroup environment.

Microsoft Fax is part of the Windows Messaging architecture and can replace any fax software you might already have installed on your computer, such as WinFax Pro. Microsoft Fax enables you to create fax messages, add cover pages, and send the messages to another fax machine or fax modem device. Because Fax is a *MAPI (Messaging Application Programming Interface)* compliant application, you can use other applications, such as Microsoft Word for Windows 97, to send faxes. Also, if you use Microsoft Fax to send a fax to a fax modem, you can encrypt it with a password to provide a layer of security for the document.

 Microsoft Fax includes fax printer drivers so you can print to a fax modem from within any Windows application.

You also can use Microsoft Fax to receive fax messages. A message can be faxed to you by the sender calling your fax number and delivering the fax. Or, if you use fax-back services to receive technical support information, sales information, or other data, you can dial the service and have it download the document to your fax modem using Microsoft Fax.

 You can store fax messages in the Windows Messaging Inbox.

A Microsoft Fax message can be sent in one of two ways:

- Binary file
- Hard copy fax

The latter option is the traditional way in which fax messages are sent and received via a fax machine, known as a Group 3 fax machine. The limitation of sending faxes this way is that the recipient cannot edit the document or use it as a binary file, unless the document is scanned or keyed into a file. A *binary file* is simply a file created in an application, such as Word for Windows or Lotus 1-2-3 for Windows. Another frustrating aspect of paper faxes is that they can be difficult or impossible to read.

When you use Microsoft Fax to send a binary file to another fax modem, the recipient can view and edit the fax in the application in which it was created and modify it. This feature is handled by Microsoft Fax's *Binary File Transfer (BFT)* capability. BFT was originally created for Microsoft's At Work program and is now supported by Windows Messaging so that you can create a mail message and attach a binary file to it. Windows for Workgroups 3.11 and other Microsoft At Work enabled platforms also can receive BFT messages.

One way in which you can take advantage of the BFT feature in Microsoft Fax is to use it with other applications, such as Microsoft Word for Windows. You can, for example, create a Word document and send it as a Microsoft Fax message to another user who has Microsoft Fax installed (and Word for Windows). The recipient receives the message and can read it as a Word document.

If the recipient doesn't have a fax modem card and Microsoft Fax and instead has a Group 3 fax machine, Microsoft Fax automatically prints the Word document as a printed fax image. A problem with sending files this way is the transmission speed and compression feature of the recipient fax machine. Fax machines are much slower than fax modems, so a large binary file (such as a 50-page Word document), can take a long time to transmit and print on the recipient's fax machine. Before you send a large attached document to someone's fax machine, you might want to test this feature first.

Fax Modem Requirements of Microsoft Fax

Besides having Windows 98 and Windows Messaging installed, you must have a fax modem installed. Your fax modem must meet the following requirements:

- High-speed fax modem, such as a 14.4 or higher Kbps fax modem
- Phone line
- Minimum requirements of Windows 95, but Pentium-based computer with 16 MB of RAM is recommended

When you install Microsoft Fax on a network, your system must meet the following requirements:

- High-speed fax modem, such as a 14.4, 28.8, or 33.6 Kbps fax modem
- Phone line

- At least an 80486-based computer with 8 MB of RAM
- If the computer will be used as a workstation, at least 12 MB of RAM

Regardless of the way in which you set up Microsoft Fax, either as a standalone or networked fax service, make sure that your fax modem is compatible with Microsoft Fax.

The following lists and describes the compatible fax modems and fax machines you can use with Microsoft Fax:

- **Class 1 and Class 2.** You need Class 1 or Class 2 fax modems to send BFT messages with attachments. These classes of fax modems also are required to use security features in Microsoft Fax.
- **ITU T.30 standard.** This standard is for Group 3 fax machines, which are traditional fax machines common in many business environments. Microsoft Fax converts any BFT fax messages to a T.30 NSF (nonstandard facilities) transmission to enable compatibility with these types of fax machines. (*ITU* is the *International Telecommunications Union.*)
- **ITU V.17, V.29, V.27ter standards.** These types are used for high-speed faxes up to 33.6 Kbps.
- **Microsoft At Work platforms.** You need Windows 95, Windows for Workgroups 3.11, or another Microsoft At Work compatible platform to use Microsoft Fax. After installed on Windows 95, Fax will work on systems that are subsequently upgraded to Windows 98.

CAUTION

Check the fax modem documentation to ensure that it adheres to the preceding requirements and works with Microsoft Fax. Beware that some fax modems on the market today do not work with Microsoft Fax.

TROUBLESHOOTING

How can I diagnose problems with Microsoft Fax and my modem? One of the ways is to see whether your fax modem is working correctly by selecting Modems from the Control Panel. In the Modem Properties sheet, select the Diagnostics page. In the list of ports, select the port to which your fax modem is connected. Click More Info to run a diagnostic of your fax modem. If everything is okay, you get a report of your modem's properties. If your fax modem is awaiting a call, you receive a message saying that the port is already opened. You need to exit from Windows Messaging and rerun the modem diagnostics to get an accurate reading.

If you still experience problems, you need to open the Modem Properties sheet and change some of the advanced settings. You might have to experiment with these settings before you find one that works for your modem. You also should make sure that you have a Microsoft Fax service set up for Windows Messaging. If not, see the following section, "Installing Microsoft Fax."

Ins

' to install the Microsoft Fax software onto your
Vizard under Windows 95. You need to have your
o add these files. Use the following steps to do this:

2. s icon in the Control Panel to display the Add/

3. e B.1).

FIG. B.1
Make sure that the
Windows Setup tab is
active.

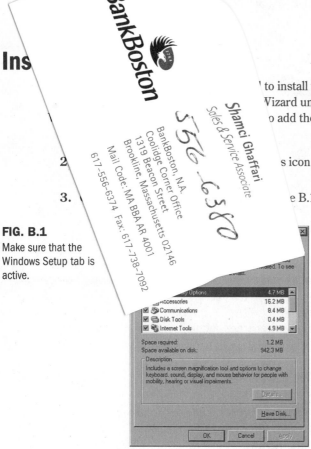

4. Scroll down the <u>C</u>omponents list box and select Microsoft Fax. Be sure not to click any
other component that is already selected, or you will inadvertently remove those
programs from your Windows 95 setup.

If Windows Messaging is not installed, Windows displays a message asking if you want
to install it as you install Microsoft Fax. Click <u>Y</u>es.

5. Click OK.

6. When Windows 95 prompts you for a specific Windows 95 Setup disk or CD-ROM, place
it in the disk drive. Windows 95 copies the files onto your hard disk and returns you to
the desktop when it finishes.

Now that you have Microsoft Fax on your system, you can configure it as a Windows Messaging information service and start sending faxes. You can do this in one of two ways: by using
the Control Panel or by using Windows Messaging. Just follow these steps:

1. Select Start, <u>S</u>ettings, <u>C</u>ontrol Panel. Double-click the Mail and Fax icon.

The Windows Messaging Settings Properties sheet appears (see Figure B.2), in which
you can configure the Microsoft Fax service.

FIG. B.2

The Windows Messaging
Settings Properties
sheet contains all the
services you configured
during Windows 95
setup or when
configuring Windows
Messaging.

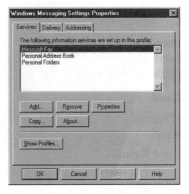

N O T E   If you do not see this sheet, click Show Profiles on the Services page to reveal the Windows
Messaging Settings Profiles set up on your system. Select the Windows Messaging Settings
profile and click Properties. ■

   2. Select Microsoft Fax and click the Properties button. The Microsoft Fax Properties
   sheet displays (see Figure B.3).

FIG. B.3

The Microsoft Fax
Properties sheet
enables you to
configure Microsoft Fax.

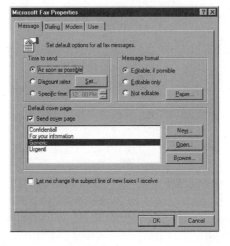

   3. Select the User page (see Figure B.4).

   4. Fill out the User sheet with the information you are asked for. For the most part, the text
   boxes are self-explanatory. The only text box that might need some explanation is the
   Mailbox (optional) item.

   The Mailbox (optional) item in the Your Return Fax Number section pertains to in-house
   mailboxes that you might have set up to receive fax messages. To fill in this box, type the
   name your administrator has assigned you, which might be your name, e-mail name, or
   some other identifier. Otherwise, leave this item blank.

FIG. B.4

Fill out the User page so that your fax recipients know who you are.

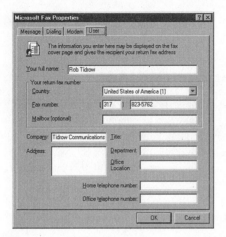

N O T E   According to Federal Communications Commission (FCC) regulation Part 68, Section 68.318(3), you must include the following items on all fax transmissions either on the top or bottom margins of all pages or on a cover page:

- Date and time fax is sent

- Identification of the business, "other entity," or the name of the sender

- Telephone number of the sending fax machine ∎

5. After you fill out the User page, click the Modem page to set up your fax modem to work with Microsoft Fax (see Figure B.5). If your fax modem already has been configured for Windows 95 (which it should be if you have an Internet or online service set up), your modem should already appear in the Available Fax Modems list.

   If your modem does not appear in the Available Fax Modems list, click the Add button. From the Add a Fax Modem dialog box, select Fax Modem and click OK. You then are walked through the Install New Modem Wizard.

FIG. B.5

You need to assign a fax modem to work with Microsoft Fax from this page.

6. If more than one modem appears in this dialog box, click the modem you want to use as the default fax modem and click the Set As Active Fax Modem button.

Configuring Fax Modem Options

Microsoft Fax is a sophisticated application that you can set up to answer your phone automatically after so many rings, let you answer it manually, or not answer your phone at all (if you tend to send rather than receive most of your faxes). As part of the configuration process, you need to tell Microsoft Fax how to behave during a call, whether it's a received or delivered call. As in most other Windows components, you do all this by configuring Microsoft Fax's properties.

 TIP You also can configure these options after you've upgraded to Windows 98.

Use the following steps:

1. On the Modem page, select your fax modem in the Available Fax Modems list and click Properties. This displays the Fax Modem Properties dialog box, as shown in Figure B.6.

FIG. B.6
Set the Microsoft Fax properties for your fax modem.

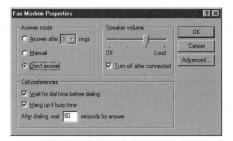

2. Set up each option, as described in the following list:

- **Answer After.** Set this option to have Microsoft Fax answer a fax call after a certain number of rings. For some reason, you cannot set this value for 1 ring or for more than 10. A good number to set this to is 2 or 3.

- **Manual.** Use this option if you want Microsoft Fax to display a message on-screen when a call comes in. You then answer the call manually. As a recommendation, use this option only if you have one phone line that you use for both voice and fax. Otherwise, select the Answer After option.

- **Don't Answer.** Why have a fax modem if you don't want it to answer incoming faxes? The reason is because you might have to share COM ports with another device. Activate this option if your fax modem shares a port with another device, such as a mouse.

- **Speaker Volume.** It's not a bad idea to set this value to about the middle of the scroll bar so that you can hear when a fax is being received. If it's set too high (such as Loud), your ears might start bleeding when a fax begins transmitting.

- **Turn Off After Connected.** Make sure that a check mark is in this box, unless you enjoy listening to two fax devices talk to each other.

- **Wait For Dial Tone Before Dialing.** For most phone systems, this option needs to be selected to instruct Microsoft Fax to wait until a dial tone is heard before making an outgoing call.

- **Hang Up If Busy Tone.** Leave this option selected so that your fax modem doesn't stay on the line if the number you're calling is busy.

- **After Dialing, Wait x Seconds For Answer.** Many fax machines and fax modems take a few seconds to synchronize after they've been called. This option sets the number of seconds Microsoft Fax waits for the receiving machine to get "in synch" after it answers the call. The default is 60 seconds, which is a good starting number. Increase this number if you notice Microsoft Fax canceling calls too soon.

 TIP Disable the Turn Off After Connected option if you want to hear if your fax transmission is still connected.

After you fill out this screen, click OK to save these configuration settings and to return to the fax modem properties screen.

If you want to configure more advanced fax modem settings, click the Advanced button and read the next section. If not, skip to the "Setting Dialing Properties" section.

 TROUBLESHOOTING

How do I turn off the fax modem speaker? Double-click Mail and Fax in the Control Panel. Click Microsoft Fax on the MS Windows Messaging Settings Properties sheet and click the Properties button. Select the Modems page and click the Properties button. In the Speaker Volume area, move the slider bar to the Off position.

Configure Advanced Fax Modem Settings

In the Advanced dialog box (see Figure B.7), you have the option of configuring more sophisticated fax modem settings.

FIG. B.7
Use the Advanced
dialog box to trouble-
shoot fax modem
problems that you
might be experiencing.

These options are detailed in the following list:

- **Disable High Speed Transmission.** High speed transmissions are anything over 9600 bps. If your fax modem is rated for higher speeds, such as 33.6 bps, you might experience transmission errors communicating with other devices. Keep this setting disabled (unchecked) unless your outgoing and incoming faxes are not being handled reliably. Select this option to slow down your transmission speeds.

- **Disable Error Correction Mode.** Fax transmissions demand a great deal of cooperation between the sending fax device and the receiving fax device. You need built-in error-correction procedures to make sure that the fax you send is received properly. This option is used to direct Microsoft Fax to send noneditable faxes, either to a fax machine or as a bitmap file, without using error correction. Keep this option disabled unless you cannot send or receive faxes reliably.

- **Enable MR Compression.** Select this option to compress faxes you send or receive, decreasing the amount of time you're online. This option appears by default and is grayed out if your fax modem does not support MR compression.

> **CAUTION**
> Compressed faxes are more susceptible to line noise and interference. If a transmission experiences too much line noise or interference, your fax might become corrupted, or your fax modem connection might be lost.

- **Use Class 2 If Available.** Select this option if you have problems sending or receiving messages using a fax modem that supports Class 1 and Class 2 fax modems. The default is to leave this option disabled.

- **Reject Pages Received With Errors.** Most fax transmissions have some sort of problem occur during sending or receiving. You can set Microsoft Fax to have a high tolerance (more errors can occur during transmission), medium tolerance, low tolerance, and very low tolerance (fewer errors can occur during transmission) for errors before rejecting the page being received. The default is to have a high tolerance for errors.

> **CAUTION**
>
> If you select the Use Class 2 If Available option, you cannot use error-correction, or send or receive editable faxes.

Click OK when these settings are ready. Click OK to return to the Modem Properties dialog box.

Setting Dialing Properties

Now that you have Microsoft Fax set up to work with your fax modem, you need to start setting user-specific information, such as how Microsoft Fax should dial your phone. Click the Dialing page in the Microsoft Fax Properties sheet. To begin, click the Dialing Properties button to display the My Locations page (see Figure B.8).

FIG. B.8

Set your dialing options, such as area code, calling card numbers, and other user-specific options, in the My Locations page.

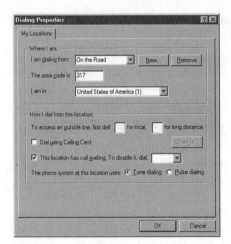

> **N O T E** The My Locations information might already be filled in if you set up your modem to make an outgoing call or if any of your Windows Messaging services previously dialed online services, such as the Microsoft Network. ▪

Microsoft Fax enables you to use several different configurations depending on where you are when you send a fax. If your computer always stays in one place (such as in your office or home), you generally need only one location configured. If, however, you use a portable PC and travel from work to home and to other places, you can configure several different locations to dial using different configuration settings.

When you are in your office, for instance, you might not need to use a calling card to make a long distance phone call to send a fax. You can set up Microsoft Fax to use a configuration that doesn't require a calling card to be entered first. On the other hand, your office phone system might require you to dial an initial number to get an outside line (such as 9). You can place this in the Microsoft Fax configuration settings that you use from your office.

Another scenario where you use a different dialing procedure is when you stay in hotels. For these calls, you might always place them on a calling card. Set up Microsoft Fax to use your calling card number to place these calls. All your configurations are saved in Windows 95 (and eventually Windows 98 when you upgrade to it) and can be retrieved each time you use Microsoft Fax.

The following steps show you how to create a new dialing location in Microsoft Fax:

1. Click the Dialing tab on the Microsoft Fax Properties sheet.

2. Click the Dialing Properties button and click New. The Create New Location dialog box appears (see Figure B.9).

N O T E Depending on the version of Windows 95 you have, you might not receive the Create New Location dialog box. Instead, you just enter the new location name in the I Am Dialing From drop-down box. ■

FIG. B.9
Enter a name for your new location in the Create New Location dialog box.

3. Enter a new name for the location, such as **Office** or **On the Road**. Click OK. You return to the Dialing Properties sheet (refer to Figure B.8).

4. In The Area Code text box, enter the area code from which you are calling. You might need to change or update this if you are not sure of the area code in which you are staying, such as when you are traveling.

   To instruct Windows on which phone numbers in your area code to dial as long distance, click the Dialing Rules button(or Area Code Rules button, in which your dialog box will differ slightly than the one shown in Figure B.10) to display the Dialing Rules dialog box (see Figure B.10). Click the New button and enter the prefix of the phone number Windows should dial as long distance. Click OK. Click OK again to return to the Dialing Properties page.

 T I P If there are any phone numbers in other area codes that you dial as local numbers, click the New button at the bottom of the Dialing Rules dialog box. Fill out the New Area Code and Prefix dialog box. Click OK twice to return to the Dialing Properties page.

5. Select the country in which you are calling.

6. Enter the number (if any) you need to dial to get an outside line (such as **9**) and to make a long distance call (usually **1**).

7. Click the Dial Using Calling Card For Long Distance option to enter your calling card information. Click the Change button to display the Calling Card dialog box (see Figure B.11). Click the drop-down list and select your card name. Fill out the Calling Card Phone Number and PIN Number fields. Click OK.

FIG. B.10

For phone numbers in your area code that Windows should dial as long distance, fill out the Dialing Rules dialog box.

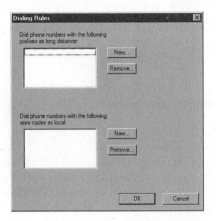

Part
IX °
App
B

  Depending on the version of Windows 95 you have, the Calling Card dialog box might display instead of the Change Calling Card dialog box shown in Figure B.11. If the Calling Card dialog box does display, you need to also fill out the PIN Number field.

FIG. B.11

Microsoft Fax can use calling card numbers to place your fax calls.

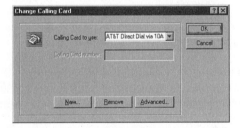

N O T E To set up calling scripts for your calling card, click the Long Distance Usage or International Usage buttons to display the Calling Card dialog box. In this dialog box, select an action from the Dial drop-down box, such as Calling Card phone number. Next, select a time or tone action in the Then Wait For drop-down list, such as 10 seconds. Continue selecting actions and times to create your calling script. As you create a script, you might need to walk through the process and write down each step. ■

8. Click the This Location Has Call Waiting. To Disable It, Dial option if your phone line uses call waiting. From the drop-down list, select the code your phone system uses to temporarily turn off call waiting. You need to obtain this code from your local phone company because each system uses a different code. Microsoft Fax provides three common codes in the drop-down list box next to this option: *70, 70#, and 1170. After you finish faxing and your fax modem hangs up, call waiting is turned back on.

N O T E Most hotels use their own phone system to get outside lines, so you need to enter those numbers when you know what they are. ■

9. Select Tone Dial or Pulse Dial to indicate which type of phone service your phone line uses.

10. Click OK when you have this location set up. You can create as many locations as you need.

Setting Toll Prefixes and Retry Options

Now that you have the locations set up, you need to tell Microsoft Fax which numbers in your local calling area require you to dial as a toll call. To do this, click the Toll Prefixes button on the Dialing page. In the Toll Prefixes page (see Figure B.12), click all the numbers from the Local Phone Numbers list to the Dial 1-*xxx* First list (*xxx* is your area code) that require you to dial your area code first. Click the Add button to place numbers from the list on the left to the list on the right. Click OK when you finish with this dialog box.

FIG. B.12
Tell Microsoft Fax which prefixes in your local calling area code are long distance calls.

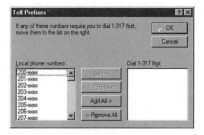

Every time you call a fax number, you're not going to be lucky enough to get through. You'll get busy signals. The fax on the other side of the line won't be ready to accept your call. Or your fax modem and the recipient's fax device won't synchronize properly.

In these cases, you need Microsoft Fax to keep retrying the number you're calling. In the Dialing dialog box, set the Number of Retries option to the number of times you want Microsoft Fax to dial the number before quitting. The default is three times. You also need to tell Microsoft Fax the amount of time you want it to wait before it tries the number again. In the Time Between Retries box, set this time in minutes. The default is two minutes.

Now that you've taken care of the dialing options, you are ready to configure the default settings for your fax messages. Click the Message page.

Configuring Message Options

The Message page (see Figure B.13) has three main areas:

- Time to Send
- Message Format
- Default Cover Page

FIG. B.13

Microsoft Fax lets you customize the way your default fax message looks by using settings in the Message page.

The following sections discuss these options in detail.

Setting Time to Send Options   You might not always want to create a fax message and then zip it off to your recipient. You might want to create a message, or several messages, and then send them at specific times, such as when you are going to lunch or when long distance rates are lower. Microsoft Fax enables you to set the time you send fax messages in one of three ways:

■ **As Soon As Possible.** This is the default selection; use this option to send faxes immediately after you create one.

■ **Discount Rates.** Use this option to send your fax message(s) during predefined hours when long distance tolls are lower. Click the Set button to set the discount rates start and end times. On the Set Discount Rates dialog box, the default discounted rate hours are set between 5 P.M. and 8 A.M. Click OK when you set the appropriate times for your long distance carrier, or keep the default settings.

■ **Specific Time.** Set this option to an exact time to send any fax messages you have in the outbox.

Configuring Fax Message Formats   Microsoft Fax can send fax messages in two primary formats: editable formats (as a binary file) and noneditable formats ("hard copy" faxes). Editable fax messages can be manipulated much the same as a word processing document can be changed. A Microsoft Fax editable fax can be received and edited only by a recipient who also has Microsoft Fax installed. A noneditable fax can be received from a "regular" facsimile machine.

In the Message format area, you set the default way in which your messages are sent. Select the Editable, If Possible option when you send faxes to both fax modems and regular fax machines. This is the default selection. If your fax messages always must be edited by the recipient, or if you want to encrypt your fax message with a password, enable the Editable Only option. (See "Setting Up Security" later in this appendix for information on using security options in Microsoft Fax.) This sends all your fax messages as binary faxes. When using this option, if the recipient does not have Microsoft Fax installed, the fax is not sent. Microsoft Fax places a message in your Windows Messaging Inbox folder telling you that the message was not sent.

When you're sure that your recipient doesn't have Microsoft Fax installed, or you don't want your fax to be edited, send it as Not Editable. Even if the receiving device is a fax modem, the fax message is sent as a bitmap image, so the recipient cannot directly edit the message. If, however, the user has an OCR (optical character recognition) program, he or she can export the faxed image or text as a file to edit in another application.

With the first and third options, you also can specify the type of paper used to print your fax message. Click the Paper button to display the Message Format dialog box and adjust paper settings, such as size, image quality, and orientation. For most faxes, the default settings are fine. Click OK when your paper settings are configured.

Configuring Default Cover Pages   You can opt to send a cover page with your fax message. Click the Send Cover Page option to send a cover page with all your fax messages. Microsoft Fax includes four standard cover pages you can use:

- Confidential
- For Your Information!
- Generic
- Urgent

Select a cover page that suits your needs. Generic is the default. As Microsoft Fax creates your fax message and prepares it to be sent, it fills in data fields on the cover page with information, such as recipient name and fax number, your name, and so on.

 Select a cover page name and click Open to see what a cover page looks like.

The New button is used to create new cover pages by using Microsoft Fax's Cover Page Editor. Also, the Browse button can be used to locate cover page files (denoted as CPE) on your computer.

Finishing Configuring Message Options   One final option on the Message page is Let Me Change the Subject Line of New Faxes I Receive. Use this option to change the subject line of any faxes you receive. Because all incoming faxes are stored in the Windows Messaging Inbox, the subject (if it contains a subject) appears in the subject field there. This option gives you control over what appears in the subject field, enabling you to organize your messages as they come in. On the other hand, you must perform one more action as each fax message is received. The default is to leave this option disabled.

Click OK to save all the Microsoft Fax properties and to return to the MS Windows Messaging Setting Properties dialog box.

Congratulations! You're ready to send a fax using Microsoft Fax.

Configuring a Shared Fax Modem

To reduce the number of fax devices and dedicated phone lines for fax services, many businesses have one centralized fax machine that everyone shares. Because of their convenience and ease of use, most people do not complain too much about walking to a fax machine to send a message or document to another fax machine. Microsoft Fax enables you to extend this sharing of fax devices by letting users in a network environment share a fax modem.

NOTE You must have File and Printer Sharing for Microsoft Networks to share a fax modem across the network. ■

The computer that contains the shared fax modem is called the *fax server* and is not required to be a dedicated PC. A fax server can be anyone's computer that is set up in a workgroup of other Windows 98 users. When a fax is received on the fax server, it then is routed to the recipient in the workgroup via Windows Messaging (or by attaching it as an email message using an email application such as cc:Mail).

> **CAUTION**
> Microsoft Fax cannot automatically route fax messages to workgroup recipients. They must be manually delivered to their recipients

Setting Up a Fax Server

Again, make sure that Windows Messaging is installed and that a fax modem is installed and working on the fax server before completing these steps.

Start Windows Messaging by double-clicking the Inbox icon and then perform the following steps:

1. Choose Tools, Microsoft Fax Tools, Options. The Microsoft Fax Properties sheet appears (refer to Figure B.3).
2. Select the Modem page.
3. Click the Let Other People on the Network Use My Modem to Send Faxes option.
4. If the Select Drive dialog box appears, select the drive that the network fax will use from the drop-down list and click OK.
5. Enter the name of the shared directory in the Share Name text box.

6. Click the Properties button to configure the shared modem's properties. The NetFax dialog box appears, in which you tell Microsoft Fax the name of the shared fax modem folder (see Figure B.14). The NetFax dialog box also enables you to set up passwords for users to connect to the fax server.

FIG. B.14

Use the NetFax dialog box to set the shared fax folder and other settings for sharing a fax modem.

N O T E   If the Properties button does not work, switch to Control Panel and double-click the Network icon. Click the File and Print Sharing button on the Configuration page of the Network sheet. Next, select both options in the File and Print Sharing dialog box for the Microsoft network service. You then need to restart Windows 95 (or Windows 98 if you've upgraded to it) for these settings to take effect. These settings enable sharing on your system, so you can share the fax modem with other users in your workgroup. ■

7. In the Share Name field, type the name of the shared folder for the fax server. Microsoft Fax displays the name of the network fax shared directory as the default. When a user in your workgroup wants to use this folder, he or she searches for this folder on your computer on your network.

8. In the Comment field, enter a string that helps users identify the shared fax.

9. In the Access Type section, select the type of access you want users to have to the shared folder. The default is Full. Select Read-Only if you want users to read, but not modify, items in the folder. The Depends on Password option is used if you want to give different people different rights to the shared folder. You can give one password—the Read-Only Password—to users who can have only read rights. You then can give another password—the Full Access Password—to users who can have full access to the folder.

10. Fill out the Passwords section as necessary, based on your selections in step 9.

11. Click OK.

For users in the workgroup to access the fax server, they must know the fax server's full network name. The name is formed by joining the server's computer name (defined in the Network option in Control Panel) with the shared folder name; for example, \\RTIDROW\FAX.

Setting Up a Fax Server Client

Not only must you configure a fax server to share a fax modem, but you also must configure the client's access to the server. The clients are those users who want to share the fax server. Start Windows Messaging on the client machine and then follow these steps:

1. From Windows Messaging, choose Tools, Microsoft Fax Tool, Options.

2. In the Microsoft Fax Properties sheet, click the Modem page.

3. In Modem properties, click the Add button to display the Add a Fax Modem dialog box (see Figure B.15).

FIG. B.15

The Add a Fax Modem dialog box includes the types of fax modems to which you can connect.

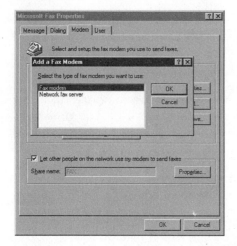

4. In the Add a Fax Modem dialog box, select Network Fax Server and then click OK. The Connect To Network Fax Server dialog box appears, as seen in Figure B.16.

FIG. B.16

To set up a client to use a shared fax server, enter the path of the shared fax server in this dialog box.

5. In the Connect To Network Fax Server dialog box, type the network name of the fax server, such as **\\RTIDROW\FAX**. If you do not know the network name, ask your network administrator. Click OK.

6. In the Microsoft Fax Properties dialog box, click the server name and then click the Set as Active Fax Modem button.

7. Click OK.

You might have to reboot your computer for the settings to take effect.

Setting Up Security

One of the most discussed topics in the computer industry is security. You hear about security and the Internet. You hear about LAN security. You hear about voice mail security. Microsoft Fax enables you to securely send fax messages using public key encryption developed by one of the leaders in security, RSA Inc. Microsoft Fax also enables you to password encrypt and use digital signatures on your messages with confidence. The security features, of course, extend only to sending digital messages and files, not to printed or hard copy faxes. These types of faxes are still subject to the eyes of anyone who happens to be walking by the fax machine when your transmission comes through.

N O T E   A *digital signature* is an electronic version of your signature. For most business transactions, such as purchase requests and employee time sheets, a signature is required to process the request. You can use a secure digital signature to "sign" requests, time sheets, and other sensitive documents. ■

One way to secure your fax messages is to password-protect them as you send them. As you create a fax message and the Send Options for This Message dialog box appears, set the type of security you want to have for your fax message. Click the Security button to display the Message Security Options dialog box (see Figure B.17).

FIG. B.17

You can set the type of security for your fax message in this dialog box.

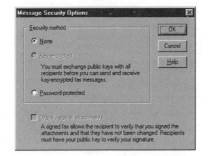

 T I P   Share your password so that the recipient can open and read your fax message.

If you have not set up public key encryption, you have to before you can use the Key-Encrypted option or use a digital signature on your message. You can, however, secure the fax message with a password by choosing the Password-protected option. Figure B.18 shows you the Fax Security—Password Protection dialog box that you need to fill out when you want to send a message with a password.

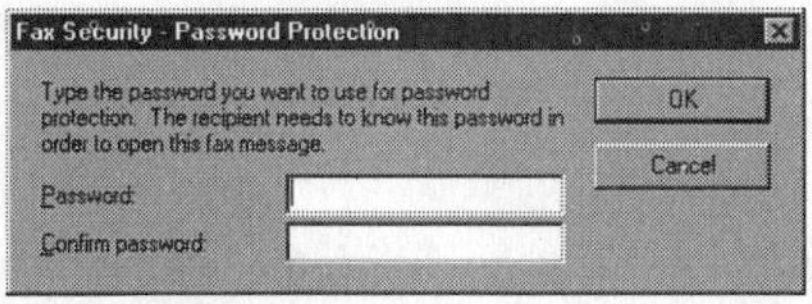

FIG. B.18

To password-protect your faxes, enter a password in this dialog box.

Setting Up Key Encryption

A *key-encrypted message* uses a public key to unlock the message for viewing. This public key is made available to your fax recipients (who must also have Microsoft Fax installed) so that only they can open your document.

You must create a public key in Windows Messaging. To do this, choose Tools, Microsoft Fax Tools, Advanced Security. The Advanced Fax Security dialog box appears (see Figure B.19). In this dialog box, if this is first time you have created a public key, the only option you can choose is the last one, New Key Set.

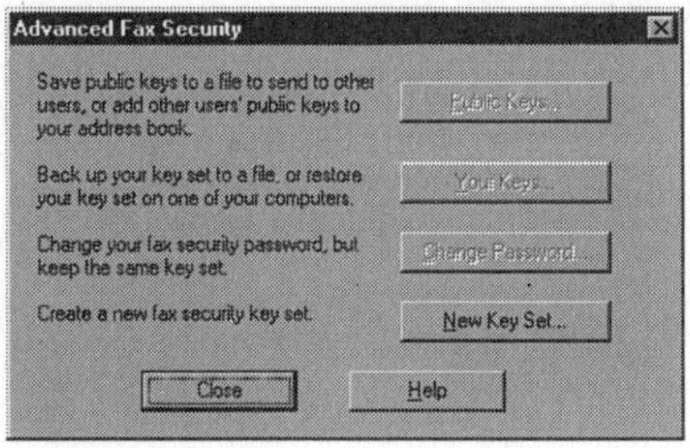

FIG. B.19

Create a public key.

In the Fax Security—New Key Set dialog box, type a password in the Password field and then retype it in the Confirm Password field (see Figure B.20). As you would expect, the password is not displayed; only a string of ***** denotes your password. Don't forget this password; it is now your public key. Click OK to have Windows Messaging create a new public key set on your system. An information box appears, telling you that it might take a few moments to create your key set.

FIG. B.20

You need to enter a new password to create a new public key.

Sharing Public Keys

After you create a public key set, you need to distribute it to your fax recipients for them to read your key-encrypted messages. Do this by clicking the Public Keys button in the Advanced Fax Security dialog box (choose Tools, Microsoft Fax Tools, Advanced Security if you've already closed this dialog box). The Fax Security—Managing Public Keys dialog box appears, from which you need to click Save. This saves your public key to a file so that you can send it to other recipients.

In the Fax Security—Save Public Keys dialog box, click the name or names of the public keys you want to share. As a minimum, you should click your name here. Click OK, and in the resulting window, select a name and folder in which to store the keys. This file has an AWP extension. To finish, you need to send this file to your recipients either via an attachment to a Windows Messaging message or on a floppy disk.

Receiving Public Keys

When you send your public key to a list of recipients, they will need to import the AWP file into Microsoft Fax. Likewise, when you receive a public key from someone, you need to import it into your Microsoft Fax settings and add it to your address book. This enables you to read key-encrypted messages from those users.

After you receive an AWP file from someone, store it on your system and click the Add button in the Fax Security—Managing Public Keys dialog box. Locate the file name that contains the public keys and click Open. Click the key or keys that you want to add. ●

Index